Jesus Is Female

EARLY AMERICAN STUDIES
Daniel K. Richter and Kathleen M. Brown, Series Editors

Exploring neglected aspects of our colonial, revolutionary, and early national history and culture, Early American Studies reinterprets familiar themes and events in fresh ways. Interdisciplinary in character, and with a special emphasis on the period from about 1600 to 1850, the series is published in partnership with the McNeil Center for Early American Studies.

A complete list of books in the series is available from the publisher.

Jesus Is Female

Moravians and the Challenge of Radical Religion in Early America

AARON SPENCER FOGLEMAN

PENN

University of Pennsylvania Press

Philadelphia

Publication of this volume was aided by a gift from Eric R. Papenfuse and Catherine A. Lawrence

10 9 8 7 6 5 4 3 2 1

Published by
University of Pennsylvania Press
Philadelphia, Pennsylvania 19104-4112

Library of Congress Cataloging-in-Publication Data

Fogleman, Aaron Spencer.
  Jesus is female : Moravians and the challenge of radical religion in early America /
Aaron Spencer Fogleman.
    p. cm.—(Early American studies)
  ISBN-13: 978-0-8122-3992-8 (cloth : alk. paper)
  ISBN-10: 0-8122-3992-X (cloth : alk. paper)
  Includes bibliographical references (p.   ) and index.
  1. Moravian Church in America—History—18th century.   2. Moravian Church
in America—Relations—Lutheran Church.   3. Moravian Church in America—
Relations—Reformed Church.   4. Moravian Church in America—Doctrines—
History—18th century.   5. Lutheran Church—Relations—Moravian Church in
America.   6. Reformed Church—Relations—Moravian Church in America.
7. Sex—Religious aspects—Moravian Church in America—History of
doctrines—18th century.   8. United States—Church history—18th century.   I.
Title. II. Series
BX8566.F64   2007
284'.67309033—dc22   2006051491

Für Vera, in Liebe

Contents

Illustrations and Tables

Maps

Figures

Plates (follow p. 110)

Tables

Introduction: The Challenge of Radical Religion

Religious freedom remains a popular, enduring image for many ordinary Americans when they think about the colonial period of their country's history. Shiploads of persecuted European religious groups found a safe haven in North America, where they hoped to carve out an existence and worship their own way in peace. Many believe that these colonists founded what became a great society based on religious and other freedoms. Some pursued utopian, millennial experiments grand and small, believing that English North America was a special place, chosen by God, where special things could and would happen. Because of founder William Penn's policies, Pennsylvania became the place where toleration, diversity, and opportunity were the most advanced, and it was here that the most religious freedom could be found in the colonial era, although it was prevalent one way or another throughout the colonies.

However, this popular image of religious freedom in colonial America does not include the fact that a number of these small, persecuted religious groups pursued beliefs and practices regarding gender that offended the sensibilities or awakened deep-seated fears among colonists then and Americans now. These groups challenged "gender order" as it was developing in most of the Protestant world in the mid-eighteenth century. Gender order refers to a community or society's beliefs and commitments regarding what proper male and female relationships and attributes should be, both in the metaphysical, spiritual, or metaphorical sense and in actual practice between men and women. It is an important component of social order, in general, as relations between men and women are critical to how a society or community functions. Understandings of what proper gender order is can change over time, but challenges by individuals or groups can provoke a rigorous response by those who are committed to preserving what they believe to be proper male and female relationships and attributes at that time. Because religion played such an important role in shaping gender order in early modern Europe and colonial America, the beliefs and practices of some of the small religious movements in this period seemed threatening, especially in territories and colonies where they appeared to flourish.

To many colonists who held orthodox Protestant beliefs, the threat to gender and social order that they had either established or were trying to establish appeared real, especially during the period of heavy immigration during the mid-eighteenth century. Some of the new religious groups dissolved the family and altered practice regarding marriage itself. They explored unusual, mystical notions of sex or celibacy. They allowed women to preach in an era when many orthodox groups demanded that women remain silent in church. And sometimes they made Jesus and other persons of the Christian deity female. Christ was a woman, or in part like a woman, bleeding on the Cross through a vagina-like side wound to give life to believers, suckling them and warming them like a mother, protecting them, and giving them sensual pleasure like a lover. No wonder they don't put this in the textbooks that shape popular images of the colonial era and explain the origins of American freedom. Yet it happened. And while most Americans have always been proud of their heritage of religious freedom and still are, they are not always comfortable with its implications and at times can and will do what is necessary to cut freedom short, to preserve social order and what most people consider to be proper values. So while in some ways there seems to have been more freedom in America than in Europe and other places, and many Americans today are especially proud of it, throughout their history there have been times when Americans have perceived that someone or some group has threatened their sense of values regarding the community, society, or nation, and this has led them to take steps to limit freedom and preserve those values.

As parts of North America became a refuge for religious outcasts and hopefuls, a growing tension emerged in colonial society when it became clear that a number of these people were quite radical, some would say blasphemous, in their religious beliefs. By "radical" I mean that these groups deviated from traditional, core beliefs in fundamental, controversial ways. Their critiques of society and alternative models of religious-social organization addressed the roots of power, authority, and legitimacy that most considered normal in Christian belief and practice. Many radical religious groups rejected traditional hierarchies in gender and/or class relations. Others altered understandings of marriage and the family, or economic relations within the community.[1] In the mid-eighteenth century the unusual combination of tolerance, diversity, and opportunity in a colonial environment, especially in and around Pennsylvania, combined with the simultaneous pressure on many radical religious groups in Europe, meant that more than the usual amount of religious radicalism was present in this society. Many colonists who cherished unbridled freedom liked it this way, but many others who clung to tradition and authority in a strange, new colonial environment did not. At times these colonists were ready to take steps to limit freedom in order to promote and preserve order. This might have been easy enough to do under normal circumstances, but now the number of radicals was growing, and what seemed most frightening was that radical religion of some form or another was beginning to look appealing to ordinary people in the large, mainstream churches. Ultimately, radical religious groups in British North America contributed significantly to the rising tensions between religious freedom and order in ways that profoundly shaped American religious culture, and still do.

And then came the Great Awakening, the grand revival movement that swept through the British North American colonies from the 1730s to the early 1750s and brought new religions and religious styles, and with this even more radical religion and more tension. The Great Awakening was the North American component of an international, transatlantic Protestant revival. Its occurrence raised questions about how far radicalism could go in America before opponents might successfully move to limit it, and with this religious freedom itself. In New England the old Puritan (Congregational) church divided among those for or against the revival, and in the fierce factional conflict that resulted some individuals and groups drifted toward radicalism. In the Middle Colonies, where tens of thousands of ethnically and religiously diverse immigrants arrived during the Awakening years, Presbyterians divided along similar lines, while a number of German radical pietist groups flourished. Throughout the colonies the growing Baptist and Methodist movements pushed boundaries in their early radical phase by allowing women to preach, by preaching to slaves and advocating their freedom, and by promoting social leveling in general. Meanwhile the Quakers, one of the most successful radical groups of the previous century, continued to allow women to preach and disavowed the concept of an established church.[2]

This is a book about the expansion of radical religion in colonial America during the years of the Great Awakening and the steps taken by European religious authorities and ordinary colonists to limit it. To many it became clear that America was a place where religious opportunity existed, but European orthodoxy might also hinder opportunity. Thus there was tension in the colonies between new, sometimes radical movements and orthodox Protestant churches, and this tension shaped early American religious culture. That tension was played out in religious communities, many of which were new and unstable, yet growing rapidly in this era of heavy immigration and natural population growth.

In some ways the development of this tension between radical and orthodox religious movements in the colonies resembled similar problems in Europe, but there were important differences in North America that potentially implied a significant threat to concepts of social order. The inability or unwillingness of the European state churches to commit fully themselves to North America meant that their establishments in the colonies would be inherently weak, thus giving more opportunity for dissenters, pietists, and radicals of all sorts to pursue their goals in the colonies than they ever would have had in Europe. Weak establishments combined with heavy and diverse immigration to represent an inherent challenge to religious order, as many orthodox Europeans conceived it. Moreover, the toleration of numerous religious groups, pursuing alternative understandings and arrangements concerning male and female roles in the community and family, seemed to threaten orthodox conceptions of gender order. This meant that orthodox religious leaders and communities in the colonies would have to rely on other means to stop any aggressive radical movement that might arise in the colonies, especially south of New England, where the state-church apparatus was weak, or nonexistent.

This study of the challenge and limits of radical religion in America focuses on four European groups and their supporters among the large immigrant populations in North America during the Great Awakening years: the Moravians, a radical group primarily from the German territories, and three of their European opponents, namely the Lutheran pietists from Halle (in Sachsen-Anhalt, recently acquired by Prussia), the state church of the Netherlands (which sponsored both Dutch and German Reformed immigrants in the colonies), and the state church of Sweden (whose authorities in Uppsala supported the Swedish Lutheran churches in the Delaware Valley). The activities of these groups, individually, and to some extent together, have been studied by numerous denominational historians, scholars of German pietism, or in a few cases students of the Great Awakening in North America, but the severe conflict between these groups, and the extraordinary level of popular religious violence in the Reformed and Lutheran communities of the Delaware Valley that resulted, has never been thoroughly investigated by historians. Also, the religious and social radicalism precipitating these conflicts has not yet been recognized by these historians. In fact, many historians of German pietism, as well as Moravian denominational historians, do not even recognize the Moravians as radical.[3] Yet their radicalism is apparent, especially when one considers their views on gender.

Of these four religious groups, the Moravians were at the center of the conflict. They were a small group of ecumenical, radical pietists known by several names, including the *Unitas Fratrum*, the Herrnhuters, and the *Brüdergemeine*. They were descended from the old Hussite movement in Bohemia and Moravia, whose roots went back to the late fourteenth century. After enduring terrible persecution and near annihilation in the seventeenth century during and after the Thirty Years War, some scattered remnants assembled on the estates of Count Nicolaus Ludwig von Zinzendorf (1700–1760) in Upper Lusatia, where they built a community called Herrnhut. In 1727 the *Unitas Fratrum* experienced a "rebirth" and quickly became a small, but important, element of the pietist movement sweeping through the Protestant churches of northwestern Europe. They were important to the larger movement because of their innovative spirituality, their missionary zeal, and their close connections to influential German nobility in the Lutheran church, like Count Zinzendorf, who became the leader of the movement.[4]

Under Zinzendorf some Moravians believed they had discovered the femaleness or androgyny of the Trinity, including Jesus their Savior (*Heiland*), with whom they developed sensual and for some even sexual spiritual relations. Zinzendorf developed an innovative spiritual view that emphasized experience over text (even though he wrote a lot), Christ as the central figure of the Trinity, and communal Christian living with an active daily liturgical program. The experiential aspects of Moravian theology included a heavy emphasis on the sensuous nature of Christ's death and resurrection and the enthusiastic joy this brought individuals and the Christian community now and forever. Led by Zinzendorf (see Plate 1), these beliefs and Moravian ecumenism fueled the group's zealous desire to develop a mission to the peoples of the world, including Indians, African slaves, and European colonists in the Americas, where the Moravians sent hundreds of missionaries and supporters in the mid-eighteenth century (see Map 1). Whether working in an overseas mission or at home in Europe, most Moravians lived in closed communities like Herrnhut in Upper Lusatia, Herrnhaag in Wetteravia, or Bethlehem and Nazareth in Pennsylvania. Here relatively large numbers of male and female nobility and clergy organized and directed a communal economy. They divided their communities by gender, age, and marital status into groups known as "choirs," in which they lived, worked, and worshiped. A liturgy of communion, baptism, love feasts, singings, foot washings, the "kiss of peace," elaborate ritual celebrations of marriage and sex between husband and wife, birthdays, and other special days filled the daily, weekly, monthly, and annual calender of the group on both sides of the Atlantic. In this sense the Moravians achieved the pietist ideal of reforming all aspects of daily life and making them more godly.[5]

None of the controversial beliefs and practices of the Moravians regarding the Trinity were unique on either side of the Atlantic in the eighteenth century, but the combination of a radical communal, ecu-

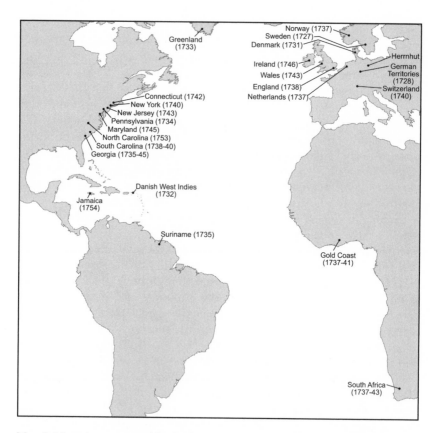

Map 1. Moravian communities in the Atlantic world, 1727–1754. The map depicts places where Moravians began missions or communities that became established and the dates this happened. Attempts to establish missions or communities that immediately failed are excluded. End dates are listed for established missions or communities that had failed by 1754.

menical, and gender order, along with the mission impulse, was perhaps unique in its time, or at least highly unusual. This was pietism, Moravian style, and it both attracted and frightened the transatlantic community of Protestant evangelicals of the period. Eighteenth-century religious authorities were familiar with radical religious groups, challenges to orthodoxy, and strange views about gender in the spiritual realm, but the combination of radical gender views and ecumenism was a difficult problem in Europe and a dangerous threat in North America, where the church establishments and institutions were weak. Moravian violations of gender order were especially threatening *because* this group was ecumenical and energetically proselytized among just about everyone.

Their ecumenism led the Moravians to infiltrate the fledgling establishments in North America at a time when some colonists and clergy wanted to erect orthodox denominational establishments with clear lines of male clerical authority, in part to promote proper discipline and to protect people from doctrinal error and threats to social and religious order that seemed to be rampant in the colonies.

The Halle Lutheran pietists shared some characteristics with the Moravians, but their increasing emphasis on patriarchy, doctrine, and maintaining the proper boundaries of Lutheranism in the mid-eighteenth century stood in stark contrast to the feminine, ecumenical piety of Count Zinzendorf's group. This part of the international pietist movement was centered at the philanthropic institutes at the university town of Halle. (These institutes are now called the *Franckesche Stiftungen*, or Francke Foundations.) In the 1690s, under the leadership of August Hermann Francke, this group promoted a reform movement within the Lutheran church that attacked the emphasis on dogma and formal worship in the church, and provided a high-profile public role for women in spiritual life, something like what the Moravians would do a generation later. The Hallensians promoted the pietist ideal of a church that became more involved in reforming individual and public life in all respects—finishing the Reformation, in their view. This included a form of religious life that stressed enthusiastic singing and preaching, emotional individual conversion experiences, small groups of men and women meeting regularly in conventicles, and correcting ills in society. Their struggle against Lutheran orthodoxy was an important part of the Protestant evangelical awakening in the early eighteenth century. After Francke's son, Gotthilf August, took over the leadership of the institutes in the 1720s, the Halle pietists began moving in different directions. These included expanding their charity schools system and worldwide mission, but also reducing the role of women and increasingly stressing dogma and respect for proper Lutheran creeds. In short, when their conflict with the Moravians escalated the Halle pietists were becoming more like the patriarchal, orthodox Lutheran church against which they had so long struggled.[6]

The state church of the Netherlands, led by the Classis of Amsterdam, paid at least some attention to the spiritual care of members in overseas colonies. At home, state church officials had struggled throughout the seventeenth and early eighteenth centuries to enforce church authority and orthodox belief and practice against internal and external dissent. In the eighteenth century they extended their support to Dutch Reformed colonists in the Americas from Suriname to New York, and eventually they provided ministers and other support for German Reformed colonists in North America. The Classis of Amsterdam promoted a patriarchal religious and social order on both sides of the Atlantic that clashed with the ecumenical, more feminine view of the Moravians. Their struggle with the Moravians began in the 1730s, when Count Zinzendorf's group moved into the Netherlands and extended to the American colonies in the 1730s and 1740s, when Moravian missionaries began working there.[7]

The Lutheran authorities at Uppsala were the heads of the state church in Sweden, one of the most ethnically and religious homogenous territories in Europe. In the late seventeenth century they revived the religious mission in the old New Sweden colony on the Delaware River and continued to support it until the second half of the eighteenth century. Until the era of the Moravian conflict the Swedish church had been more tolerant than many other European state churches, but by the middle third of the eighteenth century they too were becoming increasingly patriarchal and less tolerant of dissenters, as they built one of the strongest state churches in Protestant Europe. Like the Hallensians and the Classis of Amsterdam, they became involved in the conflict with the Moravians on both sides of the Atlantic in the mid-eighteenth century.[8]

There were other groups who contended with the Moravians on both sides of the Atlantic during this era, but these struggles never became violent as they did with the above groups in the North American colonies. English pietists like John Wesley and George Whitefield tried to find common ground with the Moravians as coworkers in the international Protestant revival, but because of the radical views and activities of Count Zinzendorf's group they could not maintain fellowship with them for long. Gilbert Tennent and the New Side Presbyterians in the Delaware Valley colonies also rejected the Moravians. Yet while these and other revivalists condemned the Moravians and published bitter polemics that vilified the group, the actual Moravian threat in Methodist, Presbyterian, and other communities was never large enough to warrant violence to remove it. The only other groups who felt truly threatened by Moravians were other small German radical pietist groups, especially in Pennsylvania, but their reaction was simply to refuse to cooperate with the Moravians' attempt to unify these many diverse groups in Europe and Pennsylvania. Violence was not needed to stop them.

This book chronicles the radical challenge of the Moravians and the orthodox response of their major enemies in the Atlantic world, and in doing so it explores the possible connections among three important themes that were a part of the conflict among these groups. The first involves confessional order.[9] In some ways this is the most studied theme to date, as historians on both sides of the Atlantic for generations have investigated how Count Zinzendorf's ecumenical views clashed with the views of Protestant orthodoxy in the period. The second major theme involves gender order. Although recent historians have investigated the importance of gender in their studies of pietism, especially among the Moravians, this study finds that violations of orthodox gender order by Moravians on both sides of the Atlantic were more extreme and controversial than previously realized. The third major theme is religious violence. In recent decades early modern European and colonial American historians have studied popular religious violence, but this study of conflict involving the Moravians uncovers extraordinary, heretofore undocumented, levels of such violence that took place during the Great Awakening among Lutheran and Reformed factions in North American communities where Moravians worked.

The question is, was there a connection among these three themes? My view is that there were important connections between beliefs and practices regarding confessional and gender order on both sides of the Atlantic and the religious violence that took place in the colonies. The connections of confessional and gender order to the conflict are clear, because religious authorities in Europe and America constantly criticized the Moravians throughout the Atlantic world on these points. Their public and private writings stress that these were the most serious transgressions of this small, radical group. Confessional and gender order became connected when fears of dangerous violations of spiritual and practical gender norms by the Moravians were used to promote the value of orthodox patriarchal and confessional boundaries. The connection of confessional and gender order to the religious violence in the mid-Atlantic colonies of North America in the mid-eighteenth century is less clear, primarily because ordinary people committed the violence, and it is more difficult to establish the motivations of such people in this era. What did they believe about gender and confessional order? Whom did they consider to be a dangerous enemy within their communities and why? No one of the "lower sort" who was directly involved in the violence left a detailed written record of why they took part, as is often the case when similar things happened in the early modern and colonial era.

To help overcome the problem of the lack of sources documenting the thoughts and motivations of ordinary Lutheran and Reformed colonists involved in the anti-Moravian communal religious violence, this book employs methodology developed by early modern cultural historians. Natalie Zemon Davis articulated the methodology well in *The Return of Martin Guerre* and in a response to criticism of this work.[10] If there are no other possibilities because of a dearth of sources, historians must work with what they have and settle for "conjectural knowledge and possible truth" to arrive at explanations for the behavior of men and women in the lower orders. The question here is why did such people attack (or support) Moravians—or really why did such people in these communities divide over the Moravian issue and attack each other? My conclusions are based upon what evidence is available and on what other historians of communal religious violence and gender have found in similar circumstances during this era. My view that confessional and especially gender issues motivated colonists of the "lower sort" to attack Moravians and their supporters cannot be proven with hard data—nor can any other explanation of the violence, for that matter—but it is certainly plausible, and I think probable that they did. If so, then the actions of these people fit into a larger transatlantic picture that this book describes in which gender and confessional issues clearly did lead to religious tensions. Other historians may explain these tensions differently, but I want to contribute to the discussion by taking the issue of gender seriously.

The book is divided into three parts. Part One analyzes concepts of gender order and confessionalism in Protestant communities of the Atlantic world as they developed in the early modern and colonial era. Part Two addresses the way the Moravians challenged the gender and confessional order that had developed by the mid-eighteenth century. Finally, Part Three addresses the furious, at times violent, response to the Moravian challenge and the defense of gender and confessional order in North America. The social and political conditions in British North America created a much greater potential for radical religion and gender violations to flourish there than in Europe in the eighteenth century; hence the need for a strong orthodox response. Because of conditions in the mid-Atlantic colonies, the Moravians were initially successful when they extended their message to the Lutheran and Reformed communities there. But the radical beliefs and practices of the ecumenical Moravians regarding gender shocked their opponents, especially when Count Zinzendorf's group attempted to penetrate the confessional walls of their churches and communities. Lutheran and Reformed colonists informed and supported by religious authorities in Halle, Amsterdam, and Uppsala could not allow this under any circumstances. Without a state church in the mid-Atlantic colonies to do their work for them, these outraged settlers took direct, violent action and drove the Moravians out of their communities themselves.

The radical challenge of the Moravians and the response of their numerous orthodox enemies is important to a number of larger topics in colonial North American and Atlantic history. The use of the transatlantic approach to the study of community conflict during the Great Awakening enhances our understanding of what caused and shaped that conflict. Further, historians of the international Protestant Awakening in the eighteenth century have not fully explored the importance of gender issues in this movement, especially regarding conflict involving the Moravians, nor are they fully aware that the policies of European religious authorities sometimes led to extreme, violent consequences in the Americas. This was an Atlantic religious conflict, fought out in peculiar ways in the mid-Atlantic communities of North America because of the conditions there, but religious people throughout Protestant Europe were interested in the outcome. Also, the religious violence that exploded in the mid-Atlantic communities of North America is relevant to the debate among historians on the relative importance of volunteerism or coercion in early American religious culture.[11] Gender issues were critical in the conflict between rival groups, and the outcome is important to understanding whether or how the feminization of religion took place in North America from the eighteenth to the nineteenth centuries. Lastly, this conflict reveals a great deal about the potential and limits of radical religion in North American religious communities during this era.

This work relies heavily on German-, English-, and Dutch-language sources produced on both sides of the Atlantic.[12] Major archival sources include correspondence, reports, protocols, and diaries kept by German Lutheran ministers at the Francke Foundations in Halle, Germany, as well as at the Lutheran Archives Center in Philadelphia. These supplement the published writings of Heinrich Melchior Mühlenberg, the Halle pietist minister whose activities in North America have been well documented by numerous historians.[13] Similar records kept by German Reformed ministers and now located at the archives of the Evangelical and Reformed Historical Society in Lancaster, Pennsylvania, as well as the Moravian records kept at their archives in Herrnhut, Germany and Bethlehem, Pennsylvania, were also used. Additionally, this work employs similar records kept by Swedish Lutheran clergy in the Delaware Valley and in Uppsala that have been translated and in some cases printed in modern editions. They provide valuable information about the course of conflict with the Moravians in the colonial religious communities originally settled by Swedes.

Among the most important manuscripts investigated in this study are the diaries of the Moravian itinerant preachers, who worked in virtually every German and Swedish Lutheran, as well as German Reformed, congregation in the colonies and recorded what they experienced. Located in the Moravian Archives in Bethlehem and Herrnhut, these German-language, handwritten records allow us to go well beyond the familiar published writings of the Halle Lutheran Mühlenberg, the Amsterdam pastor Johann Philip Boehm, Uppsala's Israel Acrelius, and a few other Lutheran and Reformed ministers, whose commentaries have long been the primary sources for studying German and Swedish communities in colonial North America. While Mühlenberg's voluminous writings reveal a great deal about religious culture among the Germans in the years before the French and Indian War, he actually worked in only a few communities in this early period and provides limited insight into many of the issues and events described in detail by the Moravian itinerants in dozens of backcountry communities in the mid-Atlantic colonies. Mühlenberg's extreme antipathy toward the Moravians, together with his relatively narrow geographic coverage at this time, mean that we must have more information about more communities than he provides in order to get a clearer picture of what was happening in the Lutheran and Reformed communities in the region as a whole. While the Moravian itinerant records provide a much broader picture of developments in those communities, they have never been adequately explored by historians, probably because they are written in the difficult German script of the period, because they have been tucked away in Moravian archives in Bethlehem and in East Germany, and because few historians have realized how much they reveal not just about the Moravians, but about the tens of thousands of Germans and others living in the Lutheran and Reformed communities of North America during this era.

Like many recent historians of the Great Awakening, my work stresses the importance of printed works in this eighteenth-century event.[14] The print medium played a critical role in promoting and documenting the revival and stimulating religious conflict. I have investigated contemporary printed sources both to understand their use as instruments in the conflict and to learn more about the conflict itself. These sources used include German- and English-language newspapers, anti-Moravian polemics, and Moravian publications published by major presses on both sides of the Atlantic. The newspapers printed in Philadelphia and Germantown provided coverage and interpretations of the conflicts in the German religious communities to eager readers in the colonies. Their biases can normally be traced quite easily to involved parties or interests that submitted stories and accounts to the editors. This is even more true for the polemical broadsides, pamphlets, and books that these same presses printed or reprinted. The enemies of Moravians in Europe and America produced hundreds of polemics that damaged the group's cause. I have relied heavily on the polemical literature, which circulated widely in the Atlantic world, in order to investigate which concerns and issues the Moravians' enemies exploited when trying to sway popular opinion against the group. Further, many of these polemics, although essentially propaganda, do contain valuable information about some of the basic events and characters in the conflict that became well known to readers on both sides of the Atlantic. Some are even histories of the conflict written as it unfolded. Above all, these works reveal the values and fears that motivated many Moravian opponents and readers of the polemics. The Moravians printed a significant amount of material themselves, mostly in Germany, that they circulated throughout the Atlantic world, much of it in defense of their beliefs and activities or to explain what they intended to do next and why.

This study also relies on unconventional sources produced by Moravians in the mid-eighteenth century, including artwork, hymns, and verse. Moravian art was prolific and reveals how important colorful, visual images were to the group's spirituality. Further, it provides insight into the mystical, spiritual qualities of the group's controversial beliefs and practices regarding gender and sex during the period of peak conflict with Lutherans, Calvinists, and others in Europe and America. Also, the group produced and published thousands of hymns during this era, most written by their leader, Count Zinzendorf. Many of these hymns include references to sensual relationships with Jesus, graphic portrayals of genitalia, and female qualities of the Trinity, all of which provoked strong reactions from enemies of the group. While these hymns appeared in numerous editions and appendices of the *Moravian Hymnal* during this era, many of the most extreme expressions appeared in the Twelfth Appendix and addenda of their hymnal, which became notorious among their enemies and was often quoted in anti-Moravian polemics.[15]

Last, this work relies on sources produced by Anglo-American observers. These include letters and printed works by outside observers who noted or commented on the conflict in the German and Swedish communities. Many of these observers were sympathetic to the Moravians, but some, like the Presbyterian minister Gilbert Tennent, expressed their fear of what might happen if Moravian influence spread outside the German and Swedish churches.

Collectively, these handwritten and printed documents in three languages on both sides of the Atlantic contain an untold story about how a relatively small group of religious radicals in the eighteenth century found a place in the Protestant Atlantic world where they could achieve many of their ambitious goals and what many of their neighbors, angered and frightened by the thought that Jesus might be female, did about it.

Part I
Religion and Gender

In the eighteenth century European immigrants came to North America and found a much different place. Initially what impressed many immigrants were a relatively weak established church, low taxes, ethnic diversity, vast distances, dispersed settlements, and opportunity. This meant that religious toleration and freedom of sorts defined life for them in ways they never could in Europe. Yet in spite of the distances and differences, North America and its new inhabitants remained connected in many ways to Europe. In addition to the migrations themselves, the Atlantic trade and religion kept them connected. Heavy immigration occurred during the era of the Protestant evangelical awakening that swept through the countries from which the immigrants came, especially Britain, the German territories, the Netherlands, and to some extent the Scandinavian lands. In British North America the revival was so intense that many historians refer to it as the "Great Awakening."

When the immigrants and the religious awakening reached North America in the 1730s, many of the attitudes, beliefs, values, and norms from Europe reached the colonies as well. This included views concerning gender—that is, people's understandings about the proper roles and attributes of males and females. Gender played an important role in spiritual affairs and always has. Tension arose in the colonial environment, where European views that had been developing since the Reformation and earlier were challenged. The same colonial environment of diversity and weak or no church establishment challenged supporters of confessional order as well. Although the height of the "Confessional Age" was in the seventeenth century, many aspects of the confessional style carried over into the eighteenth century, when orthodox theologians relied increasingly on reason and rational argument to make their points about doctrine. Yet, in the colonies, the simultaneous developments of diverse immigration and the Great Awakening spawned countless religious groups and movements that would not adhere to Protestant orthodoxy. Some of these groups were radical, challenging notions of gender and confessional order that many thought were fundamental to proper social order.

In North America the Moravians and other radicals had a chance to flourish as they never could in Europe. In fact, radical religion became so prominent during the Great Awakening that some orthodox clergy, especially in and around Pennsylvania, complained that *they* were at a disadvantage competing for the religious affections and support of the populace in this environment, and they feared that proper gender and confessional order were in danger because of it. The struggle between the Moravians and their numerous enemies in North America took place in this context. To a significant degree, clashing notions of gender and confessional order between radicals and numerous Protestant groups from Europe characterized the struggle between these groups. For this reason it is important to investigate the conditions in British North America that gave radicals like the Moravians a chance to carry out their plans, as well as the mainstream beliefs and practices regarding gender and confessionalism in early modern Europe that influenced the conflict in the colonies.

Chapter 1

Radical Religion in a Colonial Context

"Everything is different in America," the immigrants used to say (and still do). Many if not most free immigrants in the eighteenth century migrated with family members or others from their home village, remained in contact with those they left behind, and continued in America to promote important aspects of their old culture like religion and language. Yet the immigrants stressed difference more than similarity when comparing conditions in the colonies with their homelands. In North America there was a lot more land, a relatively weak state (which meant low taxes, greater geographic mobility, and religious tolerance), and in some circumstances greater chances for prosperity. In North America there were also slaves and Indians, and real dangers to immigrants from both in certain areas. For religious radicals, a relatively small but important portion of the immigrants pouring into the mid-Atlantic region and other areas in the middle third of the eighteenth century, a weak state-church apparatus or none at all, along with the vast tracts of land, meant more freedom than they could ever achieve in Europe. These groups, with their alternative views concerning gender, sex, marriage, and community, could and did flourish in Pennsylvania and other colonies, whereas in Europe they were restricted to certain small territories and always in danger of losing their rights. For immigrants belonging to the Lutheran or Reformed churches of the German territories—the vast majority of all German arrivals in the half century before independence—American conditions had a much different effect on how they might establish a viable religious life. Some Lutheran and Reformed immigrants did not care, but most did, as evidenced by the facts that the majority settled in identifiable religious communities of their home church and participation in one form or another in the local church community was high, even without a strong apparatus in place when they arrived. Some believed that the home churches were becoming corrupt and that they could do better on their own in America. But even in this case they needed pastors and other support from the Lutheran and Reformed churches in the German and Swiss territories to help them establish and preserve proper confessional and social order as they understood it. Soon after arriving in North America they realized that their home churches would not support them or maintain their stature and influence in the community and territory as they had done in Europe. The Lutheran and Reformed immigrants also quickly noticed how a large number and variety of German and other sects flourished in and around Pennsylvania, many of whom were quite radical in their views about religious and social order. The government could not or would not control these people, women preached, and people switched religions as if there were hardly boundaries between them. A tension developed between those "church" immigrants who wanted more traditional religious order, which was based upon an orthodox, patriarchal church, and those who preferred fewer restrictions, or perhaps even the radical alternative itself. The tension escalated into a severe conflict when European church authorities became more involved in the colonies during the Great Awakening. Choices had to be made in this context of revival, enthusiasm, and conflict: should ordinary people who lived in the new and rapidly growing communities of the mid-Atlantic colonies embrace the drift toward a more radical religious and social order, or should they retreat into traditional authority, as best it could be constructed in this colonial environment?[1]

The radicals were the first religious groups from the German territories to become interested in North America, and those who came were part of a controversial alternative religious-social movement that had challenged orthodox state-church authority and beliefs regarding gender, marriage, sex, and community in the German territories.[2] Many of the radicals were fairly large, well-established groups descended from the sixteenth-century "radical Reformation," like the Schwenkfelders, Mennonites, Hutterites, Swiss Brethren, and their recent offshoot the Amish. Others, like the Waldensians and Moravians, were even older. But there were also newer radical groups and individuals that formed in the late seventeenth and early eighteenth centuries. After decades of devastating warfare in central Europe many people lost faith in the ability of the confessional churches to achieve true piety. As in England at about the same time and for similar reasons, these mystics, separatists, apocalyptic millenarians, and other seekers renounced organizational structures and binding teachings of the "fallen" confessional churches and sought liberty of conscience and apostolic purity (perfection, holiness). Some were philadelphians, that is, millenarians who believed that the true church of God would gather in the end times from the fallen churches and live together in brotherly love and close spiritual communion with Christ, as described in the Book of Revelation. Some were antinomian spiritualists and inspirationists who challenged traditional views of the

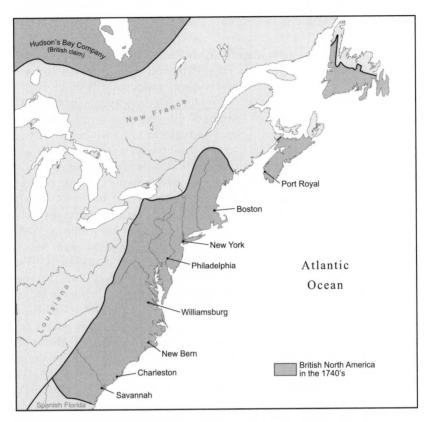

Map 2. British North America in the 1740s. Adapted from James Henretta et al., *America's History*, 4th ed., vol. 1 (New York: Bedford/St. Martin's, 2000); copyright © 2000 Bedford/St. Martin's; used by permission of Bedford/St. Martin's.

gender of the Trinity and women's roles in the community. Many were Separatists, and some of these became mystical hermits who developed into or influenced groups like the Inspired (*Inspirierten*) or the Dunkers (*Neu-Täufer,* or Church of the Brethren). Others like the New Born (*Neugeborene*) believed that after true conversion God indwelt believers and vice versa, which meant sin was removed from their lives. This led to alternative views of baptism, communion, fasting, and prayer, as well as rejection of church attendance and alms giving.[3]

The radicals flourished in some of the German territories that offered asylum and remained in contact with similar movements in England, but they maintained a precarious existence. A number of groups like the Inspired, Separatists, Dunkers, and the Mother Eva Society settled in areas like the County Wittgenstein (near the Sauerland), Frankfurt am Main, and in a region northwest of Frankfurt known informally as Wetteravia (*die Wetterau*) (see Map 3). Here religious tolerance became a mechanism to further political, economic, and state interests, and the territorial rulers offered the radicals asylum, much as William Penn did in Pennsylvania. The orthodox state churches fought against the radicals, but could not penetrate the political boundaries of these asylums and so had to rely primarily on printed attacks to convince rulers and residents to avoid them. The radicals responded by making heavy use of the print medium themselves. By the 1730s the theologian, chemist, alchemist (and possible inspiration for Mary Shelly's Frankenstein) Johann Konrad Dippel (1673–1734) became one of the most widely read radical pietists in the eighteenth century, and Berleburg (in Wittgenstein) became an important printing center for the radicals. Also, Andreas Gross of Frankfurt am Main sent a printing press to his fellow Separatist Christopher Saur in Germantown, Pennsylvania. Saur's press not only produced the most widely read radical literature, but also was the most popular German-language press altogether in North America. On both sides of the Atlantic the radicals wrote, published, and read a number of important books, newspapers, and a magazine called *Die Geistliche Fama*. The movements continued to flourish until the mideighteenth century, but in Europe they were dependent on the sometimes fickle support and protection of their local territorial rulers.[4]

In the late seventeenth century many German radicals became interested in Pennsylvania not merely as another territory that offered religious tolerance, but as a refuge from Judgment Day. William Penn recruited among radicals in the middle Rhine area before founding his Quaker colony, and a number of them joined the project, in part to pursue apocalyptic, millennial aspirations in America. Here they could witness a sure sign of the end times—the coming together of the lost tribes of Israel, represented in the Indian tribes. The end of the seventeenth century was supposed to be eventful for many radical spiritual groups in central Europe, and for some it was. In order to escape the pending doom that was about to strike Europe, Johannes Kelpius (1670–1708) of Transylvania had already in 1694 led a group of German radicals to Pennsylvania that included Anna Maria Schuchart, the prophetess who had recently been expelled from Erfurt. After a difficult journey that including in-fighting and the expulsion of Schuchart and Daniel Falkner, Kelpius's group settled in the wilderness near Philadelphia, built a tabernacle, and placed a telescope on its roof, hoping to watch the burning stars fall on wicked Europe, followed by the imminent return of Christ.[5]

When the end did not come as it was supposed to, Kelpius's group

Map 3. Centers of radical pietism in the German territories with connections to British North America, ca. 1680–1750. The broken line refers to the boundaries of the Holy Roman Empire. Adapted from Mack Walker, *German Home Towns: Community, State, and General Estate, 1648–1871* (Ithaca, N.Y.: Cornell University Press, 1971); copyright © 1971 Cornell University; used by permission of Cornell University Press.

and many other radicals in Europe became disillusioned and scattered, but Pennsylvania remained important to the movement. While some radicals returned to the Lutheran and Reformed churches, others began new movements. Pennsylvania still offered religious freedom, and the emigration to the colony continued. New Born, Inspired, Separatists, Dunkers, "New Mooners" (*Neumondler*), and other radical pietists settled in the colony, not to mention Moravians, German Quakers, and the older groups descended from the radical Reformation. In Pennsylvania the government itself was made up of English radicals, which seemed to ensure greater safety. Here tolerance, diversity, dispersal, and pacifist Quaker rule meant that the German radicals could live and worship in vibrant religious communities without fear of repression or significant restrictions. From the 1730s to the 1750s, the peak period of conflict with the Moravians in the colony, the radicals continued to arrive and maintained strong connections with their compatriots still in the German territories.[6]

By the mid-eighteenth century not only the radicals, but also many European church groups became increasingly interested in British North America, and the colonies maintained a high profile in the ongoing transatlantic Protestant evangelical awakening of the period. The center of gravity of Protestantism and evangelicalism remained in northwestern Europe, but British, Dutch, German, Swedish, and other evangelicals paid attention when their pastors went to America to preach, organize churches, and begin missions in the colonies, especially when exciting, controversial, bombastic figures like George Whitefield or Count Zinzendorf were involved. When these two met in London in 1743 to discuss their troubled relationship it was big news on both sides of the Atlantic and appeared in the newspapers. In the Netherlands, the *Haarlemse Courant* published a report about Zinzendorf's failed attempt in 1742 to unite all of the Pennsylvania religions.[7] In addition to these big names, John Wesley (who was not well known at the time he went to Georgia in 1735), Theodor Frelinghuysen, Heinrich Melchior Mühlenberg, Michael Schlatter, Charles Woodmason, and many others were sent by their respective churches to try to make something happen in America—and they did. Also, a number of religious groups like the Lutheran refugees from the Archbishopric of Salzburg, the Schwenkfelders, and the Moravians themselves made news in Europe when they migrated to America.[8]

These very migrations, the competition among pietist groups as to who would shepherd them, and the activities of these groups after arriving in America were a part of the transatlantic awakening itself. During the Great Awakening European immigrants revived the Native American mission, which had faltered by the early eighteenth century in New

England, and some began pushing for the conversion of African slaves. The European (and American) public followed the course of events in German religious journals like *Acta Historia Ecclesiastica* and *Die Geistliche Fama* or in English-language "revival magazines" like *The Weekly History*, as well as the published journals of Whitefield and Wesley, the official published reports of the Halle Lutheran pastors in North America, and the numerous works published by the radicals, especially the Moravians, about their work in the colonies. In 1748 Johann Philip Fresenius, who held the highest Lutheran post in Frankfurt am Main, even published the "American Reports" (*Americanische Nachrichten*), a documentary history of the early revival in America.[9] What the European and North American public found out was that many religious battles were being fought, won, and lost in North America, and that, unlike the case in Europe the radicals, especially the Moravians, appeared to have a real chance to influence the revival and the nature of piety among the new German and other immigrants in the colonies, as well as among Indians and slaves. While never a serious threat in Europe, in North America they seemed to have much greater opportunities for success.

Unlike the English Puritans and Quakers in the seventeenth century, Lutheran and German Reformed officials would not attempt to set up a significant church apparatus in North America in the 1730s and 1740s, even though immigration escalated dramatically in this period and many immigrants called to Europe for one. Lutheran and Reformed immigrants made up over 90 percent of the nearly 90,000 Germans arriving in the colonies from 1730 to 1754—the peak period of conflict involving the Moravians.[10] They had left their German and Swiss territories for secular reasons, often without permission in order to avoid huge taxes assessed for leaving the realm. They came from so many different political and ecclesiastical jurisdictions that few Lutheran and Reformed authorities could even imagine how they might care for them in British America, even if they wanted to. The vast majority lived in dispersed settlements in and around Pennsylvania, in which the nearest church was the center of most of the "community" that these colonists had. Among these migrants only the Salzburg Lutheran refugees, a small number of whom emigrated to Georgia, drew significant interest from major religious centers in Europe early on, and this was only because of their high profile as fellow Protestants persecuted by the Catholic archbishop of Salzburg. The Lutheran pietist center at Halle and the consistories in the German territories were more interested in the progress of the radicals and a few special projects like the Salzburgers than in the large, ongoing migration of Germans to North America. This meant that few pastors and no higher bodies of church organization existed for the tens of thousands of German Lutheran and Reformed immigrants, who nevertheless settled in these dispersed ethnic-religious communities across the landscape of "Greater Pennsylvania."[11]

Like later historians, Pennsylvanians at the time debated what kind of culture had developed in this religious environment.[12] In general the radicals did well in Pennsylvania and praised the libertine religious culture of the colony, although they often dealt with many challenges, complaints, and internal crises. Perhaps Christopher Saur, the Separatist printer in Germantown, best summed up the positive nature of the Pennsylvania religious environment from the radical point of view. Saur condemned the way immigrants were treated during passage to America and upon arrival, and he often attacked the Penn family for its political positions, but he praised the dispersed nature of society and the tolerant religious environment of the colony.[13] Flaunting his Separatist colors, Saur proclaimed in his newspaper that the Bible was the only source of truth in matters of faith and practice and that every unlearned Christian has as much right as a pastor or bishop to read and judge what it means. Moreover, every Christian has the right to practice pacifist principles without being disturbed by *anyone*, even the civil magistrates. And they have the right to publicize their beliefs and evangelize, to speak out against every depraved religious matter or false teaching, and the right to separate from any religious community not serving God and join another. Saur protested any attempt to prohibit this by anyone, especially worldly authorities.[14]

In his almanacs published during the peak years of German immigration into Pennsylvania, Saur developed a fictional dialog between a new arrival (*Neukommer*) who was confused by the new dispersed, diverse, and tolerant environment and an established resident (*Einwohner*), who explained its advantages (and thus Saur's own opinion). When the *Neukommer* complained that there were too few churches and preachers—in Germany there was a church in every city, town, and village, and everyone lived close to them—the *Einwohner* responded that it did not do them any good anyway. He asked, "Do all of the kings, nobility, magistrates, merchants, craftsmen, students, etc. live according to Christ's example just because they live close to a church and to each other?" If church here is ten miles away, go anyway, and don't fall asleep during the service, the Einwohner told the Neukommer. If your church is no good then go off alone into the woods and ask that the Holy Ghost come to you. Beware of false preachers and rely on the Holy Ghost to interpret Scripture. If you live dispersed you can contemplate your relationship with God in peace and quiet, the Einwohner explained. If you live amidst others you must put up with false teachers and sinners, as well as their pigs and chickens running through your garden. And don't worry

about getting a doctor if you or your animals get sick, he told the Neukommer: God will heal you, and you need to learn how to cure your
ailing livestock yourself. Farmers needed to be artisans and vice versa.
When the Neukommer questioned the scarcity of schools and teachers
(a product of an undeveloped colonial church) the Einwohner
responded that parents should teach their children themselves. Then
the Einwohner tried to get the Neukommer to see through all of the talk
about the chaotic plethora of religions in the land: there were really only
two—the true religion and the false one. The new fledgling Lutheran
and Reformed church establishments being constructed by the newly
arriving European clergy were not the answer, and many believed that
they actually caused the problems in the land because they taught people to hate each other. Besides, an illiterate "straw tailor" (*Stroh-
Schneider*) who looked after his flock was better in God's eyes than a
"puffed up deceiver in spirit and body who will preach for 3 pounds"
(*"Aufgeblasener geist- u. leiblicher Betrieger, der vor eine predigt 3 pfund hat"*).
The true preacher did not have to go to university—he was elected by
Christ and prepared by Him. One might interpret Saur's position as an
important development toward modern individualism, but Saur's critique of social conditions and religious culture in Pennsylvania is more
complicated and ambiguous than that. Throughout the dialogues and
elsewhere in his pamphlets and newspapers he condemns the new modern, legalistic, commercial society developing in Pennsylvania and longs
for the ancient Christian ideals of simplicity, trust, and faith.[15]

Saur and many other radicals liked "Pennsylvania religion," as some
scornfully labeled it, because it offered them the freedom they needed,
but many Europeans from the orthodox churches did not like it,
because it threatened religious and social order as they understood it.
Many Lutherans despised the "blind zeal of the many sects" in Pennsylvania, as Gottlieb Mittelberger called it. Mittelberger, the Lutheran pastor's assistant from Württemberg who immigrated in 1750 and returned
four years later, found the colony to be "heaven for farmers and artisans
and hell for officials and preachers."[16] Heinrich Melchior Mühlenberg,
the Lutheran pastor assigned by Halle to Pennsylvania in 1742, provided
a scathing critique of Pennsylvania's social and religious culture in his
correspondence and journals. Upon arriving in Philadelphia he took
one look at conditions there, saw the fledgling Lutheran churches being
overrun by Moravians and other pretenders, and complained that "Here
there is no governing authority: elders and deacons are of no account.
People do not listen to them but everybody is free and does as he
pleases."[17] A year later Mühlenberg blasted the slovenly, drunk, and lazy
people who called themselves teachers. As soon as they could read they

thought that they could preach and went around doing so. Later he wrote that some half-baked schoolmasters from Germany were going far out into the backcountry and setting themselves up as preachers to pay off their travel debts. The massive immigration at mid-century only made it worse: "Oh what a fearful thing it is to have so many thousands of unruly and brazen sinners come into this free air and unfenced country!" he wrote. Mühlenberg did not like interfaith or "mixed marriage" either, a product of the new diverse and uncontrolled environment: in New Hanover a Lutheran woman married an Anabaptist and had to bring her child in secretly to be baptized, since her husband, a crude blasphemer, was against it. Radicals like the Anabaptists were a problem not because they proselytized as a group like the Moravians, but because they were simply there, which meant good Lutheran women and men might marry them. He condemned the Quakers and Christopher Saur, both of whom attacked proper pastoral functions and sacraments. The sects constantly pointed out problems with church people, whom they referred to as worthless and dead members, but whenever some of them began to improve, Mühlenberg explained, the sectarians tried to draw them into their net with tricks and ruses. Thus Mühlenberg condemned the radical pietists and lumped them together with the "most cunning Jew."[18]

What Saur saw as freedom and an individualist paradise being threatened by the encroachments of a modern society Mühlenberg saw as godless, classless anarchy that must be replaced with proper churches, religious discipline, and respect for authority and order. Mühlenberg condemned Pennsylvania religious culture, with its uncontrolled pluralism, limitless freedom, latitudinarianism, unclear spiritual boundaries, and brutish people:

in this country Satan, who deceives the whole world, has his fully stocked fair and almost every possible type of sectarian mode, so that because of the subtleties it is almost impossible to distinguish them any longer according to the principle of indistinguishables; nevertheless they all agree in this that they give the appearance of godliness but deny its real power. This is the extent to which the unlimited, so-called freedom of conscience can lead the mortal and sinful human race.[19]

Most of all Mühlenberg complained about the lack of respect that proper pastors received from common people. Life and work in Pennsylvania were extremely difficult for these pastors: if they came without a proper call it was hard to find a good place to work. If they came with a call and received a salary, then the sects belittled them and Saur wrote them up in his newspaper. In his journal Mühlenberg cited numerous cases of callousness, insubordination, and lack of discipline among the

Germans in Pennsylvania. One man said that "in Pennsylvania neither the devil nor a parson could tell him what to do." Mühlenberg was trying to tame these wild people, but many rejected him. Why should they listen to him in this free land? Others said, "What right has the parson over me? Of course, I pay him by the year, but if his preaching does not please my taste, I'll go to another church where I can get it for nothing." And they were right: there were a lot of "Herrnhuters" (Moravians) and other sect preachers offering services for free to whom they could turn, Mühlenberg complained. The place reminded him not of some libertine paradise, but of Sodom and Gomorrah.[20]

The lack of ministerial authority and respect was linked to the problem of blasphemy, Mühlenberg discovered. In the German territories blasphemy was an offense punishable by secular authorities, but this was not so in libertine Pennsylvania, where the practice abounded. "It is almost incredible what hard and heartless expressions some bold and dissolute persons give vent to in this free, unbridled country," Mühlenberg wrote. He then related a tale of a rich scoffer in Oley, a well-known nest of radicals and misfits in the Pennsylvania backcountry, and a poor churchman who wanted to borrow money from him. "Do you know who my God is?" the rich man said. "No," the poor man replied. Then the rich man pointed to the manure pile outside his door and said, "There is my God; he gives me wheat and everything I need." When the poor man rebuked him for this blasphemy, the rich man replied, "Well, if you don't like my God, you'll have to borrow money from your own, the one you pray to and go to church for." Another man uttered similar godless expressions regarding his valuable horse and announced that he wanted to be reincarnated as a swine, Mühlenberg wrote. Later his horse was struck dead by lightning, and the man hanged himself. Another blasphemer asked one of Mühlenberg's parishioners why he went twelve miles to church to hear about the "whore's son." Additionally, Mühlenberg had to deal with Jews, who were atheists and deists, he thought.[21]

Mühlenberg described the religious condition of Pennsylvania to Dr. Joachim Oporin, one of his old professors at the orthodox Lutheran university in Göttingen, Germany: "In short, there is probably no sect in the world that is not fostered and nurtured here. There are people here from almost all the nations of the world. Whatever is not tolerated in Europe finds its place here." And he did not mean it as a compliment. The situation of the Lutherans was bad and getting worse, Mühlenberg thought. Children were growing up unbaptized and becoming heathens. Gluttony, swilling, whoring, greed, strutting, insolence, overblown pride, and the like predominated. Count Zinzendorf and the Moravians were causing confusion and "*Mischmasch*" with no end in sight. It was pitiful how people cursed, scolded, blasphemed and fought among themselves, and the Lutheran church would soon be ruined, he wrote in 1743.[22]

Mühlenberg neither wanted nor expected help from the handful of Lutheran and German Reformed preachers in the colonies, who were not properly supported and supervised by European religious authorities. In fact, these preachers were part of the problem, he thought. According to rumor, Valentin Krafft, one of his early rivals for the Philadelphia Lutheran parishes, kept two wives, one on each side of the Atlantic. The civil authorities had pressed rape charges against Caspar Schnorr, the Reformed pastor from Westphalia. And the city of Philadelphia had sued an independent Lutheran pastor named Caspar Stoever, who got drunk and vomited in an inn in front of a number of people. Christopher Saur enjoyed this sort of thing and printed it in order to discredit the churches, Mühlenberg complained. He also complained about the disorderly Lutheran colonists, i.e., those not in the Halle fold, who took on such scandalous preachers when they were already in danger of being seduced by the numerous sects.[23]

One of the most notorious Lutheran vagabond preachers who flourished in this wide open colonial religious environment was a man named Carl Rudolph, who called himself the "Prince of Württemberg." Mühlenberg and his colleague Friedrich Vigera described with disgust how the prince claimed to have been kidnaped by a ship captain and sold at Frederica, Georgia, and how he narrowly escaped the gallows there. Then the prince began his wandering preaching career and moved north into the Carolinas and Virginia. By the mid-1740s he was in Maryland, but the inhabitants at Monocacy drove him out and toward Pennsylvania, where he appeared about 1746. According to Mühlenberg the prince passed himself off as a Lutheran preacher and roved about the countryside, "whoring, stealing, gluttonizing, and swilling during the week, and on Sunday in his sermons he reviles us (the Hallensians) as horrible Pietists and refutes the Moravians in the manner of a charlatan."[24] He tried to get established in Lutheran parishes by appearing in a community wearing a black preacher's gown that he had stolen from Valentin Krafft. He then presented his credentials as a prince, behaved piously, and preached effectively. It was only after the community accepted him that he began misbehaving. Another one of Mühlenberg's enemies, a Lutheran pastor named Johann Conrad Andreae, who worked at the New Goshenhoppen, Old Goshenhoppen, and Indianfield Lutheran communities in Philadelphia (now Montgomery) County, took the prince in and assigned him to Raritan, New Jersey, in November of 1747. Rudolph won the affections of the Lutherans there, but the Hallensians eventually discovered his whereabouts and denounced him. After allegedly joining the army in Boston and spending some time in prison for defecting, Rudolph returned to preaching in New York in 1749, where he passed himself off as a prince and a doctor and plagued the Hallensians and their allies around Rhinebeck on the Hudson River. In short, the prince was effective in America because the conditions were so chaotic that he could persuade the new immigrant communities that he was a good Lutheran preacher, when in fact, he was a swindler.[25]

Christopher Saur did not like the Prince of Württemberg either, and his resentment may reflect more than Mühlenberg's the notion of old class tensions gone chaotic in the new environment. In 1753 he printed an ad in his Germantown newspaper, the *Pennsylvanische Berichte*, describing the prince and his tactics in order to warn the populace that this scoundrel had been traveling in the land for years and might try to take advantage of them. The prince was not large in stature, had a round appearance, and dressed in black in order to gain more respect. The list of his sins and shortcomings was long: he had borrowed horses without paying, and sometimes secretly rode away on them. He had also taken the fourteen- and fifteen-year-old daughters of a number of people and was supposed to have had four wives, scattered over 300 miles, who had recently died. The prince had to fly from everywhere he stayed because of his bad behavior. He traveled back and forth through the countryside preaching, administering communion, and performing marriages (or getting married himself). Beer and baptism were his forte. An official once asked him to produce proof that he was a prince and Carl Rudolph responded that the proof was in his pants.[26]

According to Saur, the prince was a learned man: he read Hebrew and Greek, spoke Latin, preached in German and English and was good at it. He talked ugly, Saur wrote, but when he preached the prince was serious, as if he actually believed what he was saying. He once made a wager with some young men that he could preach to a crowd in such a manner that those before him would cry, while those behind him would laugh, and he did it too: the prince preached a moving sermon, bringing those before him to tears. At the same time he brushed the rear flaps of his black gown to the side, reached through his torn pants and scratched his bare bottom. The audience behind him could not stop laughing. The people in front could not understand why those in the rear laughed, and those in the rear could not understand why those in front cried. The prince won this bet, but he did not always win: in the Maxatawny congregation in Berks County, Pennsylvania, Rudolph tried to lead Sebastian Zimmerman's daughter astray by secretly coming into her room through the window at night. Someone betrayed him, however, and two men lay waiting in the girl's bed instead. They pounced on the prince with a horse whip and club and "gave his highness's priestly hide a proper thrashing, so that the Herr Soul-Caretaker lost his urge."[27] The last notice about the Prince of Württemberg appeared in Saur's newspaper a year later, in 1754. The Germantown congregation had rejected him, and some Lutherans from across the Schuylkill River, a few miles away, had taken him in. He was riding his horse and singing cavalry songs before disappearing from the records, perhaps swept away by the French and Indian War and a new career as an army chaplain. His colorful story illustrates how radical separatists who embraced "Pennsylvania religion" and orthodox church builders who despised it both rejected smooth-talking, would-be (or real) nobility who were not what they seemed to be and tried to take advantage of conditions in this rapidly expanding, diverse immigrant society that offered tremendous religious freedom, for better or worse. Unfortunately for the Moravians, led by Count Zinzendorf, the other radicals and the church leaders believed they were doing essentially the same thing as Rudolph, but on a much larger scale and were therefore much more dangerous to both freedom and order in the colonies.[28]

To some orthodox European pastors women were also a part of the problem of inversion and anarchy in the social-religious order of Pennsylvania. Opportunities to preach and prophesy were more prevalent for women in the colonies than they were in Europe, and orthodox pastors considered this dangerous. Mühlenberg did not like women preachers and believed that women were more subject to "partisan zeal" and caused problems for him and his colleagues pursuing the Lord's work. Once a "miserable rabble" employed an "audacious female" to charge publicly that Mühlenberg kept two whores in Philadelphia and that Mühlenberg had attacked her. (She later admitted that this was not true and was compelled to apologize to all of his congregations.) Also, women indentured servants in one faction of a church dispute in New York complained to the city mayor that their master had assaulted them. Mühlenberg assumed the master was innocent and condemned the wicked women, comparing them to the "unscrupulous strumpets" in Pennsylvania. Sometimes gender and class worked together to threaten traditional church order as many immigrants understood it when, for example, pastors married beneath their order as well. For Mühlenberg marriage was in part a career move. When he married the daughter of Conrad Weiser, the influential political and Indian agent in Pennsylvania, it furthered the Hallensian's influence in the colony. After his marriage Mühlenberg paid little attention to his wife, who got in the way of his work, he thought. On the other hand, Mühlenberg lamented the marriage choice of another Hallensian pastor, Johann Friedrich Handschuh, who did not choose a woman who might help his career. Instead Handschuh married beneath his station and caused a scandal in his parish.[29]

While diversity and tolerance seemed to offer tremendous opportunity to religious radicals in North America, those who tried to take too much advantage of it encountered resistance from pastors like Mühlenberg and his supporters, who promoted traditional order and patriarchal authority and condemned runaway religious freedom and radical beliefs concerning gender and sex. Even though circumstances were much different and opportunity real in America, the radicals challenged a gender and confessional order that had been developing since the Reformation, if not earlier. Radicals had made such challenges before, and when the authorities and/or ordinary people considered the threat to be too dangerous, they reacted. In the recent past they had dealt with a bizarre challenge to gender order in a religious community in the German territories that had heightened sensitivity of Lutherans and other Protestants on both sides of the Atlantic to such dangers. And in case anyone had forgotten, the enemies of religious radicalism made efforts to remind them, to warn them of what happened when radicalism went too far.

Chapter 2

Gender and Confessional Order in the Protestant World

> *Regarding these dangerous matters of marriage and community I do not want readers to dwell too long in the annals of the ancient register of heresies, for the sad example (God help us!) of Mother Eva and her comrades is all too well known in our times.*
>
> —Georg Jacob Sutor, anti-Moravian polemicist, published in Frankfurt am Main, 1746

In 1700, a time of apocalyptic significance to many German radical pietist groups on both sides of the Atlantic, a new society formed in Allendorf on the Werra around a noblewoman named Eva Margaretha von Buttlar (1670–1721). The "Mother Eva Society" eventually moved to Wetteravia, one of the well-known refuges for religious radicals (see Map 3), and developed beliefs and practices concerning gender, marriage, sexuality, and the body that shocked the outside world. Their initiation, purification, and rebirth ritual was the most extreme. For women it involved what they called "circumcision" (*Beschneidung*): an initiate would be led into a room and laid on a bed. While Eva recited from the "Song of Solomon," her husband, Justus Gottfried Winter, and an associate named Sebastian Ichtershausen assured the woman that there was nothing to fear—soon Jesus was coming to cleanse her from all her sins by slaying the "old Adam" residing inside her womb. Then Winter reached into her womb, first with one finger, then two, finally with his entire hand. After a period of time he crushed her ovaries (or attempted to—the procedure did not always work), and the woman lost consciousness. When she awoke she had terrible pain and lay in bed bleeding for weeks, while her name was entered into a book indicating that she had been initiated into the Society. One mother who experienced the ritual said later that she would rather go through ten more childbirths than experience such pain again. In another case Ichtershausen needed fifteen tries, first with two fingers and then with his entire hand, before successfully completing the procedure. This brutal practice that victimized women was practiced by a group that in many ways also promoted female power, an unusual combination that heightened the growing controversy concerning the society.[1]

Members of the Mother Eva Society believed in an androgynous Christ and Adam before the Fall and the Trinity as father, mother, and son. This view was experiencing a revival in late seventeenth-century Germany, and it became the foundation of the Mother Eva Society's controversial beliefs and practices, like the above ritual "circumcision." Women played a special role in this society, whose leader was Eva herself. She taught that depravity and sexual relations began because of the Fall, when the pure, whole androgyny of Adam was lost. Only ritual purification could resolve the problem for individual believers, and this took place in different ways for women and men. For women the most important way was through ritual circumcision, and members of the Mother Eva Society learned how to achieve this through a "special inspiration." The ritual included purification of their menstrual blood and demanded subordination of their will and sexual appetite to the leaders of the group. During the ritual they swore until death to devote their lives to the Society.

For men the most important way to achieve purification was through ritual sex with Mother Eva in the presence of her husband, Justus Gottfried Winter. (Thereafter the men's names would be entered into the book of initiates as well.) A circumcised woman could transfer her new purity to a man during ritual sex. For men in the Society, sex with Eva became an initiation and purification rite, just as circumcision was for women. Further, Eva was "mother" to those in the group, because men also experienced their spiritual rebirth during the ritual with her. Ritual sex was supposed to free men of their sexual urges too, although this could take longer. Some men also subsisted on bread and water for weeks as part of the ritual.[2]

Mother Eva got into trouble for a lot of reasons, the most important of which were connected to her violations of female bodies and norms concerning gender, marriage, and sexuality, all of which were significantly shaped by religion in this era. Recently early modern European and colonial American cultural historians have made it clear that gender norms and public boundaries of action, or the German term *Handlungsräume*, as well as the mechanisms for enforcing them, were an important, dynamic part of everyday life in communities during the early modern era. Although peoples' beliefs in what proper male and female behavior was changed over time, most were committed to them. They would and did react, violently if necessary, to preserve or restore proper gender order if and when it had been challenged. Understandings of gender order were connected to concepts of power and legitimacy that reached the highest levels of authority in these societies.[3]

The most serious Moravian challenges to orthodox Protestant gender order concerned their understandings of the gender of the Christian Trinity and their alternative views regarding women preaching, marriage, and sex. Beliefs and understandings about these issues were crucial to Protestants on both sides of the Atlantic, and they were connected to their spiritual and cultural values regarding gender and power. Many Protestant men and women held strong views on these subjects that went to the core of their beliefs about religion, authority, community, and family, and this helps explain the passion with which they defended them. These beliefs and practices underwent tremendous challenges and changes in the Protestant world from the Reformation to the Enlightenment and the pietist movement of the late seventeenth and eighteenth centuries. An overview of these developments will help make it clear why Lutherans, Calvinists, and others on both sides of the Atlantic reacted so strongly toward the Moravians. The key lies in understandings of the gender of the deity and how this was used to promote female empowerment in the religious community, especially in preaching and other leadership roles.

Moravian challenges to gender order appeared even more threatening to many members of the large state churches when this radical group also began to challenge confessional order. Count Zinzendorf claimed that his followers were or could be members of those churches even when they pursued alternative gender beliefs and practices and associated with other radicals who wanted nothing to do with the state churches. In this manner the Moravians challenged the doctrine, and respect for territorial church boundaries that had developed in the sixteenth and seventeenth centuries during the Age of Confessionalism. In the mid-eighteenth century many orthodox Protestants continued to promote some aspects of the confessional religious style. To them the maintenance of sound doctrine, respect for territorial church boundaries, and patriarchal authority protected people from error, including blasphemous beliefs about the Trinity and revolting practices like those of the Mother Eva Society that resulted from such beliefs. This confessional view emerged in the North American colonies in the mid-eighteenth century in a different form as denominationalism, but its emphasis on proper doctrine, clearly delineated boundaries between churches and patriarchal authority within them was as strong in many groups or "denominations" as it had been with its confessional counterpart in Europe. The commitment to confessionalism had to be strong to protect the faith and the flock from danger.

Gender, Power, and the Trinity

The facts that members of the Mother Eva Society believed in female qualities of the Trinity and that the society was led by a woman were directly related. Religion plays a critical role in shaping understandings and practice concerning gender and power. It can be and historically has been an important dynamic in cultural perception and action—a real link from the cosmic to everyday life. Both gender and religious symbols like the Trinity operate as meaningful models in systems of cultural representation, and the two are related: religion influences the changing ways in which gender is perceived. In other words, religious symbols have practical consequences for believers, gender plays a role in understanding the meaning and function of those symbols, and practical consequences follow.[4] One of the most important spiritual symbols for Christians is the Trinity, which serves as a model for understanding power and authority in the Christian community. Throughout history, from the ancient Gnostics, to the Mother Eva Society, to recent feminist theologians, Christians who reject the complete subjugation of women to men have developed feminine language for the deity and then used this understanding of the Trinity as a model for their society, that is, to empower women. In doing so they rejected the traditional model, which stresses a male Trinity and male power in the religious community and family.[5]

So what did Protestants believe about the gender of the Trinity in the early modern and colonial era? Clearly the language and understandings were male, but we should not assume that there was uniform thought among theologians on this important subject or that it did not change over time. In fact, historical theologians stress that views on the Trinity and its importance have fluctuated over the centuries. Few, however, have investigated beliefs of Protestant religious leaders concerning the gender of the Trinity in this era.[6]

Analysis of the language and functional qualities that Reformation theologians assigned to each person of the Trinity reveals a strongly masculine view of the gender of the deity that suggests a continuation of the traditional view. Understanding the language and function they assigned to the Trinity is important: if gender is a cultural construct, that is, if gender is what people think males and females should be doing or representing, then the reformers' use of language and assignment of function reveals their attitudes about the gender of the deity. Although what prompted the reformers to write what they did about the Trinity were not questions and concerns of the day about gender, but rather challenges by Socianians, Arians, and others to the deity of Christ and the existence of the Holy Spirit,[7] their responses to these heresies reveal that they held a masculine view of the Trinity. That is, the language and the functions the reformers assigned to the different persons of the Trinity were largely male. Because their views were so influential on the development of Protestantism in the Atlantic world during the early modern and colonial era, I will briefly examine them below.

Early in his career Martin Luther commented on the Apostles' Creed in order to assuage growing doubts among some religious thinkers about the deity of all three persons of the Trinity, and in doing so he revealed his views on how gender and power worked in this critical Christian symbol. Luther's expressions concerning the power of "God the Father" are somewhat ambiguous, but the gender is clearly male. "I believe in God the Father, the All Mighty, the Creator of Heaven and Earth," he quotes from the Creed, but he does not clearly distinguish function between the Trinity as a whole and the "Father." Clearly the Father was omnipotent, but the Creation was the work of all three persons of the Trinity. He is more clear about gender, however, and not just in name: Luther declares that he is a child of the Father. Luther's description of the Son is quite male in all respects. The Son participated in the Creation; he is the redeemer; he sits at the right hand of the Father and reigns as king over the angels and all creatures and things of God in heaven, hell, and on Earth; and he will be there on Judgment Day. Thus to Luther there were no ambiguities about the gender of this male ruler, redeemer, and judge. Lastly, Luther provides a largely male description of the Holy Spirit's function. The Spirit entered the Virgin Mary, and this led to the birth of Jesus, suggesting a male function. Further, no one may come to the Father through the Son unless the Holy Spirit moved him or her, thus making them alive. Indeed, the Holy Spirit gathered and ruled the church and was responsible for resurrecting the dead and buried and making them alive as well. Giving life may be understood as a female function in modern language and belief, but in the early modern era notions that the woman was passive in conception and that it was the male who brought life to an inanimate ovum were common, especially in the German territories.[8]

Two points are clear in John Calvin's writings about the Trinity: one, the Trinity was central to Calvin's understanding of God and the relationship between God and humans, and two, the gender of the Trinity was male. Like Luther's, John Calvin's writings about the Trinity responded to heresies and doubts raised by Arians and Socinians concerning the divine essence of Christ and the Holy Spirit and the nature of the three-in-one concept. Calvin was careful about what he wrote concerning the Trinity in part because he had been falsely accused of promoting the Arian heresy. For the rest of his career, and in every revision of his *Institutes*, he carefully enunciated his views on this doctrine, pointing out his commitment to the three-in-one principle and explaining what it meant. One recent scholar even argues that Calvin wrote his entire *Institutes* on a Trinitarian pattern that illustrated his understanding of the divine-human relationship, which had direct practical consequences and meaning for believers. In other words, the Trinity mattered to Calvin, and to him specific relations and functions attributed to the Father, Son, and Holy Spirit had direct meaning for believers and their lives.[9]

While Calvin was not concerned with explaining the gender of the Trinity per se, his use of masculine language for the "Father" and the "Son," together with his descriptions of the masculine functions for all three persons, makes his position clear. His Trinitarian views and language are most explicitly stated in Book I, Chapter 13 of the *Institutes*. To the Father Calvin attributed the beginning of activity—he was the fountain and wellspring of all things. To the Son he attributed wisdom, counsel, and the ordered disposition of all things. And to the Holy Spirit he attributed the power and efficacy of these activities. Christ participated with the Father in governing the world. He performed miracles, had the power to remit sins, and his name was invoked for salvation, according to Calvin. The beauty of the universe owes its strength, preservation, and power to the Holy Spirit, thus making it clear that he believed that the Holy Spirit participated in the Creation. Further, the Holy Spirit bestowed wisdom and the faculty of speaking, and through the Spirit humans came into communion with God, so that they could feel God's life-giving power toward them. "Our justification is his work; from him is power, sanctification [cf. I Cor. 6:11], truth, grace, and every good thing that can be conceived, since there is but one Spirit from whom flows every sort of gift [I Cor. 12:11]," he wrote. From this it is clear that Calvin believed that the Holy Spirit's role was to dispense power. In fact, *power* more than anything else was the key issue to Calvin in all three persons of the Trinity, and this suggests a masculine view of the Trinity. Calvin did not indicate that the function of the Holy Spirit or the Son was to comfort or nurture in what some suggest was a feminine or motherly role.[10]

Huldrych Zwingli, the sixteenth-century Swiss Reformer, presented a clearly male view of the Trinity as well, although his depiction of the Holy Spirit was somewhat ambiguous. To him all three persons shared all major characteristics of the Trinity, but the Father was associated more with omnipotence and the Creation, while the functions of the Son were wisdom, salvation, healing, protection, and lordship—all essentially male roles. Zwingli was less clear about the Holy Ghost. In fact, he only wrote three lines about this in his "Credo Sermon," but elsewhere he did emphasize that Mary was the mother of Christ and that

Christ was born of Mary and the Holy Ghost, which suggests a male quality of the latter. On the other hand, Zwingli did attribute the functions of comforting (*Tröstung*) and initiating love (*Anzünden der Liebe*) to the Holy Ghost, which could be understood as female functions. In spite of this possible ambiguity regarding the gender of the Holy Ghost, Zwingli was one of the few reformers who explicitly addressed the possible sex of the Trinity. Since God created humans in his own image, Zwingli asked whether this meant the image of God in body or soul. He then rejected the body image, because no one knew what God looked like, and associating the human body with its male and female parts to the deity must be wrong. Thus, Zwingli concluded, the image of God in which humans were created must refer to the soul. In short, Zwingli's views of the biological "sex" of the Trinity were in some ways asexual, yet his view of gender was male.[11]

There were many voices in the "radical Reformation," not all of which can be addressed here, but one of them, Menno Simon, may help provide a sense of how religious thinkers from this side of the Reformation perceived gender and power within the Trinity. Simon was in some ways the most important of these voices because his movement withstood the test of time. In fact, by the eighteenth century there were more Mennonites in Europe and North America than any other group whose origins lay in the radical Reformation. As with Luther, Calvin, and Zwingli, Simon was concerned about violations of Trinitarian thought by those who questioned the three-in-one principle, and it is from his responses to this issue that one can glean his views on the gender of the Trinity. Here Simon used masculine language for the Father and unclear language for the Son and the Holy Spirit. The functions of the three persons were as follows: the Father played a "fatherly" role protecting children, clearly a male function. The Son's role was redemption, salvation, and mediation, none of which was intrinsically masculine. His description of the Holy Spirit's function was lengthy, but may be summed up as "distributer of the gifts of God." There were elements of the Holy Spirit's role that could be seen as feminine, e.g., consoling, pacifying, assuring, but Simon did stress the role of Mary in the birth of Jesus, and this suggests a male role of the Holy Spirit. In short, however, the functions of the Holy Spirit and even the Son were less clearly male with Simon than they were with others, which may suggest a less strongly male view of gender and power in the radical Reformation than the Lutheran, Calvinist, and Zwinglian reform movements.[12]

In the seventeenth century Protestant theologians defended their view of the Trinity against numerous challenges. Arians and Socinians continued to promote what confessional theologians considered to be heretical views. Also Jacob Böhme's explorations of the substance and essence of God, which included a view of the Trinity with androgynous elements, was extremely influential among radical pietists in the German territories, who constantly challenged state church authorities. Lutherans remained committed to defending the Trinity with Scripture, and the Dortrecht canons of the Dutch Reformed church (1618) reaffirmed the three-in-one principle. In the late seventeenth century, confessional orthodox theologians responded to deists and John Locke, who questioned how three divine entities (Father, Son, and Holy Spirit) could be one divine entity (God). Calvinist theologians became more interested in the Trinity as well.[13]

In the eighteenth century the rationalist challenge led to rigorous responses from theologians, who deeply explored the traditional view of the Trinity and developed creative interpretations that showed the meaning and importance of the three-in-one concept to believers. In part influenced by Dutch Reformed writers, Jonathan Edwards responded to rationalists, who deemphasized the divinity of Jesus and the Holy Spirit, and felt compelled to show the relevance and meaning of the Trinity to believers in everyday life—a reflection of his pietism. In doing so he employed a social model of the Trinity, in which he took gender seriously and saw the Trinity in terms of a family. To Edwards, the power relationships and deference within the Trinity were intended to work for humans and their social relations. The gendered language for the Trinity was clearly masculine: God was a father and husband and Christ was a son, husband, and brother, but Edwards was unclear about the Holy Ghost, reflecting "deep Reformed ambivalence" on this part of the Trinity. He and Reformed theologians rejected Marian devotion (i.e., God as sister, daughter, wife) and this led to the problem of an all-male family model. To resolve this problem, Edwards developed a psychological model to supplement his social model. With this he emphasized the critical role of the Holy Ghost in showing the divine love between the Father and Son, as a "comforter" carrying the delight and love flowing from the Father and Son to the church, thus making it the foundation of union between God and the saints.[14]

The heightened interest in the Trinity in the eighteenth century led to two problems. First, the three-in-one concept began to appear irrational to some. The incongruities between the early creeds and Scripture compounded the problem, and some would argue that the emphasis on reason in the critical Enlightenment left Trinitarian thinking ridiculed and rejected.[15] Second, the desire of pietists, who did not emphasize reason in their faith, to find everyday meaning and use in the Trinity led them to the question of gender in the Trinity. These pietists had either to accept an all-male Trinity as their model, or to develop a more complex model of its importance that did not consider gender, or both (as in Edwards's case). In any event it is clear that the mid-eighteenth century was a period of heightened interest among Protestant theologians in the doctrine of the Trinity. They pondered its meaning and ramifications and remained vigilant against threatening heresies, either from rationalists or radical spiritualists with alternative notions of gender and power related to the Trinity.

Women Preaching

The gender order that restricted the preaching function in the community to males was frequently challenged in the early modern and colonial era. But these challenges aroused fears of too much female power in the community, and a reaction usually followed that stifled the practice. During the early Reformation some women took Luther's notion of the "priesthood of all believers" literally and felt moved to proclaim publicly their own religious ideas through writing and preaching. But as the Protestant Reformation became more established and institutionalized, the reformers rejected the notion of women preaching and writing publicly and took action to curb such activities. Although reading the Bible was encouraged, Calvinist women were not allowed to preach. In England, Parliament even prohibited women from gathering for Bible readings, especially women in the lower orders, although many disobeyed the new law. In Germany some noble women circumvented proscriptions against women playing leadership roles in public religious authority and activity, and in the seventeenth and early eighteenth centuries, they could and did provide independent support to religious groups, especially pietists, but public preaching was no longer acceptable.[16]

Women preaching became controversial again in England in the seventeenth century, when a number of radical dissenting movements with alternative ideas concerning gender and power in the spiritual realm promoted the practice. Many of these groups attracted a disproportionate number of women into their ranks, and it was perhaps inevitable that some of them began preaching. The English Civil War provided dramatic opportunities for women's leadership and action, and a temporary relaxation in censorship allowed the publication of many religious works by female authors. The emphasis on the efficacy of public prayer and the high estimation of dramatic conversion experiences in this era gave some women the power to talk openly with others or publish how it happened to them. Ultimately women's prayers and conversion narratives became extended prophecies. Some female prophets gained significant reputations and published their warnings and admonitions. Many of these were Levellers and Fifth Monarchists, who were more open to the notion of divine revelation through lay people than were Puritans. When criticized, these women cited Old and New Testament precedents to defend their work. Those who went beyond this to actual preaching emphasized that they had been called by God to do so. Most preached spontaneously at informal or clandestine gatherings, with no one recording their words. During the Restoration, however, many Anglicans associated women's preaching with the Civil War and disorder and took measures to stop it. With this and a relative increase in peace and prosperity, most of the radical groups died out shortly thereafter.[17]

The Quakers were the most important radical group on either side of the Atlantic that survived the Restoration and continued to promote female preaching. They probably provided the most significant outlet for women to find public expression in the early modern era. Over 200 of the approximately 300 "visionary women" in seventeenth-century England were Quakers. They used gendered images of virgins, mothers, and prostitutes to praise the righteous and castigate the unjust. Quaker prophets taught hard truths in intense, emotional sermons, but they did not speak in trances like other prophets, nor were they overcome with enthusiasm. They proclaimed their message loudly at mid-century and were persecuted heavily for it. With some exceptions, early female Quaker preachers presented themselves not as possessing special authority to preach as women, but rather as spiritual equals to men, who like men received the authority to preach from the Inner Light. Some recent historians argue that Quaker women never possessed autonomous power or authority separate from men, and that even in the early years in England the Quakers were ambivalent about gender and sought to legitimize and protect the movement by curbing and controlling unruly women.[18]

In the English North American colonies during the seventeenth and early eighteenth centuries, Anglicans, Puritans, Presbyterians, and Dutch Reformed demanded that women keep silent in church. Puritan women may have influenced religious affairs in their communities by working through their husbands or village networks, pressuring ministers on policy decisions, or acting as vessels of the supernatural in witchcraft outbreaks, but they played no formal role in the church hierarchy or formal worship. The demand for silence even carried to the conversion narrative, the personal statement by individual Puritans to the congregation describing how the Holy Spirit worked within their soul to achieve their salvation. Men witnessed publicly before the congregation, while women usually described their experience privately and stood silently as a man read the narrative to the congregation. A few radical sects temporarily allowed women to exhort or prophesy, but only Quakers allowed women to preach. Anne Hutchinson, Deborah Moody, Anne Eaton, and Sarah Keayne revolted, but they were elites and never claimed the right to speak from the pulpit. Moreover, even their modest demands were suppressed.[19]

In the late seventeenth and early eighteenth centuries the radical pietists in the German territories offered increased opportunities for women, including preaching, but as in the Reformation a reaction followed. Some drew on ancient Gnostic traditions that provided alternative interpretations of God that included female qualities, and some women, like Johanna Eleanora von Merlau (1644–1724), preached and played important leadership roles in these movements.[20] In the early 1690s a wave of chiliastic-ecstatic incidents involving women took place in Frankfurt am Main, Lübeck, Quedlinburg, Erfurt, Halberstadt, and Halle that included some women who had been trained by August Hermann Francke, the leader of the newly developing pietist center at Halle. But the active participation of women who preached and taught in conventicles, wrote tracts, and interpreted Scripture was too much for religious authorities to accept—indeed, it was scandalous. So they began cracking down on this behavior, including expelling the ecstatic prophetess Anna Schuchart, who emigrated in 1694 with Johannes Kelpius of Transylvania and other German radicals to Pennsylvania. A division emerged in the pietist movement between moderates and radical separatists, who refused to give in. By the late 1690s even pietist preachers spoke out against women overstepping traditional roles. Francke led the moderates, many of whom began migrating to the new university in Halle. They concentrated on the conversion experience as the path toward salvation and were able to stay within the Lutheran church, while the others broke completely with both the church and Francke's movement. Essentially, this division removed the practice of female preaching from the Lutheran church, although noble women played important roles for a few more years at Halle in maintaining good relations between the new pietist foundation there and the male nobility. These women also served as role models for pious behavior to the youths in training there.[21]

By the first half of the eighteenth century German Lutherans had not only removed all aspects of women preaching from their church, but also associated the practice with dangerous radicalism. The pietist network in Frankfurt, in which women had played important leadership roles since the late sixteenth century, scattered under the pressure, and was marginalized in small refuges like Bad Homberg, Büdingen, Berleburg, and Laubach, where wealthy women like Katharina Elisabeth Schütz financed them. The Halle pietists continued to distance themselves from the radicals and further diminished the role of women in their movement. The Mother Eva drama became a cautionary tale about why patriarchal authority should not be abandoned. By the time the Moravians became the most significant (and threatening) radical group with alternative ideas about God, gender, and women preaching in the 1730s and 1740s their views violated firmly entrenched Lutheran views regarding proper gender order.[22]

In the eighteenth century gender remained important in Anglican rhetoric against papists and Methodists, whom they continued to accuse of seduction and sexual deviance, and who they claimed allowed women too much power. Rather than preaching, Anglican women played important roles in the religious community as clergymen's wives, sisters, and daughters.[23]

In the mid-eighteenth century the Protestant evangelical awakening sweeping through central and northwest Europe brought new, although limited, impetus to women preaching in England. John Wesley, who emerged as a leader of the new Methodist movement that was at the center of the awakening in England, was inconsistent in his support of women preaching, as he struggled to balance the needs of strong, pious women who felt called to preach and male Methodist preachers who disliked the practice. Early in his career he spoke out against it in order to distance the group from the Quakers, as he tried to keep the new movement within the Anglican church. But by 1755 Wesley cited examples from early Christianity and drew a distinction between those who could administer the sacrament, who must be ordained (i.e., males), and those who could preach, who need not be ordained and could be both men and women. By the 1760s a number of Methodist women preachers were becoming so successful that Wesley became worried about keeping both male and female preachers under control, and he asked women to confine their activities to prayer, testimony, and exhortation, without preaching. Some continued to preach, however, sometimes even in preaching-houses, and by 1771 the male preachers who felt that this violated the Pauline injunction protested. Wesley gave in to the men and decided that women could preach only with his approval, which would come on an individual basis and in recognition of an "extraordinary call" to preach. By 1780 he ordered a stop to the practice because he once again feared that things were getting out of control. After Wesley's death in 1791 Methodist officials began further restricting who could preach, and even prohibited them from publishing letters, poetry, and descriptions of their religious lives in the *Arminian Magazine*. In short, the gender order that restricted women from preaching was ultimately enforced even within the evangelical group in which the practice was most tolerated in eighteenth-century England.[24]

The international evangelical revival movement was most intense in

British North America during the Great Awakening, and here is where female preaching became the most prominent in the Protestant Atlantic world during the eighteenth century. Indeed, the rise and fall of women preaching in the colonies was in many ways connected to the rise and fall of the Awakening itself, in what one historian recently labeled "short-lived radicalism." For the first time in the English colonies, large numbers of women in several denominations and religious groups tried to establish a tradition of female ministry. They began exhorting, prophesying, and preaching, although with the exception of the Quakers and the Moravians they never pushed for ordination. It almost seemed possible in the 1740s and 1750s that they would achieve this goal. In the 1740s New Lights and Separates began making public professions of faith, praying and exhorting in public, and openly challenging male ministers' views of Scripture. In 1741 in Massachusetts, for example, the caustic tongue of an exhorter named Bathsheba Kingsley and her disdain for clergy got her into trouble when she threatened male authority in the church and in the family. In the southern colonies, Separate Baptists demanded the right to exhort and serve as deaconesses and eldresses, and Methodists promoted women's vocal participation in public spaces and religious leadership. Like the early Reformation and Luther's emphasis on the priesthood of all believers, the Great Awakening's new emphasis on experiential piety and the power of the Holy Ghost had turned the church upside down by giving virtually unprecedented authority to the laity. The Awakening removed restrictions on women's religious speech and suspended the traditional belief that it reflected a licentious, passionate nature inspired by Satan. Women's outbursts undermined clerical authority, and their emotional preaching and prophesying made the Great Awakening an open, chaotic event that included increased lay participation, spontaneous meetings, and sudden conversions. Baptist women in Connecticut participated in theological debates, discipline, and church government, including choosing pastors, and speaking in church increased. Baptist men and women spoke out and challenged authority, and lay preaching and female exhorting increased.[25]

Although people experimented with alternative gender views during the Great Awakening, gender equality never became an issue. Many women had to lose their female identity in order to justify speaking, as femaleness was still seen as a defect. As with the Methodists in England, there were detractors even in their midst. Some objected to the noisy, angry manner of women's speaking and swooning, and not just Old Lights, but also New Lights shared anxiety toward disorderly evangelical women. They continued to associate women's public speech with sexual deviance, thus blurring spiritual and sexual boundaries. Women who preached knowingly flirted with anarchy and chaos, but the chance to liberate themselves from the old religion and the appeal of evangelical religion for women (lay participation of men and women, emphasis on the emotional style with little emphasis on proper texts) made it seem worth it.[26]

The most significant proponents and practitioners of women preaching in eighteenth-century British North America were the Quakers, and they were probably the least anxious about it as well. Much had changed in the Quaker movement since the tumultuous days of George Fox and Margaret Fell, and things would continue to change in the mid-eighteenth century, as the group began an internal reform movement in America. But the movement continued to grow, and women continued to play an active role in preaching and developing its belief system, something that did not change even when Quakers began withdrawing from colonial politics in Pennsylvania and redefined themselves from 1748 to 1783.[27] Large numbers of Quaker women preached to Quaker and non-Quaker men and women in the eighteenth century. Although the group had shifted from an uninhibited, confrontational style in the seventeenth century to quietism and conservatism to achieve legitimacy after the 1689 Act of Toleration, the Quakers were still expanding. They were a strong political force in Rhode Island, New Jersey, Pennsylvania, and North Carolina and had established 250 meetings in British North America by 1750. Quaker men and women traveled throughout the colonies to preach, operating in the same transatlantic networks as Quaker merchants and traders. About 1,300 to 1,500 female preachers worked throughout the Atlantic realm in the eighteenth century, and 60 preached on both sides of the Atlantic, an achievement valued highly in Quaker circles. The call to preach could be traumatic for these women, because they were violating the gender order when they worked outside Quaker communities, but the number of traveling female preachers actually increased in the eighteenth century. Some Quaker women even had magisterial oversight that could extend to all aspects of everyday life. Traveling women preachers mediated disputes and assisted with decision making in communities. In the mid-seventeenth century Bostonians had persecuted Quaker women as witches, but in the 1760s they sometimes celebrated them even more than non-Quaker women. In this era Quaker women preached to non-Quaker crowds of men and women, and non-Quakers published their writings.[28]

But in spite of the Quaker example, the expansion of female preaching in North America during the Great Awakening ended after the Awakening ran its course. Church groups that had formerly allowed women to preach sought legitimacy and stability in the Protestant world. Female status among Connecticut Baptists declined, for example, even as their membership increased, and the practice of women speaking publicly in church was questioned. By the time of the Revolution, as their institutions matured, Baptists sought to join the mainstream, which meant adopting family, household, and patriarchal ideals. Similar patterns of declining female status owing to institutional maturation and a desire for mainstream acceptance occurred among Methodists, Separates, and New Lights as well. This decline occurred to some extent even with the Quakers, who ultimately distanced themselves from New Lights to promote their own legitimacy. Quaker women continued to preach, but the high profile of female preachers among non-Quakers receded as the group's reform movement progressed. This suggests that women's preaching was more successful in the long run when kept internal, without proselytizing to other groups. In general, Quaker and other women preachers failed to achieve legitimacy in the eighteenth century and those who did preach remained "strangers and pilgrims" in a very religious society.[29]

Thus the transatlantic revival stimulated female preaching, especially in North America, but only among certain groups, and even then the impact was temporary, except for the Quakers. Some groups, like the German and Swedish Lutherans and German and Dutch Reformed, would have none of it, and these were the groups who became the most devoted enemies of the Moravians on both sides of the Atlantic. Even some German radicals in Europe and Pennsylvania rejected female preaching and disliked the Moravians in part because they promoted this practice. Like Europeans, the vast majority of colonial Americans believed that women should not preach. This violated their understandings of gender as an expression of order and how it should define religious community. Anglican women could play important roles as pastor's wives, sisters, and daughters, and married women in German Lutheran communities guarded legal rights, and played a role in church disputes concerning, for example, pastor's wives.[30] But they should go no farther than this. Perhaps most importantly, women as well as men played active roles in enforcing these and other aspects of gender order as they understood them, even if this meant guarding nearly exclusive male access to and control of the most important positions of power.[31] At times of tremendous upheaval, spiritual innovation, and change like the Reformation, the English Civil War, the devastating warfare that swept the German territories in seventeenth century, and the Great Awakening in North America, temporary variations in the gender order or lax enforcement could follow. There was an expansion of women preaching in all of these periods, but even then it was controversial, and with the exception of the Quakers it simply did not last. Women who preached from the sixteenth to the mid-eighteenth century violated an important aspect of the gender order and sooner or later encountered significant resistance from those who could not accept this innovation.[32]

Marriage and Sexual Behavior

As with women's preaching in the early modern era, belief, practice, norms, and their enforcement concerning marriage and sexual behavior changed significantly as well. The Reformation in the sixteenth century, Puritanism and pietism in the seventeenth century, and evangelicalism in the eighteenth century shaped attitudes, but in the eighteenth century secular developments also played a role. Many historians even agree that there was some kind of sexual revolution centered roughly in the eighteenth century, and although they disagree over its precise timing and nature, most believe that the change was contentious. One thing is clear, however, and that is that changing views regarding marriage and sex were a part of much larger cultural changes taking place in early modern and colonial society.[33]

Attitudes concerning marriage began changing during the Reformation, as Protestant reformers made this institution a central issue of the movement by desacramentalizing it and stressing its importance in maintaining proper social-political order, for example to enforce morals and help control neighborhoods. They intended for almost everyone to get married, and the number of regulations governing marriage increased, as part of a move by governments to control relations between the sexes and to link moral behavior and godliness to civic responsibility, although enforcement remained difficult and took time. They ended clerical celibacy, gave husbands more authority over wives, and attacked convent women and prostitutes, who were not under a husband's authority. This was attractive to some women because they could attain status by marrying well, but the new Protestant household moralism could not furnish an enduring mode of women's public action or a distinctly feminine register of piety.[34]

Attitudes and practice concerning marriage and sex were changing as well in the early modern Protestant world, as many religious leaders struggled adequately to define and articulate an unqualified positive view of marital sex.[35] In the seventeenth and eighteenth centuries people did not think about their sexual feelings and behavior as a distinct realm of identity, the way many do in the modern era. Rather than being a product of sexuality in the modern sense—a belief in a distinct causal agency within each individual that drove sexual interaction and shaped overall personality—early modern and colonial people viewed sexual behavior as a component of spirituality, cultural identity, and social status. People never simply engaged in sex: at some level of consciousness they interpreted their physical desires and ascribed significance to their behavior. Sex was and is "scripted," as one recent historian explains, meaning that cultural norms and personal attitudes influenced how people understood sexual impulses and the circumstances under which they are enacted. Meanings attributed to sex vary over cultures, time, and place, and among individuals, and in this era religion heavily influenced these thoughts and behavior.[36]

Like those before them, most Protestant religious leaders considered marriage as the only forum for legitimate sexuality. Many believed that marriage was important to control sex, that sex was necessary to raise more good Christians, that extramarital sex and celibacy were bad, and that lust—indeed all sex—was an unhappy consequence of original sin.[37] The view of sex as necessary and acceptable if it took place within marriage, yet connected to original sin and thus inherently evil, contained problems and contradictions that troubled Christians throughout the early modern and colonial period. Most reformers were unable to absolve even marital sex of all sinful aspects, and the majority hesitated to issue unqualified endorsements of the estate. John Calvin promoted marriage but consistently resisted total rejection of the ascetic ideal. Calvin believed that sex within marriage was not just for procreation, and that God created a helper for man so that he may not lead a solitary life, but beyond this Calvin could name no explicitly positive function of marital sex itself. Instead, marriage was a "necessary remedy to keep us from plunging into unbridled lust," as he put it. Husbands and wives should have each other soberly and modestly "so as not to wallow in extreme lewdness," and he found contraception monstrous. To him marital sex was natural and necessary, but he linked the Fall to sex between Adam and Eve, who were married before the Fall. Thus even marital sex was a reminder of this unfortunate event and was connected to sin.[38]

Martin Luther also struggled to make sex within marriage something positive, since to him marriage was so important, and it implied sex—to procreate and otherwise. On the one hand, he wrote that sex was needed to encourage marriage. It was a "duty" (*ehpflicht*) which should not be regulated, and it did not imply that women (also created by God) were a necessary evil. God created women to sleep with husbands and to bear and raise their children. Sex between husband and wife was as natural as eating and drinking. Restrictions on marriage and remarriage should be eased, while those on divorce or annulment should be tightened, unless the grounds were ignorance of a previously contracted marriage, or impotence, or perhaps to maintain a vow of chastity. (According to Luther a woman should leave her husband if he is impotent, even without his consent, or she could justifiably get pregnant by another man.) On the other hand Luther could not escape the notion that sex in and of itself—even within marriage—was a sin. Christian married couples should not allow their bodies to be governed by the search for evil lust, he wrote, and while marriage was honorable, the carnal aspects of it were not. Sex was never without sin—it was something men and women had to control and God had to "excuse" within marriage. The important thing to Luther was that this sin—like all other sins of believers—was forgiven.[39] He developed his early views on sex in response to the proponents of celibacy, who rejected marriage completely because it involved sex. Later his views on marital sex were in part a reaction to infamous cases of polygamy involving Prince Phillip of Hesse and the Anabaptist kingdom established in Münster. In the wake of these developments the paterfamilias or "*Hausvater*" and his household became the model for social order, and the character and reputation of the local pastor and his household became a well-established and influential ideal in Germany. A voluminous literature projected this ideal that included the Lutheran view of marriage as a divine ordinance to procreate and avoid fornication. But the ideal included Luther's problematic view of marital sex as a positive, natural act, yet still a sin that must be forgiven. This was part of what historian Lyndal Roper aptly identified as a larger underlying instability in Lutheran doctrines of marriage and the inability of theologians to satisfactorily resolve the proper relationship between the flesh and the will. In the seventeenth and eighteenth centuries conflicts over marriage, sex, and sin continued in the pietist movements, in part the result of these difficult, unclear positions developed by Lutheran theologians during the Reformation.[40]

This ambivalence about the positive nature of marital sex also prevailed among Calvinists in the Netherlands during the seventeenth century. Most Dutch writers agreed that physical tenderness was important, but they could not agree on the "perils and pleasures of the flesh," even in the marriage bed. Strict Calvinists thought it was possible to taint the marriage bed with too much sex, and they warned against unnatural unions. To them it was even possible for a husband and wife to commit adultery with unclean thoughts or unorthodox postures. (Copulation from behind was abhorrent, for example, because it simulated the sexual acts of beasts.) On the other hand, some thought it was possible for husbands and wives to maintain purity and virginity if they had moderate sex. "The marriage bed is no gutter for vile lusts, but those who use it well, may stay a maid," wrote Johan de Brune. The Calvinist reformers had to compete with popular works on human health, some of which expressed extremely positive views of marital sex in detail, like one physician-author who set the limit for a husband at four to five ejaculations per night with his wife. It was a difficult, unclear position for the Reformers, and clearly they realized that something could be wrong with marital sex, but they did recognize that "fleshly conversation" could be an expression of married love, as well as a remedy against sin and a necessity for procreation.[41]

From the late seventeenth to the mid-eighteenth century most German pietists who were not radicals believed that marital sex should be controlled, but just how and how much was subject to a variety of interpretations. Philipp Jacob Spener, the Lutheran pietist leader, believed "moderation was the best path" ("Mittelmaß die beste Straß"), roughly following Luther's position. In the late seventeenth century Lutheran pietists at Halle struggled to distance themselves from radicals, in part because of the latter's views toward sex and marriage, but few after Spener were able to make a clear statement about it. By the mid-eighteenth century some Lutheran pietists like Carl Heinrich von Bogatzky and Johann Jacob Moser agreed with the view of moderation, but they could not escape the old problem of original sin. Others, like August Hermann Francke, Siegmund Jacob Baumgarten, Johann Albrecht Bengel, and Friedrich Christoph Oetinger could not talk about it at all. Heinrich Melchior Mühlenberg, the fledgling, future leader of the Lutheran church in North America who did not particularly like women, believed that the purpose of sex was to propagate the human race and nurture children, but he still had reservations about marriage, since wives and children restricted a man's commitment to piety. Sexuality discomforted him, and he condemned other ministers in Pennsylvania and thereabouts who tolerated dancing, which he believed led to heightened sexuality.[42]

The Lutheran pietist struggle to affirm the fully positive nature of marital sex differed markedly from the Puritan experience in both England and New England in this era. A number of historians have pointed out that, in spite of their later reputation, Puritans actually cherished marital sex in an unqualified way. It was an important and expected part of the God-ordained relationship between husband and wife, and, unlike Lutherans, Puritans did not feel compelled to justify it as necessary for procreation or as a remedy against sin. The higher value placed on marital sex can be traced to Puritan theologians' resolution of the problem of sex and sin in the Garden of Eden that had plagued Luther, Calvin, and their followers. Like Erasmus a century earlier, Puritan writers in the seventeenth century argued that God instituted the excellence of marriage and sexual intercourse *before* the Fall, not as a remedy for fornication but as a part of the paradisiacal state itself. Adam needed Eve as a companion, not merely to bear children. Their love for each other would cure each's loneliness, and because of this they made romance a duty of married life. With some exceptions. Puritan theologians celebrated the sensual-sexual aspects of marriage and asserted that sexual satisfaction came from encounters between husbands in authority and submissive wives. They described this relationship as a reflection of God's relationship with believers, which could arouse erotic feelings among the latter. Puritan theologians did call for moderation in marital sex (like Luther and Spener), but they did so as part of their overall ethic of constancy in everything, whereas Lutherans developed it specifically to control too much marital sex because they believed that there was something innately wrong with it.[43]

Throughout the early modern and colonial era the clergy and magistrates struggled to enforce new attitudes about marriage and sexual behavior on an often unwilling population. Many promoted "natural" sex, that is, use of the missionary position and privacy in sex between married couples. But it is unclear what folk beliefs were concerning positions, and privacy was a different issue for most ordinary people because of crowded living arrangements. Also, the reformers strictly forbade sodomy and bestiality, making them capital crimes in some areas, and folk beliefs did as well, but the latter were lax on enforcement, especially in rural areas where farm animals were prevalent. Compliance with the pietist ideal of moderate sex between husband and wife often lagged in village populations. For example, in Lutheran Württemberg during the sixteenth and seventeenth centuries the efforts of church and state to control sexuality had little effect on behavior—many people did not want to wait until marriage to have sex. In spite of escalating punishments in the seventeenth century, premarital sexual experiences were common, and premarital conception rates were as high as 20 percent in sample villages. Unless pregnancy resulted there was little authorities could do, and the presence of soldiers compounded the problem when pregnancy followed by illegitimacy occurred.[44] In neighboring Bavaria, many young men and women, especially in the lower orders in rural areas, simply refused to accept the view that the official Christian religious ceremony of marriage signaled the beginning of intimate relationships. With less at stake than wealthier people, youths among the lower orders did not wait for the perfect economic match. Sexual intercourse became a normal part of a relationship that led to marriage and when followed by engagement, it was considered grounds for marriage, not penance. If parents did not approve, youths could count on the church to step in and support them if the woman became pregnant.[45]

Recent demographic analysis supports the view that premarital sex was common throughout Germany during the eighteenth century, but indicates that it may have been less common in Lutheran and Reformed communities in Pennsylvania. The prenuptial conception rate in the eighteenth century was 18 percent in fourteen sample German villages, many of which were in the southwestern territories, from which most of the North American immigrants came, and these rates increased even further in the nineteenth century.[46] In mostly German Lancaster County, Pennsylvania, however, aggregate premarital conception rates were about 5 percent in the eighteenth century. This rate was much lower not only than those in Germany, but also those in England, New England, Virginia, New Jersey, and even France. They remained low even when the average age at first marriage increased, perhaps because religious, familial, and communal values were even stronger at prohibiting premarital sex than those in New England in the eighteenth century.[47]

The church in the Netherlands struggled to get its members to confine sex to marriage as well. In the seventeenth century night courting was a communally authorized encounter, and public matchmaking sometimes occurred in large groups, although there were understood limits. Over time, however, individualized courtship with accompanying games became more common, and this increased the risk of pregnancy. The result was high premarital conception rates, as in Germany. In Duiven, for example, they reached about fourteen percent from 1666 to 1730, and in Maasland they were nearly twenty percent from 1730 to 1795.[48]

In fact, high premarital conception rates seem to have been a general trend throughout western Europe and the North American colonies during the eighteenth century. In a sample of sixteen English parishes the rate rose to 22 percent from 1700 to 1749 and reached 33 percent from 1750 to 1799. Increases have been documented in France and British North America as well.[49] These generally high premarital conception rates suggest that the clergy and magistrates generally failed in their long effort to get ordinary people to wait until marriage before having sex, but that communities did ultimately enforce the practice of having a proper Christian marriage.

While villagers throughout the German territories, the Netherlands, England, and elsewhere may have resisted the assault on premarital sex, "middle-class" (*bürgerliche*) couples in eighteenth-century Germany may have come close to conforming to this "Reformation value," even if they were not pietists. Sexual experiences between engaged couples did occur, and parents considered it legitimate if a promise to marry followed, but this was a risky business, since a "fallen woman" would not do well on the marriage market if the promise fell through. Further, pregnancy was a frightening experience to many women, since mortality was high for those giving birth. Also, many *bürgerliche* people shied away from available literature celebrating sex in order to distance themselves from the perceived decadence of the nobility. Marital sex was debated: jurists and doctors agreed that men had a need for this, even if sex with prostitutes were necessary, but they were not sure if women did. Experts believed that insatiable women were insane, sex should not occur during menstruation, that it should be curtailed during pregnancy, and that male impotence was embarrassing. Thus, like the religious reformers and pietists, they concluded that moderation was the best policy.[50]

Attitudes about premarital sex varied along class and rural-urban lines. Only in small villages, for example, was premarital sex between betrothed acceptable. Urban patricians sometimes faced public shaming at their formal wedding if they had a secret marriage and sex first. Chastity was demanded by all involved during their courtship and the long, intense negotiations with kin over details of the marriage. This reflected a concern among patricians about teen sexuality, pregnancy, and syphilis—a concern that theologians, pastors, and pietists in the seventeenth and eighteenth centuries may have shared.[51]

A similar struggle over Reformation values occurred in Anglo-America and may have been linked to a sexual revolution during the eighteenth century. The key issue was the acceptance of formal marriage as a signal that legitimate sex could begin. This clashed with the traditional common view, brought over from England, that informal marriage was proper and that legitimate sex could begin with betrothal. The Church of England pushed prosecution of violators in the late sixteenth and early seventeenth centuries. This campaign reflected anxieties about order and chaos, and was extended across the Atlantic, where minister shortages south of New England compounded the problem, and where colonists resisted efforts by magistrates and clergy to enforce proper marriage and confine sex to it. Most colonists considered marriage and the family to be the basic building blocks of society, but there was no consensus on what constituted licit marriage and thus a legitimate sexual relationship. There followed a struggle between these two approaches to sexual morality, the one ideological and exclusive in its demands for allegiance, and the other more expansive and pragmatic. After early successes, Puritans ultimately tried and failed to achieve strict moral standards in New England. Judicial enforcement stumbled over issues of what constituted sufficient proof of violations, making it difficult to convict and leading to leniency. High ratios of males to females in the colonial populations, as well as minister shortages and the presence of Africans and Native Americans, in the southern colonies made it difficult to achieve sexual order there. Many, like the Anglican itinerant Charles Woodmason in South Carolina, linked sexual disorder to a general lack of civility. By the eighteenth century courts no longer enforced church views on sexual regulation in New England, parents lost at least some control over their children, and a less restrictive sexual environment developed in the second half of the century, in part encouraged by events connected to the American Revolution. The clergy lost the power to enforce sexual mores, and the traditional common view won out. This meant that sex after betrothal and before marriage increased significantly. The clergy could not stop it, and many parents condoned it.[52]

By the eighteenth century the struggle over marriage and sex took place while important changes occurred in understandings of "passions" and "emotions." Recent literature on the history of emotions emphasizes that vocabulary concerning passions and emotions is always vague and imprecise, with a troubled relationship to practice. Nevertheless a number of historians have demonstrated a growing distinction between the two by the eighteenth century. Aquinas had defined passion as negative, but early modern theorists treated emotions as positive. Passions were disordered, corrupted by the Fall, thus ethically bad, while emotions were ethically good. Passions were out of control, coming from without, ultimately from Satan, whereas emotions could be cultivated, controlled.[53]

Two aspects of this increasing legitimization of emotions in the eighteenth century that were relevant to marriage and sex were the conflict between religious enthusiasm, which promoted emotion as a divine event during conversion and revival sermons, and the rise of enlightened sentimentalism, which encouraged romantic love. A number of historians have pointed out that spiritual union with God has often been symbolized in sexual terms analogous to marital love and connected erotic spiritual imagery to the metaphor of female submission—wife is to husband as humans are to the divine.[54] But this "sacralization of emotions" was linked to new ways of imagining sex and love in eighteenth-century Anglo-America. In other words, the positive sensual, emotional experience of conversion in evangelical religion not only helped legitimize emotions, but also fostered romantic love between husband and wife, which was seen as similar to the experience with the divine, and hence as positive. A few decades earlier similar physical outbursts might have been connected to Satan and witchcraft, perhaps reflecting earlier beliefs in passion, which was illegitimate, even evil. Despite this new value placed on enthusiasm and the experiential style, they remained controversial wherever they appeared in the Protestant Atlantic world, and many vigorously opposed them. Nevertheless, the emotional, awakening style left a permanent mark on the religious landscape, especially in British North America.[55]

In Europe enlightened sentimentalism also shaped attitudes about romantic love and thus sex between husband and wife, especially in the second half of the eighteenth century. As a result of growing beliefs in natural rights and the law of reason, secular marriages increasingly competed with church weddings in the German territories, beginning in the late seventeenth century. Marriages were still "arranged," but couples did have a choice, romance was becoming more important, and women could and did decline proposals. For some, a new ethic of love was developing that emphasized marriage as a spiritual and secular union through which husband and wife could grow closer to God together. After the mid-eighteenth century, marriage practices entered a new phase characterized by idealized romantic love that was described in popular love and marriage literature. Attitudes toward marital sex probably changed as well. If legitimate sex flowed from romantic love, then procreation could hardly have been its prime purpose, nor would it necessitate limits on the quality or perhaps even quantity of sexual acts between husbands and wives. It took time, however, before very many men and women in the middle orders of society (including some pietists) were able to fully take advantage of these developments.[56]

A similar development occurred in the British colonies and early U.S. republic at about the same time. By the second half of the eighteenth century, plays and other literature no longer emphasized passive women, misogyny, and a rambunctious sexual culture. Instead, authors of seduction literature stressed sentimentalism and active women seeking true love, who defended themselves against improper advances from men. Further, British moral philosophers, who were widely read in America, contributed to the growing interest in sentimentalism by distinguishing between animal lust and civilized marital love without suppressing desire. Women gained a measure of equality with this development, which eliminated the emphasis on passive women in sexuality that had been a familiar theme earlier. Marriage became the highest form of friendship, although the notion of female obedience was retained, and sexual relations became connected to social morality. A belief in the moral value of sexual relations resulted from the elevated view of emotions (here love) that distinguished them from sympathetic affections and carnal appetites.[57] In the transition, marital sex beyond procreation was part of a reciprocal, sentimental relationship, in which humans felt toward one another something like what they felt for God.

But progressive ideas regarding romantic love, sex, and marriage did not show a significant impact in the middle and upper orders in Europe or North America before the mid-eighteenth century, and even then not everyone accepted them, especially the clergy. John Wesley held to the traditional Anglican view of three purposes for marriage (procreation, a remedy against sin, and mutual society, help, and comfort), and believed that some were better off married, but, like Mühlenberg, Wesley felt that marriage impeded piety and duty for all believers, especially preachers.[58]

One important development that shaped attitudes and practice regarding marriage and sex among all orders in the early modern era was colonization in the Americas. This brought racial challenges that Protestant colonizers struggled against, perhaps more than their Catholic counterparts in the New World, as anxieties about interracial marriage and sexual relations increased with the success of colonization. The sexual imagery used to describe America in early exploration literature was problematic: the English were supposed to dominate Indians and Africans, yet preserve civility. This literature eroticized the lush, virgin land of sexually charged and available natives and seemed to justify rough treatment of them because of their depraved, heathen nature. Yet unlike the French and especially the Spanish, the English disliked or minimized contact with Indians, fearing degeneracy and becoming "Indianized" as they sought to build civilization in the wilderness. To them, especially the clergy, Indian and African "savagery" seemed to threaten notions of order and civility. Those who did marry natives sometimes found themselves in a perilous middle ground in which they had to deal with Indian rules regarding sex. Some feared that the English would become black, if they were not careful, but other planters did not care and had sex with their slaves anyway. Some reasoned that English males could dominate African or native women, because it fitted the conquest mentality, but African and native sex with English women was threatening. In the southern colonies this was especially problematic, since in addition to significant contact with Native Americans there were many more Africans and far fewer ministers than in the northern colonies. Furthermore, indentured servants were forbidden to marry, and there were a lot of them in the south, even as late as the eighteenth century. People did not appear to care much for authority—even increasingly genteel Virginia planters did not look after their children. How were Reformation values to be achieved in this setting, not to mention civilization in general? Charles Woodmason threw up his hands in frustration, yet continued to work (and complain in his diary) about these conditions in the South Carolina backcountry. Officials tried to prohibit cohabitation, but could not. They passed laws against clandestine marriage, but could not enforce them. Religious polemics were filled with sexual content, and even the clergy themselves, like John Wesley during his brief stay in Georgia in the early years of the colony, found themselves in morality trouble. (Wesley was caught in a sex scandal and had to leave the colony.)[59]

After centuries of change and development the question is, what attitudes and norms regarding marriage and sex were in place by the mid-eighteenth century, when the Moravians made their moves in Europe and North America? Clearly many acceptable values like monogamy, marriage, and opposite-sex relations were shared by almost all groups, and these same groups rejected beliefs and practices like celibacy, bigamy, incest (although folk definitions may have differed from those of elites), sodomy, bestiality, same-sex relations, and masturbation.[60] Also, by this period same-race sex and marriage had become the norm, and miscegenation was generally condemned. And the reformers and ordinary people condemned promiscuity, although there was a gender bias, as the latter tended to be more tolerant toward men in this regard. Any individuals or groups who violated these aspects of gender order would have encountered condemnation from those promoting Reformation values, as well as those defending folk beliefs, especially if the violators appeared to be openly practicing their beliefs or proselytizing.

While those who promoted Reformation values often struggled with those who defended their folk beliefs, men and women in both groups erected external and internal mechanisms to enforce their views. External mechanisms including formal measures like courts and officials, as well as informal measures like ordinary people themselves, especially women in groups, who used gossip, ostracism, and violence to enforce their values. Internal mechanisms included the shame and guilt inculcated into individuals through education and preaching. Enforcement was much more difficult in America, as diversity, weak institutions, and new racial challenges dramatically altered the landscape of contact, control, and the possible. But gender norms and enforcement mechanisms were there, and they were ultimately very effective in the struggle against the Moravians.[61]

As early modern and colonial people developed or maintained these marriage and sex norms they occasionally faced significant challenges from radical groups practicing alternative views. The most important challenges that shaped the way Lutheran and Reformed people on both sides of the Atlantic reacted against the Moravian threat during the mid-eighteenth century came from religious radicals who promoted alternative views of gender and power, marriage and sex. From the late seventeenth to the mid-eighteenth century, church pietists and others in central Europe and Pennsylvania who stressed moderation faced challenges from radical pietists, who provided "dangerous" interpretations of sex and the sacred, thus continuing long traditions and old conflicts. Some radicals like Johann Georg Gichtel promoted celibacy, which mainstream Protestants by then viewed as unnatural, Catholic, and heathen (hence evil). In Pennsylvania, a mystical communal celibate movement began among the Dunker immigrants that eventually led to the founding of the Ephrata cloister in the 1730s. It started when members of the group began to follow Conrad Beissel, the wandering preacher who had immigrated in 1720. Beissel had been banished from Strassburg for having a lusty, scandalous affair during his baker's apprenticeship. He joined a small radical group and went to Pennsylvania to find the remnants of the old flock of Johannes Kelpius that had scattered in that colony two decades earlier. Beissel was a hermetic, mystical seeker who sought solitude, but enjoyed company when it came. He achieved a following among some of the Dunkers and apparently a few Jewish mystics and others in Pennsylvania, who followed him to Cocalico in the backcountry to build an hermetic cloister. In spite of severe internal tensions, challenges to Beissel's leadership and to the celibate ideal of the commune, unwanted attention from outside, and other problems, the cloister flourished for decades and became a landmark for contemporaries, as well as for later historians and authors who have celebrated Pennsylvania's checkered religious landscape and pondered the sexual culture of this area.[62]

Protestant Orthodoxy and Confessional Order in the Eighteenth Century

From the mid-sixteenth to the mid-seventeenth centuries, an era historians refer to as the "Age of Confessionalism," Protestant scholar theologians in the various churches developed detailed written statements that defined their faith and distinguished their respective churches from each other and from radical groups they considered to be dangerous. These theologians regarded Scripture as normative and confessions as a useful "working out" of Scripture's teaching. Thus the authority of the confession was ancillary to that of Scripture, and therefore undermined when a departure from Scripture was detected. Major confessional statements these theologians produced included the Lutheran Augsburg Confession (1530) and Formula of Concord (1577), the Book of Common Prayer for the Anglican church (1549), the Heidelberg Catechism for the German Reformed church (1563), the canons of Dordrecht for the Dutch Reformed church (1618–1619), and the Westminster Confession for the Puritan (especially Presbyterian) church (1647). These and other confessions, which became teaching tools within communities, were designed to distinguish theological "truth" from "falsehood" and clarify the distinctions between churches.[63]

The confessions produced in this era became an important part of Protestant orthodoxy in the seventeenth century. This orthodoxy included a confessional order, or style of religion and social-political order that stressed doctrinal purity as defined in creeds, patriarchal authority within the church, morality, and conformity to the state and its established church. In addition to clear lines of authority within the state church and distinct boundaries separating it from dissenters and other confessional churches, Protestant orthodoxy promoted exclusively male leadership in the church and male authority in the daily life of families, as well as proper Christian clerical marriage and the criminalization of extramarital sex. Both the clergy and the laity were expected to conform and to promote these ideals in their communities, and confessional leaders employed the pulpit, plays, pageants, and other means to spread the word. State and church authorities built establishments designed to enforce confessional beliefs, the state, and a patriarchal religious, social, and household order within their respective state boundaries. Although the confessions themselves were perhaps not implicitly intolerant, their emphasis on purity of doctrine and the establishment of distinctions between churches made them compatible with the developing political-religious-social order that Protestant orthodoxy helped to promote in the territorial churches. In this manner church authorities hoped to fight error, promote morality and conformity, and thereby extend the Reformation to all peoples in their territories and to all aspects of society. They worked with state authorities to suppress separatist movements within their churches and to keep radicals and other dissenters at bay.

By the late seventeenth and early eighteenth centuries confessionalism was under attack from the Enlightenment and pietism, and some historians even refer to its demise in this era. Enlightenment thinkers who emphasized reason over revelation and tolerance over conformity attacked the confessional churches and ushered in the beginnings of modern secularization, which hindered the efforts of the churches to reform society according to the confessional ideal. Further, many orthodox theologians embraced the power of reason and new scientific developments because they felt it helped them understand and explain Scripture, their churches, and their programs. In the eighteenth century science still supported religion, yet the old confessions seemed to have lost much of their significance, supplanted by reason as a means of better understanding Scripture in the new Protestant orthodoxy. In some ways, then, confessionalism seemed to have run its course by the mid-eighteenth century.

The growth of pietism during the same period also helped to undermine confessionalism. The pietists rejected the confessional style of religion and social-political order. Some were separatists who believed the state churches were hopelessly lost. To them true Christian faith, worship, and life could only be achieved by withdrawal. Others wanted to remain within their church, but see it operate in a less confessional manner. They deemphasized dogma and stressed a more emotional, enthusiastic form of religious worship and life that could be shared with members of other faiths. This pietist ideal that deemphasized doctrine, promoted porous boundaries between churches, and sought to achieve unity among different churches was in many ways the antithesis of confessionalism and reflected aspects of what came to be called ecumenism in the twentieth century.

In the German Lutheran territories a huge conflict developed in the late seventeenth and early eighteenth centuries when the pietist movement challenged the orthodoxy of the church. Many pietists developed views so incompatible with the Lutheran church that they eventually separated, and Lutherans were glad to be rid of them. Johann Philip Fresenius, who held the highest Lutheran position in Frankfurt am Main, made his career by attacking such radical groups and defending the church in this imperial city.[64] Others, like the movement centered in Halle or a parallel movement in Württemberg, rejected the confessional vision and pursued pietist ideals, but remained within the church, insisting that they, not the orthodox theologians and leaders of the institutional church, carried the banner of true Lutheranism. The struggle between orthodoxy and pietism defined the Lutheran church to a significant degree until at least the mid-eighteenth centuries.[65]

But although the Enlightenment and pietism had led to significant changes in Protestant orthodoxy since the Age of Confessionalism, it is my view that many aspects of "confessional religion" or the "confessional style" remained an important part of the dynamic of religious conflict in the Protestant world in the mid-eighteenth century and reflected a response to the challenges of pietism, especially from the radicals. In the mid-eighteenth century orthodox theologians continued to emphasize doctrine to define themselves and exclude others (especially radicals), using the old creeds and now rational approaches to help explain their positions. Further, defining and policing theological-institutional boundaries between state churches and clear lines of authority within them remained important, and many orthodox authorities continued their attempt to enforce conformity and discipline within their territorial churches. Orthodox theologians and church leaders condemned spiritual enthusiasm and antinomianism as irrational, and they rejected ecumenism, latitudinarianism, separatism, and theological "indifference" because they did not properly respect the confessions and dogma of the church. They believed that the problem of irrational antinomianism and indifference toward proper dogma and confessional boundaries led to blasphemous beliefs about the Trinity and revolting practices regarding men and women that threatened gender order in the communities. They continued to emphasize instead patriarchy (exclusively male leadership in the church and male predominance in the household and community) and opposed female empowerment (preaching and other office holding, or alternative family and household arrangements). Thus while the success of pietism and the continued existence of radical religious movements challenged the authority of the confessional state churches, they reenforced their orthodox opponents' need for confessionalism to stop them.

In the mid-eighteenth century some aspects of the confessional religious style also reemerged in a surprising place, namely the extremely successful pietist movement centered in Halle. The 1730s and 1740s marked the beginning of the most extensive and impressive expansion in the movement's history. The Hallensians fulfilled many pietist ideals by establishing schools and expanding their publishing program and missions throughout the world, but at the same time their leaders began moving away from their old emphasis on female piety and leadership, tolerance, regeneration, and repentance expressed by pious believers meeting in small groups, or conventicles. Siegmund Jacob Baumgarten, Halle's leading theologian in this era, stressed instead using reason to understand Scripture. He used mathematical concepts of precise definitions and syllogisms to demonstrate theological points concerning the doctrine of the Trinity (vigorously defending the traditional view against all opponents), Christology, and the sacraments. Baumgarten's seven-volume theological exposition appeared from 1742 to 1750, putting him on the cutting edge of Halle's new move toward enlightened dogmatism, intellectualism, and moralism, for which there was no room for the pietist ecumenical ideal. Now even the Halle pietists were becoming more orthodox.[66]

Denominationalism, which became an increasingly important part of British North American religious order during and after the Great Awakening, also appears to have both challenged European confessionalism and provided an outlet for its continued existence in the eighteenth century. In North America the confessional churches did not do well, except for the Puritans early on in New England, and even they had to deal with many runaway nonconformity in Rhode Island. The Anglican establishment was weak throughout the other colonies, although it was not unimportant in places like Virginia. The Dutch Reformed church had some success developing its confessional order in New York, ironically more in the eighteenth century after the English conquest than earlier when it was a Dutch colony. Because of the inability of any one church south of New England to control the religious-political-social order of its colony, many church leaders began to accept the presence of other faiths within their colony as legitimate. But while church leaders could accept other churches within their colony, they intended to build establishments with distinct boundaries separating them from other churches, like the confessionalists in Europe. Colonial clergy and lay leaders also hoped to enforce adherence to dogma and clear lines of proper patriarchal religious-social order within these denominational walls. Their desire for distinction and proper boundaries that reflected the European territorial churches from which they had come was so strong that they rejected union efforts, even between different ethnic groups that shared the same religious creeds. The new denominational style in North America was in many ways successful, as numerous lay and ordained religious leaders slowly developed clearly delineated establishments that created their separate confessional identities and proper clerical authority within their boundaries.[67]

Most of the tens of thousands of Lutherans, Reformed, and other immigrants arriving in the colonies in the mid-eighteenth century were familiar with an orthodox church and its attempts to establish and maintain religious and social order in the community. Those immigrants who wanted a proper Lutheran or Reformed establishment could not have it in their colony as a whole, but the denominational concept developing in America meant that they could achieve many aspects of it at the local level, in their religious communities, dispersed and bounded by other religious communities as they might be. Those immigrants who did not want a local orthodox establishment in America could either stay away from the Lutheran and Reformed communities and do as they pleased, or join one of the numerous radical groups flourishing in the colonies.

In colonial North America the environment of relative freedom and extreme diversity meant that radicalism could flourish and opportunities for the pietist dream of unity seemed real, and this too promoted the resurgence of Protestant orthodoxy. Those who rejected radicalism demanded that confessional walls be built around their churches to protect them from the radicals and their dangerous religious-social order. Appearing orthodox (hence governable) improved their chances to receive more support from European religious authorities, primarily pastors, supplies, and money. If radicals tried to infiltrate the boundaries of a community with an able and regular pastor and lay leaders who were committed to establishing the orthodox Lutheran or Reformed ideal as best they could in America, then there would be trouble. In other words it was the radical challenge, much more significant in the colonies than in Europe during the mid-eighteenth century, that helped demonstrate the need for Protestant orthodoxy and confessionalism to many Lutherans and Calvinists in colonial communities. As the Great Awakening was the period in which many such immigrant communities were just becoming established, it was not always clear during the course of this movement, especially early on, just how committed people were to European orthodoxy. In fact, in many ways it was the course of conflict in the Awakening itself that determined this.

What happened to the Mother Eva Society in the German territories at the beginning of the eighteenth century should be evaluated in the context of the development and enforcement of Protestant gender, marriage, and sex norms of the early modern and colonial era. Female mutilation and Mother Eva's alleged ritual sex with multiple partners could not go unnoticed by the outside world. People called them the "Buttlar Gang" (*Buttlarsche Rotte*), and the group's enemies wrote polemics against them that shaped views of the Society to the present. They labeled Mother Eva's ritual sexual practices as holy whoredom and sacred prostitution. Many details came out at Eva's well-publicized trial. One man even described how during passionate sex between Buttlar and Winter she grabbed his "private member and maneuvered it around herself" ("Schamm, undt selbst damitt handthiret").[68] Eva denied all this, and even denied that she had ever had sex with anyone besides Winter, but her enemies did not believe her. The book that the Society kept suggested that Eva had slept with nineteen men and that Winter and Ichtershausen had circumcised twenty women. This was enough for most contemporaries, who paid little attention to Mother Eva's religiosity and developed their views of the group based on these graphic descriptions of promiscuity and ritual mutilation of the female body.[69]

Was Mother Eva a noblewoman mad for power and bent on dominating or exploiting men and women beneath her rank? Or was she a pious woman who responded to a special calling from God like many other women of her day, a calling that included promoting a higher female role in the Trinity and society? To her enemies it did not matter. She might have been a mad woman victimizing other women beneath her class in shocking, blasphemous ways. Or, even if these stories were not true, she clearly was promoting a blasphemous female view of the deity and acted upon it by leading the group and preaching herself. In fact, many could not separate the two views: if women held too much power, evil things connected to the work of Satan like sexual depravity and abuses of marriage and the body would follow. To them Mother Eva was clearly guilty on all counts, and something had to be done to stop her.

The Mother Eva drama occurred at a time when the Lutheran and Reformed churches promoted the confessional ideal, in part to protect people from such dangerous threats to gender order. State church authorities instructed the clergy in their respective territories to enforce proper church marriage and confine sex to it in the general population—something many people of the lower orders in German villages were not always willing to accept. But even stubborn German peasants were committed to male dominance and monogamy. They rarely if ever thought about the finer points of the doctrine of the Trinity, but they did believe that their deity was male and could not accept the alternative. Nearly everyone believed that overactive female sexuality somehow reflected the influence of Satan, and ritual female circumcision or mutilation appeared to be a bizarre, gruesome affair of female bodies out of control or in danger, all the result of too much female power in the community.

But while authorities eradicated the Mother Eva problem, the memory of the group and its dangerous threat to gender order lived on. When the Moravians began their expansion throughout the Protestant Atlantic world in the 1730s and 1740s, the memory of the Mother Eva nightmare came back to haunt them. German Lutherans and Calvinists had not forgotten Mother Eva—the anti-Moravian polemicists would not let them. They were especially worried about the Moravians because, unlike Mother Eva, these challengers to proper gender order insisted that they were or ought to be a part of the state churches. The polemicists made direct comparisons and references to the Mother Eva Society when condemning the Moravians. Georg Jacob Sutor, an ex-Moravian Separatist, described Moravian marriage and sexual practices, including forced marriages, whoredom, and debauchery in "Venus Temples," and reminded his readers that they had experienced this sort of thing a generation earlier with the Mother Eva Society. Johann Philip Fresenius affirmed this comparison in a footnote to Sutor's work, which appeared in Fresenius's four-volume anti-Moravian polemic that circulated widely on both sides of the Atlantic. The Halle pietist theologians also picked up on the dangerous Moravian-Mother Eva comparison and employed it in their polemics. Siegmund Jacob Baumgarten cited the historical litany of heresies from the ancient Gnostics and heathen Phallus and Priapus cults to the Mother Eva Society and argued that the Moravians represented yet another example of this old problem. In short, younger church members received history lessons from these influential writers—lessons that instructed them in the dangers of female power. The writers hoped that tales of female woe and a direct comparison of the Moravians to Mother Eva would be enough not only to discourage groups from joining Zinzendorf's group, but also to drive out the count's emissaries if they ever appeared in their communities.[70]

The Mother Eva Society had become an important part of the narrative and warning about female power. Like witchcraft and Quakerism, orthodox writers explained in their polemics, the Mother Eva tragedy seemed to be yet another case of uncontrolled female leadership leading to uncontrolled bodies and sexuality, which could only be the work of Satan. The early modern and colonial era is filled with examples in which this narrative was played out, as numerous groups reinterpreted the gender of God and gendered power in the community. When they did, ordinary people often took extraordinary, even violent actions to defend their communities against groups that appeared to threaten common understandings of spiritual gender and power and what it meant in the lives of men and women.

In Europe and New England, with their strong state church establishments, people knew how to deal with radical challenges to gender and confessional order, but what would happen in the mid-Atlantic colonies? There boundaries between churches appeared to be meaningless, which meant that violations of the gender order by the radicals were even more threatening. When the Moravians entered the stage in the 1730s there were already groups in the colonies, especially in Pennsylvania, who had challenged both confessional and gender order, including the traditional views of the gender of the Trinity, female preaching, marriage, and sexual behavior. Moreover, immigration to the mid-Atlantic colonies of radicals and especially of vulnerable Lutheran and Reformed church people was increasingly dramatically. Transatlantic gender and confessional norms were strong, but changing in the colonies. Because of the differences in America, opportunities for European radicals and others were clear, but the limits were less clear. How far could one go in America?

Part II
The Moravian Challenge

By the 1740s the Moravians had become one of the best known radical groups challenging the religious and social sensibilities of the Protestant world. Their views regarding the gender of the Trinity and the resulting influence this had on male and female activity and relations in their communities were quite radical, but not unique in the history of Christianity or the Protestant Atlantic world at this time. What made the Moravians appear so dangerous to their enemies was that they attempted to carry their threat to proper gender order to others. The ecumenical Moravians zealously pursued a mission to all peoples of the world, from throughout Protestant Europe to immigrants in America, to African slaves, Native Americans, and Africans throughout the Atlantic world, and even to some people in the Indian Ocean region. In Europe and the Americas they proclaimed that they were or ought to be Lutherans or members of the Reformed church, even as they practiced their radical views on gender in their separate, closed communities. To their enemies in the state churches, who were just then stressing patriarchal, confessional order in a more rational way and demanding adherence within the boundaries of their respective churches, making Jesus female while claiming to be a good Lutheran or Calvinist represented a dangerous challenge to religious and social order.

Chapter 3

The Challenge to Gender Order

I ask you to examine the Twelfth Part (Appendix) of their hymns (published hymnal) where you will discover that these obscene birds (the Moravians)— with your permission—have compared women's genitalia, vagina of the uterus, with the side of the Savior of the world which on the cross had been pierced by a spear."

—*Heinrich Melchior Mühlenberg, German Lutheran pastor in Pennsylvania, 1750*

A few years after the close of the Mother Eva drama, the Moravian movement began to take root on the estates of Count Zinzendorf in Upper Lusatia. In 1722 the first "Moravian" refugees settled there and began building the town of Herrnhut. By 1727 their numbers had grown significantly, the town was complete, and they celebrated the renewal or "rebirth" of the Moravian church. From this point until the count's death in 1760 the Moravians experienced the most dramatic, innovative, and productive period in the modern history of their church, yet at the same time it was their strangest and most controversial period. Beginning in the late 1730s, the center of spiritual exploration, controversy, and leadership of the movement shifted from the town of Herrnhut to their new settlements in Wetteravia, especially Herrnhaag—not far from where the Mother Eva Society had been active a generation earlier. Here the tolerant Count Büdingen offered them a refuge, and the group began to explore alternative notions of gendered power and authority and dramatically expanded their ecumenical missionary efforts throughout the Atlantic world. Most Moravian historians since the eighteenth century have preferred to emphasize the sometimes dazzling, even heroic accomplishments of their missionaries during this era, while deemphasizing the spiritual innovation regarding gender, which they have linked to a regretful episode of extreme mystical spiritualism and "blood and wounds" beliefs that they call the "Sifting Period," or "Sifting Time." But recently historians have begun exploring and revealing much of what did happen in their closed communities during this era. Moreover, it is now clear that the spiritual innovation and alternative views of gender and sexuality energized the missionary movement of ecumenical Moravians to peoples in North America and throughout the Atlantic world. It was a time of spiritual exploration for Moravians by their own accounts—a time in which virtually anything was possible in the realms of gender, sex, and spirituality. These radical Moravian views and activities provoked a furious response from the group's many enemies in the eighteenth century, and were controversial even within the group, which explains why careless, perhaps embarrassed, Moravian church officials later burned many records from the period. Enough has survived, however, to indicate what many of their controversial beliefs and practices at the time were.[1]

A Female Trinity

The Moravians altered the gender and structures of power within the Trinity first by dis-empowering "God the Father."[2] To most, this male figure was the omnipotent creator and ruler of the universe and all things in it. The Moravians did not alter the gender of the Father, but rather took away much of his power by assigning the function of the Creator entirely to Jesus. In his "Seven Last Sermons" before departing for Pennsylvania in the summer of 1741, Zinzendorf referred to Christ as the Creator, and he even announced it in Benjamin Franklin's newspaper upon arriving in the colony. August Gottlieb Spangenberg, who ultimately became the second most important leader of the group, defended the view in print ten years later. Lower-ranking Moravians also became familiar with the idea in the group's hymns and litanies: one-fourth of the hymns available in Bethlehem during this period explicitly identified Christ as the Creator or Jehovah, and none designated the Father as such. Moreover, the litanies establish this principle as a central feature of their beliefs concerning the Trinity. This unusual but not unique idea did not go unnoticed by the outside world. The Moravians suffered repeated attacks in widely circulated polemics for this view. Johann Philipp Fresenius called this minimizing of the Father's role in the Trinity a dangerous Satanic belief. In Pennsylvania, the German Reformed pastor Johann Philipp Boehm attacked the Moravians for praying to the Savior only, and not the Father. In Amsterdam, Gerardus Kulenkamp (a member of the Reformed church council and the principal leader of the assault against the Moravians in the Netherlands) blasted Zinzendorf for overemphasizing the Savior as the only God, for teaching that the Old Testament books were primarily about Jesus, and for believing that Jesus provided the revelation to men about those books.[3]

The Moravians next reordered the Trinity by feminizing the Holy Spirit, which became a "mother." Zinzendorf developed the idea in his sermons, and it is present in many Moravian hymns as well. During his Pennsylvania tour in December 1741 Zinzendorf articulated this view during a sermon at Germantown, in which he used a relational model of the Trinity and the human family, describing the Holy Spirit as the true mother of Jesus and "all of us." "It can be no other way," he wrote, "that his (Christ's) Father must also be *our father* and his mother also *our mother.*" During the Creation the Spirit "hovered about the waters as the common Mother" and made all things living. In 1746 he preached a sermon in London called "On the Maternal Office of the Holy Spirit" ("*Vom Mutteramte des heiligen Geistes*"), and in the following year another entitled "On the True Evidence of the Maternal Office of the Holy Spirit" ("*Von dem eigentlichen Grund-Beweiß des Mutter-Amts des heiligen Geistes*"). Zinzendorf explained that calling the Spirit a mother, or labeling her role a "maternal office," was Scriptural and applied to all Christians. He also argued that since a title for the Holy Spirit was unclear within Christendom anyway, they should use the family analogy, and the Spirit was nearer to a mother. Further, before the birth of Christ pagans had had vague, confusing notions of a foster mother or nurse of humanity, i.e., goddesses who nurtured heroes and became mothers of all humans. With the birth of Christ it became clear what all of this meant: the Holy Spirit exercised a motherly, nurturing function over him, and whatever belonged to Christ must belong to all Christians too. The Holy Spirit became the mother of Jesus more than Mary by preparing her womb, and by protecting and bringing the Savior into the light. The Holy Spirit was also the mother of all living souls and the mother of the reborn.[4]

Moravian belief in the Holy Spirit as mother flourished in the 1740s and 1750s. The Bethlehem, Pennsylvania, community diary has several references to the idea during this period, and one of the European community diaries in 1747 included a cantata describing the marital relationship between the deity and believers that included references to the Holy Spirit as a mother, an idea that their enemies soundly condemned in published polemics. In 1756 they published a work entitled *A Booklet on God the Holy Spirit of the Eternal Wisdom and Our Complete Mother,* which contained a list of daily readings on the subject, one for each day of the year 1757.[5] The concept of the Holy Spirit as mother appears in the addenda of the Twelfth Appendix of the *Moravian Hymnal* as well. See, for example the following, which Zinzendorf composed for his wife on her birthday in 1745:[6]

Das nennet er sein Ehgemal,
ist herrschaft der naturen,
die frau der geister ohne zahl,
und aller creaturen:
Gott seinen Vater gibt er an
als ihren Vater,
sich als Mann, *den Heiligen Geist*
als Mutter.

This he calls his spouse,
is lord of all things,
the wife of countless spiritual beings
and all creatures:
God his father he declares
as her father,
himself as husband,
and the Holy Spirit as mother.

(Hymn 2175, verse 8, Twelfth Appendix addenda,
Moravian Hymnal, emphasis mine).

The Moravian belief in the Holy Spirit as mother was so strong during this period that Spangenberg aggressively defended it in his *Apologetische Schluß-Schrifft,* where he responded to more than a thousand accusations against the Moravians in question and answer format. To the question whether the Moravians believed in the maternal office of the Holy Spirit, Spangenberg responded, "Amen, Amen, and that is indeed true about the Holy Spirit." He rejected the notion that this was dangerous Gnostic doctrine or that it contradicted Martin Luther's views.[7]

The numerous published polemical attacks against the view of the Holy Spirit as mother that circulated on both sides of the Atlantic provoked a response from Zinzendorf that reveals the problematic difference between metaphor and reality, as well as the difference between sex and gender. Zinzendorf argued that by proclaiming the Holy Spirit was a mother he did not mean to imply that this referred to the biological features of a woman, that is to any *"distinctio sexus."* Instead he used the concept metaphorically (in the ways described above). Similarly, Spangenberg argued that the maternal office of the Holy Spirit did not refer to *"sexum sequiorem,"* but rather to Scriptural allegory. Zinzendorf and Spangenberg thought that they were safe using metaphors because they had not changed the physiological sex of the Holy Spirit. To their opponents, however, metaphor *was* important, even sacred. These metaphorical distortions were blasphemy. The crucial issue was the gender of the Holy Spirit, i.e., how the attributes, functions, expectations, and relationships associated with males or females were assigned to it. As shown in the previous chapter, most theologians believed that the Trinity was revealed in Scripture as male (including the Holy Spirit) and from this the order of creation with men superior to women was derived, something the Scriptural prohibition on women preaching reflected or confirmed. Thus the Trinity was an important metaphor or symbol for power and authority in the Christian community. Metaphors mattered, and with theirs the Moravians had violated the gender boundaries in this most crucial point of Christianity.[8]

Gendered metaphors mattered when Moravians began assigning

female characteristics to Jesus as well.[9] Zinzendorf never developed a fully explicated theological view of a female or androgynous Jesus as the ancient Gnostics or later mystics like Jacob Böhme did. Moreover, he and other Moravians never abandoned a view of the body of Christ that stressed its male features, which can be seen in their crucifixion artwork of the period. But in the realm of metaphor—the attributes, qualities, and functions of the Savior, they employed female as well as male imagery. Many of their protocols, poems, and hymns, and much of their iconography suggested female qualities of Christ, including sensuous descriptions of body fluids, adoring descriptions of a nurturing, motherly Savior, and even graphic portrayals of the side wound, apparently in the form of female genitalia. This view of the Savior, which was developed both by Zinzendorf and other leaders and elaborated by lower-ranking young men and women, influenced the lives and piety of many Moravians in the closed communities and provided their enemies with material for polemics.

Zinzendorf and Spangenberg also employed the metaphor of Jesus as mother. In Zinzendorf's fourth (published) discourse on the Augsburg Confession, in which he comments on the nature of Christ and the relationship between the body and the soul, he directly assigns the function of spiritual birthing to Jesus. While many in the early modern era believed that giving life was a male function, it is clear that Zinzendorf had adopted the modern view of females giving life by referring to the side wound as a womb. He came to this conclusion by carefully reasoning from the premise that the Savior was the center of the universe and all things. This meant that the Holy Spirit dwelt within him, and so was released or "born" at Christ's death through the side wound. Since the spiritual rebirth of believers occurs through the indwelling of the Holy Spirit, then they are born of Christ and *through* him. Finally, if the Holy Spirit was born through the side wound and this led to believers' rebirth, then the side wound (or hole), must be a *womb* (*Matrix*), because it gives birth, or as Zinzendorf put it, "his side is the womb in which my spirit was conceived and carried."[10] In his *Apologetische Schluß-Schrifft*, Spangenberg publicly defended the Moravian notion of a maternal Jesus. After explaining to his imagined inquisitor that the Holy Spirit was a mother, Spangenberg extended the idea of a motherly, nurturing role to Jesus Christ, insisting that this reflected no Gnostic heresy. In fact, Spangenberg even implied that the motherly qualities reflected the nature of the entire Trinity—including God the "Father."[11]

A number of Moravian hymns referred to motherly qualities of Jesus as well. In the following example the Moravians altered a pietist hymn by the seventeenth-century mystic, Gottfried Arnold, and introduced the Jesus as mother theme:

Mein König! schreib mir dein gesez ins herz,	My King, write Thy law in my heart,
das meinen Geist ergezt;	that will delight my spirit;
dein königlicher trieb zünd mir	Thy royal desire kindles in me
das sanfte feuer an;	the mellow flame;
und fuhr mich auf der streiter bahn,	and leads me on the militant path
durch mütterliche lieb.	*with motherly love.*

(Hymn 820, verse 1, *Moravian Hymnal*, emphasis mine)

Here "My King" refers to Christ, suggesting that Christ's love was motherly love. In their hymnal of 1731 the relevant passage refers to "angelic love" ("engelreiche lieb"), but by 1735 the Moravians had made the change. From then until 1753 Moravian hymnals used the new version; however, later editions (after 1778) dropped the Jesus as mother theme. Clearly this was a point of emphasis by Moravian hymnal editors only from the mid-1730s to the 1750s, the peak period of conflict between them and their numerous enemies.[12]

Moravians not only assigned motherly female qualities to Jesus, but also erotic qualities to their relationship with the Savior. Many Moravian men and women celebrated a sensuous relationship and produced hymns, poetry, and other writings that suggested erotic impulses toward Christ. Like many Puritans, Methodists, and others in Europe and North America a mystical marriage concept contributed to these views.[13] Zinzendorf adopted the Biblical view of Christ as the bridegroom of the church and marriage as a heavenly union of the soul with Christ. Marriage on earth served as a theological illustration of the union of Christ with individual souls and the entire community, and the husband became Christ's representative, or a "vice Christ." As with other pietists, a personal relationship with the Savior through a recreated heart was central to Moravian religious beliefs. In 1746 Zinzendorf wrote, "Therefore by faith and love we must so enter the Saviour, that we can no longer see or hear anything else above or beyond Him, that we and He remain inseparably together. . . . He knows my danger and my security; in short, I can be nowhere better than in His arms."[14] Such bridal mysticism exploited and encouraged analogies between spiritual and sexual themes. This kind of imagery can also be noted in Moravian hymns of the period like the following:

Seiten-hölgen! Seiten-hölgen!	Little side hole! Little side hole!
Seiten-hölgen, du bist mein:	Little side hole, thou art mine:
allerliebstes Seiten-hölgen	most dear little side hole
ich verwünsch mich ganz hinein.	I wish myself entirely inside.
Ach mein Seiten-hölgen!	Ah, my little side hole!
du bist meinen seelgen	thou art my little soul
doch das liebste plätzlein;	yes the dearest little place;
Seiten-schrein!	Side shrine!
leib und seel fährt in dich nein.	body and soul passes into thee.

(Hymn 2281, *Moravian Hymnal*)

Like many others before them, when the Moravians began to take seriously the view of an erotic union of believers with Christ, even if only in the metaphorical sense, then they had a problem: believers were both male and female. One solution to the problem was to emphasize that the entire church community was female (i.e., the bride of Christ), but this detracted from individual experiences with the Savior, which pietists often stressed. Another solution, evident in their hymnology and poetry, was to make all souls female, as some medieval mystics and English Puritans had done. (The Moravians were severely attacked in the polemics for this view as well.[15]) Thus a union with the male Son of God could be presented in ways consistent with a traditional gender and sexual order stressing male-female unions.

One way to overcome the problem of how male believers could have intense sensual relations with a male Savior was to deny that this was a problem and embrace the concept. There is evidence of homoerotic relations between women and especially between young men in Moravian communities in this period, perhaps in part the result of the strict segregation by sex in their living quarters, and a few members extended their desires to their spiritual relationship with Christ. Conceiving the relationship between Moravian men and their Savior as a same-sex erotic bond was another solution, and there is some evidence that this occurred. The single brothers of Ebersdorf seemed to be suggesting this when they poetically encouraged the Savior to kiss "so very extraordinaire" ("so gantz extraordinair") Christian Renatus Zinzendorf on his birthday and to take him into the *Cabinet* (the special chamber where married couples met to have sex), where they could talk, caress, and kiss each other, inspired by the flame of love. Also, Zinzendorf's reprimand to the Moravians in Herrnhaag in 1749 suggests that opposite- and same-sex kissing as a Christian greeting were becoming too passionate during services.[16] Although some Moravian leaders warned against same-sex intimacy, they saw it as no worse than other expressions of lust, and there are numerous examples of such intimacy occurring in the eighteenth century—including the "ritualized homosexuality" in which an inner circle of young men in Herrnhaag closely connected to Christian Renatus Zinzendorf penetrated the side-wound-anus of Christ in spiritual ceremonies. Metaphorical and real homoeroticism were part of at least some Moravian explorations of spiritual-gender-sexual boundaries during the Herrnhaag era, and were known to their enemies: in 1747, during discussions in the English Parliament about whether to formally recognize the Moravians as a religious denomination, an older Whig member claimed he wanted nothing to do with such "Enthusiasts and Sodomites," and in 1751 an ex-Moravian named Heinrich Joachim Bothe published a polemic in which he accused a Moravian prayer group in Berlin of committing disgraceful acts, "even a man with a man" ("ja so gar Mann mit Mann").[17]

Still another solution to the problem of how both men and women could have a spiritual-sexual union with the Savior was to change the metaphor, or regender Jesus as both male and female. Christ was born as the Son of God (the Father) and the Holy Spirit (the Mother), but at the crucial point of his death on the Cross "he" became female by giving birth through the side wound, which in portraiture, speech, and hymnology became a womb. Indeed, in their emotionally and erotically laden expressions of spirituality during this period, at least some Moravian men, including Christian Renatus Zinzendorf, began to question whether the gender of their Savior was male or female. If "he" could be both male and female, then men and women believers could have a sensuous spiritual relationship with their Savior without resorting to metaphorical, spiritual homosexuality, which only a few were willing to do.[18]

Moravian iconography of the period assigned both erotic and maternal qualities to the side wound of Jesus.[19] Members inscribed colored expressions about an erotic relationship with Jesus on hundreds of colorful small cards, many of which contained sensuous expressions about penetrating the side wound. The originals were inscribed in green and red with attractive script (see Plate 4):

Ich lieg im (Seitenhölchen) grad und schlief ein paar Millionen Claffter tief.	In the (little side hole) I lie just right and sleep a couple of million fathoms deep.
Momentlich da der Stich geschah, fuhr ich heraus Halleluja!	The moment the stab occurred, I leapt out, hallelujah!
Tief nein! *Tief nein!* Tief nein ins Seitlein!	Deep inside! *Deep inside!* Deep inside the little side!
Aufs Seiten Höhlgen *Zitterlich.*	*Trembling* in the Side Wound.

Many of these little cards also contain striking water colors depicting the side wound in the form of female genitalia, and/or showing daily activities—eating, sleeping, going for a walk, etc.—*inside* the "womb-like" wound (see Plate 5). Mariane von Watteville (see Figure 1), who lived most of her life in Herrnhut without ever marrying, produced some of the artwork. Her father brought her to Herrnhaag form Bern, Switzerland, in 1749 when she was fourteen years old. She remained for a year before being sent to Zinzendorf's estates in Upper Lusatia, where she remained the rest of her life, without marrying. At some point she painted an unusual side wound image in which she stitched thread for

Figure 1. Mariane von Watteville (1736–1810), born in Switzerland, later moved to Herrnhaag and Herrnhut, never married. Von Watteville painted at least some of the Moravian devotional side wound images. Oil painting by Johann Valentin Haidt, mid-eighteenth century. GS 076, Unity Archives, Herrnhut.

a three-dimensional effect (see Plate 6). It depicts Watteville kneeling inside the side wound and being sprayed by the blood of Christ with the expression. "O, I rejoice, I rejoice so much that I have found the sea from the wound, where I am a blessed little sinner. I have everything."[20]

The way Moravians employed images like those depicted in Plates 4–6 reflects their understanding of both maternal and erotic female qualities of Christ. The images in Plate 5 emphasize the maternal aspect of the side wound of the Savior: believers appear to celebrate Christian joy in everyday life within the safe, protective confines of the womb. But there was an erotic quality and function of the little cards as well, and this supports a side wound as vagina interpretation. This is apparent not only in the numerous cards with verses such as those depicted in Plate 4, but also in the way the Moravians employed the cards in their explicit, detailed instructions on how married couples should have sex. The instructions explained that the husband blessed the wife during ejaculation and suggested that he read aloud an appropriate verse while this is happening. At this point in the instructions one of the little cards was pasted in the margin, with the inscription "Little Side Hole's Marrying" (S:Hölches Ehelich) and a bed and a bench (suggesting the two methods of intercourse preferred by the Moravians) painted inside the side wound-vagina. Thus the Moravians directly linked an erotic female image of the side wound of Jesus to human male orgasm during ritualized sex between married couples. Indeed, the Moravians produced the artwork depicted here at the same time that their theology emphasized bridal mysticism and their new hymnology celebrated a sensuous relationship with a Savior who had female qualities. They used artwork liberally during their community services and festivals, including paintings of Christ bleeding on the Cross or being placed in the tomb. At a Single Sisters festival in Bethlehem in 1758 they decorated their meeting room with green leaves, flowers, slogans about Christ written in white and green, and portraits of Anna Nitschmann, Anna Johanna Nitschmann, and the corpse of Christ. "It looked right lovely and pretty," one of the sisters noted. Iconography such as this was likely the product of the same mentality as Moravian theology and hymnology.[21]

An interpretation of the erotic quality of the Moravian side-wound image is compatible with the views of many art historians, who emphasize that throughout history devotional images often connected spirituality and sexuality. Such images can come "alive" for Protestants as well as Catholics and awaken powerful responses in beholders like empathy, which might help the believer, or they can arouse desire for an intense, emotional, and sensual relationship with the Savior. This was important for pietists, who stressed contemplation of the wounds of Christ as part of their individual, personal experience with their Savior. Many cloistered men and women who produced devotional images believed that the path to salvation lay through the side wound (a strong Moravian theme, as well), through which one must pass to achieve union with Christ. The nuns at St. Wallburg in Bavaria, for example, kept small images on their bodies and considered them keepsakes, tokens of affection or gratitude meant for exchange—something Moravians easily could have done with the little side wound cards. Some medieval poetry contains erotic imagery from the Song of Songs and images of the body of Christ as open, passive, suffering, and hence feminine. In such cases the side opening invites its beholders to penetrate, introspect, and enter the womb-like interior of the heart. In these "ready made images of a secret place of mystical communion," as one historian called them, an intimate colloquy took place between Christ and the soul, and while they can suggest sensual, female qualities of Jesus, they do not necessarily serve to sublimate sexual desire. Instead they can function as an access to the divine. Such imagery can call into question the gender of Jesus, which has not been constant historically. In addition to radicals, who assign female imagery to Christ, the view among mainstream Christians has fluctuated over time, ranging from a gentle, ethereal, and effeminate Savior to a rugged, violent man's man.[22]

The Moravians did not invent the female Jesus—the concept can be traced back as far as the ancient Gnostics. This far-flung, unorganized mystical movement flourished within Christianity from about 80 to 200 A.D. The Gnostics believed in mystical revelation and hidden divine wisdom, which they personalized in the term "Sophia." Dualism shaped their views, including the belief that the Godhead was a complex unity of male and female entities emanating from a single transcendent One. Adam and Eve together were created in the image of God, revealing that both genders existed in the deity. Although many Gnostics maintained a negative view of femaleness and believed that salvation meant in part becoming male, they promoted an active role for women with Eve and Mary Magdalene as two of their models, and some saw the virile woman as a powerful sign of redemption. Most Christians repudiated this version of mystic spirituality. As early as 150 A.D. the enemies of Gnosticism associated the movement with sexual promiscuity, and in 297 A.D. the Edict of Diocletian proscribed the Gnosticizing religion known as Manichaeanism. By the fourth century Gnostics were forbidden to hold meetings, although the movement continued to survive in the next century. Thereafter "Gnosticism" was considered a dangerous heresy, and many used the term to denounce individuals and movements within the church that appeared to resemble these early groups.[23]

Images of Jesus with female characteristics were prevalent in the medieval period as well. Maternal imagery was often applied to male religious authority figures, especially abbots, bishops, the apostles, God, and Christ during the Middle Ages. For Cistercian monks in the twelfth century it was connected in part to their ambivalence about authority and to their conception of community. Their sermons and letters contain explicit imagery alluding to suckling Christ's breasts and erotic images of the side wound (including kissing it and hiding in it)—similar to Moravian images six centuries later. The image of Christ that the monks should imitate was that of a compassionate, loving, nurturing mother who creates and sacrifices. They also used female imagery for God and Jesus to express a (metaphorical) sexual union with the deity. The monks wanted to avoid a male-male relationship with the deity (although there is some evidence for a homosexual subculture among them), and they did this sometimes by describing themselves or their souls as the brides of Christ, and sometimes by describing God or Jesus as female. The Jesus as mother theme appears in thirteenth- and fourteenth-century imagery, as well, especially in the theology developed around it by the anchoress, Julian of Norwich, who died sometime after 1416. Indeed throughout the medieval era the image of woman as Christ emerged, and it was connected to powerful female figures who were seen as vessels of divine expression and knowledge.[24]

Female imagery of Jesus became part of the spiritual life of numerous radical pietist groups in the early modern period as well, including prophetesses and visionaries in England and mystics in Germany and some Puritan theologians in New England. The Fifth Monarchist Anna Trapnel used maternal imagery to describe Jesus, exhorting "sucklings" to take in the milk that ran through Christ's breasts, and Eleanor Davies portrayed God as female. The ancient Sophia tradition was alive and well in these areas, some of its most important proponents being Jacob Böhme (1575–1624), Gottfried Arnold (1666–1714), Johann Georg Gichtel (1638–1710), Johanna Eleanora von Merlau (1644–1724), Johann Wilhelm Petersen (1649–1727), and the Mother Eva Society in Germany, and Jane Lead (1623–1704) and John Pordage (1608–1681) in England. In New England Thomas Shepard used graphic maternal imagery to describe Jesus and God as a whole.[25]

Jesus became female in North America and elsewhere in the Atlantic world during the eighteenth century as well. At the Ephrata commune in Pennsylvania (not far from the Moravian communities of Bethlehem and Nazareth), for example, some German radical pietists who had been strongly influenced by Jacob Böhme produced devotional books that portrayed an androgynous God, with Sophia representing God's femaleness. Sophia gave birth first to Adam (who was androgynous until the creation of Eve from his side) and then to Christ, who was also androgynous. The latter appeared in the form of a man, but in essence was female. His male form died on the Cross, which had cosmic significance, for in it all maleness was overcome. Sophia, who had been compelled to leave Adam, hovered near all human beings in order to win them to herself. But the fiery will of man to rule made such a union impossible. Spiritual struggle resulted within humans, with Christ as the model for both male and female in perfect balance. Only as humans became mystically united with Christ did their maleness die with his, and Christ's death became life for them.[26] From a different theological tradition, Samuel Davies, the Presbyterian awakener who itinerated in Virginia during the mid-eighteenth century and published poems full of erotic devotional imagery likening sexual love to the love of God, was attacked in newspapers for sexualizing and feminizing God. Also, at least some Native American converts seem to have adopted the Moravian view of a Christ with female qualities, like the Mahican woman named Rachel, who understood the breast-feeding of her own child as similar to the way Christ provided blood to sustain herself and other believers. A few years later the leader of the Shakers, Ann Lee, also promoted the view of a female Christ, and in the early nineteenth century a Freewill Baptist, later Methodist preacher named Salome Lincoln used maternal imagery from Deuteronomy 32:11–12 to describe God and justify female preaching. Also, around 1800 Christians in the Soyo province of the Kongo produced brass and bronze crucifixes showing Christ as a woman, sometimes nursing a child.[27]

Since the use of female imagery of Christ was neither new in the history of Christianity nor unique in North America, why did it matter so much to the enemies of the Moravians that they too regendered the metaphors and qualities of Jesus? How did this contribute to the religious conflict involving the group that raged in the Atlantic world in the mid-eighteenth century? It certainly mattered to the anti-Moravian writers in Europe like the Prussian court advisor Heinrich Rimius, who mocked Moravian references to "Mamma Jesua" and described their side-wound devotion as if he had seen some of the little cards decorating their trees and illustrating their sex manuals: they kiss the side wound, repose in it, breathe, lie down in, and sport in it—lengthwise, crosswise, etc. "There is his Country," Rimius wrote, describing a typical Moravian's feelings toward the wound, "his House, his Hall, his little Bed, his little Table: There he eats, there he drinks, there he lives, there he praises the dear little Lamb."[28] Alexander Volck, the city scribe and notary in Büdingen who was a former Moravian, found evidence in the Twelfth Appendix of the group's hymnal that suggested these "present-day Gnostics" and "mystic swine" compared the female "birthing member" to the side wound of the Savior.[29] Gerardus Kulenkamp, a member of the church council (*kerkeraad*) in Amsterdam, bitterly condemned the Moravian notion of a female or androgynous Jesus, which he believed resembled mystical teachings.[30] In Pennsylvania Heinrich Melchior Mühlenberg, the pastor from Halle who led the Lutheran fight against the Moravians in that colony, read the Twelfth Appendix of their hymnal and blasted the erotic qualities of their hymns and their comparisons of the side wound to women's genitalia (see the quote at the beginning of this chapter). Moreover Mühlenberg explicitly cited Moravian references to this in their hymns when arguing with opponents in the field, thus bringing the ideas in print about a female savior directly into the local field of conflict.[31] The religious leaders and polemicists in Europe and America were shocked by this regendering of the Savior that had reemerged, this time among the Moravians, and saw it as part of Satan's ageless attempt to threaten God with blasphemous female qualities and notions.

To many the Moravians appeared to represent another reappearance of the old Gnostic heresy and the more recent Mother Eva nightmare of a female Trinity and too much female power. In the eighteenth century Jesus had become female again, and as in the past, church leaders were prepared to take significant steps to stop this Satanic heresy, especially since it came from a group that was expanding and tried to proselytize among everyone.

Communal Living and the Challenge to Patriarchal Authority

Most Moravians lived, worked, and worshiped in closed communities throughout the Atlantic world, and in places like Herrnhut and Herrn-haag in Germany, s'Herrendijk in the Netherlands, or Nazareth and Bethlehem in Pennsylvania, they worked out the meaning of their views on the Trinity and developed radical practices regarding gender that challenged those living around them.[32] On both sides of the Atlantic, nobility and especially clergy dominated the upper ranks of these hierarchical Moravian communities. During the mid-eighteenth century they directed a "General Economy" in many of the communities, regulating all economic activity and implementing a system of collective ownership of the means of production. Members received no wages, and the church provided housing, food, and other provisions. For a while some of these communities became thriving centers of industry and commerce, especially in Pennsylvania and North Carolina.[33]

Liturgical life and the "choir" system were central to Moravian closed communities throughout the Atlantic realm, from Herrnhaag to London and from Bethlehem to the Delaware missions in Pennsylvania and the Ohio, and they reflected the group's theological views on gender. Zinzendorf developed a "community marriage" ideal, in which Moravian believers were divided, cloisterlike, into living, work, and worship groups called choirs, based on age, sex, and marital status. The system was central to the organization and direction of Moravian society, which had a top-down, compartmentalized look. (Moravian clergy and nobility sometimes even directed the migration of members in communities called "sea congregations" or in choirs.[34]) Married women, married men, single women, single men, widows, older girls, older boys, younger girls, and younger boys lived, worked, and worshiped in these groups, often in well designed and crafted architectural structures that still exist. Each choir had its own leadership, kept its own diary, and organized its own work schedule and liturgical life. This meant that women had considerable opportunity to play leadership roles in community religious life. Indeed the Moravian daily, weekly, quarterly, and yearly calendars were filled not only with traditional Christian liturgy, but also with special events and practices few Christians performed. These included love feasts, foot washings, singing hours, and group marriages, as well as events unique to the Moravians, such as liturgical celebrations honoring individuals or important events in Moravian history. The choir system and special liturgy predominated even in death, as Moravians read aloud written memoirs of those who had died and then buried them not in family plots, but in straight rows and columns, marching toward heaven in chronological order of death and sectioned by choir.[35]

The most controversial Moravian community during the period of conflict was Herrnhaag (see Figure 2), the center of most innovative beliefs and practices concerning gender, marriage, and sex.[36] Construction of the baroque style buildings on Count Büdingen's estate in Wetteravia began in 1738. The inhabitants were a mixture of old artisan refugee families from Moravia and young, single students, nobility, and high-ranking "middle-class" citizens (*Bürger*) who were charged with energy, piety, and hormones. Also present were Inspired, Separatist, and other radical pietist seekers who participated in the controversial communal life there and later reported on it in polemics that significantly damaged the Moravian cause. The new piety, often described as the "blood and wounds" litany and lifestyle, emerged in Herrnhaag. By 1739 various forms of terms like the lamb (referring to Christ), blood and wounds, and the side wound as a shrine permeated daily speech and hymnology. This was typical pietist language, but the Moravians went further than what many Protestants then and now who are familiar with hymns like "Rock of Ages," "Are You Washed in the Blood?" or "O Haupt voll Blut und Wunden!" ("O Sacred Head Sore Wounded!") found acceptable. Moravians began describing themselves as "little worms" ("Würmlein") who swam and bathed in the blood of Jesus, or as little doves fluttering in and out of the pierced side.[37]

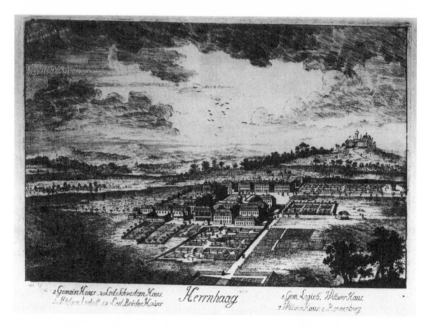

Figure 2. View of the community of Herrnhaag in Wetteravia, center of the Moravian movement from 1738 to 1753 and the place where many of the group's innovations concerning gender and sex took place. Copper etching, artist unknown, mid-eighteenth century. TS Mp.88.a, Unity Archives, Herrnhut.

After Zinzendorf departed for Pennsylvania in 1741, a clannish inner circle of extremely pious young men and women raised the "blood and wounds" beliefs and lifestyle to new levels and challenged the older leadership in Herrnhaag. Zinzendorf embraced the movement upon returning in 1743, and they began playfully using the new "little lamb" ("Lämlein") speech, as it was called. Development of the "wounds litany" ("Wundenlitanei") accelerated in 1744, with poems and hymns taught in school that celebrated it. A new term appeared, the "Cross Air Birdies" ("Kreuzluftvögelein"), that represented believers as little birds fluttering around the Cross and sinking into the body of Christ. This sensuous language was connected to the new Moravian views on marriage and the spiritualization of sexuality. Wearing new clothes, singing new songs, painting and composing new themes, and erecting new baroque buildings, the Moravians in Herrnhaag celebrated life as a grand liturgical festival. The playful language continued, now more about the "Cross Air Birdies" and the "little side hole" than the little lamb.[38] The side hole became a vagina-like tunnel, inside which one might find a safe, womb-like room with a bed and table. In early December of 1748 the spiritual ecstasy and innovation among the circle of young men devoted to the count's son, Christian Renatus Zinzendorf, reached new heights, as a young man named Johann Christoph Becker described gender transformations in his diary:

> A few days earlier the brothers in Herrnhaag with astonishing feeling were *all* accepted and declared as single sisters, and we experienced this astonishing thing ourselves this evening and were blessed by the dear Hertzel, with (Christian) Renatus, Rubusch, and Caillet singing and laying on hands. There was also Communion and foot washing.[39]

Gender transformations, kissing in public among single men and women, and sensuous, private liturgies strained relations between generations in Wetteravia to a breaking point and made their way into anti-Moravian polemics. In response to the growing crisis in Herrnhaag Zinzendorf wrote an open letter to the community from London in 1749, warning them that they were going too far. But the Herrnhaag experiment did not end until 1753, when the new Count Büdingen heeded the pleas in the polemics and his own instincts and ejected the Moravians from Wetteravia.[40] Not surprisingly, the pressure against the Moravians throughout the Atlantic world began to subside after this happened.

Many young Moravians in Herrnhaag migrated to Bethlehem, Pennsylvania, before and after their forced removal from there and the other Wetteravian communities in 1753.[41] After a rough beginning the communal society in Bethlehem began working well, and at least some of the controversies from Herrnhaag reemerged in this New World community. Ties with Europe were close, as leaders were sent to Pennsylvania on lengthy assignments to direct the community. Also, Bethlehem received hundreds of publications; in 1755 its bookstore had fifteen different hymnals and over 5,000 volumes for the community, which was nearly completely literate. Bethlehemers always wanted the latest editions, including the controversial works about the conflicts in Europe and the Twelfth Appendix of the hymnal, which they received in 1748. They possessed thousands of published and unpublished hymns and litanies that were central to their everyday life. Many of these works emphasized Christ as the Creator and husband and the Holy Spirit as mother. Worship of the mother intensified in the 1750s, when Bethlehemers developed a "Mother Festival" (*Mutterfest*) that they continued to celebrate until 1774.[42]

Zinzendorf's theology played a tremendous direct role in everyday life in Bethlehem, where all life became a liturgy. Ritual life connected the secular to the sacred (linking everyday life to the death of Christ), and it kept the inhabitants focused on their mission and held the community together. Community litanies became a form of corporate prayer. Death was a holy moment, when believers entered the side wound and their marriage with Christ was consummated, accompanied by singing and deathbed litanies. Funerals followed with strict gender separation, lively music, and prayers for the dead. Annual commemorations in the graveyard, called "God's Acre," celebrated the Resurrection, and at Easter they read aloud the names of all who had died that year.[43]

The choir system, not the traditional nuclear family household, shaped the structure of life in Bethlehem. Children lived and learned in choirs separated from their parents. The process began early with a "Baby Choir" and continued through childhood, as young Bethlehemers learned to develop an intimate spiritual relationship with Jesus that informed their behavior. Parents, including women busy with ministering, set out to do mission work without their children. Female piety flourished in the Single Sisters Choir, where ceremony, liturgy, an erotic marriage with Christ, adoration of the Holy Spirit as mother, and even a view of Anna Nitschmann as the Virgin Mary shaped life. Each choir used a different aspect of the life of Christ as a model for their own lives, much the way theologians (including Zinzendorf) employed the Trinity as a model for understanding power relations and life in the community.[44]

The choir system had profound, some thought sinister, implications for family life and patriarchal authority. Because children did not live with their parents in proper nuclear families dominated by the father, the old Reformation ideal that was supposed to be the bulwark of good Christian society appeared to be threatened. Women could live separately, to some degree independent of male control, and there were numerous positions as choir leaders that women could and did fill. This too violated the Reformation ideal. The fact that some husbands and wives lived separately in their choirs, away from each other and their children, outraged the group's enemies, who saw this as a direct threat to the family and patriarchal order. Moravians not only did this to themselves, they also did it to others they had attracted to their communities. Polemicists viciously attacked the group for such perversities and conjured up images for eager readers of women and children in danger, Moravian women misusing too much power, sexual orgies, and the like behind closed (sometimes even opened!) doors. The threat in many ways was real—the choir system made the nuclear family practically obsolete, and it did empower women, within limits. Worst of all for the Moravians, it provided their enemies with ammunition to attack the group for what they saw as gross, Catholic-like perversities, and female power gone astray.

Marriage and Sex

Within their closed communities Moravians developed beliefs and practices concerning marriage and sex that shocked many of their enemies. While many Protestants in the early modern era (Puritans and a few others excepted) had come to believe that marriage was important to control sex, that sexual intercourse was necessary to raise more good Christians, that extramarital sex and celibacy were bad, and that lust—indeed all sex—was an unhappy consequence of original sin, the Moravians defied these and other mainstream views concerning marriage and sex.

Although Zinzendorf and the Moravians upheld monogamy, controlled sex in their communities, and did not promote sex outside of marriage, they defied prevailing Protestant notions about marriage and sex, especially those of church pietists (as opposed to radical pietists), by changing their theological, metaphorical meaning, making both sacred and positive events. They resacralized marriage and declared that sex between husband and wife was holy, a service to God, and a part of their liturgy. This was in part a consequence of their view of marriage between men and women as an image of the mystical marriage between the church and Christ the bridegroom that was common in Christian belief, but the Moravians went well beyond this. Zinzendorf taught that the husband acted as a proxy or procurator for Christ, and the wife should regard him as acting in the name of the Creator (Christ). Husband and wife became partners in the struggle to do the Lord's work on earth and were sometimes called "*Streiter.*"[45] Such partnerships were often sealed by use of the lot. The lot was originally employed to determine leadership posts in the community, and the group eventually began using this "communication from God" (*Herablassung Gottes*) as a mechanism to prevent false decisions from being made because of imagined problems or prejudices. The most common method they used was to write two statements expressing the Savior's will, one of which was drawn from a container. This they ultimately extended to a number of liturgical matters, including marriage. Choir leaders sought good matches and then put them to the lot for approval. If the persons involved did not want to marry, they could refuse. In some cases a dozen or more couples chosen by lot were wedded in a single mass ceremony (see Figure 3).[46]

In addition to marriage itself, sex among married couples also became an important spiritual event in the church, as man and wife received a blessing from the Savior during intercourse, and Moravian hymns portrayed the glory of sexual organs. By emphasizing the gendered, sexual character of the deity the Moravians took away the shame

Figure 3. The marriage of twelve Moravian couples in Marienborn (Wetteravia) in 1743. TS Mp.372.15, Unity Archives, Herrnhut.

and sin of sex at a time when church pietists and "middle-class" (*bürgerliche*) inhabitants increasingly emphasized a more private sex life between husbands and wives. As Zinzendorf explained in the forward to their hymnal, if the Creator had a male organ (*männliches Glied*), and if the female organ (*weibliches Glied*) was honored for all eternity in the person of the holy mother, then why should they be ashamed of their sexual parts?[47] Thus the genitalia of men and women were venerated, not hidden, and the act of procreation became not a necessary evil or impure act, but rather a majestic one that should not be kept secret but sung publicly in hymns like the following:

O brächt uns unser Ehe-Freund
die blutbesprengsten glieder,
die zu dem bunde nöthig seynd,
in ihre Unschuld wieder!

O bring us, our marriage friend
thy blood speckled member,
which is needed for the union
with our innocence once again.

(Hymn 2121, verse 6, Twelfth Appendix, *Moravian Hymnal*)

Wenn ich Ihn essen kan,	When I can eat him,
so ist mirs am gesündsten,	so it is best for me.
und wenn mein lieber mann	and when my dear husband
sein öl läßt in mich dünsten;	lets his oil sizzle in me;
weil aber diese gnad in einem	since this grace is a sacrament
sacrament,	
das man nicht immer hat,	that one cannot always have
dem leib wird zugewand.	my body is turned toward (him).

(Hymn 2085, verse 1, Twelfth Appendix, *Moravian Hymnal*)

Moravians not only challenged prevailing views concerning marital sex in the theological or metaphorical realm, they also developed real, tangible practices that other pietists found unacceptable, including a view of marital sex that violated the traditional view of moderation. Like the mystical pietists who promoted celibacy and the radicals such as the Mother Eva Society who appeared to promote promiscuity, the Moravians took a stand on sex and made it central to their religious beliefs and ritual. They discouraged sex outside of marriage (although there was a rumor that Zinzendorf had an extramarital affair with Anna Nitschmann), but they made sex within marriage a positive, sacred practice—even when it was not for procreation. In their communal societies they controlled opposite-sex relations by keeping single men and women apart and by regulating and ritualizing contacts between married couples. They upheld monogamy and controlled who married whom through the lot. Their choir system and sacralization of sex allowed them carefully to regulate sexuality and relations between the sexes, and Zinzendorf developed a fine distinction between "necessary feeling" in sexual relations, which was positive, and "sinful lust" derived from impure intentions. Zinzendorf taught that sex between husband and wife was a positive thing for its liturgical value and spiritual meaning, rather than as a matter of lustful pleasure.[48]

Moravians believed that since sex was positive and married believers received a blessing during intercourse, then it should be encouraged and openly discussed so young men and women would know what to do and when. Before leaving for Pennsylvania in 1741, Zinzendorf left instructions on how married couples should be brought together, after various religious ceremonies, and left alone for sex.[49] With this, marital sex literally became a part of their liturgy, and detailed instructions were drawn up explaining how members of the married "choirs" (i.e., living, work, and worship groups) were to teach sexual procedures and practice to newly wedded sisters and brothers. In Bethlehem the "Married People's class" spoke openly about matrimony, how Christ and not the "rules of reason" should instruct them on it, and how they must avoid the "lust of the flesh." Zinzendorf's instructions emphasized the importance of consent by both parties in marriage, properly informing young men and women before and after their marriage about sex, how and why their bodies and sexual organs were made holy through Jesus, the methods of sexual intercourse, and how often it should be performed. Two methods of intercourse were suitable—sitting or lying, and couples should choose according to their own taste, using a chair or bench and towel with the first or a pillow with the second. After they finished couples prayed and discussed the liturgical importance of the event with others. Couples should have sex about once per week, but not during menstruation or nursing, on communion days, or when either of them was feeling ill or down. However, couples should not let small problems like toothaches, headaches, or dizzy spells stop them, and they should continue into the sixth or seventh month of pregnancy, at least on holidays. Further, they should continue to have sex, even when they could no longer have children.[50]

Because of their special living arrangements in the closed communities and the liturgical nature of their sexual practices, the logistics of how Moravians actually came together for this blessed event were unusual as well. In some communities married couples were housed barracks-style, separated by gender, so there was nowhere for them to meet alone indoors to have sex unless the church leaders designated a special place and made arrangements. Thus male and female "bed masters" (*Bettmeister*) and "curators" (*Caplainen*) scheduled times for married couples to meet in special sleeping quarters (a *Schlafsaal*) with a double bed (there were two in the married sisters' dormitory in Bethlehem), so that they could have sacred sex in what they called their "marriage quarter hourlies" (*Eheviertelstunden*). In Bethlehem a Mahican woman described in a letter to Maria Spangenberg how she spent time in the *Cabinet* (chamber) with a brother and what a blessed sensuous experience it was. There is a reference in the Moravians' own records to couples in Herrnhut having sex "in the presence of everyone," but it is not clear if this meant that they entered and departed the *Schlaafsaal* or *Cabinet* with others watching, or if others actually observed their sexual intercourse. To their enemies, however, these were minor details scarcely worth mentioning.[51]

Resacralizing marriage, singing about sex, and incorporating it into liturgy provided more than enough material for the enemies of this group to attack them as dangerous, satanic, promiscuous perverts. Even though Moravians actually emphasized the traditional ideals of controlled heterosexual sex in monogamous relationships, they shocked their enemies by sacralizing marital sex and publicly discussing and celebrating it, as well as the sexual organs of Christ and humans. While many villagers who had been busy having premarital sex followed by a public marriage ceremony may not have had a problem with semipublic consummation of marriage, and the clergy sometimes formally blessed the marriage bed of newly wedded couples, the above practices of open sex in a special, crowded place just for this purpose suggested scandalous promiscuity, which they condemned in their writings. As with Quakers, the Mother Eva Society, and other radical religious groups, opponents could and did associate the Moravian movement with sexual perversity and dangerous, uncontrolled female power, hence evil. Moreover the sacramental, liturgical aspects of Moravian marriage and sex seemed too bizarre and Catholic for most good Protestants to accept in the eighteenth century.

The Moravian challenge to orthodox views concerning marriage and sex and the furious response of their enemies played an important role in the transatlantic conflict among these Protestant groups, which recent interpretations of marriage and sex cannot adequately explain. Many historians have stressed the clerical assault on premarital sex as central to religious conflict in this era and have overemphasized the positive evaluation reformers and pietists held of marital sex (see Chapter 2). The Moravian conflict shows, however, that marital sex could be a problem in religious tensions during this period. Pietists who struggled to believe that sex between husband and wife really could be without sin (many concluding that it could not) simply did not accept a view that celebrated this act in such an unqualified, sacred, and ritualistic way. They became convinced that this was yet another manifestation of Satan's work among the Moravians and attacked them vigorously for it.

Moravians and Women Preaching

One of the most dangerous violations of gender boundaries perpetrated by the Moravians, according to their enemies, was allowing women to preach.[52] Like the dissenting churches and the early pietists in Europe, as well as the Quakers, the new German commune at Ephrata, and others in North America, the Moravians on both continents sought to end the utter subjection of women in formal religious worship and communities. While in Pennsylvania, Zinzendorf began developing a special, important role for women in Moravian communities. In his "Address to Women" given in Philadelphia, he emphasized that the New Testament speaks of a special love that the Savior has for the female sex. In the Old Testament women were meant for service and work. They were considered foolish, unworthy of respect or honor, and were held responsible for the Fall and bringing unhappiness into the world. But since the Savior was brought into the world by a woman, Zinzendorf said, women should now be respected and honored, like Mary Magdalene, to whom Christ first appeared after the Resurrection. The sisters were stronger and had more character than men. They were more noble, innocent, humble, honest, and true ("a sister's heart is a true heart," he wrote).[53] These were traits associated with and promoted by Jesus Christ—what more could one ask? Women should rejoice in their sex, and they should be honored, respected, and celebrated in song, as the Savior expected.[54]

While Zinzendorf, like the Quakers in the seventeenth century, used the Bible to justify women preaching and holding office, he distanced himself from that group on one important Biblical interpretation, and this suggests that the Moravians were less radical than the Quakers on the subject. Unlike George Fox and Margaret Fell, Zinzendorf accepted the idea of women's subordination to men in 1 Corinthians 14:34–35, but creatively interpreted it in order to give women as much responsibility as possible without violating the Pauline principle. At the 1740 Moravian synod in Gotha he explained that *wives* (*Weiber*) were forbidden by Paul to speak in services because this was disrespectful to their husbands, but at meetings they could witness or express religious knowledge and wisdom (*weissagen*), as long as they did not discuss dogma. He also reasoned that young single women (*Jungfern*) could preach and that widows (no longer *wives*) could teach young women and girls in the choirs. Zinzendorf did not believe that women should have full equality with men, and men should (and did) hold all of the highest positions in all of the Moravian communities. He too believed that if women ruled, confusion would follow. Thus when Anna Nitschmann preached, for example, part of her message was that women should be obedient to men.[55]

In spite of Zinzendorf's limitations on women preaching, significant evidence exists of Moravian women doing just that in Europe and America. From 1740 to 1742, just as they began organizing their communal settlements in Nazareth and Bethlehem, there were a handful of Moravian women in the colony, and at least three of them preached and worked with non-Moravians. All three were young and two were noblewomen—qualities that attracted attention among non-Moravians. Anna Nitschmann was 25 upon her arrival in 1740, and the baroness Johanna Sophia Molther was 22, while Benigna Zinzendorf (the count's daughter) was only 16 when she came the following year.[56] Molther and Nitschmann arrived in 1740 and provided badly needed female leadership to the struggling Moravians in the colony. Nitschmann was the leader of the single women in Herrnhut. Eventually she became the most powerful and respected woman of the movement, Count Zinzendorf's travel companion, and ultimately his wife. She arrived in Philadelphia on December 5, 1740 with Molther, the bishop David Nitschmann (her father), and the Indian missionary Christian Fröhlich.[57]

This was a critical time of the early Moravian mission in the colony. Until then things had been going badly for the group in Pennsylvania. Remnants of their failed community in Georgia had been trickling into the northern colony and continued their squabbling—or refused to speak with one another. Negotiations with the Schwenkfelders were going badly, and a year earlier Spangenberg had been recalled from Pennsylvania to Europe and was not happy about it. Moreover, after failing in Georgia the Indian mission in New York was just beginning, as was the construction of a closed Moravian community in Nazareth. (Work on nearby Bethlehem would begin the following year.) In her diary and correspondence Nitschmann described her initial impressions and activities in the colony and how they developed until her departure in July of 1742.[58]

Upon arriving in Pennsylvania, Nitschmann wrote that she immediately began meeting with women from the numerous sects, as well as with other Moravians (see Plate 7). In 1740 she preached to men and women at a Quaker meeting "to the greatest astonishment of those present" ("mit höchster Verwunderung der Anwesenden").[59] Nitschmann commented on how poorly the Moravians were doing in the colony at this early date, including the problems they were having with the numerous sects. But she worked hard, preaching to Indian women, and by April 1741 she worked with 20 young Christian women outside of the Moravian settlements who were searching for the Savior. People were always asking her to come and preach, and she wrote to Benigna Zinzendorf that there would be plenty of work for her upon arriving, especially with children, as they planned to open a school. Progress was slow, but hopeful, Nitschmann wrote to other Moravian women at home, as she attempted to pave the way for some of them to work in the colony. She also wrote to Moravian men, informing them in an authoritative way of conditions in Pennsylvania and what needed to be done about it, which demonstrates the legitimacy of her work and leadership in Moravian circles. Nitschmann described the numerous sects in the land and their errors to Isaac LeLong, the Moravian business contact in Amsterdam. She asked Count Zinzendorf to send more sisters to work in Pennsylvania and in Maryland and Virginia, and she noted that Andreas Frey was unsuited for public preaching—thus acting as a *judge* toward Moravian men and one of their male preachers. Nitschmann buried herself in her work, which she compared to spiritually burying herself in the side hole of Christ—typical Moravian talk of the period—and complained about constantly traveling and working in winter weather. There was hope in this wild, desolate land, and there was certainly a place for Moravian women to preach there. In fact, she called for more women to help, as the work load was exhausting, what with dealing with weekly public sermons, serving the Moravians in the country, working the Indian mission, dealing with problems involving George Whitefield, and other Moravian activities in the colony.[60]

In late 1741 help arrived, as Count Zinzendorf appeared with his daughter, Benigna (see Figure 4), and others. The party arrived in Philadelphia on December 9. A week later, while her father and others traveled, Benigna stayed with Johanna Sophia Molther in Germantown, where she had the opportunity to speak with a number of people, mostly children, about the death of the Lamb. On January 1 Benigna rode with two Moravian brothers and a sister to Oley, then Falkner's Swamp, visiting along the way with the daughters of affiliated families. She attended the first ecumenical conference in Oley (see Chapter 6) and did the "work of the Savior" while in the town. Benigna worked hard with children there and by April had 31 under her tutelage. Later she moved back to Philadelphia, where she had trouble because she could not speak English, but eventually began to learn the language and then spoke to young "English" women. At one point she was meeting with 25 girls and young women, telling them what the Lamb had done for her. She also worked with Indians when she accompanied her father on his first tour into "Indian country," and she spent time in Nazareth and Bethlehem.[61]

Women played important roles as itinerant workers in the revival, whether with their husbands or with other women. Anna Nitschmann, Benigna Zinzendorf, and Johanna Sophia Molther were not the only Moravian women who did this. In 1753 Anna Ramsberger and Maria Catharina Binder worked in Lancaster and York Counties, Pennsylvania, and in western Maryland, usually escorted from place to place by local Moravian men or supporters. After attending the synod in Lancaster they began their tour in the country. While overnighting at a tavern in York they had to endure a visit by three drunken men who came to sing for them. At Monocacy, Maryland, they met with their local contact, Captain Ogle, and spoke to his three daughters, and after the Sunday sermon in the school house they met with a number of single women. It became a successful, high-profile tour in which Ramsberger and Binder not only visited, but also led some quarter-hourly meetings. Then they concentrated on spreading the message about the blood and wounds of the Savior while visiting young non-Moravian women in the largely German countryside around Monocacy. Ramsberger and Binder worked in the school house at York on the way back as well. Around Lancaster and Warwick they visited young women and held love feasts for women and girls in school houses. They also traveled to Donegal, Quittopehille, and Balthasar Ort's, working in schools, holding love feasts, and visiting.

Figure 4. Henriette Benigna Justine von Watteville (1725–1789), daughter of Count Nicholaus Ludwig von Zinzendorf. Along with Anna Nitschmann and Johanna SophiaMolther she took part in the Moravian women's preaching tour in Pennsylvania from 1740 to 1742. Oil painting by Johann Valentin Haidt. GS 099, Unity Archives, Herrnhut.

Then they went to Tulpehocken, Heidelberg, Allemaengel, the Delaware mission at Gnadenhütten, and finally back to Bethlehem.[62]

Moravians often sent teams of husbands and wives to work among Europeans, Africans, and Native Americans. A small army of male and female itinerant preachers, teachers, and their assistants worked out of Bethlehem and other communities. Each husband and wife team, or "wheel," as Moravians sometimes called their married itinerants, might work a circuit of four or five communities and visit in surrounding areas of those communities. The wives usually worked with women in groups, while their husbands pursued their own work in the community. They traveled almost constantly, not only around their circuit, but back and forth to Bethlehem, to relieve colleagues in trouble on another circuit, or to complete a special mission anywhere from the upper Hudson to the upper Shenandoah Valley. The teams of itinerant workers possessed maps like the one used by Matthias and Anna Maria Hehl in their tour of Pennsylvania (see Plate 8). The map marked communities and trails in the "Pennsylvania field."

Moravian men and women working together delivered important pastoral care to Lutheran and Reformed immigrants flooding into the colonies during the Great Awakening, but it was not easy. Johann and Anna Maria Brandmüller, for example, worked effectively as a team, traveling in a covered wagon. They set up a school at Swatara, where Anna Maria taught sixty boys and girls with a German "ABC Book," probably the one printed in Germantown by Christopher Saur in 1738.[63] When they announced that boys and girls would meet on opposite days, however, no one showed up. After a visitation tour by the Brandmüllers failed to win over the local inhabitants, the couple compromised and allowed boys and girls to have school together, separated by a curtain. Johann was miserable over this development, but it worked, and he and his wife went on to become important figures in the area. Many people came to visit Anna Maria, and in 1745 she attended the synod in Lancaster. Visitors from Bethlehem supported the couple by bringing greetings and exchanging information. After the death of their daughter and the school problem, the synod gave both of them a much needed boost. To many Reformed and Lutheran immigrants in the communities unused to care in America by regular pastors, this sudden infusion of pastoral activity and male and female attention gave the impression that whoever was behind it was serious about supporting the new flocks in the colonies.[64]

Many other Moravian women worked in tandem with their husbands, or other men, visiting, problem-solving, teaching, and holding informal or liturgical meetings with other women. Rosina Almers and Sister Nobel made the trip with Rosina's husband, Heinrich, and another

Moravian man to New York in the summer of 1742. They started a
"band" (something like a choir) of single women in Manhattan and
held a service in which they discussed the holy five wounds of Christ on
the Cross. The group then visited the Mahican mission upriver at Shekomeko. In May/June of 1743 Judith Meinung met separately with women
at Oley while Andreas Eschenbach met with the men. Women played
an important role in the revival at Muddy Creek in 1745, where Rosina
Nitschmann Münster, wife of the itinerant Johannes, held several spiritual meetings with fifteen to twenty women. And in Dansbury Elizabeth
Payne and Anna Ramsberger worked with groups of single women and
girls in 1753, while Elizabeth's husband, Jasper Payne, preached in the
area.[65]

Like the Quakers, Shakers, the Mother Eva Society, and others, the
Moravians endured severe criticism for allowing women to preach, even
in an era and place where the practice was increasing. In a polemic sent
to North America Joachim Lange, the aging Halle Lutheran theologian,
questioned the Moravian practice of sending women and unqualified
men to do missionary work in America, which was against the teachings
of the Gospel. Even Zinzendorf's wife was doing missionary work, he
complained. Johann Georg Walch, the theology professor at Jena, connected female preaching to other Moravian practices that threatened
the orders in society. Fresenius printed a description of Moravian activities in this period that included Nitschmann, Zinzendorf, and Molter's
preaching tours, which he described with disdain in his "American News
of Herrnhuter Matters" (*Americanische Nachrichten von Herrnhutischen
Sachen*), a kind of documentary history of the rise and fall of the Moravian movement in America. When Anna Nitschmann traveled around
the colony, meeting with groups, preaching and recruiting, she
attracted some women because she could sing so well and because she
exploited the innocence of unknowing children. Molther and Benigna
Zinzendorf were guilty too, Fresenius wrote. Benigna held meetings in
Oley, Pennsylvania, especially with young people, and took down their
names. And although this writer believed that her methods and strange
attitudes and speech about the Savior's blood and poor sinners repelled
many of her listeners, she still represented a threat that must be
addressed. Benigna and other Moravian women proselytized in Philadelphia under the pretext of learning English from them, according to Fresenius. Other Europeans, such as Ernst Salomon Cyprian and Georg
Jacob Sutor, condemned Moravian women preaching without further
comment to this obvious malpractice, the latter claiming to have seen
for himself the ordination of Moravian women, complete with the laying
on of hands. The issue resonated in the Delaware Valley as well. Mühlenberg complained that everyone in this country was becoming a Quaker

and ignoring God's word in favor of "what this or that woman preaches from her own imagination (*Fantasie*) or inspiration." Gabriel Naesman, the Swedish Lutheran pastor who was a fierce enemy of the Moravians in the Swedish congregations on both sides of the Delaware and was involved in violent attacks on them in New Jersey, furiously denounced the group with harsh rhetoric that revealed his deep fears about women preaching and taking over the pulpits of the region. Thus fears and slander promoted about the Moravians in polemics and the tension and violent conflict in the communities were connected to Moravian women preaching.[66]

Although condemned in anti-Moravian polemics as a dangerous violation of gender boundaries, female workers may have helped to draw other women to the Moravian cause. A third of the immigrants and half of their children were women, and many of them found the Moravians appealing. Watching Anna Nitschmann preach or Catharina Binder hold a love feast attracted pious women who wanted to play a more active role in their Lutheran and Reformed spiritual communities. Male Moravians were not always aware of this, or at least did not highlight it in their diaries, as their female counterparts did.

Immigrants and others in the Lutheran and Reformed communities of the colonies did not usually see Moravian liturgical practices regarding marriage and sex and other controversial aspects of their choir system that took place within their closed communities, but what they did see when Moravian preachers came to their communities was an emotional revival style of preaching and speech, as well as women playing important leadership roles in the mission. The contrast to what their orthodox opponents offered these communities was striking: male pastors sent by European state church authorities to work in America did not take their wives or any other women with them when they visited these communities, and they preached in a scholastic style, usually from notes.[67]

The overall number of Moravian women who preached and held other important offices in the colonies and Europe was significant. Of the 270 known female Moravian immigrants who settled in British North America, seventeen did at least some preaching, mostly as missionaries, and thirteen of these arrived between 1740 and 1752, during the peak period of conflict.[68] In addition to preaching, hundreds of Moravian women held other offices in Europe and America, including eldresses, teachers (who instructed men and women), overseers, group leaders, and 47 ordained deaconesses who worked in the mid-Atlantic colonies before independence. These officeholders looked after the spiritual and material needs of Moravian women without the support of men. They ran the choir houses and attended conferences, synods, and other meetings with men—not as mere observers, but as full participants who spoke, argued, and voted.[69]

Thus while the Moravians were not as radical as the Quakers on the point of women preaching, the efforts of Zinzendorf, Anna Nitschmann, Benigna Zinzendorf, and many others meant that Moravian women clearly had more opportunities to participate in formal church rule and decision-making than women did in Lutheran, Reformed, and most other communities, and people in North America knew it. The high-profile preaching tours of elite Moravian women early on in Pennsylvania highlighted to friend and foe that the Moravians had come to the colony and that both women and men intended to preach there. Those who missed the tours could read about them in the *Pennsylvania Gazette*. In 1743 Franklin ran an article explaining Moravian beliefs and practices that included citations from John Wesley's *Journal*, in which Wesley noted that Moravian women could preach and hold other offices. Perhaps more importantly, men and women in the German and Swedish Lutheran and Reformed communities with little formal pastoral care could see Moravian women effectively preaching, teaching, and otherwise assisting with the mission.[70]

It is rare that a religious group with such radical views on gender strives so hard to engage other Christian and non-Christian peoples. Groups that believe in a largely female Christian deity and use this belief to develop and justify reordered gender relationships in the community, including leadership, marriage, and sexual behavior, usually prefer isolation, or proselytize in limited areas. Yet the Moravians expanded dramatically throughout the Atlantic world in the mid-eighteenth century and took these beliefs with them. In fact, one recent historian argues that it was these beliefs that *energized* the mission. These beliefs should not be associated with some marginal, misguided pursuit of an internal faction that must be somehow excused by later denominational historians, but rather understood as central to their beliefs and activity during this period of dramatic expansion of the modern Moravian church. Without the commitment of so many Moravian men and women to these views, their mission probably would not have been as successful as it was.[71]

Yet pursuing such radical views of gender was dangerous in the Protestant world. Promotion of a female Trinity, communal living separated by gender, the sacralization of marriage and sex, and women preaching violated fundamental aspects of gender order that had been developing since the Reformation, if not earlier. Their enemies, that is, theologians and writers of the orthodox churches, compared the Moravians to the Mother Eva Society, which had been one of the most dangerous threats to the churches in the German territories in the early eighteenth century, many thought. They exploited fears of gender disorder represented by the radicals to promote the value of traditional confessional order. Throughout the early modern and colonial era ordinary people in communities reacted strongly, if need be violently, to such warnings and removed people in their midst who appeared to threaten gender and confessional order.

The Moravian challenge to mainstream gender order was a transatlantic event in the Protestant world during the mid-eighteenth century, but by the 1740s many realized that North America would become a special setting in which this radical challenge and an orthodox response would take place. The polemics published on both sides of the Atlantic played an important role in the growing conflict, as did the pastors sent by the European churches to America, but ultimately the stage on which the battles over gender order would be fought were the new immigrant religious communities in the colonies. As with confessional order, there were clearly differences in how gender order might develop in North America, but it was unclear during the Great Awakening how or to what extent old views from Europe would take root and shape behavior in the new American communities. Would radicals succeed in fundamentally overhauling the older gender order? Would the radicals be able to go beyond the mere tolerance and precarious safety they enjoyed in certain European territories? Would they be able to shape religious life in mainstream communities without losing their radical edge? Or would the new communities develop in such a way that they would establish and protect traditional order and ward off violators, violently if necessary, the way they always had?

Chapter 4
The Ecumenical Challenge

And if we hold fast,
that the Community of God in the Spirit
continuously remains our house,
then it is in America
that we are on the right footing
my brethren!

und wenn wir fest darauf halten/
daß die Gemeine GOttes im Geist
unser beständiges Hauß bleibt/
so sind wir in America
auf den rechten Fuß/
meine Brüder!

Now I am convinced in my heart. . . . that America must be dipped in
the blood of Jesus

Nun bin ich in meinem Hertz versichert gewesen. . . . daß America
nothwendig ins Blut Jesu getaucht werden muß
—*Count Zinzendorf to Moravians in Philadelphia, 17 March 1742*

Moravian ambitions in North America were motivated by a zealous ecumenism that they attempted to extend to other radical groups and
churches alike, and it challenged or threatened those groups for a number of reasons. Unlike other radicals who pursued the philadelphian
ideal, it was not enough for Moravians to separate themselves from the
fallen institutional churches in order to unite with other like-minded
Christians. Instead, they embraced both radical separatists and the
established churches, hoping to find a way to unite all of them. Unfortunately for the Moravians, few Protestant Christians truly desired this kind
of unity at this time. Some found it offensive because Moravians spread
radical views on gender that threatened religious and social order. It was
the existence of dangerous groups like the Moravians, they argued, that
made it even more important to protect church boundaries. Others,
especially the radicals, came to believe that Moravian ecumenism, especially the views and activity of Count Zinzendorf himself, represented a
challenge to their very existence. Living in relative freedom in their asylums in Wittgenstein, Pennsylvania, and elsewhere, the radicals took a
great risk if they joined any kind of larger organization, especially if any

hierarchy or commitment to specific principles were involved. When the Moravians vigorously pursued their ecumenical program among the radicals and others, they encountered the old problem of how to achieve unity without losing freedom. To many orthodox Lutheran and Reformed people, ecumenism itself was a problem under any circumstances, because it challenged their continued commitment to distinct boundaries and recognition of dogmatic differences between churches. This was true even among some church pietists like the Hallensians, who a generation earlier had themselves deemphasized dogma and sought contacts with other groups. For the Moravians, however, the key issues were not defining and defending institutional boundaries and dogma, but rather understanding the meaning and death of Christ and expressing this to as many people as possible. This could be done while at the same time honoring liturgical and other traditions in the state churches, they thought.[1]

The Plan to Unite the Radicals

Zinzendorf's ecumenical thought and endeavors began long before the renewal of the Unitas Fratrum on his estates in Upper Lusatia. He grew up in the house of the Halle pietist leader August Hermann Francke, dining regularly with him and his wife, and had considerable contact with other leaders of the pietist movements in the German territories.[2] By 1717, when he was only seventeen years old, Zinzendorf was already thinking about a union of all awakened Christians, and in the early 1720s he presented an ecumenical plan to a Tübingen theologian. He was influenced by the philadelphian ideas of radicals and the pietist principle of "separating to unite." At a time when ecumenism and separatism were closely related because of political conditions, many pietists saw their work as a revival of primitive Christianity. Like the Puritans and Philip Jacob Spener, they distinguished between the true and the false church, the former being the intolerant, institutional, "visible" church that stressed dogma and compliance, and the latter being the "invisible" church of those in all groups who lived in intimate communion with Christ. These people must separate from the "false" state churches and unite with each other. The beauty of the invisible church lay in its plurality and diversity. Individuals could belong to a visible, organized church and also to the invisible religious community. Zinzendorf believed that the Moravians' role was to assist making the invisible church visible, thus creating a true philadelphian community in an increasingly intolerant, confessional, or secular world. Unlike most radical pietists, who were separatists, Zinzendorf thought that individuals and groups could achieve this in some semiformal way without separating from their home churches. In this way he strove to achieve the unity of all Christians.[3]

Throughout his career Zinzendorf maintained contact with major religious leaders in Europe, from pope to patriarch to Protestant awakener, and he attempted to realize his ecumenical vision by working with radicals. In the 1720s and 1730s he corresponded with the French Quietist, Cardinal Noailles, and he traveled to Prague and Silesia to make contacts with Schwenkfelders and others. Philadelphian ecumenism motivated the Moravian mission in the Netherlands, which began in 1736, as the group worked with Anabaptists, Old Flemings (*Oude Vlamingen*), Danzigers, Flemings, and Waterlanders, and to some extent with the Socinian Collegianten, all the while trying to be a part of the Reformed church—a controversial stance that the state church rejected. In the 1730s Zinzendorf also made contacts with radical pietists like Johann Konrad Dippel, as well as Separatists and Inspired, and he tried to build communities with them in the Sorau and Wittgenstein. Ultimately Dippel and other radicals not only rejected Zinzendorf's plan, but also deeply resented his meddling and communicated this to their radical compatriots in Pennsylvania.[4]

Zinzendorf's ecumenical failures in the 1730s continued to mount, as he and the Moravians embarked on an ambitious project in Georgia. From 1735 to 1740 the Moravians sent 41 men and women (including Spangenberg) to Savannah to lead Lutheran refugees from the Archbishopric of Salzburg and Schwenkfelders from Upper Lusatia to the new British colony. They also intended to preach to Indians in Georgia and to slaves in nearby South Carolina. But the Halle Lutherans took over the Salzburger project, and the Schwenkfelders decided to go to Pennsylvania. Moreover, few Indians or slaves understood German or English, and those who did cared little for the Moravian message. Eventually the Moravians began quarreling among themselves so badly that their community centered in Savannah collapsed, and its members trickled away to Europe and the northern colonies.[5]

Before the failure in Georgia had completely played out, the Moravians began planning their next ecumenical adventure in tolerant, diverse, and disorganized North America, this time in Pennsylvania. Spangenberg moved north from Georgia to Pennsylvania, where he joined other radicals in a grass-roots philadelphian ecumenical movement known as the "Associated Brethren of the Skippack" (*Vereinigte Schippach-Brüder*). In 1736 an Inspired immigrant named Johann Adam Gruber published a call for a union among the diverse religious parties in Pennsylvania, and in the following years Waldensians, Moravians, Schwenkfelders, Inspired, Dunkers, Separatists, and others responded. They met at the house of a Schwenkfelder named Christoph Wiegner and talked about how to achieve the philadelphian, ecumenical ideal. George Whitefield raised the stakes by preaching a number of emotional, ecumenical sermons in the area in 1739 and 1740, including one to at least 2,000 people at Wiegner's house in Skippack and another to about 3,000 people a few miles away at the house of Heinrich Antes, a Lutheran who had joined the Skippack Brethren and would later join the Moravians. Anna Nitschmann arrived in 1740 and used the Wiegner house as a base during her successful two-year preaching tour of Pennsylvania. Thus, Moravian women preaching became a part of the excitement in the new ecumenical movement. Encouraged by these developments, Count Zinzendorf decided to journey to Pennsylvania himself, where the Moravians now hoped to make a major effort to achieve their ecumenical ideal. By late 1741, as the arrival of the count, his daughter Benigna, and other Moravians was imminent, Heinrich Antes issued a circular letter that announced that the meetings of all interested parties to discuss how they might realize the philadelphian ideal and make the true invisible church visible in tolerant, diverse Pennsylvania would begin on 1 January 1742 in Germantown.[6]

The "Seven Ecumenical Synods" of Pennsylvania in 1742, an incredible gathering of diverse Protestant Christians, became, for better and worse, a showcase on both sides of the Atlantic for Zinzendorf's ecumenical program. By the time the first meeting took place in Germantown, Moravian influence on the movement had increased dramatically. In addition to Count Zinzendorf and other Moravians, Lutherans, German Reformed, Presbyterians, Anglicans, Quakers, Mennonites, Dunkers, Sabbatarians, Inspired, and even Separatists attended the synod. It was a striking, colorful display of the new social conditions of diversity, toleration, and immigration into the colony. Over one hundred people met at the conference—more than attended the initial sessions of the grand ecumenical Council of Basel in 1431. Newspapers covered developments in the conferences, Johann Jacob Müller recorded the minutes in German, and the entrepreneurial Benjamin Franklin, who correctly sensed that these meetings were going to make a big splash in the colony, printed and quickly sold them. Across the Atlantic in Frankfurt am Main Fresenius printed anti-Moravian responses to the minutes.[7]

The first two meetings of the ecumenical synods of 1742 were so successful that for a moment it appeared that there was some chance to realize Zinzendorf's goals, at least partially, and create the body of Christ in Pennsylvania. Attendance was high, and a spirit of cooperation reigned as Zinzendorf was named syndic of the conferences, allowing him to play a major role in defining the purpose and nature of this "Community of God in the Spirit" (*Gemeine Gottes im Geist*), as they called it. The conference declared that Christ had begun his work in all evangelical religions and that the conversion of thousands of souls in all lands and religions was legitimate. Further, those who pursued the work of the Lord should be supported in spite of their differences with one another, but they must relinquish personal interests and not worry about differences in the various "households." They must unite on the important points, making sure no one takes advantage of another, and they should judge others only to benefit the community. The synod addressed the question, "How diverse is the community of saints?" ("Wie mancherlei ist die Gemeinschaft der Heiligen?") and concluded, "The Community of God in the Spirit, throughout the entire world, which is His (Christ's) body, namely the fulness of him that filleth all in all, is innumerable, and its members are to be found in places where one never would have sought them."[8]

Zinzendorf used the metaphors of the body of Christ and the household to explain how relationships should work in the Community of God in the Spirit, that is, how unity could be achieved without sacrificing religious freedom. According to him, the so-called sects were compartments of a great house and should not be overlooked. All are members of a great body, Zinzendorf explained, and they could not afford to lose any of its members. If the small churches remain true to Christ as they build this spiritual house, then "their diversity is their beauty" ("so ist ihre Mannichfaltigkeit eine Schönheit"). At the Pennsylvania synods Zinzendorf essentially saw the union of the Community of God in the Spirit as a federal association of different religious groups. If the various groups could just agree on the main points, Zinzendorf thought, then such a federation in faith in which every household maintained its particular rights could be attempted. The spiritual metaphor of the body of Christ remained strong to the end. After the last session Heinrich Antes sent an open letter to the inhabitants of Pennsylvania, in which he noted that, "We, altogether, constitute the body of JESUS in Pennsylvania." ("Wir alle zusammen machen den Leib JESU in Pennsylvania aus.")[9]

After these promising beginnings in early 1742 the philadelphian, utopian ecumenical movement in Pennsylvania collapsed within a few weeks, and most historians believe that Count Zinzendorf's bombastic intervention was at least partially responsible for its demise. The Pennsylvania radicals, who had experienced more religious freedom there than they had ever imagined in Wetteravia or elsewhere in the German territories, did not want the pompous count or his federation. They believed that Zinzendorf wanted to dominate the movement at the expense of their religious freedom—much as he had tried to do with the radicals in Germany—and they published a number of polemics attacking Zinzendorf on this point (see Appendix 1).[10] Quarreling, absenteeism, and noncompliance increased at the synods, and the philadelphian spirit was lost. With this, yet another attempt by Europeans to create a utopia in the American wilderness had failed, and the Moravians had failed once again as well.[11]

Another failure did not deter the Moravians, however, and before Count Zinzendorf returned to Europe in January 1743 there were once again encouraging signs for what they might accomplish in British North America. The small Moravian contingent working in Pennsylvania had been reinforced by the "First Sea Congregation," a ship full of Moravians that had landed in Philadelphia and moved inland to build up the new closed communities at Nazareth and Bethlehem. German immigrants were pouring into the colony, most unattached to a strong, well organized church and many seeking spiritual guidance of some sort from Europe. The count and other Moravian leaders drew up detailed plans for new missions in America. The mission to the Mahicans in Shekomeko, New York, and Pachgatgoch, and Wechquatnach, Connecticut, was beginning to show progress. Energized by their newly developing theology that emphasized the female characteristics of the deity, the importance of women, and an invigorating communal life with innovative liturgical celebrations that stressed the importance of the sensual, emotional aspects of their relationship with the Savior and each other, at first dozens and then hundreds of Moravian men and women arrived in Pennsylvania, ready to work on new projects.

In his last speech to the Moravians before returning to Europe, Zinzendorf told the group gathered at Stephen Benezet's house in Philadelphia that in spite of their recent setbacks he was optimistic about the future of their mission. He reminded them that the sole purpose of their endeavors of the past twenty years had been to seek the truth and serve their Savior. Zinzendorf told them that he was convinced in his heart of two things: one, "that America must be dipped in the blood of Jesus just like Europe" ("daß America nothwendig ins Blut Jesu getaucht werden muß wie Europa") and two, that this must be done differently in America than in Europe. Pennsylvania was the key to all of America, and they had accomplished more in one year there than in the previous twelve years in Europe. But the very thing that had made their task possible in America, namely diversity and tolerance, also hindered them from achieving their final goal. Nevertheless, they could still take the first step toward achieving the Community of God in the Spirit in America, not Europe, as they celebrated in the verse at the beginning of this chapter.

The New Plan for the Churches

Even as the effort to unite the Pennsylvania radicals faltered, the Moravians were already developing new ecumenical plans, and their enemies

Plate 1. Nicolaus Ludwig von Zinzendorf (1700–1760), illuminated by the side wound of Christ, as the teacher of the peoples of the world. Oil painting by Johann Valentin Haidt (1700–1780), 1747. GS 583, Unity Archives, Herrnhut.

Plate 2. Moravian men and women at the Cross, beholding the blood of Christ. Watercolor, artist unknown, mid-eighteenth century. TS Mp.375.9, Unity Archives, Herrnhut.

Plate 3. The Crucifixion of Jesus Christ and Worship of the Exalted Lamb of God. Two colored copper engravings pasted together, artist unknown, ca. 1740. TS Mp.375.11.b, Unity Archives, Herrnhut.

Plate 4. Erotic Moravian side wound verses.
Watercolor on card stock, artist unknown, mid-eighteenth century, 6.2 × 3.5 cm. M 135 13, M 159
4–6, Unity Archives, Herrnhut.

Plate 5. Moravian miniatures with scenes of piety
in everyday life depicted inside the side wound,
represented as a womb. Watercolor on card stock,
artist unknown, mid-eighteenth century, 6.2 × 3.5
cm. TS Mp.375.4.d, TS Mp.375.d.e., M 135 1, 3, 5,
11, 12, M 159 2, Unity Archives, Herrnhut.

Plate 6. Other Moravian devotional artwork depicting the side wound. Top to bottom: watercolor on card stock, artist unknown, 6.5 cm × 5 cm; watercolor on card stock by Antoinette D., 6.5 cm × 4 cm; watercolor with thread sewn in by Mariane von Watteville, 16 cm × 11 cm; all mid-eighteenth century. M 161 f and g, and M 163, Unity Archives, Herrnhut.

Plate 7. Anna Nitschmann (1715–1760) preaching in a Quaker meeting house in Pennsylvania during her controversial tour in 1740–1742. Detail from a mural depicting important scenes in her life painted by Paul Adam Schöpfel. Gouache on parchment, 1747. GS 703, Unity Archives, Herrnhut.

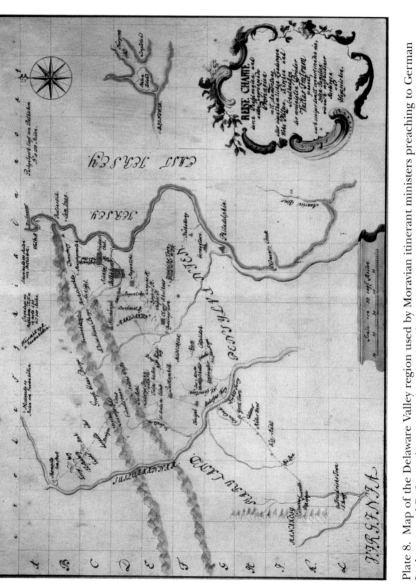

Plate 8. Map of the Delaware Valley region used by Moravian itinerant ministers preaching to German Lutheran and Reformed congregations in the 1740s. The map labels the locations of many settlements where Moravians preached at the time. Moravian Archives, Bethlehem.

were bracing themselves for the expected onslaught. The key target of their efforts now would be the German, Swedish Lutheran, and German Reformed communities in the Delaware Valley, where thousands of immigrants were arriving every year. These immigrants came without pastors and found themselves in unimaginable circumstances in America—spiritual and otherwise. To the Moravians this appeared to be a wonderful opportunity to labor for the Lord among people who desperately needed it and seemed to appreciate it. But after the recent fiascos in Georgia and Pennsylvania, not to mention tensions with Wesley and Whitefield in England, controversies with the slave and Indian missions on St. Thomas and in Suriname, and problems with the Lutheran and Reformed churches in Europe, much of the leadership in Protestant world carefully watched what the count and his people would do next in the Delaware Valley. What the Moravians needed, if they were to succeed in the Lutheran and Reformed communities, was a sense of legitimacy in those communities. They needed to find a way to convince themselves and others that it was proper for Moravians to preach and otherwise serve in these church communities.

Within a year after returning to Europe in early 1743, Zinzendorf developed a new ecumenical plan called the Tropus concept (*Tropenidee*), which he thought could allow Moravian men and women to work legitimately in the German and Swedish Lutheran and German Reformed church communities of the Delaware Valley. His plan was based on the notion that confessional boundaries could be transgressed without destroying the integrity of the church in question. It focused on three groups: the Lutherans and Reformed on both sides of the Atlantic, and the true "Moravians," who were descendants of the ancient church dating back to Jan Hus and others over a hundred years prior to the Reformation. As with the Pennsylvania ecumenical synods that focused on the many radical groups in the colony, Zinzendorf hoped to establish a loose confederation of churches and communities. Lutheran, Reformed, and Moravian communities would send their leaders to synods, which met regularly to have Christian fellowship, discuss progress, and work out problems. Zinzendorf hoped to achieve legitimacy for the movement by recognizing the teachings and confessional identity of all three groups. Each group maintained its own hierarchy within its community and remained a part of its larger church. Theoretically Lutheran and Reformed members kept their confessional identity and did not become Moravians, nor were they both Lutheran/Reformed and "Moravian."

But Zinzendorf's manner of creating hierarchy and organization in the new Tropus scheme raised suspicions. The count did not consider himself a "Moravian," but rather a Lutheran, and had managed to get himself ordained as a minister in that church in Tübingen (Württemberg) in 1734. Also, soon after creation of the Tropus system Zinzendorf became the head or Ordinarius Fratrum of all three Tropi, which together adopted the new name Unitas Fratrum. Lastly, when choosing leaders of the Lutheran and Reformed communities and representatives at synod meetings the count was careful to choose people who had spent time at Herrnhaag, Herrnhut, Bethlehem, or other Moravian communities and were sympathetic to the movement. To most Moravians these points were not problematic, but logical: Zinzendorf had been raised in the Lutheran church and never left it. His abilities, piety, and ecumenical mentality, along with his status as an imperial count, made him the perfect choice to lead the new movement. As for those chosen to represent their communities in the new system, if they were not truly pious, ecumenical, and hence sympathetic to the Moravians, then the movement would not work anyway. In short, a Lutheran count adopted a small radical pietist group, became their leader, initiated one ecumenical scheme after another, and still claimed to be a Lutheran.[12]

To orthodox Lutheran and Reformed authorities this was too much: now Count Zinzendorf was directly challenging their confessional ideal by saying essentially that the clergy and laity could be members of the state churches and simultaneously participate in the Moravian heresy. The count was in the field, claiming that he was a Lutheran bishop and ordaining Moravians into the Lutheran priesthood, and his Moravian preachers in North America were actually working in Lutheran and Reformed communities, administering the sacraments and claiming to their congregants that they were upstanding, properly ordained members of those churches. To their enemies, Count Zinzendorf's people appeared to be dangerous, deluded liars. Like wolves in sheep's clothing, they claimed they were Lutherans or Reformed, yet really were part of a Moravian conspiracy. As Moravian enemies learned more about the group's views on gender, marriage, sex, and women preaching they appeared to be even more threatening. The confessional leaders desired solid walls separating their churches and distinct organization and hierarchy within those walls. They did not allow their members to go back and forth between groups, something they considered to be a sign of theological "indifference," and they certainly did not want people whom they considered to be dangerous, secretive radicals penetrating the walls of their church.

The Moravians must have expected stiff resistance as they began their new plan, but America needed to be dipped in the blood of Jesus, as Zinzendorf put it, and they intended to make every effort to do just that. By 1743 the Moravians had more German, Swedish, and English-speaking preachers in the "Pennsylvania field" than all other Lutheran and Reformed European authorities combined in order to accomplish this sanguinary task. The Moravian advantage in numbers continued throughout the 1740s: by May 1745 they were already in a position to hold a meeting with 68 men and women involved in spiritual work outside Bethlehem.[13] By 1748 they controlled or had significant influence in most of the communities where thousands of German Lutheran and Reformed immigrants were settling, as well as in the Swedish communities in the Delaware Valley, and among the Mahicans and Delawares. From 1740 to 1754 the Moravians worked in at least 194 communities from Suriname to Greenland, of which 186 were on the North American mainland (see Table 1). They labored primarily among Germans (in at least 127 communities), but also among ethnic English groups, Swedes, and other Europeans, as well as among Africans and Native Americans. During this period 148 Moravians (111 men and 37 women) worked in 171 communities in the "Pennsylvania field" (from New York to Virginia), and they heavily influenced the German Reformed and Lutheran congregations that were then expanding dramatically due to record levels of immigration. In 1742 there were 68 pastors working in 52–63 German Lutheran and Reformed congregations, and 46 of them (68%) were Moravian. By 1748, when the Moravians reached the peak of their influence among European colonists, 73 of the 112 pastors working in 108 German Lutheran and Reformed congregations were Moravian. Although their influence was waning by 1754, there were nevertheless 122 Moravians working in the Pennsylvania field. They also opened or worked in at least 22 schools for German children.[14] And, in addition to Germans, the Moravians wielded significant influence in the small number of Swedish Lutheran communities in the Delaware Valley during the 1740s, and they worked in 27 ethnically English communities there and in New England.

Moravian Communities, Preachers, and Tactics

One of the appeals of the Moravians in the mid-Atlantic colonies was their support community in Bethlehem (see Figure 5), along with nearby Nazareth. Moravian architecture, organization, and community life impressed many Delawares, Mahicans, Germans, English, and others, and the Moravians effectively used the community as a headquarters for the planning and execution of their missions in North America. Founded in 1741, Bethlehem quickly became the economic, spiritual, and communications center, as well as a training base for the movement and the mission. In June of 1742 the early arrivals divided themselves into two groups: the "Pilgrim Communities" (*Pilgergemeine*), made up of 24 men and 16 women (including 12 single women) who would go out

Sources: Moravian synod minutes, itinerant minister diaries, and correspondence by and about itinerants in Moravian Archives (Bethlehem), Archives of the Evangelical and Reformed Historical Society (Lancaster), Unity Archives (Herrnhut), *Bethlehem Diary*, vols. 1–2.

TABLE 1. NUMBERS OF COMMUNITIES IN WHICH MORAVIANS WORKED IN THE AMERICAS, 1740–1754, BY ETHNIC GROUP AND COLONY

	German	English	Swedish	Irish	African	Delaware	Mahican	Mohawk	Inuit	Arawak	Mixed	Total
Pennsylvania	84	9	7	2		5					1	108
New Jersey	6	3	4								4	17
New York	9						1	1				11
New England		12					2					14
Maryland	11		1									12
Delaware		3										3
Virginia	16				1					2		19
South Carolina					1							1
Georgia	1											1
Danish West Indies					3							3
Jamaica					1							1
Greenland									2			2
Suriname					1					1		2
Total	127	27	12	2	7	5	3	1	2	3	5	194

Figure 5. "A View of Bethlehem" from the south. Pen drawing by Nicholas Garrison, Jr., 1754. Moravian Archives, Bethlehem.

into the colony and extend the mission to Native Americans, slaves, and other colonists, and the "House Community" (*Hausgemeine*), made up of 36 men and 13 women who would stay in Bethlehem to provide material support to the whole. (Six were in both groups.) Within a few years their industries became profitable, but even before then Bethlehem provided rest, spiritual solace, and safety for weary itinerant preachers who were often disconsolate because of resistance and failures to their plan and at times even found themselves in physical danger. Often they returned to the field after a brief stay in Bethlehem, refreshed and energized, with instructions and advice about how to deal with their problems. No high level of support like this existed on this side of the Atlantic for their Lutheran, Calvinist, and other opponents.[15]The most important appeal of the Moravian mission to the mid-Atlantic colonies was their small army of male and female itinerant preachers, teachers, and workers, most of whom worked out of Bethlehem. Each husband and wife team or pair of male preachers might work a circuit of four or five communities and visit in surrounding areas of those communities. They traveled almost constantly, not only around their circuit, but back and forth to Bethlehem, or to relieve colleagues in trouble on another circuit, or to complete a special mission anywhere from the upper Hudson to the upper Shenandoah Valley. Trusted Moravians like Leonhard Schnell, Christian Rauch, or Johann Philip Meurer moved into strategically located houses across the countryside, providing safe havens for weary and sometimes frightened preachers. Also, the preachers often met on the trail, exchanging information, instruction, mail, and greetings. They expressed feelings of blood and wounds and Cross Air Birdies in services and to each other when meeting, which was uplifting.[16] Schnell and Rauch worked closely together but separately—crossing paths, meeting every two or three days to work together for a while and discuss plans and problems.[17] The preachers were flexible and changed their plans based on intelligence received from their colleagues. Sometimes several came together to demonstrate strength in a key area. Their maps marked communities and trails in the "Pennsylvania field." Some were novices who struggled and failed, and others were powerful, effective figures like Jacob Lischy or Spangenberg, who could intimidate and challenge opponents from the pulpit. Intimidation of enemies in front of audiences with powerful rhetoric and posturing often persuaded fence straddlers to support the cause, a tactic all sides employed in the struggle for control of the Delaware Valley communities.[18]

The large number of Moravian male and female itinerants, along with Bethlehem and other closed communities for Europeans and Indians, represented a major commitment by the Moravians to North America, and many colonists and Indians found this appealing, especially since

Halle, Amsterdam, Uppsala, and other European religious centers showed little or no interest in the colonies early in the Great Awakening. The Moravians sent their best leaders and workers, their money, and their energy to the colonies and tried to make something of them. Count Zinzendorf and other Moravian leaders developed strategic goals, plans, and tactics that they outlined in their "America Plan" and elsewhere. They were flexible, and the details of the plans and tactics they employed were based on the experiences of people working in the American field, rather than distant Europeans who had no intention of ever traveling to the colonies. In contrast, the only plan their rivals developed in the early years was to stop the Moravians. While the Moravians made a major commitment of their resources and leadership to North America, their enemies initially sent minor expeditions after long delays, quarreled about money and jurisdiction, and did not always adequately support those they did send to America. The Moravians carefully planned and managed the migrations of nearly nine hundred members from Europe to North America during the colonial era and lost only one person in transit. No other religious or secular immigrant group could match that record. And shortly after arrival in the colonies, most Moravian immigrants proceeded to Bethlehem or Nazareth, where individual immigrants received work and location assignments that fit into some larger plan.[19]

With their army of male and female itinerant preachers and workers, the ecumenical Moravians attained an overwhelming early advantage over their orthodox opponents, and this impressed those immigrants who were looking for pastoral care, not dogmatic purity. In the early years the Moravians simply outgunned the Reformed and Lutheran preachers sent from Halle, Amsterdam, and Uppsala. From 1727 to 1748 the number of organized, recognizable German Lutheran and Reformed congregations in the Pennsylvania field expanded from 17 to 108, paralleling the tremendous immigration of these groups from the German and Swiss territories in this period (see Table 2). By 1748 only 283 Moravian men, women, and children had immigrated into the North American colonies,[20] yet at least 132 (including a few recruited in the colonies) were involved in preaching or other mission work in the mid-Atlantic colonies, of whom at least 112 worked among the German Lutheran and Reformed colonists in the Pennsylvania field. In other words, the Moravians had more individuals active among the Lutheran and Reformed settlements than there were organized congregations. In contrast, there were only 13 Lutheran preachers and teachers working in the field in 1748, and only six of these were Hallensians—the most aggressive and best organized of the Moravians' Lutheran opponents. Similarly, there were only 11 German Reformed preachers, of whom

TABLE 2. GERMAN LUTHERAN AND REFORMED CONGREGATIONS IN THE "PENNSYLVANIA FIELD," 1742–1748

	Lutheran	Reformed	Total
1727	3	14	17
1736	12	22–23	34–35
1742	22–28	30–35	52–63
1748	53	55	108

Note: The "Pennsylvania Field" included Pennsylvania, New York, New Jersey, Maryland, and Virginia.
Source: Glatfelter, *Pastors and People*, vol. 2, for 1742 and 1748 (tables, 52–53, 138–39); earlier numbers calculated from individual community entries in vol. 1.

TABLE 3. GERMAN LUTHERAN, REFORMED, AND MORAVIAN PREACHERS IN THE "PENNSYLVANIA FIELD," 1742–1754

	Lutheran		Reformed			
	Hallensian*	Other	Amsterdamers†	Other	Moravian‡	Total
1742	1	8	2	11	46	68
1748	6	13	9	11	73	112
1754	8	25	11	22	122	188

Note: The "Pennsylvania Field" included Pennsylvania, New York, New Jersey, Maryland, and Virginia.
* Those sent by Halle, including unordained assistants.
† Germans sent by the Classis of Amsterdam, or associating with them, including unordained pastors.
‡Includes some non-Germans who did not preach to Germans, but excludes a few who joined the Moravians in America and did preach to Germans.
Sources: Glatfelter, *Pastors and People*, on Lutherans and Reformed; Fogleman, *Hopeful Journeys*, 111n14.

nine were sponsored by the Classis of Amsterdam (see Table 3). For the period 1740–1754, there were 148 Moravians who worked in the mid-Atlantic colonies and New England, of whom 126 worked the Pennsylvania field of Lutheran and Reformed communities.

The large numbers of Moravian men and women working in the mid-Atlantic colonies in the 1740s were part of the Great Awakening then sweeping through the colonies, and they shared many of its ecumenical characteristics. By 1745 the Moravians conducted a full-fledged revival in the classic sense in and around Pennsylvania, with traveling preachers, emotional sermons, singing, and conventicles that targeted mixed audiences and made heavy use of travel and communications networks, including the print medium. The Moravians offered emotional sermons any day of the week, with singing in churches, barns, and open fields, while daily visiting, meetings in small groups, active women, big crowds of mixed ethnic and religious groups, sometimes including Indians and slaves, were the order of the day. Like George Whitefield and other revivalists, the Moravians wanted to preach to *everyone*, and to a significant degree they did.

The Moravians offered the immigrants the emotional, revivalist style of preaching, often by larger than life figures. One of the most imposing figures in the area at the time was August Gottlieb Spangenberg, who rapidly ascended the ranks of the Moravians and ultimately became their number two man, after Count Zinzendorf. Spangenberg was not intimidated by adversaries and difficult situations, as other Moravian preachers sometimes were, and he did not hesitate to use his position and reputation to influence a crowd. His return from Europe in 1744 stimulated excitement in Bethlehem, and the country preachers and other workers were anxious to go out with him into the field to work.[21] With one or two exceptions, Spangenberg and other Moravian pastors did not appeal to the intellect of their listeners with doctrine, catechism, salvation theories, and enlightened inquiries into the nature and work of God. Instead they kept their focus on what the blood and wounds of Christ on the Cross meant to believers. Zinzendorf's sermons in Pennsylvania also emphasized the choice of life or death, conversion, faith, understanding the Bible, and the Holy Spirit as a mother-like figure that cared for and nurtured them.[22] Church attendance in Pennsylvania was high, and many colonists wanted more of the revivalist George Whitefield's style in their sermons and less dogmatic, rational confessionalism and control, and with Zinzendorf and the other Moravian preachers they found it.[23] The result was that many people were being *erweckt*, or "awakened."

Like other awakeners, Moravians preached to ethnically, religiously, and linguistically mixed crowds in church buildings, houses, barns, and open fields. Sometimes their itinerants preached in several languages on the same day to achieve this purpose. (German, Swedish, English, Dutch, Mahican, and Delaware were the most common languages they used.) In 1743 John Oakley preached in an orchard near the Maurice River, New Jersey, to one hundred members of the Swedish community there.[24] In April 1746 in Maxatawny, Pennsylvania, Christian Rauch preached to a large crowd of Reformed, Lutherans, Mennonites, Dunkers, Separatists, Catholics, and New Born and visited with them thereafter, and in the autumn of 1749 Leonhard Schnell and Johann Brandmüller completed a long, successful tour preaching to many different groups in Pennsylvania, western Maryland, and Virginia.[25] In the

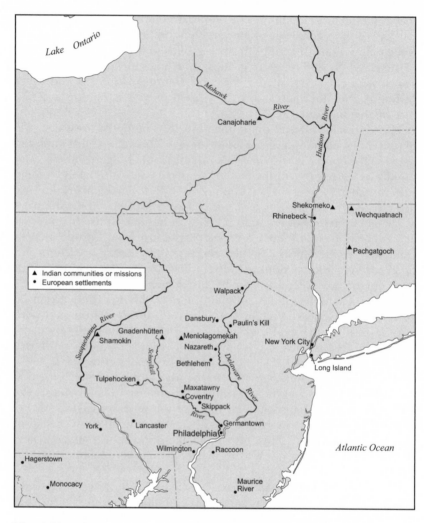

Map 4. Moravian expansion in the mid-Atlantic colonies, 1740–1754.

summer of 1753 Abraham Reincke worked the circuit of Wechquatnach, Pachgatgoch, Rhinebeck, Nine Partners, Oblong, and Lewistown in New York and Connecticut. In Oblong, near Wechquatnach, he preached in a barn 20 times in eight weeks to 300 listeners from nearby Sharon and Salisbury, Connecticut. Many of them were New Lights who had been awakened years earlier by George Whitefield and then separated from the Presbyterians. In Oblong Reincke claimed that he had 400 listeners at one sermon. He also preached twice to German Lutheran and

Reformed inhabitants in Rhinebeck and visited the Moravian mission to the Mahicans at Pachgatgoch.[26]

From the summer of 1748 to the summer of 1749 Sven Roseen, a Swedish Moravian, worked in a frontier area on the upper Delaware where blacks, Indians, and whites lived and intermingled. Roseen's diary describes a generally successful mission in Dansbury, Pennsylvania, and Pawlin's Kill, New Jersey, and problems in Walpack, Pennsylvania. He preached to Germans, Dutch, English, Welsh, blacks, and Mahicans, including among these groups Presbyterians, New Lights, New Englanders, Quakers, Lutherans, and others, often in the same crowd. In the autumn of 1749 he preached in German, Swedish, and English in Hagerstown, Maryland. Roseen never preached to huge crowds, partly because these areas were not densely populated. He worked in a frontier area and was in constant contact with Indians and blacks, even though it was not his mission to preach to them. Roseen overcame what resistance there was to Moravians in the upper Delaware settlements, which consisted mostly of rumors, but no direct attacks—physical or otherwise. But he and the Moravians did not dominate these communities: this was shared space on the frontier, shared with other religions, and Moravians shared or extended services to all racial, religious, and ethnic groups. Roseen saw it all and worked with everyone.[27]

Like all good itinerant revival preachers during the Great Awakening, the Moravians developed and exploited excellent travel and communications networks, in this case from the upper Hudson Valley to the Potomac River. With their maps, strategically located support families, and numerous preachers, workers, and other travelers, they kept each other informed of events, possibilities, and dangers in the field. Moravian communications and travel networks worked so well that they could quickly assemble a number of their best preachers in the field at a given location to accomplish some specific purpose. In May/June 1743, for example, five Moravian itinerants descended on Lancaster, preaching fourteen days at a time, as they tried to win over this important community. In early 1746 Johann Hantsch, Jacob Adolph, Christian Rauch, Jacob Lischy, Johann Brandmüller, and Leonard Schnell frequently crossed paths as they worked in Lancaster and Philadelphia counties during the height of Moravian success in the area. Schnell and Rauch worked closely together there later in the year as well. Crossing the Schuylkill in a canoe, they met every two or three days, worked together for a while, discussed their plans, and then split up, only to meet again in two or three days.[28] Johann Brandmüller, David Bruce, Christian Fröhlich, John Oakley, and others worked closely with Lischy in Lancaster, York, and Philadelphia Counties, sometimes appearing together with him for services and at other times preceding or following him in these communities, visiting, preaching, singing, and holding communion in English and German for good crowds.

Like George Whitefield, Gilbert Tennent, James Davenport, and other revival preachers the Moravians also used the printed word to announce their pending meetings and other activities. Heinrich Antes used a printed circular to announce the beginning of the ecumenical synods in 1742,[29] and when opponents in Bern, Pennsylvania, challenged the authenticity of Jacob Lischy as a Reformed preacher, Lischy produced printed copies of his "Declaration" signed by 38 upstanding members of the Reformed church, and this helped his cause in Bern and elsewhere.[30] Also, the Pennsylvania Moravians often responded in kind to printed attacks against them, with either broadsides, pamphlets, or newspapers. Christopher Saur's *Hoch-Deutsch Pennsylvanische Geschichts-Schreiber*, Benjamin Franklin's *Pennsylvania Gazette*, and Andrew Bradford's *American Weekly Mercury* in the 1740s were filled with articles and ads that charted Moravian actions and the reactions of their enemies on both sides of the Atlantic, along with the activities of Whitefield, Wesley, Tennent, Davenport, and others.

As well staffed and organized as they were, even the Moravians could not provide all of the growing number of immigrant communities with enough care to win them over, so they targeted certain high-profile communities in strategic locations. Lancaster was a crucial inland town that all rival parties, especially the Hallensians, wanted to control. In order to influence the surrounding communities one had to control Lancaster, which by 1746 had about 1500 inhabitants and 300 houses.[31] The Moravians did well there initially, assigning Laurentius Nyberg, who also had an appointment by Swedish authorities in Uppsala to work in the colony.[32] York, Pennsylvania, was another strategic location where the Moravians made a great effort. Christian Rauch preached to two hundred Reformed colonists there one morning in 1746, and Leonhard Schnell spoke to one hundred Lutherans in the afternoon in their new building. Lischy and others spent a lot of time in York as well.[33] The Moravians sometimes made a major effort in communities that supported their own goals, but were of little interest to their enemies, and here resistance was light. They made a major effort in the small community of Macungie, for example, which lay on the road to Bethlehem. Numerous preachers cared for the congregation there, making the one-day trip to insure that Macungie always had a preacher. This meant that weary Moravian itinerants and other travelers coming in from the field in Pennsylvania always had a secure place to stay if they could get within a day of Bethlehem.[34]

Although many Moravians preached in multiple languages to diverse audiences, others employed a controversial tactic that I call "ethnic preaching," in which they targeted certain ethnic-religious communities, especially German Reformed and German and Swedish Lutheran communities. The Moravians developed this tactic to help implement their new ecumenical plan under the Tropus concept. Most of the new Lutheran and Reformed communities had no pastor; the Moravians sent men and women who had a similar ethnic-religious background before they had become affiliated with the Moravians. Under the Tropus concept, these people remained Lutheran or Reformed and so could legitimately pastor these communities, remain affiliated with the Moravians, and continue to call themselves Lutheran or German Reformed clergy. For example, they sent Swedes like Paul Daniel Bryzelius and Abraham Reincke to preach to the Swedish Lutherans on either side of the Delaware River, and sent Swiss and German Reformed preachers like Jacob Lischy and Johann Brandmüller to work among communities of those ethnic-religious groups in the Delaware Valley. The Moravians also expanded the practice of ethnic preaching to groups outside their Tropus system. For example, David Bruce, whose background was Scottish Presbyterian, preached to English speakers in Pennsylvania, while John Oakley, who was raised an Anglican, preached to English Quakers, Anglicans, and Presbyterians in Pennsylvania and Delaware, and John Wade worked among Quakers and Presbyterians in Pennsylvania, Delaware, and New Jersey. In one case they sent a former Dunker named Abraham Müller out on a kind of diplomatic mission to Pennsylvania Dunker communities of which he had once been a part because he knew the individuals in them so well.[35]

Many of the Moravian ethnic preachers became flamboyant revivalists who could sway crowds with emotional sermons and intimidate rivals who doubted their legitimacy in the Lutheran and Reformed communities. One of the most effective early on was the Swiss immigrant, Jacob Lischy, who arrived with the First Sea Congregation in the summer of 1742.[36] Lischy was a persuasive, charismatic figure who knew how to sway a big crowd and how to deal with opponents who might doubt his background and connections. He toured tirelessly through the Reformed communities in York, Lancaster, and Philadelphia counties, preaching in the communities of Bern, Heidelberg, the Blue Mountains, and Tulpehocken. Lischy then continued on to Millbach, Muddy Creek, the Gegese River, Conestoga, and a popular preaching place at the house of Balthasar Ort, where he preached to a crowd of Reformed and Mennonites that came from up to twelve miles away to hear him. Warwick, Lancaster, and Oley were also on his list. He reported good crowds in most places in 1743, including an overflow crowd in a barn at Coventry. Following Zinzendorf's instructions from the previous year, Lischy avoided the Reformed congregation in Philadelphia, where their adversary,

Johann Philip Boehm, was working, but he met with fifty people at Johann Bechtel's house in Germantown for a singing hour. After a brief stopover in Bethlehem, Lischy set out again and worked over the same communities with similar results. The next year he extended his work to include Donegal, Quittopehilla, Cocalico, Earl, Kissel Hill, Upper Tulpehocken, Goshenhoppen, Cacusi, and York. Lischy was so successful through 1744 that he frequently had to turn down offers from congregations to become their regular preacher. By early 1745 his luck was still holding: accompanied by Christian Rauch, he preached to three hundred listeners at the Seltenreich Reformed congregation in Earl township of Lancaster County. Donegal was on fire spiritually, and Lischy preached for three hours there in an open air service to 100 Lutherans, Reformed, and Mennonites. He added Oley, Falkner Swamp, Schwartzwald, Farni, Klee, Manheim, Philadelphia, Balthasar Ort's, White Oaks, and Kreutz Creek to his list as the revival peaked in 1745. By the late summer Lischy centered his activities at his new home in Muddy Creek, where he worked closely with his wife and Rosina Münster, who met separately with women in the community. Lischy may have exaggerated some of his claims, because rumor had it that he was about to be reassigned to South Carolina and he wanted to stay, but in Bethlehem at this time he clearly had a reputation of being one of the Moravians' most effective itinerants in Pennsylvania. Apparently his preaching style was effective, and he handled adversity well. He also understood the Moravian ecumenical position and tactics and used them to his advantage, along with his printed tracts. Lischy talked to Mennonites, Dunkers, Separatists, and others who confronted him, but he sought out only the Reformed colonists. Moravian ministers like Lischy and Johann Philip Meurer met on the trail from time to time and expressed uplifting blood and wounds feelings in services. Unlike other Moravians, he usually did not travel with his wife and covered a lot of ground quickly, overcoming obstacles, marrying and baptizing along the way. Lischy described how the religious culture was working in Pennsylvania before the Lutheran and Reformed churches organized the Germans along confessional, denominational lines. This included lay groups meeting without preachers and Moravian women meeting with women's spiritual groups.[37]

Christian Rauch was also an effective ethnic preacher in German Reformed communities, but he had his low moments and sometimes needed help from Bethlehem. In his tour of Lancaster, York, and Philadelphia counties in 1746 Rauch helped establish schools and preached to large mixed crowds, overcoming numerous local adversaries and bringing many to tears, he claimed. His success at Oley, where there was always a tough crowd, suggests that in some cases people would turn out for a good sermon even if it came from an enemy. Rauch understood the importance of communication and advertising in a revival: he wrote numerous letters informing communities that he was coming, and he often met with other Moravian itinerants like David Bruce and Johann Philip Meurer on the trail to discuss plans. But after several months on the trail and a dangerous crossing of the Susquehanna River, Rauch grew weary and the crowds dwindled. While at Heidelberg he went to a mountain top, prayed for guidance, and then returned aimlessly to Bethlehem. Two weeks later he was on the road again with Leonhard Schnell and pursued once again the "Country Preachers Plan" (*Land-prediger Plan*), now faster and with more energy than ever. The renewal for Rauch carried over into the next year, when he conducted a success-ful five-month tour in the area, even as some of his colleagues began to fail.[38]

In trying to win over Lutheran, Reformed, and other settlers, Mora-vians offered a number of community services, one of which was doctor-ing. There was not only a minister shortage, but also a doctor shortage in the colonies, which meant that those few available were expensive. At least two Moravian itinerants, Christian Rauch and Leonhard Schnell, frequently doctored people in their communities, probably for free. Like Jesuit missionaries in New France or their rivals among Germans in Pennsylvania (Mühlenberg, for example), Moravian ministers some-times found that doctoring was part of the job and that it could help win over people to their cause. However, Zinzendorf warned Moravian pastors not to compete directly with Hallensians on medical concerns, as the latter were much stronger.[39]

The Moravian emphasis on schooling appealed to many Reformed and Lutheran immigrants as well. In general, the Germans were a rela-tively well-educated populace—the immigrants probably more so than those born in America. (About 70 percent of the men could sign their name when taking the loyalty oath upon arriving in Philadelphia.)[40] However, living dispersed across the American landscape presented two problems: one, how would they be able to school their children, and two, how would they be able to school them in German? The twenty-plus schools with instruction in German that the Moravians established were not nearly enough, but they were more than anyone else was offering at the time, and, like their preachers, Moravian teachers worked for free. As with medicine, Zinzendorf warned the Moravians early on in Pennsyl-vania not to compete directly with the Hallensian schools either—they would lose. Halle was famous for its schools, and children in them could learn as much in eight weeks as they could in a year from the Moravians, he told a group of Moravians in Philadelphia in 1743.[41] But within two years it was clear that Zinzendorf had overrated the ability of Halle to replicate its renowned school system in North America. And the Hallensians were expensive: Johann Nicolaus Kurtz charged 5s per child per quarter in 1745 and made disturbingly too much money from it, according to his colleague, Mühlenberg.[42] Mühlenberg lamented the squabbling over teacher salaries with which he had to deal and was envious of the Moravian teachers who worked without pay.[43] He badly needed money for schools, especially to help the poor and orphaned children. The Moravians had schools, Mühlenberg wrote in his journal, where they instructed and boarded children for free or for a modest fee. Many wanted Mühlenberg to do the same, but he could not, since he was not getting money from Halle for this.[44] Mühlenberg's counterpart working among the German Reformed congregations, Michael Schlatter, lamented shortly after his arrival in 1746 that these communities had enough teachers, but that they were of poor quality and badly paid.[45]

Last, the Moravians assisted financially with the erection of a number of church buildings in the Lutheran and Reformed communities, for example in Tulpehocken and Lancaster. Church buildings and parsonages were at the center of most of the Lutheran and Reformed communities, and the Moravian itinerants who helped build them contributed significantly to the sacralization of the colonial landscape. They were expensive, controversial propositions in the mid-eighteenth century (and still are), and Moravian generosity in this respect attracted many supporters and aggravated their enemies. The Lutheran congregation in Philadelphia was plagued with debt because, as Mühlenberg put it, the Herrnhuters had forced them to build such an expensive church so that they could compete with them. In the face of sectarian threats Lutherans needed a new church to help promote the appearance of order, civility, and loyalty to their English-speaking neighbors and government, but such expensive building projects became the source of severe internal conflicts in the Lutheran and Reformed churches during the late colonial era. Schlatter reviewed the state of Reformed church buildings in Pennsylvania in 1746 and found seventeen wooden structures, mostly poorly constructed, and three stone churches, in Philadelphia, Germantown, and Old Goshenhoppen. All of the congregations with stone churches were heavily indebted. Philadelphia's new church, which was still under construction, was needed because all other religions and sects in Philadelphia had nice churches, Schlatter wrote.[46]

The Moravian ecumenical mission appealed to many German, Swedish, and other colonists, because the group offered good preachers who did not charge for their services, and because they were simply *there*. On the other hand, Lutheran and Reformed ministers were seldom there and often appeared arrogant, incompetent, and expensive. Some tried to exert too much European authority on parishioners and others not enough. Many unattached Lutheran and Reformed preachers like the "Prince of Württemberg" led scandalous careers and exploited their congregations. Funerals, marriages, baptisms, communion, and sometimes even sermons cost money. The Moravians never asked for any of this, and these kinds of conflicts were absent in congregations that accepted them.[47] Jacob Lischy once told Johann Bartholomäus Rieger, the independent Reformed preacher in Lancaster, that Rieger worried too much about collecting money from the people and that this was part of his problem with the congregation there. (Rieger had complained that people were more willing to spend their money in a tavern than on the church.)[48] According to the Swedish Moravian Laurentius Nyberg, when his rival John Dylander, rector of the Swedish church at Wicaco parish in Philadelphia, went to Lancaster and Conestoga he advertised his visits to the Germans in the newspaper, charged one shilling per person for the sacrament, and got rich from it.[49] Mühlenberg confirms in his correspondence that he and other Halle Lutherans were at a disadvantage competing with Moravians in the 1740s because they did charge for their religious and other services. Mühlenberg often complained during these years to his superiors in Halle that he was having difficulty competing with the Moravians because they worked for free. The Moravians and other sectarians always said that the pastors should support themselves with their own work, and it was hard to argue against them.[50] The German Reformed preachers sponsored by Amsterdam were committed to pastor salaries and resented the Moravian practice of preaching for free as well.[51] Instead of asking the settlers for money, Moravian nobility relied on contacts with Dutch creditors to bankroll the construction of their closed communities, and then used the industries in those communities to support their missionaries. Individual Moravians found the offer to work hard at no pay attractive because they became elites, even heroes or "pilgrims," in the eyes of the others in these well constructed closed communities, and the missionaries lived in the best quarters there. Ecumenism was expensive, but the Moravians were willing to make the sacrifice.[52]

In the growing battle between the ecumenical Moravians and their rivals sent from Halle, Amsterdam, and Uppsala, one important weakness of the Moravians that their enemies often exploited was their apparent tendency to conceal their identity when working in the Lutheran and Reformed communities of the Delaware Valley. Because of their ecumenical Tropus view, the Moravians could send pastors into the American communities, present themselves in the image parishioners wanted, and reply honestly if questioned that they were Lutheran or Reformed ministers. In their own minds there was no contradiction, but, when their enemies discovered their Bethlehem connection and revealed it to the communities where they worked, there was trouble. Now it appeared that they were really lying, deceitful Moravians and not true Lutherans or genuine Reformed, and many of their preachers had to withdraw from those communities. Sometimes during the heat of battle Moravians took elaborate steps to protect their pastors from such accusations, but this could make matters worse. When Laurentius Nyberg traveled from Europe to Pennsylvania in 1743 to take up a position preaching at the Lutheran community in Lancaster, the Moravians would not let him travel with the "Second Sea Congregation" in order to avoid prejudice against him (or blowing his cover, to put it another way). Upon arriving in Lancaster Nyberg never told his parishioners directly that he was affiliated with the Moravians. This tactic worked until he hosted a large Moravian-directed synod in 1745, which tipped his hand. The Moravians probably thought that Nyberg's position was so strong that holding the synod in the courthouse there would secure their position in the whole area, but they were quite wrong, and their troubles in the area date from this point, when Nyberg was forced to show his colors.[53]

It is also clear that there were limits to how much of their radical spiritual beliefs Moravian preachers would reveal in the Lutheran and Reformed communities where they worked. Privately, in their diaries or when they met each other on the trail, the male and female itinerants expressed their enthusiasm for the blood and wounds of the Lamb. Leonhard Schnell, Johann Brandmüller, Christian Rauch, and Johann Christian Friedrich Cammerhof all enjoyed the bloody stream from the side hole at their meeting on the Catores, near York, in 1749, and they wrote often in their diaries about this and the Cross Air Birdies as they ventured into the Shenandoah Valley thereafter. Also, at least some of this came out in their sermons. Nathanael Seidel and John Eric Westman preached blood and wounds and visited Cross Air Birdies as they slogged their way through deep snow in Lancaster County in 1747. In the same year Johann Georg Hantsch preached blood and wounds at York, even when he was warned not to.[54]

There is no evidence that the Moravian itinerants openly promoted the controversial aspects of their beliefs in a female Trinity, marriage, or sexuality in European communities. In fact, for the most part they insisted they were Lutheran or Reformed preachers, not Moravian, so the itinerants could not be linked to radical views about the gender of the Trinity that appeared in the Moravian published hymnal or Zinzendorf's sermons in Pennsylvania about the Holy Ghost. Also, while they often enthusiastically preached and discussed the blood and wounds of Jesus on the trail, the Moravian itinerants limited the practice of special liturgical celebrations like love feasts, "community day" (*Gemeintag*), foot washing, and the kiss of peace to special places like Heidelberg, Oley, and Monocacy, where hard-core Moravians had gathered and begun fledgling closed communities, from which they might work the surrounding countryside. How far they might have gone with ritual marriage and sexual activities, as well as some of their more extreme practices in the period, is unclear from the itinerant preacher diaries, but the itinerants do not seem to have promoted these practices even in these communities, and certainly not in the large number of Lutheran and Reformed immigrant communities in which they worked. What Lutheran, Reformed, and other colonists did see when Moravian preachers came to their community was an emotional revival style of preaching and speech, rather than a scholastic or rational style. And they saw women playing important leadership roles—both controversial yet prolific activities in the larger Great Awakening that swept through the British colonies in the 1740s. But when their Lutheran and Reformed pastors were revealed as Moravians, parishioners immediately connected them to the dangerous, radical practices of which they had been warned. In most cases the Moravian preachers could not recover from the damage such revelations caused to their position in the community.[55]

But as long as Lutheran and Reformed people were unaware of the Moravian connection and its meaning, many were satisfied with the pastors from Bethlehem because they offered these communities so much more than what the pastors from Halle, Amsterdam, and Uppsala offered. Without reservation the Moravians offered ecumenism, communalism, and an organized religious life with ministers and a recognizable Lutheran or Reformed liturgy. For the large and rapidly growing Lutheran and Reformed population, the Moravians offered seemingly real Lutheran and Reformed church life, with pastors, church buildings, and the like—a strong appeal to many. Johann Christoph Pyrlaeus came from Lutheran Vogtland and knew how to offer a Lutheran service to parishioners in Philadelphia. Jacob Lischy came from Mühlhausen in Switzerland and could do the same for German and Swiss Reformed colonists. If Moravian preachers were unfamiliar with Reformed or Lutheran liturgy, there were experienced people in Herrnhut, Herrnhaag, or Bethlehem who could train them. Many colonists seeking proper religious care were not concerned when a Moravian connection was revealed in their pastor. They had what they wanted—something resembling a proper Lutheran or Reformed service with a pastor, and if this came from so-called "Moravians," then this was not a problem. For ultrapious men and women the Moravians offered places where they could live, work, and worship in safety, relative comfort, and nearly total spiritual devotion and self-fulfillment, namely Nazareth and Bethlehem.

In the latitudinarian mid-Atlantic colonies Moravian ecumenism was appealing to many. In dispersed Pennsylvania, New Jersey, and western Maryland the Moravians offered religious community, and this appealed to many new immigrants, many of whom had migrated in family and village networks and settled in Lutheran and Reformed church communities.[56]

To Zinzendorf and the Moravians in the eighteenth century ecumenism meant porous church boundaries and true believers from all faiths establishing communion with one another. This ran counter to the orthodox and denominational ideals found in the major Protestant churches in Europe and North America. Moravian ecumenism challenged critical issues concerning authority, legitimacy, and power, just as their challenge concerning gender and the Trinity had done. They questioned conventional notions of the church and its authority. Many pietists found the ecumenical ideal attractive, but the radicals who had found a degree of toleration in some German territories and significant religious freedom in Pennsylvania were jealous of their rights and feared a Moravian takeover. On the other hand, by the middle third of the eighteenth century the church pietists had given up on ecumenism and sought to achieve their goals of reforming life and society within the bounds of the confessional churches. Any radicals like the Moravians who entered into their denominational sphere represented a threat to the church and its authority. In the Moravian conflict of this period the old question of how to achieve unity without losing freedom was played out once again.

With their radical views on gender and their ecumenism the Moravians challenged transatlantic norms of power and authority in ways that provoked a response from orthodox Protestant leaders and community members. The ecumenical challenge to the other radicals in Europe and especially Pennsylvania was serious, and their reaction stopped the Moravians from taking over the philadelphian utopian movement. The challenge to the Lutheran and Reformed churches in America was also serious, but the question remained, would the ministerial need being filled by well organized, devoted Moravians enable them to overcome the fears, prejudices, and commitments to confessional order? Would their ecumenism allow them to dip America in the blood of Jesus, or would the confessional church leaders be able to successfully mobilize resistance and stop them?

Part III
Religious Violence and the Defense of Order

The Moravians' flagrant transgressions of gender and confessional order gained the attention of religious leaders and writers throughout the Protestant world, and it is not surprising that these utterly condemned Count Zinzendorf's followers as agents of the Devil. Christian writers often viewed threats to religious and social order that involved women and gender as Satanic, and to many this was an important reason why confessional boundaries had to be maintained—to protect their church from such blasphemous error. By the 1740s European religious authorities began sending pastors and books to North America with the emphatic message that the Moravian threat in the colonies must be stopped. They were able to get their warnings against Moravian ecumenism and the threat to gender order to the North American communities, but it was uncertain how ordinary people in those communities would respond. In fact, the earliest pastors arriving in the colonies reported that the Moravians were gaining ground in the mid-Atlantic colonies, and they complained about having to work with no state support. For them the problem was that many colonists *liked* the Moravians. Count Zinzendorf's followers offered the colonists countless hardworking male and female field workers who had a reputation for good preaching and piety, charged no fees for it, and even helped erect expensive church and school buildings. On the other hand, the pastors sent from Halle, Amsterdam, and Uppsala were badly outnumbered and ill-trained to deal with colonial conditions during a revival, and had to be paid. These pastors believed, however, that if they could convince the people in these Lutheran and Reformed communities of who the Moravians really were and Count Zinzendorf's real intentions toward them, then those people would surely come to their senses and get rid of the Moravian intruders in order to protect their true churches. Since the state could not or would not act to stop such dangerous radicals, then it would be up to these Reformed and Lutheran colonists in dispersed, far-flung religious communities to remove the Moravian danger. The question was, would the small number of pastors from Halle, Amsterdam, and Uppsala, with their inflammatory sermons and books, be enough to offset the advantages of the ecumenical Moravians, who were sweeping through the Lutheran and Reformed immigrant communities? Would they be able to turn the tide against radical religion and motivate ordinary people in these rapidly expanding immigrant communities to take action against the dangerous Moravians and drive them out of their communities?

Chapter 5

The Orthodox Response

The struggle against the Moravians that began in the 1730s played an important role in the transatlantic Protestant awakening until the 1750s. One of the most important weapons the Lutheran, Calvinist, and other rivals employed in the battle against the Moravians was the printing press. They published and circulated hundreds of polemics in numerous languages on both sides of the Atlantic that warned innocents of the dangerous Moravian threat at hand. For example, in Frankfurt Johann Philip Fresenius published a widely read anti-Moravian polemic in 1746 that included an "autobiography" written by a renegade mystical seeker living in Pennsylvania named Jean François Reynier. Reynier included extremely inflammatory material about the marital and sexual practices of the Moravians. He had been a member of this religious group and lived in their communities in Georgia, Germany, London, Suriname, St. Thomas, and Pennsylvania before leaving them in 1743. Reynier provided Fresenius and his readers with graphic descriptions of Moravian marriage and sexual practices, in which he claimed to have participated, hoping that this would help destroy their movement. Reynier himself was married in 1740 to Maria Barbara Knoll in Herrnhaag, near where the Mother Eva Society had operated a generation earlier. Fresenius was too shy to print some of the most graphic scenes portrayed by Reynier, but others were not, especially Alexander Volck, the city scribe and notary in nearby Büdingen, who carefully printed and commented on everything Fresenius had censored. Reynier wrote that before the Moravian marriage ceremony Count Zinzendorf watched the brides get dressed and fondled their breasts. After the ceremony communion was celebrated, and then the new couple had their first sexual experience—sitting on a bench, wearing colorful robes. Reynier claimed that in his case, he and his wife began talking instead, in order to get to know one another first. August Gottlieb Spangenberg and his wife peeked through the cracked door, saw this, and sprang into the room, insisting that Reynier and Knoll get on with the task at hand. After they had finished and were getting dressed, the Spangenbergs slipped away, and the Reyniers retired to separate chambers, convinced that if the wife was impregnated while on her husband's lap then their child would have been conceived in a spiritual way. The next day Frau Spangenberg began talking openly about this (which was common among the inner circle of militant married Moravians, called *Streiter*), encouraging them to "come together" once a week—not just to have children, but to receive this spiritual blessing. The Reyniers learned from the Spangenbergs and others how the marriage blessing flowed from the male organ of the Savior, that is, how the blood from Christ's circumcision was the semen, or mixed with the semen of men to form the material from which children came. Reynier, Fresenius, and especially Volck very likely stretched the truth significantly when they described the procedure Moravian couples went through in order to receive this blessing: according to them they stood in line, two-by-two, to go into their portable "blue chamber" (*das blaue Cabinet*). The first couple entered the contraption, had sex for fifteen minutes, and then departed. Then the next couple entered, and so on. According to Volck the blue chamber, which he called a bordello, had windows so others could observe.[1]

Polemics like these played a critical role in the transatlantic struggle against the Moravians. In 1747 Johann Christian Sieberberg and Andreas Frey, who had recently deserted the Moravians in Herrnhaag, arrived in Philadelphia carrying polemics by Fresenius, Reynier, and others, as well as the controversial Twelfth Appendix of the *Moravian Hymnal.* Johann Adam Gruber, who was a member of a group called the "Inspired" (*Inspirierten*), and the Separatist printer Christopher Saur distributed the books. Gruber reported that the demand for them was so high that he had to read them quickly and pass them on. He believed that the work of the Herrnhuters and their leader was becoming so well known there that they must all be put to shame. He wrote that from their hymns and other materials it "becomes increasingly more clear, and revolting, what they really intend to do, such that one is ashamed to be near them and wonders, could it get any worse than this?" ("wird ihre Sache redlich Gesinten immer klärer, auch eckelhafter, daß man sich vor sie schämet und dencket, obs auch noch ärger werden könte?") Gruber feared that Moravian successes among the Lutheran and Reformed immigrants in the Delaware Valley would embolden Count Zinzendorf's followers to renew their offensive against the radicals, and he wanted to use the polemics to stop them. Sieberberg and Frey had made Moravian abominations public in the colony, and they were worse than anyone had thought, Gruber believed. Sieberberg reported that he and Frey were harassed by Moravians upon landing, and rumor had it that they had whisked Frey away to Bethlehem in a chaise and held him against his will. The arrival of a new set of anti-Moravian polemics from Europe was a highly anticipated event in Pennsylvania, and those who wrote and/or circulated them succeeded in getting the books and their message into circulation in British North America.[2]

Lutheran and Reformed church leaders revealed their fears regarding the count and his clan in the polemics they wrote or circulated, and the themes they emphasized the most were the Moravian threats to gender and confessional order. Their female Trinity, communal lifestyle, strange marriage and sex beliefs and practices, and women preaching, as well as their ecumenism and emphasis on irrational, enthusiastic spirituality, threatened the patriarchal confessional ideal of the Lutheran and Reformed churches in Europe. Something had to be done to stop the radical Moravian challenge, and church leaders argued in European courts for removal of the sect, flooded their populations with hundreds of anti-Moravian polemics, and tried to keep individual Moravians out of universities and church government. America seemed to be the place most vulnerable to the Moravians, so they sent polemics, pastors, and other materials to their flocks from Suriname to New York to stop them. The Moravian challenge to gender and confessional order was not the only problem that Lutheran and Reformed church leaders had to address in this era, but their own writings reveal that from the late 1730s to the early 1750s the Moravians were their biggest threat, and the challenge by Count Zinzendorf and his followers concerned them most. The orthodox response was vigorous, as state church authorities attempted to reassert proper gender and confessional order where they believed the Moravians were doing serious damage.

Gender, Confession, and the Problem with the Moravians

In the 1740s orthodox theologians in Europe went public about the Moravians' new views concerning the Trinity, gender, marriage, and sex, blasting them for real and imagined violations of their views of gender order and the threat to the church and state implicit in these violations. Authors offered "proof" to readers that they were dealing with a dangerous, Satanic sect that threatened women, children, communities, and even governments with their blasphemous abominations. The writers described and embellished on Moravian marriage and sexual practices, thereby hoping to incite their readers either to guard against the sect or to attack and remove them. They accused the Moravians of abusing the marriage ideal, labeling their practices a "mysterious evil" and a whoredom that was denigrating to men. One author wrote that to the Moravians the husband was no more than a chamberlain to his wife.[3] Another condemned their dangerous sacralization of marriage and sex, as well as their shameless, graphic portrayals of male and female genitalia.[4] And a former Moravian criticized their mass marriages and use of the lot in choosing marriage partners, including matching people who do not even know each other.[5] All of this meant that the Moravian movement was a slithering Satanic serpent, wrote one polemicist. Jean François Reynier, writing in North America, proclaimed that Zinzendorf infused the spirit of Antichrist into the group and their work.[6] Throughout the 1740s the increasingly vicious and available polemics heightened public "awareness" of the Moravians, skillfully describing and exaggerating their beliefs and practices involving the Trinity, marriage, sex, women, and children, and warning readers to keep Moravians out of their homes, communities, churches, and territories.

Many anti-Moravian polemicists also emphasized the group's threat to proper doctrine and boundaries of the churches. While most church historians now recognize Moravian beliefs and efforts to achieve Christian union as an important phase in the history of ecumenism, in the mid-eighteenth century the Protestant world (especially its leadership) was not with the group on this point, in spite of the ongoing international evangelical revival, and they attacked the Moravians without mercy for this in their polemics. Many enemies viewed Moravian ecumenism as a reflection of their lack of reason (*Vernunft*), their doctrinal indifference, their antinomianism, and even authoritarianism—all related problems that no orthodox church leader could tolerate. To them, when a Moravian claimed to be a Lutheran or Reformed pastor he or she was really an irrational liar, trying to manipulate the community into the Moravian fold. Zinzendorf's so-called "*Tropus* concept" was a senseless farce and a cover for their lying and manipulation—common characteristics of Moravians, they thought. Moreover, the problem of irrational antinomianism and indifference toward proper dogma and church boundaries led to their blasphemous beliefs about the Trinity and the revolting practices regarding men and women in their communities.

Historians should use polemics with caution when assessing the mentality, beliefs, and practice of their authors, because they were (and are) essentially propaganda, in this case motivated by a burning desire to stop the Moravian threat at all costs. But most historians agree that printed works played a critical role in inciting and sustaining the transatlantic awakening in the mid-eighteenth century, and polemics were an important part of the body of literature that emerged during the revival. In North America, for example, literacy among German immigrants was high, and the number of imported works and those printed in the colonies in their language expanded tremendously in the early 1740s, paralleling both increasing German immigration and the Great Awakening. The vast majority of these works were religious in nature, and many were polemics directly related to the conflict investigated here. It is important to use these and other polemics—carefully—when studying religious conflict in this era. Since the seventeenth century deviant practices concerning women and sex were almost always emphasized in polemics against radicals, but this does not mean that these issues were a cover for the "real" reasons that people attacked radicals or that historians should ignore them as a source for understanding the conflict. These polemics reveal a great deal about the fundamental values of the writers and the readers that were at stake, as well as the gravity of the situation. The polemics were a medium for expressing dissatisfaction with an opponent, but for them to be effective, some deeper problem must be there. Gender and sexuality issues had often been a fundamental part of the problem with radicals like the Moravians, and polemicists quickly referred to this whenever a problematic group seemed to gain ground. Gender order had been violated, and through the polemics alarmed religious leaders did succeed in getting this message out to ordinary people, including those in the North American communities.[7]

During the struggle against the Moravians, Lutheran and Reformed church leaders and many others employed hundreds of polemics against the group.[8] In addition to publishing their own works, Lutheran and Reformed leaders circulated polemics written by political theorists and religious radicals who disliked the Moravians as well. Some of the most important anti-Moravian polemics in the struggle in North America were published in Amsterdam, Frankfurt am Main, Halle, Leipzig, London, New York, Philadelphia, and Stockholm. Most of the authors were Lutheran or Dutch Reformed theologians in Europe, radical pietists in Pennsylvania, or former members of the Moravian movement. They used militant rhetoric to attack the Moravians viciously for a wide variety of abuses related to gender and confessional issues, and they employed classic polemical strategies intended to stir the deepest fears of their reading public and arouse them into action.

The Halle Lutheran theologians were among those who attacked the Moravians in polemics for their trangressions regarding gender and confessional issues. Joachim Lange (1670–1744), the aging Hallensian who had experienced challenges and strife throughout his long career and battled the Moravians to the last year of his life, described numerous Moravian errors in a polemic sent to Pennsylvania in 1744. Lange (see Figure 6) accused the Moravians of promoting both separatism and improper forms of worship and doctrine among Protestants near and far and among non-Christian peoples in their mission throughout the Atlantic world. He condemned the Moravians for their antinomianism, their enthusiasm, their indifference to proper church doctrine, their ecumenism, and their blind obedience to Count Zinzendorf's authority. To Lange these people were neither good Lutherans nor true followers

Figure 6. Title page of an anti-Moravian polemic written by Joachim Lange (1670–1744) and published in Halle and Leipzig in 1744. Lange (pictured) was a professor of theology at the university in Halle. His work circulated in the German territories and in North America. Photograph courtesy of the Library of the Francke Foundations, Halle.

of the old Moravian traditions established by Jan Hus and his followers in the fifteenth century. But when citing examples of Moravian confessional violations, Lange consistently referred to gender transgressions, thus showing the connection between the two in the Moravian threat. His list of Moravian problems included their sensuous "little lamb" and "blood and wounds" speech, their views on marriage, their communal ownership of goods, and their use of women preachers in North America and elsewhere. Proper Lutherans would not pursue such dangerous beliefs and practices, and anyone who did and claimed to be Lutheran was a threat to the church. Lange was particularly worried about North America and attributed these Moravian sins to the free and diverse nature of life in Pennsylvania, which he also condemned.[9]

The two most important polemical writers in Halle, however, were

Carl Heinrich von Bogatzky (1690–1774) and Siegmund Jacob Baumgarten, who probably exercised more influence on North American Lutherans and their struggles with the Moravians than the head of the Halle institutes, Gotthilf August Francke, who was not a theologian and did not publish. Francke disliked Zinzendorf and the Moravians intensely, but his influence was filtered through Mühlenberg and other Halle pastors, who often ignored his advice and did things their own way. But the colonists could read Bogatzky and Baumgarten for themselves, and Francke made sure that their books reached the pastors working in the embattled Lutheran communities in the colonies. What these Hallensian writers told their readers on both sides of the Atlantic was that the Moravians were a dangerous threat to both confessional and gender order.

Bogatzky was the author of the *Golden Treasury* (*Güldnes Schatz-Kästlein*), perhaps the most widely read Lutheran pietist work on either side of the Atlantic in the eighteenth century.[10] He first encountered Moravians in Breslau in 1734 and was dismayed at the sensuous nature of their singing and their tendency to confuse the excitement of natural feeling with the work of the Holy Spirit. In 1739 Bogatzky attacked Moravian errors in the new edition of the *Golden Treasury*, which included 120 remarks against the group. He wrote that the Moravians were not true Lutherans, in spite of Zinzendorf's claims, because they did not hold to the law, the true Gospel, proper repentance and conversion, justification, and sanctification. Moreover, they undervalued and distorted the Bible; one of the most important examples Bogatzky used to demonstrate this point was the Moravian view of the Trinity. He was especially critical of the way Zinzendorf deprecated or ignored the Father, in part by teaching that Jesus was the Creator of all things. Belief in the Scripture, not the experience of the blood and wounds of Christ, must be the basis for all belief and understanding of God, according to Bogatzky. In addition to their unscriptural view of the Trinity, he dwelt on issues related to gender, marriage, and sexuality, like the Moravian belief in the "marriage mystery" (*Ehegeheimnis*) coming from the blood flowing out of the side wound. Their disgusting, intolerable manner of talking about this made a mockery of what Christ really did on the Cross, Bogatzky thought, and led to sexual and marital fantasies that were apparent in their writings and hymns. The Moravian single brethren behaved like fools, and the entire group raised their children in degenerate ways. In short, this popular Halle Lutheran writer believed that the Moravian refusal to follow proper Lutheran creeds led to dangerous distortions of proper beliefs about the Trinity, marriage, sexuality, and the relations of believers to their Savior, and these distortions would threaten the church, unless the Moravians were kept out of it.[11]

While Baumgarten (see Figure 7) was not as popular as Bogatzky, he was the leading theologian of Halle's transition from pietism toward the new Enlightenment theology that stressed using reason to understand Scripture, and was prepared to defend it against any detractors, especially Moravians, who were trying to destroy the future of the good Lutheran church. His seven-volume theological treatise appeared from 1742 to 1750, during the period of peak conflict with the Moravians in the Atlantic world, and Halle quickly exported the volumes to the British North American colonies as they appeared. The works represented a full expression of the theology of Halle during this critical transition period in its history, and they contained lengthy sections on the Moravian problem, demonstrating that the Hallensians were shocked by Moravian symbolic and practical distortions of gender order.[12]

Baumgarten provided the most damaging criticism from Halle of the

Figure 7. Siegmund Jacob Baumgarten (1706–1757), professor of theology at Halle and author of a widely read multivolume work that criticized the Moravians severely. Photograph courtesy of the Library of the Francke Foundations, Halle.

Moravian transgressions of confessional order. His critique of the Moravians was a product of his emphasis on doctrine, maintaining proper boundaries around the Lutheran church, and his "rational" theology. He began by rejecting their ecumenism. Baumgarten refused to recognize the Herrnhuters as part of the Lutheran church because they did not hold to Lutheran confessional works, but rather to those of ancient Moravian brethren, and had even sought out and accepted Reformed teachers, Quakers, and Mennonites. They were not and could not be Lutherans, he thought, because they associated with all sorts of error-prone spiritualists and even papists. If the Herrnhuters wanted to preach to unbelieving peoples and work with the sects he did not mind, but they could not be allowed to work within the Lutheran church. Baumgarten attacked their antinomianism as well, which prevented them from understanding proper dogma. He rejected the Moravian belief in creating a visible church within the larger church, as well as their blind, childish obedience to the "community" (*Gemeine*), their dark, unclear expressions about Scripture, distorted piety, undervaluing good works, and enthusiasm. All of these Moravian views were improper because Baumgarten could not see clear, mathematical-like expressions of doctrine, belief, and practice or a "purity of doctrine" (*Reinigkeit der Lehre*) in them.[13] He followed his attack on the Moravians in volume one of his *Theologische Bedencken* (1742) with continued assaults in subsequent volumes, adding theological "indifference" to his list of Moravian errors in volume three (1744).[14] By volume four (1745) Baumgarten responded to Zinzendorf's counterattacks with a more personal retort to the count, condemning his false claims, misleading statements, and scandalous, frivolous writing style, liturgy, and litany.[15] In short, the Moravians could not present logical, rational arguments about who they were, and their connections with the Reformed and radicals (i.e., their ecumenism) proved that they could not be a part of the Lutheran church.

In the fifth and sixth volumes of his theological treatise (published in 1747 and 1748) Baumgarten directly attacked symbolic and actual violations of gender order by the Moravians and the sensuous, sexual nature of their worship. He condemned the Moravian infatuation with the side wound of Jesus, their explicit hymns that stressed a sexual relationship with the Savior, and their feminine Trinity (as seen in those hymns). All of this led him to compare the group to the Mother Eva sect from the previous generation, and the ancient Gnostics and heathen Priapus cult.[16] As the war against the Moravians continued, Baumgarten stepped up his attack on their activities in Pennsylvania and issues involving gender, sex, and the Trinity. The number of their irritating hymns was increasing, Baumgarten complained, calling number 2085 (see Chapter

Three) "the most completely maddening female hymn."[17] Their blasphemies and deepening, uncontrolled enthusiasms (*Schwärmereien*), and their shameless assertions about the sacramental nature of marital sex, in which the husband took the place of Christ during sex, disgusted Baumgarten. He also condemned their distortions of the gender of the Trinity, their belief that all souls were female, the views that men became women after death, that the joy of eternal life was associated with sleeping with Christ, and their ridiculous view of marriage as seen in their hymns, as well as their shameless, graphic portrayals of male and female genitals. In short, the leading theologian at Halle launched an all-out assault against the Moravians for their gross violations of gender order, as demonstrated in their beliefs in the Trinity and their practices in their communities. It was to guard against this kind of gross error that firm confessional walls were needed. Baumgarten's goal was to discredit the group so severely that no one could ever again consider them to be a part of the Lutheran church.[18]

The state church of the Netherlands also used polemics to attack Moravian violations of confessional and gender order. At least 26 anti-Moravian polemics were published in Amsterdam in this era, along with at least nine German and Dutch Reformed works in North America. The most important of these was Gerardus Kulenkamp's *De naakt ontdekte enthusiastery* (*The Naked Exposed Enthusiasm*) a large, two-volume work published in 1739 and 1740 and exported to Reformed readers throughout the Atlantic world, including Suriname, Pennsylvania, and New York. Kulenkamp (see Figure 8) was actually from the northern German city of Bremen, but he studied in Utrecht and chose to remain in the Netherlands to pursue his career in the church, which he advanced greatly by attacking the Moravians. Kulenkamp studied Moravian published works and their Dutch-language hymnal and concluded that these were works of dangerous, hysterical enthusiasts, and gruesome liars who must be stopped. Kulenkamp criticized the Herrnhuter "warship" ("*Oorlogs-Schip*"), armed with its songbook of Babel and Sodom, because its members believed in universal grace and perfectionism and were theologically "indifferent," a grave sin to orthodox church leaders. The Herrnhuters claimed that they wanted to be part of the church, but they hardly knew the Bible and Dutch Reformed creeds, relying instead on experiential, mystical truth that they developed after associating with sects indwelt by the Devil himself.[19]

Kulenkamp's attack on Moravian violations of gender order was explicit, and he believed that these were among the gravest threats that the group presented. Kulenkamp was most shocked by the horrible secrets Moravian writings revealed about the nature of humans and God. The Moravians, he explained, removed the distinctions between the Cre-

GERARDUS KULENKAMP. Bremenſ:
V. D. M: AMSTELODAMENSIS. Aetat: 39.

Ora KULENKAMPI Custodis in Aede JEHOVAE
Sistit Apellaeâ picta tabella manu.
Umbra est. Sed labiis ſancto flagrantibus Igne
THEIOLOGUM Cathedris cernis in Amsteliis.
Viva BOANERGIS coeli tuba terreat hostem,
BARNABAM cupiens Hunc pie lasſus adi.
Supplex ante Thronum jungens pia thura precanti,
Aspicies olim, Tuque Vigilque DEUM.

Figure 8. Gerardus Kulenkamp (1700–1775), theologian and member of the
Kerkenraad, or church council of the state church of the Netherlands.
Kulenkamp was the most vocal and active critic of the Moravians in the
Netherlands during the 1730s and 1740s and authored inflammatory polemics
that damaged the Moravian cause on both sides of the Atlantic. Collectie
Verhuell no. VH0016, Verhuell 1/A/12, Streekarchief Voorne-Putten en
Rozenburg, the Netherlands.

ator and his creatures, and this opened the door to terrible conclusions about each.[20] To begin with, they promoted the perfectionist idea that humans return to the godly nature possessed by Adam before the Fall.[21] This mystical view of humans and the deity carried over to their understanding of Jesus, who was something between angel and man, with a double body essence—male and female: one of God and one of Mary— that dwelt bodily in believers and thus assumed human nature.[22]

Many other church officials in the Netherlands believed that the Herrnhuter view of the gender of humans and God represented the deepest penetrations of Satan into their teachings. In 1750 fifty-eight members of the church council in Amsterdam signed a polemic that condemned the Herrnhuters in four articles: 1) because Zinzendorf mistranslated the New Testament and demeaned the Old Testament writers,[23] 2) because Zinzendorf scandalously distorted the nature and meaning of the Trinity by teaching that Christ was the Creator, the Holy Spirit was a mother, and the Father was a grandfather or father-in-law,[24] 3) because Zinzendorf belittled the concept of a (male) sovereign God sitting in judgment upon people,[25] and 4) because Zinzendorf demeaned the dominant role of the husband in marriage and sex, emphasizing instead that children can be born without a man (as Mary gave birth to Jesus), that a wife need not subordinate herself to her husband to have children, and that all souls were sisters.[26] The writers concluded from this that "It is now a foregone conclusion that an anti-Christlike dominion of people has a place in the community, and that the Count has been commissioned with a more than papal authority."[27] In short, Dutch Reformed authorities, who had been struggling against the Moravians for a decade, recognized that the group had made the Trinity female and used this symbol of gender and power in Christianity to empower women in their communities. To them this meant that the true male God had been demeaned, and with it male dominance in marriage and in the community. Like the Hallensians and others, the members of the Classis of Amsterdam made it their business to ensure that the Reformed world at home and abroad knew about the Moravian errors. The Moravians had dramatically violated gender order, and these writers correctly perceived that they could stir up deep resentment against the group by publishing this and circulating it widely in the Reformed Atlantic world, as they did.

The heads of the Lutheran church in Uppsala, Sweden, also condemned the Moravian assault on proper gender and confessional order. Swedish authorities in Uppsala did not publish as many polemics as the Germans and Dutch, but they made their views clear in instructions sent to pastors in North America. For example, they condemned the *Moravian Hymnal*, which "contains, not only a quantity of dark and ambiguous expressions, but also all kinds of Popish, Calvinistic, Fanatic and other similar gross heresies." They condemned their emphasis on individual experience and authority, deemphasis on Scriptural authority, doctrinal problems, refusal to recognize the political authority of the state, and separatist spirit, as well as their strange ceremonies and church discipline and their devaluation of communion. In North America, the Uppsalan pastors rejected Zinzendorf's Tropus concept and the notion that his people could also be Lutherans. Gabriel Naesman described how the Moravians sent out their apostles in great multitudes, going from house to house and preaching everywhere, and then lied about who they were and conspired against proper clergymen who did not side with them. "He who has an opportunity to come to know the Moravians will have to admit that there are not more glib lying and sly creatures in existence than their scheming minds," he wrote. Naesman also mocked their enthusiastic, extemporaneous mode of preaching and their improper use of Scripture.[28]

At the heart of Uppsala's criticism of the Moravians were gender issues. They rejected the Moravian view of the Trinity, because Zinzendorf did not recognize three separate persons, but rather names that designated certain qualities of God. Moravians were so ambiguous in these views, Uppsala authorities believed, that one could not distinguish their position from ancient or recent heresies concerning the Trinity. Uppsala did not specifically mention gender issues regarding the Trinity, but the consistory recognized and critiqued the foundation of those views, namely the emphasis on the function of the three aspects of the Trinity. Uppsala authorities were familiar with the *Moravian Hymnal* and its contents, as well as the polemics written against the group that stressed gender issues. They specifically condemned the Moravian belief that God created all creatures from his own being and that humans belonged to God's nature and became divine after conversion. Since humans were male and female, this suggested a belief in God's similar qualities. The consistory went on to excoriate Moravian distortion of the doctrine of the "spiritual conjunction of the faithful with Christ," referring to their sensual spiritual relationships with the Savior. And they denounced the Moravians' overemphasis on the crucifixion and mortification of the flesh in their beliefs about the new birth, justification, and regeneration—a reference to the Moravian emphasis on the blood and wounds of Christ and salvation. Lastly, they allowed all members of the church to conduct priestly functions—"without distinction of class, freedom and right." That is, the Moravians allowed anyone to preach, including women.[29]

Working under the guidance and instructions of Uppsala, Swedish pastors in North America also criticized the Moravians for their transgressions against the gender order. Gabriel Naesman attacked their sensual liturgical and spiritual practices, where they expressed their love for Christ with kisses and embraces, foot washings, and love feasts that led to wives stealing from their husbands. His condemnation of their marriage practices and relationships reflected Naesman's misogyny. Moravian women were too powerful within the household, and women who wanted too much power tended to be drawn to the Moravians—a dangerous trend, Naesman thought. According to him, one Swedish husband had to leave his Lutheran community in New Jersey because of his wife's "spite and haughtiness." She wanted to domineer over everyone, including her husband. So the congregation was glad to get rid of them. Later she became a Moravian, and her husband followed her, but he became melancholic and died, according to Naesman. Here was an example of how the Moravians threatened proper patriarchal household order: "If anyone of the inmates of a house converted to their creed, matrimonial love, filial and menial obedience is violated, and made war upon . . . ," Naesman wrote.[30]

In addition to the three main opponents of the Moravians in North America, many other polemicists linked the group's violations of gender and confessional order, and their views became important to the struggle for the Lutheran and Reformed communities in North America when the religious authorities in Halle, Amsterdam, and Uppsala began exporting their works to the colonies. Some writers argued that Moravian beliefs and practices represented a political threat to the state and communities. They were especially concerned about the group's assault on patriarchal families, proper marriage, and proper (male) preachers, all of which were important to building a strong state. Johann Georg Walch, a theology professor at Jena, accused the Moravians of deviating from true (Lutheran) religion with their secret, papist ceremonies, ecumenical tendencies, and female Trinity. Further, they attempted to erect a new papacy by subjecting others to their rule, by building cloisters, and by their pilgrimages to Herrnhaag. By recruiting rich people into their fold and exporting their money the Moravians destroyed the orders and the economy of the state, Walch wrote. They allowed anyone to teach, preach, or do missionary work, including women, children, and untrained men. They controlled marriage and took away the rights of parents over their children. In the view of Walch and other political theorists the state should support the church and vice versa, and Moravian gender violations threatened both. He concluded his work with advice to rulers on how to deal with the Herrnhuter problem.[31]

One of the most important printed collections employed in North America by the Hallensians was written by Johann Philipp Fresenius (see Figure 9) in Frankfurt am Main. Fresenius made his career during the

Figure 9. Johann Philip Fresenius (1705–1761), pictured here in 1749, held the top Lutheran post in Frankfurt am Main and edited one of the most critical anti-Moravian polemics that circulated widely on both sides of the Atlantic and was quoted by numerous authors. Photograph courtesy of the Library of the Francke Foundations, Halle.

period of peak conflict with the Moravians by striking out against them and other non-Lutheran deviants. Frankfurt was an important center of publishing and pietist activity—an appropriate place for the tough, intolerant Fresenius to go to work for the Lutheran cause. This included instigating the public burning of the works of a "free spirit" named Johann Christian Edelmann.[32]

Fresenius published a series of works in the 1740s in which he presented the nature of the Moravian threat to gender and confessional order to German readers throughout the Protestant Atlantic world.

These included a number of short works, most of which appeared in other publications, and his massive, four-volume collection dedicated to the destruction of the Moravians called *Bewährte Nachrichten von Herrnhutischen Sachen (True Reports on Herrnhuter Affairs)*.[33] This publication highlighted events in North America (especially those involving Moravians) to eager readers. Fresenius attacked the Moravians for their ecumenism,[34] abuses in their missionary work,[35] and their authoritarianism.[36] His most flagrant charges regarded their irrational beliefs and practices concerning a female Trinity,[37] marriage and sex,[38] their empowerment of women,[39] and their threat to women and children.[40] Fresenius concluded at the end of volume one that "This super holy community looks more like a gang of robbers and public swindlers than a holy people, if one looks at them properly."[41] He blasted fanatical Moravian beliefs about the Savior and sex and shuddered to think what was really going on behind closed doors, especially in their closed married choirs.[42] He often used such harsh rhetoric against the Moravians or quoted or reprinted many others who did.[43] Fresenius was a superb editor who gained the confidence of many major religious leaders in Europe and brought together fascinating accounts of important people and events in the awakening by otherwise little known participants. He skillfully manipulated their presentation, sometimes reversing the chronological order to give the appearance of desired cause and effect relationships to his readers. The Moravians were his favorite subjects— clearly there was a significant demand in his readership for his electrifying material regarding this group.

Some of the most ferocious and influential attacks against the Moravians came from other radicals who were former members of the group and whose writings leaders of the confessional churches reprinted and circulated throughout the Atlantic world. Frey, Reynier, Sutor, and Volck were all ex-Moravians who demonstrated a special insight and animosity toward the group. When Reynier wrote his polemic in Pennsylvania, he was extremely angry at the Moravians because he believed that they had abandoned him and his wife during their mission in Suriname. Many of the polemics written by radicals reached Lutheran and Reformed settlers in the Delaware Valley by way of Christopher Saur, who published and sold them cheaply in Germantown. Fresenius also reprinted many of the radical writings and sent them to Pennsylvania.[44]

The radical polemicists sometimes wrote in a rowdy, bawdy style, clearly aimed at audiences in the lower orders on both sides of the Atlantic, and they did not hesitate to exploit gender, marriage, and sexual issues. Volck's work, which Saur sold for one shilling in Germantown, described a Moravian marriage ceremony in Herrnhaag involving fourteen couples, including a man and woman that Zinzendorf paired because they each had one eye. He mocked their extreme reverence for the side wound by describing one of their crucifixion paintings that, if illuminated from behind with a candle, revealed the face of the Moravian Baron von Watteville peeking through the side wound. Volck also accused Zinzendorf of sexual perversions with brides, and he elaborated on the "blue chamber" ("das blaue Cabinet"), the special room where Moravian couples met to have liturgical sex. "Have you been in the blue chamber?" ("Bist du im blauen Cabinet gewesen?") and "Won't you be coming soon to the blue chamber?" ("Kommst du nicht bald ins blaue Cabinet?") were expressions that referred to sexual intercourse.[45]

While the above examples of Moravian sins were obviously intended to appeal to a wide audience with humor, the overall message of the Moravian threat to proper gender order was serious, even chilling. The sixty-three-year-old Frey claimed to have been badly mistreated by the group and often referred to their magical powers.[46] Volck hoped his work would warn readers of the "enthusiast spiritualist regiment" (*Schwarm-Geist Regiment*) that was endangering the souls of hundreds of people, and was especially worried about Moravian hymns and what they revealed. The Moravians were a theological amphibium, like frogs, that dwelt in the stinking mud of error rather than in the graceful bounds of truth, Volck wrote. They were like the false Christs and prophets of the New Testament, as well as the ancient Gnostics and the Mother Eva sect. Volck attacked Moravian beliefs that all souls were female and Christ was an androgynous being with a vagina-like side wound. Their marriage beliefs allowed their women to become too strong, so they could be used like whips against their husbands, Volck explained. Moreover, the sensuous nature of their worship led to men misbehaving toward women who were not their wives, he wrote. They tricked innocent young women into joining their community, where they might be abused. While the radicals appear to have been more egalitarian than the Moravians regarding class issues, and some like the Mother Eva Society and the Ephrata cloister shared the Moravian tendency to empower women, many others rejected any hint of gender equality or female empowerment in their communities.[47]

The radicals who wrote against the Moravians were important in the struggle between the orthodox churches and Zinzendorf's group for a number of reasons. Many of them were seekers who had been members of Moravian communities and gave detailed accounts of important beliefs and practices largely unknown to orthodox clergy. Also, the radicals wrote in a common style that may have been more appealing to ordinary Lutheran and Reformed men and women than the rhetoric of theologians. These were the very kind of people the authorities in Halle, Amsterdam, and Uppsala hoped to mobilize against the Moravians in the North American communities. Further, the misogyny present in some radical writings very likely resonated among many Lutheran and Reformed people in those communities and was certainly shared by many of the patriarchal orthodox authorities. Moreover, like the state church theologians, the radicals rejected Moravian ecumenical efforts, although for different reasons. The radicals had no interest in promoting doctrinal purity or in protecting confessional and denominational walls, but they did resent Zinzendorf's authoritarian ways and feared that what he really wanted to do was take over the small radical groups on both sides of the Atlantic and unite them under his control. So in addition to publishing their own anti-Moravian polemics, many radicals cooperated with orthodox religious authorities and printers so that their stories could be printed in Frankfurt, Halle, and Amsterdam as well. And the authorities from those religious centers used radical works effectively in their struggle against the Moravians.

By the 1740s a long list of orthodox church leaders were attacking the Moravians along a broad front for a number of transgressions that they believed Count Zinzendorf and his followers were committing. The sins against the proper order of male and female relationships and hierarchy, authority, and boundaries within and between churches could not be overlooked, especially in a group that was so actively pursuing their ecumenical mission in Europe and overseas. The conflict was both intense, because of the issues driving it, and extensive, because of the mission work of the Moravians throughout Protestant Europe and overseas.

The Atlantic Conflict with the Moravians

The orthodox response to the Moravian challenge was centered in Protestant Europe but spread throughout the Atlantic world and even to the Indian Ocean. Tensions between Moravians and church authorities developed in Württemberg, Lower Saxony, Norway, and Finland, and especially in European states and religious centers that had overseas interests, These included Halle, the Netherlands, Sweden, Denmark, and England.[48] In each case conflict began in Europe and spread overseas, especially to the colonies in the Americas. These transatlantic connections and conflicts became an important part of the international Protestant awakening during the eighteenth century. Those involving Halle, and the state churches in the Netherlands and Sweden, influenced the conflict in North America the most.

The conflict between the Moravians and Halle was one of the most important in the transatlantic awakening, and it occurred during a period of expansion and increasing radicalism for the Moravians and a time of expansion and increasing conservatism for Halle. Because Count Zinzendorf was raised in Halle, yet embraced the Moravians and other elements of the radical movement, a collision was inevitable, especially since the Halle pietists continued to distance themselves from their radical past. Although the roots of the conflict went back in some ways to Zinzendorf's childhood, it came to fruition and shaped the course of pietism and revival in the Atlantic world during the period of Moravian ecumenism and as they began their dramatic mission movement in the 1730s and 1740s. During this time Halle, under the leadership of Gotthilf August Francke from 1727 to 1769, was undergoing its own period of expansion and redefinition of its goals. Halle's schools, world-wide mission, and publishing expanded dramatically during this era. Thus, unlike Moravians, who took their radicalism with them when they expanded overseas, the Hallensians had renounced theirs before sending their pastors to America and elsewhere. Wherever the two groups met, the energetic, ecumenical Moravians challenged the Hallensians with the radical notions and practices that they had recently buried in their own movement. Most historians agree that the rivalry between the two groups that extended from the Baltic to America to the East Indies significantly shaped the second generation of the transatlantic evangelical revival.[49]

Convinced that the Moravians were not only a lost cause but downright dangerous to the Lutheran church, the Hallensians went to great efforts to undermine the their mission wherever they encountered it. Both groups worked in Denmark and the duchies of Schleswig and Holstein, where the Moravians initially did well. But Zinzendorf was never able completely to gain the favor of the court in Copenhagen, while the Halle pietists did and skillfully used their alliance with the state to attack all of their enemies there, including the Moravians.[50] The Halle pietists and Moravians also clashed in Georgia during the 1730s, as Francke and Zinzendorf competed over which group would lead the Salzburg Lutheran refugees to that colony. The Hallensians eventually received the assignment, but the Moravians went anyway, and the two groups had several tense encounters in the colony that were written up and published for eager audiences by both sides.[51] The Moravians and Hallensians clashed in the Indian Ocean region as well: the Moravian mission to the Danish East India Company station at Tranquebar that began in 1760 met stiff resistance from Hallensian missionaries already working there, who appealed to the government to have the Moravians removed.[52]

The Dutch Reformed church also fought the Moravians at home and then carried the conflict into the Atlantic world. Early Moravian successes in the Netherlands came at a time when the state church there was still dealing with internal divisions and worried about the numerous dissenting groups challenging their authority from without, including Lutherans, Anabaptists, and Roman Catholics. The circular pastoral letter issued by the church council in 1738 against the Moravians quickly reached Reformed communities throughout the Netherlands. Its purpose was to warn good Reformed people of the growing Moravian threat throughout the Netherlands and Europe. The pastoral letter, along with the blistering polemic by Kulenkamp published in Amsterdam the following year, discredited the Moravians and alarmed enough people in the Reformed church to take the steam out of the Moravians' philadelphian, ecumenical cause in the Netherlands.[53]

The Dutch Reformed officials carried their anti-Moravian campaign overseas wherever Moravians appeared to threaten the true Reformed church with their erroneous ways. When Georg Schmidt singlehandedly began the Moravian mission to the Hottentots in South Africa in 1737, Dutch Reformed authorities there questioned his credentials, and the colonial government forced him to return to Holland for verification. Schmidt left his congregation of 47 Hottentots in 1743 and after arriving in Holland was refused permission to return.[54] In 1740 two Moravians tried to open a mission in Ceylon, but after a few months of success they met stiff resistance. Dutch Reformed clergy and members of the Dutch colonial government who had read the 1738 circular pastoral letter warning against the Moravians ultimately forced the Herrnhuter missionaries to leave. Another attempt by the Moravians in 1767 was also rejected by the government.[55]

The most intense overseas conflict outside North America between the Dutch Reformed church and the Moravians occurred in Suriname. The Moravian mission began in that Dutch colony in 1736, when they sent artisan missionaries to work in and around the capital at Paramaribo and others to work with plantation slaves one hundred miles inland on the Rio de Berbice. The Paramaribo mission encountered resistance from clergy and colonial officials influenced by the conflict with the Moravians in the Netherlands. Here the Moravians worked among European colonials, slaves, and natives, early on attracting good crowds of Lutherans, Jews, and others to their singing hours, love feasts, foot washings, and other ceremonies in their house. Their initial success provoked a reaction from both civil and religious authorities, however. Colonial authorities summoned one of the missionaries (who happened to be the later polemicist Jean François Reynier) and threatened to use force if he and the other Moravians did not stop holding services. The church council summoned Reynier the next day, told him his services were forbidden, and questioned his theology. Only proper salaried missionaries were allowed to direct religious services, they explained—an important issue that would resurface in the North American conflict.

That evening a patrol sent by the church council interrupted the Moravian service and threatened them with imprisonment. The missionaries continued, however, even though French and Dutch pastors began denouncing them from their pulpits. By 1741, pressure from their enemies, the government pressure on them to bear arms to defend the colony, the extreme climate, illness and death, and internal dissension began taking their toll on the mission. Their plantation failed as well, and the indifferent natives began walking away from their preaching. The Suriname adventure became a miserable failure for the Moravians, at least temporarily, for many reasons, but here the Dutch Reformed church could claim a victory in the transatlantic struggle against Count Zinzendorf and his people.[56]

The conflict with the Moravians in Sweden also influenced developments in North America. Moravians began moving into Sweden as early as 1727, and one historian refers to a "great Herrnhuter awakening" there beginning in 1740. While an atmosphere of enlightened tolerance assisted their efforts, especially in Stockholm, Främmestad, and in southern Sweden, the blood and wounds enthusiasm of the Moravians ultimately provoked a reaction that would have profound consequences for the Swedish Lutheran communities in the Delaware Valley. Many Moravian leaders were exiled, and the state Lutheran authorities began monitoring events in North America and instructing their pastors there to stop the Moravian intrusions into the Swedish Lutheran communities.[57]

By the 1740s, as the Moravians centered in Herrnhaag deepened their commitment to beliefs and practices that transgressed mainstream Protestant gender and confessional order and extended their mission overseas, the orthodox response escalated, turning local conflicts against a small radical religious group in Saxony into a transatlantic struggle that for a time grasped the attention of much of the Protestant world. This Atlantic struggle became the most intense in the Delaware Valley, where colonial conditions favored the Moravians and where the orthodox church leaders and their members took extreme measures to stop the count and his movement.

Chapter 6

The Confrontation in the Middle Colonies

The struggle against the radicalism of the Moravians that began in Europe in the 1730s spread across the Atlantic to Georgia, Suriname, and the Caribbean and intensified in the mid-Atlantic colonies in the 1740s, where thousands of Lutheran and Reformed immigrants were settling and building new religious communities. All sides used military rhetoric to describe the growing conflict. Count Zinzendorf established a "corps de reserve" in Philadelphia in 1742 to assist any threatened Moravians, and in 1743 the Moravian itinerants held a "Warriors' Communion" in Bethlehem. Fresenius described people in Philadelphia who had fled the Herrnhuters, yet were still plagued by them: "some began shaking in their arms and legs, some began to wail and cry out in their sleep, and as they awoke said that Count Zinzendorf was there and was trying to get them into his clutches. Others said that troops and crowds of Herrnhuters stood before them and terrified them."[1] Gabriel Naesman, the Swedish pastor sent by Uppsala to fight against the Moravians in the Delaware Valley, once described pro-Moravian women attacking their enemies like a "battalion of horsemen" whose "war cry" prevented him from speaking for over two hours.[2] Heinrich Melchior Mühlenberg described the confrontation as follows:

For the last twelve years the lot has fallen to me to be in their neighborhood, to note their movements, plans, writings, and attacks, and to observe the defense and preparations of our Lutheran church. With sadness I have learned that we did not seem to be a match for their stratagems of war and their serpentine deviousness, because they advanced mightily and like a plague creeping in the dark they gained the upper hand. The commanding officers and generals of our church were in part badly trained to stand against such a crafty enemy, because they had learned only the theoretical part of the divine knowledge and had not encountered the praxis; also they had more military exercises on paper than in their hearts.

Consequently they often beat the air, and when they thought they were on target they lacked the right judgment, insight into the point of the controversy, the most essential truths, and the power of godliness. Thus, they often opened the door and gate to the enemy, put the sword into his hand, or themselves fought against the heart of our Christian religion when they dared to do battle and attack.[3]

By the 1740s the Moravians faced numerous enemies in Europe and the Americas, as Protestants everywhere reacted angrily toward the group's deepening radicalism and their aggressive ecumenical program of expansion. The crisis escalated for the anti-Moravian clergy and their supporters in the mid-Atlantic colonies when the Moravians overcame their numerous early failures and began to succeed in their missions to Delawares, Mahicans, and Lutheran and Reformed immigrants in the region. The radical threat was rising in the colonies, and numerous orthodox groups and even some Awakeners took steps to stop the Moravians. The most important confrontations that emerged in the 1740s, however, involved the clergy sent by Halle, Amsterdam, and Uppsala, as they attempted to rally support against the radical threat in the Lutheran and Reformed communities and institute their own form of patriarchal, confessional religious culture.

Deepening Mistrust and Tension in Colonial Society

The success of Moravian radicalism during the Great Awakening aroused resentment, fear, and mistrust among a large and growing number of colonial authorities, religious groups, and individuals. Authorities in Connecticut and Virginia worried about Moravian and other itinerants within their borders and drove them out in both cases. In 1745 and 1746 the Moravians made another attempt to work with the German Dunkers by sending two former Dunker missionaries back to their old communities to canvass support for collaboration with the Moravians, but Dunker colonists rejected them for a number of reasons, including their "horrible matrimony" developed by their "abominable leaders" in the Twelfth Appendix of their hymnal and their "perverted principles . . . , 'marriage-bands,' blue chambers (*blaue Cabineten*)", etc. Andrew Bradford, the newspaper printer in Philadelphia, became angry with the Moravians and published a number of letters in his *American Weekly Mercury* in 1743 that suggested they were trying to take young women forcibly from their parents. Collectively, these enemies damaged the Moravian cause with widely publicized government lobbying and polemics.[4]

Even the Awakeners in the colonies rejected the Moravians' deepening radicalism and turned against the group.[5] The Presbyterians worried that the Moravians were getting too close to their flocks and took action: Gilbert Tennent was repulsed by the radicalism not only of James Davenport, but also that of Count Zinzendorf. He and Samuel Finley published inflammatory polemics against them, and Samuel Blair had a sharp exchange with a Moravian pastor. All of them were truly worried about the nature of Moravian beliefs and practices. Concern about the

Moravians among the Presbyterian, German Reformed, and Dutch Reformed clergy led to talk of an interethnic Calvinist union of the three groups. But the Presbyterians rejected this move because they recognized the growing Moravian influence in the German Reformed congregations and feared that, rather than alleviating the threat, a union would provide Count Zinzendorf's band with an opportunity to infect their own congregations. After the Presbyterians discontinued participation in the union talks their concern with Moravian activities declined. The Dutch Reformed and German Reformed clergy ultimately broke off union talks because they wished to protect their ethnic-religious identities and the confessional creeds associated with them.[6] John Wesley had been close to the Moravians in London, undergoing his famous "Aldersgate" conversion experience while associated with them there. He journeyed to Georgia with them in 1736 and visited Herrnhut in 1738. By late 1739, however, Wesley began having doubts about Zinzendorf and rejected a proposed union between his group and the fledgling Methodists in England. Ecumenism had its limits, even for Awakeners, who also found the need for confessional or denominational walls to protect their churches from dangerous error.[7]

George Whitefield also embraced the Moravians early on, but later renounced and attacked them. Historians have normally linked this conflict to doctrinal differences and a dispute over property in Pennsylvania that Whitefield had made available to the Moravians, but as the larger conflict with the count deepened, the Grand Itinerant grew more concerned with Moravian radicalism and their threat to gender order as well. Whitefield's correspondence suggests that he was disturbed by Moravian practices regarding women and gender. His letters to and about the group are entirely positive until June of 1739, when Whitefield condemned their community in London known as the "Fetter Lane Society" for allowing a woman to preach, or "prophesy," and linked this to the influence of Satan on the group. He continued to work with other Moravians, but the strain in Pennsylvania in late 1740 took its toll on his relations with the group, and he tried to have them ejected from his tract. By March of 1741 (after returning to England) Whitefield was bitter that the Moravians had "drawn away" his London publisher, James Hutton. A few months later he no longer wanted to dispute with Moravians, Wesley, or anyone else and sold the tract of land in Pennsylvania to the small Moravian colony there, but the truce was only temporary. After more than a decade of conflict involving the Moravians in Whitefield's transatlantic world, he too joined the parade of polemics against the group. In 1753 he accused Zinzendorf in a published letter of being manipulative, misusing financial resources and his power over the Moravian communities, and inaccurately proclaiming that the Moravian movement was descended from the ancient *Unitas Fratrum* and the worthy Jan Hus of Bohemia. Further, Whitefield accused them of leading honest-hearted Christians astray, ruining many families, and introducing superstitions, and "idolatrous fopperies" into the English nation, very likely a reference to accounts of unusual spiritual and physical practices between Moravian men that were appearing in polemics. The eventual opposition of Whitefield to the Moravians, along with that of Wesley and Tennent, suggests that leaders of the evangelical revival were not prepared to accept the radical views regarding gender that the Moravians were developing.[8]

Moravian successes in their African slave mission on St. Thomas and among Mahicans and Delawares in New York and Pennsylvania in the 1730s and 1740s also engendered tense opposition to the group. Their mission successes (and many failures) came at a volatile period of escalating rebellion and warfare in colonial history, when most Protestant evangelicals and others approached the mission to slaves and Indians cautiously, if at all. The Moravian newcomers, however, rushed headlong toward these groups to win their souls for Christ, with little regard for the growing fears and anxieties of white colonists. The Moravian slave mission in South Carolina, New York, and the Chesapeake occurred concurrently with the Stono Rebellion of 1739 in South Carolina and the alleged great slave conspiracy in New York of 1741. It failed, due to white resistance and the rejection of their message by the slaves, but this was not the case with their Indian missions in the Hudson River Valley and Pennsylvania.

Unlike the slaves in colonial North America, many Mahicans and Delawares accepted the offer of Moravian missionaries, and this heightened white hostility toward the Moravians considerably in the mid-Atlantic colonies during the 1740s. The Moravians were dissenting itinerants, which was a problem for some, and they were also pacifists and non-British immigrants, which during wartime was even more problematic to many colonists. Their insistence on promoting the mission to the Mahicans and Delawares led many colonists to conclude that the Moravians were a threat to the security of colonial society that must be stopped. Consequently, Moravian missionaries working in New York and across the border in Connecticut faced harassment, arrest, and incarceration for continuing their work. In 1743, for example, a company of "English soldiers" detained the missionaries and questioned them about their work. The next day the sheriff and three other riders from Connecticut arrested them and took them to a room full of people for interrogation. What is your name? Where did you come from? How long have you been here? Have you preached to the Indians? Did you have a proper call to do this? Did you not know that this was against the law in

Connecticut? Do you want to appear before the governor? Later the male missionaries did appear before the governor at Old Millford, while a female missionary was released because of illness. While they were waiting to see the governor, a New Light minister, who had earlier supported them, now denounced the Moravians in front of his students. The missionaries were held in a tavern packed with curious people who wanted to ask them a hundred questions designed to detect whether they were spies. When they met the governor, an Anglican and a Presbyterian minister were present, along with two military officers and curious onlookers. They told the missionaries that they had violated the colony's anti-itinerant law and questioned them about Moravian doctrine. After deliberations ended three days later one missionary was dismissed because he had broken the law by accident, but two others were found guilty and fined £100 New England currency. The missionaries protested, but to no avail, and were lucky to get out of Connecticut without further harm from the authorities or an increasingly angry crowd.[9]

When war broke out in 1744 the pressure on the Moravians from the authorities increased. That summer three Moravian missionaries working at Shekomeko were summoned before the governor and his council, questioned, and ordered to depart the colony. In December a sheriff, deputy sheriff, and justices of the peace came to Shekomeko with an order from the New York governor forbidding their replacements from public and private teaching. Christian Rauch and Johann Martin Mack had to appear before a judge at Poughkeepsie, who acquainted them with the particulars of the new law that forbade preaching to Indians and required them to swear loyalty to the King. The entire affair was civil, but the judge told the missionaries that if they refused to swear the oath, they would be fined £20, and if they did not stop teaching the Indians (openly or secretly) they would be fined £40 or face six months in prison. Rauch refused to do either, and after he debated with the judge about whether Christians should swear oaths, the judge gave in and let them go.[10] A few weeks later Christian Post and David Zeisberger were arrested while at the "Mohawk Castle" at Canajoharie. After a death threat authorities took them to Albany, where they declared their loyalty to the British Crown and were released, but ordered to leave the province. The mayor threatened them with a whipping if they returned. Still suspicious, guards escorted Post and Zeisberger to New York City, where Conrad Weiser (the famous Indian agent who was then an ally of the Moravians) spoke on their behalf, but they were jailed anyway, brought before the governor and council, fined, and released.[11]

The rumor about Moravian duplicity on the frontier with their Indian mission would not die, however, and two years of warfare magnified it. The war in New York and Moravian mission activities there made Pennsylvanians anxious that the Indians might attack their colony. In 1744 several merchants visited Bethlehem to investigate a rumor that hundreds of Indians were gathering there to make war on Pennsylvania.[12] In 1746 the Moravian Heinrich Antes, himself a justice of the peace, was arrested in Bethlehem and ordered to appear in court in Lancaster, where someone had accused the Moravians of taking in "French Indians" who were preparing to attack Pennsylvania. A number of justices questioned Antes in a crowded courtroom, demanding to know if the former Lutheran was really a Catholic and if it were true that the Moravians now had 3,000 men armed with muskets and bayonets about to attack. But cooler heads prevailed—hundreds of armed Indians might have been possible, but *thousands* was ludicrous. The man who made the charges was embarrassed, and they were dropped.[13]

The presence of ministers during the trial against the Moravians in Connecticut in 1743 suggests a link between the problems with the Indian mission and other problems colonists had with the Moravians. Because the missionaries worked with the Mahicans, there was growing popular resentment against them because people thought they were dangerous spies—as they would during later conflicts between colonists and Indians. The New Lights and Presbyterians connected Moravian religious practices to the problem of their Indian mission, thereby feeding the growing antipathy toward the group. The two problems fed off each other and made things worse for the Moravians during this peak period of conflict for them in North America: their Indian mission led people to mistrust them for secular reasons (i.e., espionage), but because of the growing mistrust of them for religious reasons—the polemics said that they were deceptive, secretive, and sent out irresponsible, untrained men and women to the heathen—people could easily believe that especially the Moravians would turn into spies when working with Indians during wartime.

In some cases the link between the conflicts involving the Moravians, other Europeans, and non-Europeans was more direct. When the Delaware leader Shickellamy negotiated a deal with the Moravians in 1747 to provide them protection and allow them to build a mission at Shamokin on the upper Susquehanna River, this caused many colonists to mistrust the Moravians and their missionaries. The problem was that Shickellamy required the Moravians to build and operate a forge that might be used to repair Iroquois and Delaware weapons. When Shickellamy became a Moravian convert and visited Bethlehem in 1748, this incurred the ire of Conrad Weiser, who had switched sides by this time and now was a bitter enemy of the Moravians and a strong ally of the Hallensians in the Tulpehocken area of the Pennsylvania backcountry. Weiser denounced the Moravians to the government and provided officials with anti-Moravian polemics from Europe—the kind of polemics then circulating in many if not most of the Lutheran and Reformed communities.[14]

One incident that occurred in New York during wartime demonstrates how the issues involving Moravian conflict with colonists and Indians were linked and shaped religious conflict involving the Moravians in mid-eighteenth-century America. On 27 November 1744, after the outbreak of war, the New York council ordered the Moravians to cease their Indian mission and leave the province, and they sent instructions to the sheriffs of Albany, Ulster, and Dutchess Counties to enforce the order. (This was the same order used to arrest the missionaries discussed earlier.) Zinzendorf protested to the Board of Trade in London and won temporary sympathy: the board requested that Governor George Clinton look into the matter and explain the council's action against the Moravians. The chairman of the council and supreme court justice, Daniel Horsmanden, responded in May of 1746 to Governor Clinton, who forwarded Horsmanden's report without comment to the Board of Trade. Horsmanden's response reflects a view of the Moravian threat when the group was at the peak of its influence in the colonies, that is, what one opponent believed the future held for them all if they did not immediately take measures to stop the Moravians.[15]

Horsmanden's criticism of the Moravians was extensive and linked the problems with their missions to Europeans and "heathens." Itinerants ("Suspicious, Vagrant, Strolling Preachers") had debauched the minds of people with "Enthusiastical Notions," created schisms in Protestant congregations, and ruined families by getting followers to devote themselves entirely to their community efforts. Based on what he thought was credible hearsay evidence, Horsmanden implied that Moravian missionaries were at least indirectly linked to the slave conspiracy of 1741, the so-called "Negro plot" in New York, about which he was an acknowledged expert, and probably the Stono Rebellion in South Carolina and other threats in the South, he thought. Writing in an atmosphere of instability, fear, and suspicion in New York City during the 1740s, Horsmanden argued that Moravians worked with Spanish agents, disguised themselves as schoolmasters, dance teachers, physicians, and the like to infiltrate families in order to "have an opportunity of debauching & Distracting the minds of the people, in order to carry on their wicked purposes, of Creating Disturbances & Occasioning Revolts among his Majesties Subjects." The Moravians were indistinguishable from Catholics and hence connected to the papist threat up and down the frontier. They have "Compassed Sea & Land to make Proselytes, & have so far succeeded" in Pennsylvania and other colonies. They dispatched their simple, illiterate strolling preachers with abandon—bricklayers, carpenters, tailors, and others unsatisfied with these callings and infatuated with enthusiasms and folly. It was not enough for them to convert Europeans: now they targeted the heathen with unqualified missionaries at Shekomeko, New York. White colonists who lived in the area feared that these unnaturalized, uninvited pacifist Germans would seduce the Indians into renouncing their loyalty to the Crown. They refused to swear an oath of loyalty, and when ordered to leave the province for these reasons, one of them threatened authorities by saying their Indians would go with them and thus become part of the communications and intelligence network emanating out of Bethlehem that reached into other colonies and threatened the frontier. In short, these strange, manipulative papist-like aliens deluded the ignorant savages, threatened the frontier (especially in wartime), and had to be stopped.[16]

Horsmanden described the entire spectrum of the Moravian threat and showed how the group's religious deviance threatened colonial society. The problem with the Moravian Indian mission in New York, according to Horsmanden, was not that the Moravians were preaching to the enemy, but that they were deluding and leading astray *friendly* Indians (the Mahicans), as they did white colonists whom they proselytized. It was the nature of their papist-like ways to operate as foreign agents—to serve governments whose religion resembled theirs. Their refusal to swear an oath of loyalty to the King, give up the German language, or marry English colonists made them suspect, and their strange communities, itinerant preaching, and deemphasis on the family reflected the corruption of their religion. New Yorkers felt vulnerable in the 1740s to the standing threat of the French and Indians on the frontier and to infiltration of their agents into their communities and even their families. The nuclear, patriarchal family was the bulwark needed to settle the frontier and maintain proper order in colonial society. Strong patriarchal families were needed to maintain order in colonial society—to protect them from the French and Indian threat and slave rebellion. By undermining the patriarchal family with the choir system and empowered women the Moravians served the interests of belligerent Indians and rebellious slaves. The vulnerability and fear felt by white New Yorkers in the 1740s spread to Pennsylvania (hence Heinrich Antes's arrest because of the rumor about the Moravians arming 3,000 Indians) and raised tensions among ordinary colonists, many of whom were just then deciding whether to embrace or repulse the pacifist Moravians.

Warfare and state authority dealt the Moravians a severe setback in New York and Connecticut, but this was not the case in the Delaware Valley. In spite of the opposition from Gilbert Tennent and George Whitefield, the Moravians enjoyed tremendous success among the German and Swedish speakers in this region, where religious toleration, heavy immigration, and relative peace could be found. The opponents of the Moravians attempted to use the courts to stop the group, and they usually won their cases, but this was not enough to stop the movement. In at least fifteen cases in British North America from 1742 to 1747, pursuit, arrests, court hearings, trials, and jail time resulted from the conflict with the Moravians (see Appendix 2). In seven of those cases the Moravians either were found guilty, or pressed assault charges against their enemies and lost. In another six cases Moravians were released after arrest, questioning, and threatening courtroom or other legal situations. Only twice were the Moravians or their supporters able to win. In other words, their enemies were able to mobilize the legal machinery to support their cause, while the same machinery generally failed the Moravians when they tried to use it. Yet the courts or other aspects of the colonial establishment would not decide this issue: while the Moravians were losing in the courts at this time, they were actually *winning* the battle for the Delaware Valley communities. As Moravian successes in this region increased, so did the opposition from Halle, Amsterdam, and Uppsala, as pastors and their supporters from these European religious centers struggled to stop the Moravian movement.

The Opposition from Halle

The Lutheran Francke Foundation in the German city of Halle was a major philanthropic organization and center of Protestant pietism in eighteenth-century Europe, building a worldwide mission, but its leaders had to make strategic choices about where they would send their support. The foundation ran a large charitable and educational establishment, famous throughout Europe, that took in orphans and others and trained them to be teachers, doctors, druggists, printers, pastors, and missionaries. They sent their missionaries throughout the Atlantic world and beyond—from Siberia to the East Indies. In North America they were especially interested in Georgia because of the Salzburg Lutheran refugee presence there, and had energetically supported that mission since 1734. But early on Halle showed little interest in the growing Lutheran population in Pennsylvania and the surrounding mid-Atlantic colonies, and even rebuffed their calls for pastors, claiming they were incapable of supporting them, financially or otherwise. Unlike Georgia, the rest of North America had a low profile in the transatlantic awakening at this time, and Halle remained uninterested in the Lutherans in sectarian Pennsylvania. Their attitude changed when they noticed increased Moravian interest and activity there, and they finally realized that something must be done about the growing number of Lutherans in the Delaware Valley. If Zinzendorf's ecumenical plans succeeded in Pennsylvania, he would gain enormous credit and standing in the transatlantic Protestant awakening. Halle could never work with Zinzendorf because of his ecumenism, irrational theology, and dangerous attitudes about gender. But ignoring him might allow him to have too much success among the Lutherans in the Delaware Valley.[17]

Halle finally began providing limited support to Pennsylvania by sending their first pastor, Heinrich Melchior Mühlenberg, in 1742 (see Figure 10). The Hallensians ultimately established an umbilical cord of support that stretched from Halle to Hamburg to London to Philadelphia, to their pastors in the field, and they channeled pastors, books (from Bibles to polemics), and medical supplies through the umbilical cord. Seven other pastors and assistants followed Mühlenberg to the Delaware Valley before the French and Indian War (see Appendix 3) and were centered in in the Philadelphia-New Hanover-Providence area (see Map 5).[18]

Halle also sent large quantities of medical supplies and books through the umbilical cord to North America, including anti-Moravian polemics. The books and medicines followed the same channels of trade, and the two markets were sometimes directly linked: Halle took orders from pastors in North America, usually via a representative in London, and shipped both books and medicines to pastoral agents.[19] Halle exported polemics written by their own theologians, as well as those written by radicals and other authors, and they wanted their pastors in North America to make heavy use of them when battling the Moravians. Francke felt that the pastors needed all of these works since "Count Zinzendorf appears to have turned with all of his might toward Pennsylvania, but God with his even greater might will resist him" ("der Graf von Zinzendorf sich mit aller Macht gleichsam nach Pennsylvanien zu wenden scheint, dem aber Gott mit nach größerer Macht wiederstehen wird"). The key pastor responsible for their distribution in the Delaware Valley was not Mühlenberg but Peter Brunnholtz, who was stationed in Philadelphia in 1745. Halle sent all of its supplies to Brunnholtz, who then distributed them to the other pastors in the field. They sold these materials at moderate prices in order to raise money to support their mission efforts.[20]

There is ample evidence that the Hallensian pastors followed Francke's instructions and made use of the polemics in North America. In 1750 Mühlenberg, for example, borrowed Conrad Weiser's copy of Alexander Volck's inflammatory polemic, and Johann Friedrich Handschuh noted one day in November of 1750 that he had just received a copy of Volck's *Das entdeckte Geheimnis der Bosheit der Herrnhutischen Secte* (The Mystery of Evil of the Herrnhutisch Sect Revealed) reprinted in Philadelphia and read it that afternoon. A year later Handschuh met Brunnholtz in Philadelphia to go over materials that had just arrived from Europe, including Johann Georg Becherer's *Nöthige Prüfung Der*

Figure 10. Heinrich Melchior Mühlenberg (1711–1787) became the leader of the Halle pietist mission and opponent of the Moravians in Pennsylvania and surrounding colonies after his arrival in 1742. Later etching by J. W. Steel of original portrait by Charles Willson Peale. Reproduced with permission of the Lutheran Archives Center, Philadelphia.

Zinzendorfischen Lehr-Art Von der Heil. Dreyeinigkeit (Necessary Examination of the Zinzendorfian Doctrine of the Holy Trinity).[21] Johann Albert Weygand referred to Baumgarten's *Theologische Bedencken* as a reference to help resolve a church dispute. Although the dispute did not involve

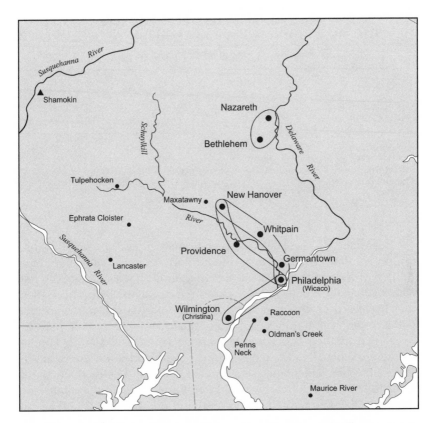

Map 5. Centers of power of the four European religious authorities competing for Lutheran and Reformed communities in the Delaware Valley, 1740–1754. The centers of power of the four groups were as follows. *Moravians*: Bethlehem and Nazareth; *Uppsalans*: Wilmington (Christina Parish) and Philadelphia (Wicaco Parish); *Amsterdamers*: New Hanover and Whitpain under Johann Philip Boehm (until 1746) and Philadelphia and Germantown thereafter under Michael Schlatter; *Hallensians*: Philadelphia, New Hanover, Providence.

Moravians, this shows that Weygand possessed Baumgarten's work and used it in his work. Also, Hallensians in the Delaware Valley sent material on the Moravians to Halle, where it was published in polemics.[22] In Georgia the battle against the Moravians had been won, but the Hallensian pastors were concerned about Moravian successes elsewhere in the Atlantic world and still received polemics in the late 1740s and early 1750s.[23]

Although the supplies Halle sent were significant, they sent only six pastors to the Pennsylvania field during the period of peak conflict with

TABLE 4. NUMBER OF LUTHERAN CONGREGATIONS IN THE PENNSYLVANIA FIELD
WHERE HALLENSIAN PASTORS WERE ACTIVE, 1742–1752

Year	Pastors*	Under control	Contested†	Visited	Total
1742	1	2	1	0	3
1745	4	4	2	5	11
1748	6	8	6	8	22
1752	8	16	2	16	34

* Including assistants who were not ordained.
†Not necessarily contested with Moravians.
Source: Diaries and correspondence of Halle pastors in Lutheran Archives Center
(Philadelphia), Archives of the Francke Foundations (Halle), and Glatfelter, *Pastors and
People*, vol. 1.

the Moravians, so the Hallensians stationed themselves in key battleground communities. Strategic interest and the personality and ability
of the pastors, not the needs of the community (for example, who had
been waiting the longest) often determined assignments. The Hallensians preferred to stick together (often two per parish), in or near the
battleground communities, and they usually did not stray very far for
very long from their contacts to Halle. They visited surrounding families
and congregations, held meetings in the field, and often traded places
with each other. The Hallensians reacted slowly and deliberately to formal calls by congregations for a minister, because they did not have very
many available and wanted to be sure that those they sent would be well
taken care of and might serve a functioning congregation. They did
send ministers on numerous occasions to help resolve disputes and
schisms throughout the Pennsylvania field, but those ministers returned
to their home congregations as soon as possible. Thus their coverage
was much more limited than that of the Moravians, and progress was
slow. Mühlenberg worsened the odds against the anti-Moravian cause
early on by stubbornly refusing to work with a number of Lutheran
preachers from Europe already in the colonies, including some who
were ordained and did not like the Moravians either. His early diaries
and correspondence suggest that he was a hard-working, competitive,
territorial man who thought he knew the right course of action and
insisted on following it, even when flexibility might have led to a better
solution at times. By 1748, six years after Mühlenberg began, the Hallensians worried constantly about what the Moravians and other foes were
doing, as he and his colleagues worked regularly in only fourteen of fifty-
three known Lutheran congregations in the Pennsylvania field, and six
of these were contested (see Table 4).[24]

Although the Hallensians were badly outnumbered by the Moravians in the contest for the loyalty of the Lutheran communities, they welcomed direct encounters with Moravian leaders, which often became tense, high-profile showdowns working in their favor. The best-known confrontation took place on 30 December 1742, when Count Zinzendorf and Heinrich Melchior Mühlenberg met in the parlor of Stephen Benezet, a merchant in Philadelphia. Surviving documents produced by both Mühlenberg and the Moravians detail a long, intense, carefully orchestrated argument between the count and the future leader of the Lutheran church in North America. More than anything else, this showdown that began the conflict between Halle and the Moravians in the Delaware Valley reflected the larger struggle between the two groups over who was or could be a proper Lutheran. To Zinzendorf, Mühlenberg was an interloper, an intrusive, trouble-making vagrant, and a manipulator who played a significant role in causing a deep, permanent schism among the Pennsylvania Lutherans. He had come to undermine his work and violate the viable Lutheran consistory in Pennsylvania that the count had set up when no one else in Europe cared. Thus the young Hallensian destroyed a wonderful opportunity for Pennsylvania Lutherans and widened a tragic schism. In many ways the count was correct in this assessment: Mühlenberg really was there in part to undermine the work of Zinzendorf and the Moravians, and he was quite successful at it. To Mühlenberg, the pietist sent by Halle to stop Zinzendorf and save the good Lutheran church from the sects, the count was a dishonest, confused manipulator because he simply could not understand that a Moravian could not be a Lutheran. Neither side was going to give in, because for each the stakes were too high and their positions were completely incompatible. It would be a long, difficult struggle for control of the Lutheran communities of the mid-Atlantic colonies.[25]

There were other unpleasant encounters between Hallensians and Moravians, although for the most part they avoided direct confrontations.[26] The Lutherans in Lancaster made up a battleground community that neither side could control, although both tried very hard. In 1746 the embattled Moravian Laurentius Nyberg complained that Mühlenberg had come during this difficult time to fish in troubled waters, but they did not meet. Two years later Nyberg did meet Johann Friedrich Handschuh, and it was not pleasant. Handschuh claimed that Nyberg warned him to stay out of his circle in Lancaster, to which the Hallensian replied that the Moravian had no business telling him in which circles he might work.[27] As late as 1754 tensions were still high when the two groups met. In that year Brunnholtz accompanied two Uppsala Lutheran pastors and a German lay leader on an uninvited visit to Bethlehem that was marred by heated disputes about Moravian beliefs and practices. They even brought up the old conflict between Mühlenberg and Zinzendorf from December of 1742. Mühlenberg himself expressed nothing but scorn for the Moravians until after they had been massacred by Delawares at Gnadenhütten, Pennsylvania in 1755, when he displayed sympathy for them. By then the Hallensians had defeated the Moravians anyway.[28]

One tactic Mühlenberg and the other Halle pastors employed in important, contested areas was to ride in groups as a show of force when moving into an area—essentially to disguise their weakness in numbers. This involved a major commitment of their meager resources, but it could be an effective demonstration of confessional, patriarchal power. When six men—five Hallensians and Conrad Weiser, the intimidating justice of the peace, colonial Indian agent, and father-in-law of Mühlenberg—rode into a community where a Moravian husband and wife team worked, they took over a church by force, and read aloud pronouncements declaring to parishioners their legitimate authority and the illegitimacy of the Herrnhuters.[29]

While the Hallensians achieved some local successes against the Moravians with these tactics, they could not defeat the Moravians throughout the Delaware Valley. In the 1740s and early 1750s the Hallensians failed to organize most of the Lutheran congregations in and around Pennsylvania and bring them under their influence, in part because support from Halle was insufficient. They did not have enough pastors (Mühlenberg constantly complained of being outnumbered by the Moravians), and Halle refused to send a printing press and other materials that Mühlenberg badly wanted to carry out the struggle. In fact, there were significant problems between Halle and Mühlenberg, as the latter resented their limited support of his mission, while Halle doubted their young pastor's abilities from the beginning. The Hallensian ministers could at times converge in individual communities for a show of force, but the Pennsylvania field was simply too large—too many immigrants were pouring into the mid-Atlantic colonies, and the Hallensians could not cover all of the rural parishes. They even lost some key town parishes like Germantown, and sometimes found themselves retreating. Handschuh ultimately failed in Lancaster as well, and the Hallensians lost this key parish in 1751—a stunning defeat that set them back in surrounding parishes as well. The umbilical cord system had allowed the Hallensians to make inroads into the mid-Atlantic colonies, and it did help to defeat the Moravians and other enemies, but it did not enable them to control most of the Lutheran congregations or build an extensive denominational establishment.[30]

Mühlenberg and the other pastors may not have succeeded in replicating a Hallensian establishment in Pennsylvania, but they were able effectively to raise doubts in the minds of parishioners about the legitimacy of the radical Moravian alternative and offer instead a denominational church that stressed patriarchy and order. As the group of male Hallensian pastors and supporters rode through an area, drawing big crowds, it must have been impressive to many and shocking to the Moravians and their supporters or any other challengers. It was a striking display of male power, as no women rode with these men to work in the field, and it impressed many parishioners in these communities. People who demanded a clear, easy to understand sermon with a time limit from a proper male pastor with impeccable credentials from Europe favored the Hallensian pastors over the Moravians. With this style and message for religious and communal order, the Hallensians succeeded in the 1740s in dividing Lutheran communities that Moravians had previously won over. The Great Awakening had forced members of these new immigrant communities to choose between two incompatible alternatives from Europe: an ecumenical, more feminized form of religious and communal order, or a patriarchal, confessional, denominational order. Nearly every Lutheran community in the Delaware Valley was eventually faced with this choice, and compromise was not possible, as the alternative was too dangerous in either case.

The Opposition from Amsterdam

The impetus for stopping the Moravians and building a German Reformed establishment in the colonies came from Amsterdam. For years German Reformed settlers in the colonies had appealed to various religious governing bodies in the German territories for support, but these authorities proved unwilling to start a mission, send pastors or significant aid, or otherwise build and support an apparatus in North America. Ultimately the Dutch state church agreed to do so, at first hoping to combine the German Reformed apparatus with that of the Dutch Reformed colonists there, but when the German and Dutch colonists refused to join with one another in 1738, the Classis of Amsterdam sponsored each separately. They recognized the German lay preacher Johann Philip Boehm as early as 1728 and six years later asked him to begin sending reports on conditions in Pennsylvania.[31] They also corresponded with Peter Heinrich Dorius and Georg Michael Weiss, whom they later fully charged to work in the colony. The German Reformed population was growing rapidly during this period due to heavy immigration, but the religious leadership was divided and struggling for legitimacy. A number of new preachers arrived, but none could establish himself, save Boehm, and even he was constantly challenged because he did not have a "proper" European background. In 1738 Dorius and Weiss reported that they were rapidly losing good Reformed people to the sects, especially the Quakers and Ephrata.[32] As late as 1743, however, Amsterdam still dismissed or ignored calls from Pennsylvania congregations.[33]

In the early 1740s Amsterdam's interest in the Delaware Valley and Moravian activity there grew slowly. A number of Reformed leaders went over to the Moravians, and Moravians of Reformed background worked successfully in many Reformed communities. In response Amsterdam charged Boehm to carry out the fight against the Moravians in the German Reformed communities. This extremely confessional pastor began the fight against Zinzendorf and the Moravians during the ecumenical synods in 1742 and made it clear that, while he did not care what Zinzendorf did to Lutherans or others, the count should stay away from the German Reformed people of Pennsylvania. Boehm worked out of the New Hanover-Whitpain area (see Map 5), but zealously pursued the anti-Moravian cause throughout Pennsylvania, eagerly devouring the polemics Amsterdam sent and even writing two himself.[34] With rumors, sermons, and polemics he hurried about the numerous congregations in the colony, warned his audiences of the Moravian dangers, and probably played a significant role in keeping the Moravians from influencing even more congregations than they did in the early to mid-1740s. In 1744 Amsterdam tried again to implement a union between the Dutch and German Reformed settlers, and maybe even the Presbyterians, but would not send pastors to the Delaware Valley. Meanwhile the interethnic Calvinist union effort had failed, and the Moravians continued to gain ground—they were winning the contest for the Reformed parishes throughout Pennsylvania and beyond.[35]

When Amsterdam finally responded to the Moravian threat and German Reformed needs in 1746 by sending pastors and other support, they did much more than Halle in trying to establish confessional order in the colonies. Michael Schlatter (see Figure 11) was the first of eleven pastors sent to Pennsylvania by 1752 to organize the German Reformed communities formally, and he was the early leader of the group (see Appendix 3). Schlatter arrived in September 1746 and worked out of the Philadelphia-Germantown area. He intended to use Amsterdam's personnel, money, and authority to build a denominational apparatus in and around Pennsylvania that would complement and receive support from the similar Dutch Reformed apparatus in New York and New Jersey, yet remain distinct from it. Schlatter wanted to bring "order" to the German Calvinists in America, and to him "order" meant not feeding off a tenuous connection to Europe, but establishing a network of male pastors, trained in Amsterdam, and placed equidistant from one another in congregations that had pledged in writing to pay them a salary he had approved. Amsterdam should subsidize their salaries, Schlat-

REV.ᴰ MICHAEL SCHLATTER,
one of the first Missionaries and founders of the German Reformed Church in America
Anno Domini 1746

Entered according to Act of Congress in the year 1847 by J. Hellmstan Jr. in the clerks office of the District Court for the Eastern District of Pennsylvania.

Figure 11. Michael Schlatter (1716–1790) succeeded Johann Philip Boehm as the leader of the German Reformed pastors in and around Pennsylvania, who were sponsored by the Classis of Amsterdam. He arrived from Europe in 1746. Engraving dated 1847. Reproduced with permission of the Evangelical and Reformed Historical Society, Lancaster, Pennsylvania.

ter thought, and also send books and money for church buildings and teachers' salaries (although not teachers themselves). All of this would be regulated by a governing synod or coetus of pastors and elders that represented the highest authority on the American side of the Atlantic. After surveying the situation and speaking with Boehm, Schlatter concluded that eight or nine additional ministers would be sufficient, but he later decided that they needed three more. He was certain that such an impressive display of European authority, hierarchy, and financial strength would impress the colonists and attract them to the Reformed church, away from the sects.[36]

From the beginning Schlatter was more interested in financial matters than in directly confronting the Moravians or other detractors. This focus hurt Amsterdam's cause in the colonies, where many immigrants struggled financially and the ecumenical Moravians preached to Reformed congregations for free. Schlatter believed, however, that people wanted good confessional order (or should have it whether they wanted it or not) and that this rested on the financial support of proper pastors. If the Amsterdam pastors could build up this kind of apparatus in the colonies, governed by a coetus, then Reformed people would forget about the Moravians and others and support their church. After preaching his first sermon at the Reformed church on Arch Street in Philadelphia in 1746, Schlatter informed the congregation that they would have to unite with Germantown and guarantee him in writing a fixed salary if they wanted to have him as their pastor. Schlatter believed that the Amsterdam pastors needed £65 Pennsylvania currency per annum to live decently, and that he could never in good conscience recommend anyone to come there unless he knew he was going to get at least £60. He also noted that he wanted a higher salary for himself, since the cost of living in Philadelphia was much higher than in the rural communities. Within weeks Schlatter had canvassed all of the communities to see how much they could pay and pushed Amsterdam for more pastors and financial support. He did not want the new pastors to overwork themselves by taking on additional congregations to meet their salary needs. The contrast between this and the Moravian pastors, who worked tirelessly for free throughout the region, was striking, but Schlatter was certain that his kind of order would both extend the Reformed faith and defeat the Moravians.[37]

Amsterdam intended to extend its authority and care to the Delaware Valley communities via pastors, books and money. Like Halle, Amsterdam sent hymnals and religious books to North America: Schlatter brought 130 Bibles with him, and shortly thereafter he asked for 5000 copies of *Contents of Wholesome Words*, as well as New Testaments, hymnals, and short catechisms. He found at least thirty Reformed church buildings in Pennsylvania, but only three were built of stone. The rest were wooden, and many were dilapidated, including his own in Philadelphia. If Amsterdam subsidized building more stone churches, Schlatter was sure that they could further impress the colonists and draw in more members. Most important, however, were the pastors. When Amsterdam delayed sending them, the Philadelphia congregation sent Schlatter back to Holland in 1751 to get them, along with other supplies they needed and money. Schlatter placed the pastors in a network, focusing on key communities, and then traveled frequently to visit and supervise them. The Amsterdam pastors also received assistance from the Dutch Reformed establishment in New York, which could ordain pastors and sent assistants to the Delaware Valley. Schlatter traveled tirelessly to install the new pastors and monitor their progress, and on long itinerant journeys to New York and up the Shenandoah Valley, and sometimes it paid off.[38]

Like the Hallensians, the Amsterdamers also made good use of polemics in their struggle against the Moravians in America. The Classis of Amsterdam sent Kulenkamp's *The Enthusiasms Exposed* and the 1738 pastoral letter to Boehm, and he made heavy use of them. (The latter was published in German translation in Leipzig and Amsterdam in 1739.[39]) Of course, the German Calvinists could also read other polemics imported from Europe or printed in America, and, unlike Lutherans, German Reformed pastors themselves published their own anti-Moravian polemics in America (see Appendix 1).

Part of the "order" that Schlatter and the other Amsterdamers intended to establish among the German Calvinists in the mid-Atlantic colonies was a gender order. Schlatter wanted to impress the Americans with a denominational apparatus of European authority, hierarchy, and money, and only *men* could be a part of that apparatus. He promoted a patriarchal, confessional order, and wanted to defeat the male and female Moravian workers in the Reformed communities with male power. Women not only did not preach, hold office, or attend coetus meetings of the Reformed congregations, but Schlatter did not even mention them in his diaries. Indeed, no women were ever listed in any of the reports, petitions, coetus meetings and letters, or the available correspondence of Boehm—a striking contrast to the Moravian alternative.[40]

Schlatter's early efforts seemed impressive and worried the Moravians, but it was not easy to establish this kind of confessional-gender order when it rested on such a large financial commitment from the immigrants. Schlatter was good at collecting pledges of financial support for his planned network of Amsterdam pastors, but this did not mean that the Pennsylvanians would actually *pay* him. In fact, they did not. Even his own congregation in Philadelphia refused to pay Schlatter for over a year. Eventually he had to deal with a growing internal crisis and factionalism within his own ranks. As with the Lutherans, many resented the Amsterdamers' authoritarian ways and Schlatter's attempt to build an apparatus dependent on European authority, while demanding a lot of money from them. Ultimately the Amsterdamers also had to compromise under pressure and consent to more lay influence, although, as with Lutherans, there was still a net loss in lay power in Reformed communities after the Amsterdamers arrived and settled in.[41]

During the Great Awakening the Amsterdam pastors offered German Reformed colonists in the Delaware Valley, who had been used to nearly complete lay rule with no connection to European authority, a confessional, patriarchal order that contrasted starkly with the ecumenical, more female Moravian alternative. Both choices meant surrendering at least some lay control to European clergy and authority and with this gaining at least some of the familiar ways they had left behind in their old Reformed churches of Switzerland and the German territories. The question for the colonists was, should they accept and defend the Moravian notion of order, which meant plenty of revival pastors, porous confessional boundaries, a heavy dose of mystical pietism, and a high profile for femaleness and women in their communities, or should they embrace Amsterdam's notion of order, which meant a patriarchal, confessional establishment with heavy financial contributions and fewer pastors, but no questions about the legitimacy of the pastors they did receive? Amsterdam's efforts to influence the decision with polemics, pastors, and other support were significant, but ultimately the immigrants in the Delaware Valley communities would have to decide for themselves. Like the Hallensians, the Amsterdamers could only divide communities against the Moravians during this early period, not win them over.

The Opposition from Uppsala

When the Moravians began working in the Swedish communities of the Delaware Valley in 1742, they found well established communities that dated back to the period of Swedish political and military hegemony in the region in the mid-seventeenth century. But by the mid-eighteenth century the Delaware Valley Swedes were a struggling ethnic group. In 1754 there were only about 1,250 members in the four largest communities—Christina (in Wilmington, Delaware), Wicaco (Philadelphia), and Raccoon and Penns Neck in New Jersey. Additionally there were perhaps about one hundred at the Maurice River settlement in southern New Jersey, and some others in Kingsessing, Upper Merion, and Manatawny townships in Pennsylvania, and at Hagerstown, Maryland. But the "Swedes" were still there, even if they lived and worshiped with English colonists, German immigrants, and others in their communities. So many still understood the language that successful itinerants among them had to be able to preach in Swedish, as well as English, and perhaps German.[42]

The Swedish Lutheran church played the most important role in holding these small ethnic communities or congregations together in the late seventeenth and eighteenth centuries, but support from Uppsala ebbed and flowed during this era. Unlike the Lutheran consistories in the German territories during this period, Uppsala generally supplied their American ethnic-religious compatriots with pastors (whose expenses they paid), schools, Bibles, and other religious reading materials. Because of their government's earlier colonial interests, religious authorities in Uppsala felt compelled to send pastors and provide Swedish confessional education in the Delaware Valley. But the period after 1730 was one of general decline in the Swedish Lutheran parishes on the Delaware. Uppsala's pastors came and went, many rejected by their parishioners because of their salary demands or other problems, and others did not handle ethnic sensitivities very well. Coming from one of the most ethnically and religiously homogeneous states in Protestant Europe, where the Lutheran church ruled nearly unchallenged, the pastors Uppsala sent to the Delaware Valley must have been even more shocked than the Hallensians and those sent by Amsterdam at the social and religious chaos developing in the region in the mid-eighteenth century. In short, proper Swedish Lutheran authority was collapsing in the old parishes in the 1730s and early 1740s, as the small number of overworked ordained ministers could not keep up with new developments in the Delaware Valley.[43]

It was during this period of weak control and declining authority that the Uppsala ministers faced the Moravian challenge.[44] From 1743 to 1748 the Moravians sent at least thirteen preachers to work in the ten Swedish communities of the mid-Atlantic colonies. They overwhelmed the five Uppsala preachers, who were centered in the Philadelphia-Wilmington (Delaware) area (see Map 5), and worked around or ignored the two independents. In fact, one of Uppsala's five pastors during this period (Nyberg) became a Moravian, and two did not arrive until 1748, one of those dying shortly thereafter. So during most of the conflict before 1749, only two Uppsala pastors were available to guard the ten Swedish communities from the Moravians (see Table 5 and Appendix 3).[45]

With this numerical advantage, the Moravians struck hardest in the three parishes where there were no regular Swedish Lutheran pastors, namely Wicaco, Raccoon, and Penns Neck, and they avoided Christina Parish in Wilmington, where one of the two Uppsala pastors worked. The German Mühlenberg tried to cover Wicaco in Philadelphia, but he could only be there once every eight days. He complained that in

TABLE 5. UPPSALAN, MORAVIAN, AND INDEPENDENT PASTORS WORKING IN THE
SWEDISH LUTHERAN COMMUNITIES IN NORTH AMERICA, 1743–1755

Dates	Uppsalan	Moravian	Independent	Total
1743–1748	5	13	2	19
1749–1755	6	1*	0	7

*The one represented here, John Wade, only worked in 1749. Six other Moravians worked
at Oldman's Creek, which by then was a separate Moravian congregation, no longer
Swedish Lutheran.
Sources: Acrelius, *History of New Sweden*; *Bethlehem Diary*, vols. 1–2; Paul Minotty, ed., *The
Records of the Moravian Church at Oldman's Creek, Gloucester County, New Jersey* (Woodbury,
N.J.: Gloucester County Historical Society, 1968); Moravian itinerant diaries and reports
in Moravian Archives (Bethlehem) and Unity Archives (Herrnhut).

between the "Herrnhutisch Jesuits" were trying to run him out. The
Swedish Moravian Bryzelius told parishioners that Mühlenberg was an
"arch pietist" and used his ethnicity against his German rival. By the
time Gabriel Naesman arrived from Sweden in 1743 to take over the
Wicaco congregation in Philadelphia, many parishioners had already
gone over to the Moravians. Naesman was able to bring Wicaco into the
Uppsalan camp, but the parishioners complained whenever he traveled
across the Delaware to Penns Neck and Raccoon to round up the faithful
and defend them against the Moravians.[46]

To resolve the problem of the minister shortage, some pro-Uppsala
Swedes proposed a confessional, interethnic alliance with the German
Halle Lutherans in order to fight their common enemy, the "Zinzendorfers." But the Lutherans were no more capable of achieving this kind
of union than the Calvinists, and after a bitter, two-day conference, in
which a Moravian-Lutheran pastor resisted the union, the attempt
failed. Neither Calvinists nor Lutherans were prepared to compromise
their ethnic heritage at this time, and this actually assisted the Moravians, whose brand of ecumenism under the "Tropus system" meant
that they had penetrated the circle of confessional pastors seeking ethnic unity and could send preachers to the very communities that the
European authorities had targeted for care in order to stop them.[47]

While the confessional union attempt was failing, the Moravians
extended their influence in the Swedish communities. Their itinerants
completed successful tours throughout the Delaware Valley, and they
scored a major victory when Gustavus Hesselius, the painter whose two
brothers had earlier served in Uppsala's mission in the Delaware Valley,
seems to have publicly announced he had joined the Moravians by hanging a crucifixion painting on his door. Naesman labored against the
growing Moravian presence, but he was largely alone. He served the

English and Swedes within his own parish and struggled to intervene across the river to help counter the Moravian threat there, preaching to English and Germans in Cohansey and English and Swedes at Raccoon, "which was vacant, and suffering from the intrusion of the Herrnhutters," as he put it. In his reports to Uppsala, Naesman described himself as under siege, battling against the Moravians, who "have tried in various manners to molest me and by vast harassments when I have plainly shown inclinations to side with them." Peter Tranberg, the only other Uppsala pastor in the Delaware Valley at the time, refused to confront the growing chaos the Moravians were causing in the Swedish communities of the region and shut himself up in Wilmington. At least this one congregation could be kept safe from the Moravians, he believed, and at this, anyway, he succeeded.[48]

There was still scattered resistance, but by 1745 the Moravians were so confident that they felt it was time to introduce women into the Swedish New Jersey field to help with the mission. This sent Naesman reeling into a misogynist paranoia. Now that their women were working in the field, Naesman was truly worried that the Moravians, with their female hosts and manner, would overwhelm the Swedish communities. Matters worsened when the other Uppsala pastor, Peter Tranberg, made peace with the Moravians, which left Naesman alone in the field to fight the count's people. By November he expressed his worst fears to Uppsala. Perhaps Naesman had read some of the polemics that emphasized that women were not safe around the Moravians. Whenever he had a female servant in the house, twenty female Moravian apostles would appear to convert her and bring her into the Moravian church, Naesman wrote. If they succeeded in converting his servants, then the slander against him would only escalate, which he feared would ruin his chances of finding a wife. Naesman feared that the "whole Moravian ant hill" would descend upon her. What might they not be able to do to a wife he might have, since "well nigh thirty of their petticoated prophets with all their eloquence and profound reasons" were already trying to convert him? "I have seen and found how several other clergymen here have had to place a Moravian spinning wheel on the very altar," Naesman continued. Thus in 1745, at the height of the Moravian offensive on the Swedish communities, as the last active representatives of orthodox Lutheranism from Sweden, Naesman feared the power of Moravian women preachers and prophets to control both women and men from the pulpit and by infiltrating families. Most of all he now feared that they were out to get *him*.[49]

In 1745 the Moravian plan was working among the Swedes in the Delaware Valley, and this startled the authorities in Uppsala. The Moravians were winning, not just because their male and female itinerants energetically outmaneuvered their outnumbered opponents, but because they employed their ecumenical Tropus concept in such a way that their pastors did not inform their parishioners about their Moravian connection. When Uppsala finally became aware that even some of their own pastors were tainted by Moravianism, they responded more rigorously to events occurring in the Delaware Valley. When lay leaders and pastors called for help, Uppsala responded by sending them a scathing critique of Moravian beliefs and practices and informed their constituents in North America that the Moravians were not in good standing with the Lutheran Church in Sweden, as they had claimed. Moreover, Uppsala named names of pastors then working in the Delaware Valley who were not true Lutherans, as they had claimed, but actually members of the count's group. They also cited polemics and described in detail Zinzendorf's errors and the dangers that this wicked, Satanic group represented. Uppsala warned the American leaders to "keep a watchful eye upon the herd, that the enemy take not advantage of this to sow tares there." With this the full weight of the criticism by European theologians of Moravian beliefs and practices was brought into the conflict among the Swedes in the Delaware Valley.[50]

Beginning in 1748 a new wave of Uppsala pastors, armed with anti-Moravian polemics, began arriving and attempted to save the Swedish Lutheran church in the Delaware Valley. In 1748 John Sandin arrived and was named by Uppsala as the provost of all the Swedish churches on the Delaware, but he died within a year of his arrival. As a temporary replacement, the anti-Moravian factions engaged Peter Kalm, the well-known Swedish naturalist, who was then traveling in the area. The unordained Kalm responded enthusiastically to the vacuum left by Sandin's early demise, preaching nearly every Sunday to hold back the Moravian threat and marrying Sandin's widow a few months later. Israel Acrelius (see Figure 12) and Eric Unander arrived in 1749, Acrelius to replace Sandin as provost. He immediately sacked Naesman, who had done so poorly against the Moravians and otherwise, and began distributing fifteen copies of the new Swedish translation of Ernst Salomon Cyprian's *Vernünftige Warnung vor Irrthume von Gleichgültigkeit der Gottesdienste* (*Reasonable Warning against the Error that all Religions Are Equally Good*),[51] a German polemic directed at Moravian ecumenism. It included an introduction by the Swedish translator, Eric Beckman, entitled "Touching the Sect of Herrnhutters" (*Angående Herrnhutiska Secten*). In 1750 Olof Parlin brought thirty copies of the new Swedish translation of the Hallensian Johann Georg Walch's *Theologisches Bedencken von der Beschaffenheit der Herrnhutischen Secte* (*Theological Considerations on the Nature of the Herrnhuter Sect*).[52] Uppsala had been sending reading materials to the Delaware settlements since the late seventeenth century, but these mate-

Figure 12. Israel Acrelius (1714–1800) was sent by the Lutheran state church authorities in Uppsala to the Delaware Valley in 1749 to organize the resistance against the Moravians in the region and to reinvigorate the struggling Swedish parishes there. In 1756 he returned to Sweden and two years later published a history of the Swedish Lutheran settlements in the region. Photograph courtesy of Holy Trinity (Old Swedes) Church Foundation, Henrickson House, Wilmington, Delaware.

rials had consisted primarily of Bibles, catechisms, and hymnals. Now, in the heat of battle with the Moravians for the soul of those settlements, they began employing the same weapon that the German opponents of the Moravians had used so effectively—inflammatory propaganda that railed at Moravian abuses, perversities, and threats against authority, decency, and the proper order and relationships between men and women. The distribution of these publications throughout the Swedish Delaware communities provided invaluable material for inflammatory sermons and gossip aimed at the Moravians and their supporters in the region.[53]

Uppsala's reaction against the Moravians in the Delaware Valley was bitter and reflected their patriarchal confessional position. Like their counterparts from Halle and Amsterdam, the Uppsala pastors used harsh, militant, animalistic rhetoric to describe the Moravians and their activities, hoping to incite popular resistance against them. Acrelius called Penns Neck a Moravian "nest" and wrote that Bryzelius "crept" into the Swedish houses at Raccoon. Immediately after Whitefield's preaching tour, Zinzendorf came "with his pernicious sect called Herrnhutters, and spread out his net to catch all at one time."[54] Also similar to Halle and Amsterdam, the Uppsala pastors were denominational: they wanted clear lines of authority established from Uppsala, through them, to the parishes on the Delaware. Like Mühlenberg and many other clergy from Europe, Naesman disliked the libertine atmosphere of the Delaware Valley, which included everything from the numerous Quaker congregations to the Moravians and other radicals. He did not even like other Lutheran pastors like Mühlenberg, who was problematic not only because he was a Halle pietist, but also because he was German, not Swedish, which meant that a union with him would contribute to the further erosion of the ethnic-religious ideal of a true Swedish Lutheran church on the Delaware. The Uppsala pastors were trying to bring stability and confessional and gender order to the Delaware Swedes, and many parishioners found the renewed emphasis and support from Sweden attractive. They preferred the patriarchal, confessional alternative, although they resisted overbearing authority. As in Halle and Amsterdam, the Uppsalan vision of proper order included no leadership roles for women. The radical, ecumenical Moravians with their aggressive female preachers represented disorder to Naesman, and both had to be stopped. The fact that Uppsala never employed or even referred to women in leadership positions unless condemning the practice by the Moravians suggests how important an all male hierarchy was to them. But North America was different, and the Uppsala pastors and their supporters would have to fight to achieve and preserve this kind of order in their badly divided communities.

The tense confrontation that developed in the Delaware Valley colonies in the 1740s was part of the transatlantic conflict with the Moravians that was largely defined by gender and confessional issues, but the outcome was uncertain. The outnumbered pastors sent by Halle, Amsterdam, and

Uppsala struggled to build patriarchal denominational establishments without the support of the state. The Moravians promoted their worldwide ecumenical mission with a more female piety in an area that the Lutheran and Reformed state churches in Europe seemed to have neglected. Meanwhile, most of the Lutheran and Reformed immigrants in the Delaware Valley wanted an organized congregation with at least a part-time pastor. They did not always know that the "Lutheran" or "Reformed" men and women working in their communities were part of the Moravian movement, but they did know that these people worked hard and effectively for them, even helping them build churches and schools when no one else would. In fact, the Moravians succeeded early on in the region because of the high demand for pastors, fueled by massive immigration, that only they were in a position to meet. But when these men and women laboring in the Lutheran and Reformed communities were unmasked as "Moravians," the people in the communities had to decide if this mattered.

What did Lutheran and Reformed community members really know about "Moravians," "Herrnhuters," or "Zinzendorfers," as they were called, and their radical beliefs and practices on gender, marriage, and, sexuality? They knew what they had seen among the male and female workers in their communities, and this was impressive. But they also knew what the anti-Moravian polemics, sermons, and rumors that circulated in all of these communities told them, namely that Count Zinzendorf's people believed that the Trinity was largely female and that they lived in strange ways in their nearby communities of Bethlehem and Nazareth, where bizarre marriage, sexual, and other liturgical rituals took place.

The small number of pastors from Halle, Amsterdam, and Uppsala had only managed to divide the Lutheran and Reformed communities in the Delaware Valley over the Moravian issue. Now it was up to the people who lived there to decide which form of religious authority and style would serve them best in the new environment. Should they choose the Moravian alternative, which brought them the immediate results of good preaching, schools, church buildings, and a recognizable liturgy for free, as well as a high-profile role for women in the community, porous confessional boundaries, and a radical spirituality that feminized the sacred? Or should they choose the confessional-denominational alternative, which offered them a "true" (*echter*) Reformed or Lutheran preacher (if they waited long enough), clearly delineated religious boundaries, a clearly male hierarchy, access to more familiar authority in Europe, and Jesus as a man, the way they always knew him to be? The Moravians and their supporters had gained an early advantage, in part because people in the communities were unaware of their connections to Bethlehem and Count Zinzendorf. Once the men and women in these communities discovered these connections, the question was, would the Moravians and their supporters be able to hold on to these communities, or would the anti-Moravian factions succeed in driving them out?

Chapter 7

Religious Violence Erupts

In the 1740s the conflict between the Moravians and the Lutheran and Reformed clergy and their supporters raged from Virginia to New York, but it was most intense in the German and Swedish communities of Pennsylvania and New Jersey, where widespread religious violence erupted, and a typical pattern of community conflict emerged throughout the region. Moravians sent one or more preachers to a community where there was no other regular Lutheran or Reformed pastor, who gained acceptance by most congregants, as well as the elders and church council members. They often focused on new, unestablished immigrant communities, or old communities experiencing factional conflict and neglect. Often the Moravian preachers won over a hard core of upstanding community members and elders who later supported them the most when their enemies began attacking them. Tensions, conflict, and schism followed when pastors and lay leaders from the churches supported by Halle, Amsterdam, and Uppsala used polemics, inflammatory preaching, and rumor to discredit the Moravians. In many cases pro- and anti-Moravian factions fought violently for control of their communities. As long as enough members supported them, the Moravian preachers kept returning to the community, but eventually the anti-Moravian factions defeated them and they were permanently expelled. The religious violence following this pattern was extensive and occurred during the peak years of what one historian labeled the "Moravian threat" to the new Lutheran and Calvinist immigrant communities.[1] The physical fighting usually took place between lay men and women competing for control of their communities, although sometimes preachers were attacked. The elders and councils of the churches were heavily involved in the conflict as well.

Few historians have recognized the extent of the communal religious violence in the Delaware Valley during the Great Awakening, because most of the records describing it are in the old German script in the Moravian Archives in Bethlehem or the Unity Archives in Herrnhut. The Hallensian pastors documented some of it in their diaries, and for the most part these manuscripts lie in the Lutheran Archives in Philadel-

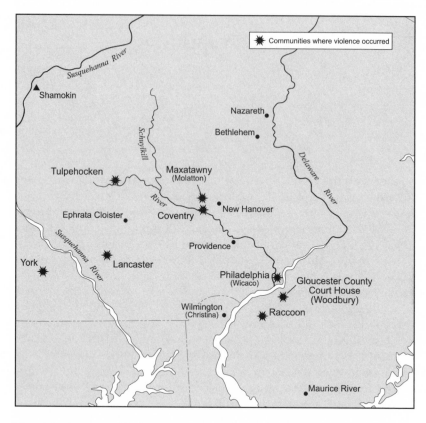

Map 6. Lutheran and Reformed communities in the mid-Atlantic colonies in which religious violence involving Moravians occurred, 1742–1748.

phia and the Francke Foundations in Halle. The printed sources so often used by historians (e.g., Mühlenberg's journal and correspondence, as well as the "Halle Reports" (*Hallesche Nachrichten*) or translated published records of the Reformed pastors) provide only heavily edited, incomplete versions of events. The exception is Mühlenberg, whose published works are complete, but in these early years he was not directly involved in the communal violence, as his colleagues were, and Mühlenberg's printed works are thus not as helpful as the records kept by other Hallensian pastors. Below are some examples that demonstrate how widespread the religious violence was in many of the Lutheran and Reformed communities of Pennsylvania and New Jersey during the 1740s.

In February 1743 the Moravian pastor Paul Daniel Bryzelius visited the

Swedish Lutheran community at Manatawny Creek in Amity township (now in Berks County), Pennsylvania, and there was trouble. Swedish pastors from Philadelphia had been visiting the area for decades, including Samuel Hesselius and Gabriel Falk, both sent by Uppsala. But Hesselius went back to Sweden in 1731, and Falk's parishioners in Philadelphia had rejected him shortly after his arrival in 1733. For the next ten years Falk worked independently, partly at the log church called Molatton that the Swedes in the Manatawny community had built in 1737.[2] He had been preaching against the Moravian itinerant, Bryzelius, who had recently come from Sweden and had been sent by Bethlehem to work in the area. According to Bryzelius, Falk stole the key to the log church in order to keep him out. Bryzelius managed to get in anyway, and one day during his service Falk burst in wielding a large whip, and cried out, "You are coming into the sheepfold as a thief and a murderer!" Falk then struck Bryzelius hard in the mouth and tried to thrash him with his whip, but he was so furious that he could not hit his target. Finally some of Bryzelius's supporters in this divided community rushed in and threw Falk out of the church. The Moravians had won, at least for a time. Falk, the independent Swedish minister, was discredited, and Bryzelius was able to continue preaching at Manatawny, as well as in other Swedish Lutheran communities on the Schuylkill, Wicaco in Philadelphia (where he overcame significant resistance), Kalckenhucken, Ammas Land, Matthony, and Hagerstown in Maryland.[3]

In 1743 a tense showdown took place in the Reformed community of Coventry between the flamboyant Moravian revival preacher Jacob Lischy and the Amsterdamer Johann Phillip Boehm. For a time Lischy was one of Bethlehem's most popular itinerant preachers to the Reformed communities—probably their most popular preacher. Shortly before arriving at Coventry he completed two electrifying revival tours, the first of which covered nine Reformed communities in ten days and the second eight communities in two weeks. But rumors were growing that Lischy was really a Herrnhuter, not a true Reformed preacher. Lischy insisted to his audiences and in a published "Declaration" that he really was a Reformed preacher and denied that he was a Moravian— employing the logic of Zinzendorf's Tropus concept, which meant that there was no contradiction in his ecumenical way of thinking on this point. Meanwhile Boehm sensed something was wrong with Lischy's credentials and published a letter attacking him. One day during the summer of 1743 Lischy and Boehm both raced to the Reformed church building at Coventry to try to win over that important community. Apparently they both arrived at about the same time, but while Lischy went to the church and began winning over the crowd, Boehm went to the authorities to get them to ban any non-Reformed pastor from preaching in the Coventry church. It was a bad move on Boehm's part, as he encountered a hostile crowd in the church when he arrived later. Lischy was in the pulpit and had already persuaded them that he was a true Reformed preacher and that Boehm was the real threat to their community. Something was terribly wrong, Boehm realized. He had to find out more about the eloquent, persuasive Lischy and be sure that he really was a Moravian before he could attack him head-on in that crowd. While Lischy read aloud his published "Declaration" Boehm tried to leave the scene, but the crowd demanded that he remain and face Lischy to settle the issue. They forced him back into the church, and only by a clever ruse was he able to escape the angry crowd and flee on his horse, with parishioners running after him, calling him a liar and a fraud. For the time being the community had chosen the Moravians, even though they were not fully aware of Bethlehem's backing of their choice.[4]

Muddy Creek in Lancaster County, Pennsylvania, was another trouble spot, and here women played a large role in the conflict, as they often did in the battle for the mid-Atlantic Lutheran and Reformed communities. In 1744 Jacob Lischy worked in this area and reported tensions and threats of violence. Here were the most wicked and godless people in the whole country because of their drinking and dancing, he wrote. The Separatists were against him, and at one point some members of the anti-Moravian Reformed faction planned to beat him in the church, with women leading the way. Yet the Moravians and their supporters were able to turn the tables and win a victory at Muddy Creek. By February 1745 Moravian reenforcements arrived, namely Christian Rauch and Rosina Nitschmann Münster. Some women in Muddy Creek had complained that they were not getting enough attention from Lischy, and Münster addressed their complaints by holding numerous spiritual meetings with them. All of the Moravians preached the emotional, revival message of the blood and wounds of the Savior. Later Spangenberg came, along with Johann Philip Meurer, and by spring the Moravians had won over Muddy Creek.[5]

In York, Pennsylvania, a long struggle between pro- and anti-Moravian factions of the German Reformed community erupted in 1746. York was a key community deep in the backcountry surrounded by Kreutz Creek, Conewago, and several other satellite communities. Whoever controlled York controlled these other communities as well, since the pastor at York usually served the others. In October Jacob Lischy was that pastor, and he received assistance from three other Moravian itinerants, Christian Rauch, Heinrich Beck, and Jacob Adolph. The Amsterdam Reformed preachers led by Boehm and later Michael Schlatter could not match this, nor could anyone else. This advantage in numbers, along with

Lischy's abilities as a revival preacher, meant that the Moravians were winning in the York area. But that October the anti-Moravian faction finally took a stand and fought back. Having read the Reformed polemics and heard the rumors that circulated in the colony, they claimed that Lischy was not a Reformed preacher, but really a Zinzendorfer. The anti-Moravian faction in York demanded the church door key, and when Lischy refused, they broke the lock, replaced it with their own, and threatened to do the same at Kreutz Creek and run out their schoolmaster as well. The next day Lischy and his people knocked the new lock off the door and went into the church. Lischy's colleague, Christian Rauch, feared what would happen next and went into the woods to pray. Later all four of the Moravian preachers met to discuss strategy. The next day, October 26, a large crowd from the anti-Moravian factions of many surrounding communities gathered at the York church and fought over control of the building with the pro-Moravian faction. One of the other Moravian itinerants described how the Devil had been at work in York—the Moravian had never seen so many people from the bush gather for a free-for-all, or *Tumult*, as they called it. The anti-Moravian faction blocked Lischy and his followers from entering the church, while "cursing and blaspheming in indescribable ways" ("und haben unbeschreiblich gescholten und gelästert"). They forced Lischy to have his service in the woods nearby, where a large number of people sat on the ground for his sermon. In the following weeks Lischy lost the battle for the York community and had to leave in disgrace. Even though enemies of the Moravians had removed him by force, a year later Moravian itinerants passing through the area noticed that people were still afraid of them.[6]

In 1747 the Hallensians won an important victory at the old Lutheran community of Tulpehocken, deep in the Pennsylvania backcountry, after a tense struggle that made the transatlantic pietist news when Fresenius published the story in his "American Reports." Tulpehocken was a much older Lutheran community, founded in 1723. It had been plagued by factional conflict long before Zinzendorf arrived in 1742 and offered the Lutherans a pastor. Many were tired of the constant maneuvering, intimidation, and fighting that had characterized religious life there and supported the Moravians, who sent seven men and two women to work at the Lutheran church and school building during the next four years and openly admitted their Bethlehem connection. High tide for the Moravians came when they built a new stone church for the community that Spangenberg consecrated in 1746. But the Moravians could not win over both of the old factions, and by the following year the Hallensians not only moved in to organize the opposing faction, but also attacked the pro-Moravian Lutherans as well. As they demonstrated time after time in the colonies, the Hallensians would not tolerate Moravians working in a Lutheran community near them, regardless of whether a church building was the focal point of that community. They sent one of their pastors, Johann Nicolaus Kurtz, to work in Tulpehocken, and they won the allegiance of Conrad Weiser, the local justice of the peace. Weiser had been friendly toward the Moravians earlier, but now was in a bitter dispute with the group. (At one point he wrote Spangenberg an angry letter, claiming that he had to disarm two Moravians who had come to his house with ill intentions.) The new alliance between this powerful man and the Hallensians was sealed when Mühlenberg married Weiser's daughter. In the same year the Hallensians helped their faction build a new stone church, just two miles from the new pro-Moravian Lutheran church. Now firmly entrenched in Tulpehocken, the Hallensians, Weiser, and their supporters were ready to heal the old schism by force, drive the Moravians completely out of the community, and purify the good Lutheran church once and for all. The Moravian Bishop Johann Christian Friedrich Cammerhof and Spangenberg visited Tulpehocken to try to save the Moravian half of the Lutheran community, but to no avail. The pro-Hallensians began the takeover by breaking into the pro-Moravian school building, claiming possession and leasing it. Next, on 25 September 1747, "our people," as Kurtz wrote in his diary, namely Conrad Weiser and a group of men, broke into the church built and paid for by the Moravians and their supporters. As the pro-Moravian faction looked on helplessly, Weiser proclaimed to Kurtz that the church was his. It was a total victory for the Hallensians, who now controlled two stone churches in Tulpehocken. The Moravians could not fight off a direct Hallensian assault supported by the ranking law enforcement officer in the area and withdrew. Bitter memories about the forceful takeover of the church lingered for years, and Kurtz later showed some remorse, but he remained the pastor there until 1770.[7]

For a long time most historians who studied the struggles for control of religious communities during the Great Awakening were unaware of the level of religious violence that occurred in the Middle Colonies. Many focused instead on lay-clergy relations to explain the communal conflict that they did find. A number of them have argued that the democratization of religion, or the acceleration of lay involvement in local rule, began during the Great Awakening and developed in ways that would become important during the Imperial Crisis and American Revolution in the subsequent generation. One of these historians, A. G. Roeber, stresses the importance of church property issues among the Lutherans in these struggles. He and other historians for the most part support what one might call the "layman's progress" thesis, which emphasizes that the laity successfully challenged clerical authority during the Great Awakening, and that this led directly or indirectly to further challenges from below during the crisis with Britain beginning in the 1760s and in the Revolution itself. The Revolution, according to this representation, was in part a successful continuation of local struggles for more freedom (religious and otherwise) by ordinary Americans that began during the Great Awakening.[8]

But the conflict between the radical Moravians and their enemies that erupted in nearly all of the Lutheran and German Reformed communities of the mid-Atlantic colonies during the Great Awakening was of a fundamentally different nature. Until the early 1750s, the laity in these communities contended most of all, not with the clergy over control of their affairs, but rather with each other over whether they should accept the Moravians in their communities. In this region the radical Moravian alternative was spreading so rapidly and the orthodox response was so vehement that both views could not coexist in one religious community. The stakes were high for both sides: achieving Christian unity and providing badly needed service in a colonial situation on the part of the Moravians, and stopping the work of the Devil on the part of their orthodox opponents, who associated Moravian threats to gender and confessional order with Satan.

The question is, what caused ordinary men and women in these communities to attack the Moravians and their supporters with words and weapons? We do not know the thoughts and motivations of most people in these communities during these violent episodes, because they did not write them down—or if they did, they were not preserved. We only know what these men and women *did*. To assist in an interpretation of why they acted as they did, we can consider how people in similar circumstances during this era reacted and what we know about the times and the place in question here (i.e., the Middle Colonies in the mid-eighteenth century). This, combined with evidence that is available for these specific communities, makes it possible to conjecture what roles confessional and especially gender issues may have played in motivating the violence. Consider the following:

Both historical, cultural developments in early modern Europe and new conditions in the colonies influenced these Lutheran and Reformed immigrants and their descendants. Early modern historians demonstrated long ago that men and women involved in community violence often believed that their actions were not only legitimate, but necessary, normal, and expected, even though not officially sanctioned by civil or ecclesiastical authority. This was how people in early modern and colonial communities defended their sacred space and values (including values shaped by religion and gender) when they believed something or someone threatened them.[9] Also, consider that the mid-eighteenth century was a period of rapid change and increasing ethnic and religious diversity that resulted from heavy immigration in the mid-Atlantic colonies. Under these conditions tensions developed between those who promoted freedom on the one hand, and those who sought to bring more order in their colonial society (see Chapter One). Further, it is clear that gender and confessionalism played an important role in the larger, transatlantic conflict involving the Moravians and their numerous enemies in the mid-eighteenth century.

Consider also the evidence available for these specific communities in the Middle Colonies. The beliefs and activities of the Moravians themselves are relatively clear, as is the fact that they won over many supporters in these communities, especially in the initial phases of the conflict. Further, we know what their enemies said about the Moravians, and what people in the Delaware Valley congregations read and heard about Zinzendorf and his followers. These were mostly literate people in a colonial society undergoing a "Great Awakening," for which printed materials played an important role. Yet though most were literate, few if any committed to paper their views on "gender," or how this might have motivated them to attack the Moravians and their supporters, nor is it realistic for historians later to expect them to have done so. Further, we know what alternatives people in these communities were offered: a patriarchal, confessional one presented by the Hallensian, Amsterdam, and Uppsalan pastors, and an ecumenical alternative presented by the Moravians that offered a higher profile for women and female qualities of the Trinity. These two views were fundamentally incompatible, and ordinary colonists had to decide which they wanted.

We know all of this, and we know how men and women in the Lutheran and Reformed communities responded to the Moravian presence. From this, and the absence of clear evidence supporting other views, the question can be raised about what role beliefs and values concerning gender and confessional issues may have played in motivating many ordinary Lutheran and Reformed men and women to attack the Moravians and their supporters, whom they perceived as trying to take over their communities. The three case studies that follow show how deeply mid-Atlantic communities were affected by violence and allow us to assess the possibilities that issues concerning gender and confessionalism caused it, instead of something else.

Philadelphia

In the summer of 1742 a violent struggle for control of the Lutheran and Reformed union church on Arch Street in Philadelphia erupted, and the Moravians (including Count Zinzendorf himself) and the Amsterdamer Johann Philip Boehm were involved. Tension had been growing for months among rival factions of the church, as Zinzendorf won over Reformed people in the area and the Lutherans at Arch Street, where he installed Johann Christoph Pyrlaeus (see Figure 13) as their pastor. (Pyrlaeus was a trained Lutheran from Vogtland-Sachsen who had recently joined the Moravians at Herrnhaag.) On the other hand, Boehm influenced the faction that controlled the Reformed congregation. Thus, a pro-Moravian Lutheran faction and an anti-Moravian Reformed faction controlled the sacred space in the same building, which they rented and took turns using on Sundays. But because of the persuasive revival tactics of the Moravians on the one hand, and the passionate rhetoric against them from Boehm on the other hand, there was growing tension between the two groups sharing the building, and the situation was becoming increasingly unstable during the late spring and early summer months.[10]

The violence began in July, and the two sides could not agree on who started it or why. The numerous surviving accounts provide conflicting reports as to the details, but it is clear that it began in the Arch Street church on Sunday, 18 July 1742, and that what happened that day shaped the future of the community there. Lutheran, Reformed, and Moravian clergy and laity all told their stories in ways to support their causes. Published accounts of the violence appeared in newspapers, polemics, and pamphlets on both sides of the Atlantic. But, through the smoke and fire of religious fear and hatred that swirled around the controversy, there was some general agreement on the basic course of events that Sunday and in the following days.

Sunday, 18 July, was a Lutheran day at the union church, so Pyrlaeus and the Lutheran congregation assembled before the meeting house, but found it locked. In recent days some of the Lutherans had been showing displeasure with Pyrlaeus and questioned the validity of the Moravian connection, so he was not entirely surprised to find the door locked. They sent for the key, but the council member in charge refused to give it to them, according to a newspaper account, because the man with the key had gone to Germantown and left it with the church warden and his wife, who were not home. The pro-Moravian accounts say that they brought in a locksmith to open it, but the anti-Moravian accounts say that they broke it open with irons and tongs. After breaking through the door, the pro-Moravian faction filed inside and Pyrlaeus began the Sunday service. While the pro-Moravian group was singing, an anti-Moravian crowd began to gather in the street outside the church. After some time four men in the crowd decided that they had had enough of crypto-Moravians trying to take over their church and went

Figure 13. Johann Christoph Pyrlaeus (1713–1785), the Moravian preacher who in July 1742 was attacked during a sermon in Philadelphia, dragged from the pulpit, and beaten in the street by a crowd of German Reformed settlers. Oil painting, artist unknown, mid-eighteenth century. GS 264, Unity Archives, Herrnhut.

inside. Just as Pyrlaeus was beginning to preach, one of the four demanded that he stop and leave immediately, but Pyrlaeus refused. Then one of the crowd cried out, "Strike the dog dead!" ("*Schlag den Hund todt!*"), and the four men grabbed Pyrlaeus by the arms and dragged him out of the pulpit and into the street. Johann Adam Gruber's anti-Moravian account, published by Fresenius, says that "that tremendous noise and a lot of cursing and pushing from both sides took place" ("große Lermen, viel Scheltworte, auch einige Armstöße beyderseits gab"). Boehm described a "great tumult" that arose, and Mühlenberg later reported that "they trampled, pushed, and knocked each other about, and the women began to scream" ("sie haben einander unbestehens gedrängt, getreten, die Weiber geschrieen"). The pro-Moravians wrote that there were "the most horrible expletives and yelling" ("horribelsten Ausdrucken und Geschrey") as Pyrlaeus, who did not resist, was dragged into the street and beaten by the crowd.[11]

The confrontation on Arch Street quickly became a major story in the colony's newspapers. In Franklin's *Pennsylvania Gazette* Zinzendorf declared his and Pyrlaeus's work in the Philadelphia church to be legitimate and that he knew of no opposition to it. Because the Calvinists resorted to violence, he would stand by his declaration not to leave unless the law required it.[12] A week later Zinzendorf's opponents published a point-for-point refutation of his claims in Andrew Bradford's *American Weekly Mercury*. Zinzendorf and Pyrlaeus had not received a call from the majority of the members in the church, and Pyrlaeus was a Moravian, not a Lutheran, as Zinzendorf claimed. The Moravians were trying to divide and weaken their church. They wanted no Moravian ministers among them, especially if appointed by the count.[13]

After the religious violence of 18 July matters quickly escalated in Philadelphia. While each side had a number of their opponents arrested, Count Zinzendorf heard the news about Pyrlaeus and hurried back from a meeting with members of the Six Iroquois Nations in Tulpehocken, seventy miles away. He arrived in Philadelphia on the Saturday evening after the Pyrlaeus beating. The next morning he led the Moravian-Lutheran faction to the church, but it was so crowded with Reformed worshipers that they could not get in. (This was their Sunday in the union church.) Meanwhile, inside, the noisy Reformed congregants declared that they were no longer sharing the building with the Lutherans. Zinzendorf's group filed in anyway, and a tense quiet spread through the room as the tall European nobleman stood opposite the lay reader, hoping to intimidate him. He did, but the count bade him to continue.

The Reformed service ended, but someone told the people to remain in their places. Zinzendorf then addressed the Calvinists, demanding to know who had attacked Pyrlaeus the previous Sunday. Showing no deference to the European count, several members openly declared that they had done it, and they threatened to do the same to Zinzendorf if he did not leave. Then the count tried to shame them. He declared that they may have the church—he did not want to fight over it. Quoting Scripture about not trying to take back what people have unjustly taken, he said that they would build another at his own expense, and if they tried to take it, they might have that church too. But then Zinzendorf provoked them: if they had done their injustice in an orderly manner, the count went on to say, they might already have the church. But, since they used force and attacked Pyrlaeus in an uproar without warning, they would have to wait until the new church was built. The count said he was a great enemy of uproars in the commonwealth and was afraid of no one, and despised those who would intercede for the transgressors. He would show them that nothing was to be gained by violence. The anti-Moravian Reformed elders replied that they had nothing against his preaching to the Lutherans, but they resented his attempts to take over the entire church. Zinzendorf snapped that they were not competent judges in the matter. This outraged the anti-Moravian Reformed audience, and people began shouting at Zinzendorf. According to the pro-Moravian account, which seems unlikely, both parties settled down and departed quietly, but according to an anti-Moravian account a number of people, especially women, shouted at Zinzendorf, ran him out of the church, and warned him never to return.[14]

Reports of violence between the factions continued. The day after Zinzendorf's confrontation with the Reformed group in the meeting house, he and others in the pro-Moravian group met at the count's quarters in Stephen Benezet's house to discuss what to do next. Among other things, they were writing down their version of what had just happened.[15] According to an anti-Moravian report, a half-drunken man came to the house and wanted them to remove his name from their membership lists. He would not be quiet, so a newcomer to the pro-Moravian faction went out into the street and beat him with a club. Later the same source reported that Zinzendorf himself was attacked.[16] Tensions and accusations continued, and both sides met, but could not come to an agreement.[17]

The action in Philadelphia that July generated a number of court cases. Apparently Zinzendorf managed to win a slander case against Jacob Bauerle of Lancaster, who had circulated a fabricated story that the count would see to it that the four men who attacked Pyrlaeus in Philadelphia would hang. The most important case, however, involved the trial of the men accused of attacking the pro-Moravians on 18 July. Pyrlaeus refused to press charges against those who assaulted him, but other injured parties in the pro-Moravian faction did. The judgment issued on 16 November 1742 was mixed, but essentially Zinzendorf and his supporters lost the case. Only one of the men was found guilty of assault, and none were found guilty of rioting. Further, in a lawsuit decided in February 1743 the court ruled that the Moravians had no legal right to be in the church anyway, as it had been rented to the "old Lutherans," not the "new Lutherans," or Moravians.[18]

The verdicts concerning the 18 July incident meant not only that the pro-Moravians lost the church, but that Zinzendorf had lost the moral high ground he had won when facing down the anti-Moravian Reformed faction the week after the Pyrlaeus assault. To Philadelphians it now looked as though the anti-Moravian faction had been right all along: Zinzendorf and the Moravians never had a right to be there in the first place. It was a crushing blow to the Moravian cause and meant that they permanently lost the German Lutheran and Reformed communities of Philadelphia. The Moravians did build a new church in Philadelphia within a few months, but while they caused some problems for Mühlenberg, Boehm, and others, they never again seriously contended for influence in the big Lutheran and Reformed congregations of the city.[19]

The Moravians were bitter after losing Philadelphia, and they joined the chorus blaming Boehm for instigating the Reformed attack on Pyrlaeus. Peter Böhler also blamed the Amsterdamer for the "mutiny" that led to the violence against his colleague. Richard Peters, an Anglican minister and secretary of the colony's land office, agreed with the Moravian assessment. Peters knew Boehm well from their work together on land issues for the Penn family and was essentially a neutral in the religious conflict. He summarized the July 1742 incident in a letter to Thomas Penn and blamed the Lutherans for causing the riot, but had harsh words about Boehm and his hatred of the Moravians, even stating that Boehm helped the crowd remove Pyrlaeus from the church. There is a "mortal aversion between Behme's congregation & ye Count's People," Peters wrote, "but the whole of the Count's Party gains ground, having made considerable converts," which was something that Boehm could not bear. When Peters counseled Boehm not to be so harsh, Boehm's eyes "struck Fire, & he declared with great passion he would as soon agree with the Devil as with the Count."[20]

The struggle in the union church on Arch Street was not about property or a clash between the clergy and the laity. The sacred space in which these people fought was a dilapidated wooden house that they rented. The Moravians had no interest in property and later built a new church in Philadelphia anyway. Also, while there was class-based resentment against Zinzendorf involved in the conflict, the main problem with the count and Pyrlaeus was that they were Moravians, not that they were clergy trying to expand their power in the community. Many of the lay men and women in the Arch Street community supported these pastors, while many others listened to Boehm and attacked them because they were Moravian.

Confessionalism and ecumenism, however, do seem to have played a critical role in the violent struggle for control of the union church on Arch Street. The Moravians never attempted to conceal who they were in Philadelphia: Count Zinzendorf preached openly in the Arch Street meeting house, and initially the Lutherans accepted him and Pyrlaeus, which meant that they accepted the ecumenical view that a legitimate Lutheran preacher could be associated with the Moravians. The Reformed parishioners, on the other hand, did not accept the Moravian ecumenical view, and it was they who led the attack on Pyrlaeus. Instead they chose the orthodox position offered by Boehm. The Reformed parishioners might have been willing to share the building with another group like the Lutherans, who respected confessional boundaries, but they were not willing to share sacred space with the ecumenical Moravians, who they feared would not respect those boundaries. When the Halle Lutheran Mühlenberg arrived that December, faced Zinzendorf personally, and wrestled leadership of the Lutheran community from the count, it became clear from that point that the Philadelphia Lutheran members would also support the orthodox position and sever all relations with the ecumenical Moravians.

Gender was probably an important issue motivating lay members of the union church in the conflict as well. Direct evidence is lacking, but it is clear that at least some of the Moravians' controversial beliefs and practices had been made known in Philadelphia. Zinzendorf had recently preached open sermons on the Trinity, including emphasizing Christ as the Creator and the Holy Spirit as mother, and Moravian women had recently preached in and around Philadelphia, gaining a lot of attention. Those members of the pro-Moravian faction must have been aware of this when they accepted Zinzendorf and Pyrlaeus into their church. Also, Boehm passionately attacked the Moravians in the colony, making their gender transgressions known to ordinary people in Philadelphia. (He had been reading Kulenkamp's polemics, in which the Amsterdam clergyman condemned Moravian views of the Trinity and their use of women preachers, labeling both as the work of the Devil.) Many Reformed people in the Arch Street church followed the patriarchal, confessional order offered by Boehm and Amsterdam as a way to protect their community from the blasphemous, more female piety of the Moravians. They likely believed Boehm when he told them that the Devil was at work in their community and Count Zinzendorf was his instrument. Sharing a church with Satan and his hosts was more than some Reformed members could bear, so they removed the problem and felt justified using force to do so.

Members of the anti-Moravian faction violently removed the Moravian threat from the Reformed community, sealing their victory with the court decision, and the Lutherans soon removed them as well. Mühlenberg arrived in December 1742, after the violence but before the court hearings, and helped to shore up the Arch Street Lutheran community against the Moravians. It was an early double defeat for the Moravians in Philadelphia, but many more battles would be fought before the larger issue of what kind of religious and social order would reign in the Lutheran and Reformed communities of the Delaware Valley would be settled.

Raccoon, New Jersey

While the importance of confessionalism in causing the religious violence in Philadelphia is clear and the role of gender must be inferred, there is evidence that both played a role in the violence that took place in the Swedish Lutheran community of Raccoon, New Jersey, in 1743 and 1744. The crucial difference was that in some cases the Uppsalan and Moravian pastors faced each other with their supporters gathered about them when the violence erupted. (Boehm, on the other hand, never faced Zinzendorf directly in Philadelphia and was not present when the violence took place.) This meant that the very people who so rigorously and articulately condemned the Moravians on the points of gender and confessional order were present during the violence, helped instigate it, and clearly had a following in the community.[21] In the case of one Uppsalan pastor present during the violence at Raccoon, Gabriel Naesman, it is also clear that he was motivated by a near paranoia of Moravian women and gender practices.

The religious violence at Raccoon was part of the power struggle between the Swedish Moravian Paul Daniel Bryzelius and his supporters on the one hand, and the Uppsalan pastor Gabriel Naesman and his supporters on the other hand. Bryzelius began work at Raccoon after his tense scouting tour among the Swedish communities in the Delaware Valley in early 1743, that included Gabriel Falk's violent attack on him with a whip in Manatawny and accusations by New Lights that Bryzelius was trying to get the Uppsalan Peter Tranberg's wife to join the Moravians. Unlike those in Philadelphia, the parishioners at Raccoon apparently were not aware of Bryzelius's connection to the Moravians. Tranberg, the only other Uppsalan pastor in the region, was probably unaware of this when he recommended that Bryzelius go to Raccoon and Penns Neck, New Jersey, where the Swedes needed a pastor. Both communities, located fifteen miles apart, had been the difficult step-children of the Uppsalan pastors, who did not want them but found themselves obligated to do something with them anyway. Raccoon had one of the densest populations of Swedes in the region, but was also a mixed ethnic community, with English, Irish, and Germans making up part of the congregation. Uppsala had sent only two permanent pastors to the community since the late seventeenth century, neither of whom stayed for long, and the Uppsalan pastors sent to Wicaco and Christina did not visit Raccoon often.[22]

The Moravians had their biggest success among the Swedes in Raccoon and also encountered the most resistance in this community. Bryzelius began preaching there in March 1743, but a pro-Uppsalan faction formed around an older trustee, who condemned Bryzelius and invited Gabriel Naesman to visit Raccoon. Naesman arrived in October 1743 and found a divided community, with the Moravians holding the upper hand. Naesman was so worried about the ground the Moravians were winning in the area that he agreed to visit when he could, even though he was overworked and fending off Moravians elsewhere. For the Raccoon community this meant that pastors from both Bethlehem and Uppsala would attempt to serve them, as they had in Philadelphia, presenting them with the ecumenical, more feminine religious order on the one hand, and the confessional, patriarchal order on the other. When Naesman journeyed from Philadelphia and preached his first sermon in Raccoon on 9 December 1743, this touched off a schism and violence in the church. Both Naesman and Bryzelius left detailed, widely varying accounts of what happened that day in the church.[23]

When Naesman and his supporters faced Bryzelius and his supporters in the church during Sunday services that December day, their encounter represented a dramatic showdown between confessional, patriarchal and ecumenical, feminine religious order in the colonies. Naesman reached the chancel first for the Sunday service on 9 December and stood in the door to prevent Bryzelius from taking it. Following the orthodox Swedish style, he began his reading and singing, followed by a sermon in which he denounced Bryzelius. Meanwhile Bryzelius occupied the minister's chair a few feet away and waited patiently. It was the first time the two had ever seen each other, and there were no formal introductions. After the sermon Naesman stepped down so that a layman could read the creed, but Bryzelius would not let him sit in the parson's pew, "looking fiercely at me as if he wanted to frighten me," Naesman wrote. After the sermon an "astonishing uproar" broke out—Bryzelius claimed it began as soon as Naesman stepped down from the chancel, but Naesman claimed it began after a pro-Uppsalan elder asked everyone to stay after the service for a meeting. Both agreed that it lasted a long time and became violent. Sometime during the commotion the pro-Uppsalan elder announced that they wanted Naesman to preach in Raccoon once per month. Then Bryzelius cried out that he would come every fortnight. To this a pro-Uppsalan elder, who had studied in Sweden and knew the archbishop, responded that Bryzelius was incapable of conducting services correctly and was not a properly called pastor. Then a number of Bryzelius's supporters crowded into the chancel and proclaimed that they wanted him as their preacher. A former Catholic, who had married a Swedish Moravian woman and converted to get her land, yelled that God had sent Bryzelius. Then the shouting really began—Naesman wrote that he never thought that such howling could take place in a church.[24]

Women on both sides played a central role in the violence at Raccoon, but the misogynist Naesman believed that those who supported the Moravians threatened proper gender order. Like Quakers, Moravian women wanted to have the most say in the parish, he thought. The pro-Moravian women were in passionate contention with women in the anti-Moravian faction, who supported the confessional, patriarchal alternative offered by Naesman. The pro-Moravian women also shouted and charged at the pro-Uppsalan men in the church. It was as if "a battalion of horsemen had pulled each other by the hair," he wrote. Naesman tried to get to two women who wanted him to baptize their children, but the pro-Moravian faction prevented him for two hours. He managed to press his way to the chancel and begged for silence, but the pro-Moravians shouted even more loudly and attempted to goad him into an angry outburst. Then they charged against a pro-Uppsalan elder, and that faction began to waver.

After listening to the shouting for about an hour Naesman began shouting himself, got the crowd to quiet down, and began questioning Bryzelius on his background and authority to preach in Raccoon. Naesman then showed his university diploma, and, according to Bryzelius, declared that whoever did not have one was not a true teacher. In a scene that was repeated often in the Swedish and German churches of the mid-Atlantic colonies during this period, competing pastors appealed to higher authority in Europe for legitimacy and used written documentation to impress their congregations and win support. Those parishioners who were impressed by this sort of thing usually supported the orthodox pastors when this happened, as they did with Naesman at Raccoon that day. As some of the crowd began to rally to his side he lashed out at Bryzelius, claiming that he had been gathering the sheep there so that he might devour them like a wolf. Then one of the pro-Uppsalan members grabbed Bryzelius by the hand, spun him around, and told him he was a devil for doing what he was doing.

Naesman may have had the legitimacy of Uppsala's documentation, but Bryzelius had gotten to Raccoon first and acquired legitimacy from the people by working for them. An Irish Catholic whom Naesman called a "Moravian" and who had been laughing at the Uppsalan pastor during his sermon cried out that Bryzelius had been sent by God, not men, and that was enough for them. This rallied the pro-Moravian crowd, which rejected Naesman's orthodox position, and the authority of Uppsala behind it, in favor of the Moravian alternative. The crowd forced itself toward Naesman and his supporters "to assault and frighten us," Naesman wrote. Whenever he spoke they laughed and shouted him down. Finally a Swedish immigrant and a few other "dauntless comrades" advanced to shield Naesman, and the dialogue continued. Naesman believed that he had pointed out several other lies by Bryzelius, but the Moravian only laughed at him scornfully. He called Bryzelius a liar and a thief and called for a formal examination of him. Naesman then called on all who supported Bryzelius to step forward and sign a petition to the archbishop in Uppsala, but this was shouted down. So he asked all who were against Bryzelius to step forward and sign, and about thirty did. With this Bryzelius left the church laughing, perhaps because the number that signed against him was so small (150 to 200 usually attended services at Raccoon), and promised to come back in a fortnight to preach.

At this point most of the Raccoon parishioners were pro-Moravian, but pro-Uppsalan men dominated the church council, and the clergy were divided—Bryzelius was an ecumenical Moravian and Naesman was an orthodox Uppsalan Lutheran. The clergy, the council, and the rest of the laity competed for control of the community, as happened frequently during the Great Awakening, but in this case they did not compete with each other for power.[25] Instead, each of the three groups was divided, and they competed among themselves for either the patriarchal confessional ideal represented by Naesman, or the radical alternative offered by Bryzelius. For months the clergy, especially Bryzelius, struggled to hold services while opponents in the audience shouted at him. On the other hand, church officers attempted to lock out their opponents when it was time for them to hold services.

Raccoon was deadlocked over its two choices, and, after months of tension, the anti-Moravian faction decided to force the issue. When Bryzelius arrived to preach one Sunday in January 1744 as scheduled, members of the pro-Uppsalan faction were waiting for him. Fifteen Swedes, Germans, and Irish with clubs, led by a pro-Uppsalan elder, stood in the church doorway and refused to allow Bryzelius and his faction to enter. When the Bryzelius group tried to force their way in, the fifteen men began swinging their clubs. One of them grabbed Bryzelius by the neck, while another held his club to him, but the elder intervened and told them to let Bryzelius go. The Moravian pastor was so frightened that he announced he would not preach at Raccoon any more, made his way to Philadelphia to see his Swedish compatriot Laurentius Nyberg, and then hurried back to Bethlehem. The pro-Moravian faction reported the attack to the governor, who chose not to get involved, but a justice of the peace responded. Thirteen men of the pro-Uppsalan faction were indicted and scheduled to appear before the Gloucester County court in March. The contest for control of the church at Raccoon was far from over, but for the moment the pro-Uppsalan faction relied on brute force and was now winning. A few days later they tried to consolidate their victory by stacking the church council with their supporters, thus insuring that Moravian preachers could not be formally asked to return. It worked, and now the pro-Uppsalan faction had complete control of the church offices.[26]

The pro-Uppsalan faction was winning, and when Bryzelius returned to the field of conflict in Raccoon in March 1744, after a few weeks in Bethlehem to regain his courage and receive instructions on how to handle the situation, he was promptly arrested for breaking the King's peace with his preaching and was confined in a tavern. The Raccoon parishioners remained divided: the wife of one of Bryzelius's accusers came to the Moravian pastor crying and apologized, but a crowd of men and women gathered at the tavern and began to ridicule and question him. When Bryzelius stood before them in silence (as instructed by Zinzendorf in these matters), the crowd became even more angry. Why did he come back, when he knew they had a warrant out for his arrest, they asked. Why did he not take a different road? Why did he not leave and never come back?[27]

At Bryzelius's grand jury trial at the county courthouse in Woodbury, twenty miles away, the drama between proponents of the two competing religious and gender orders continued. In the hearing immediately preceding, the judge fined and discharged thirteen of the men who had attacked Bryzelius, then dealt with the charge against the Moravian. The pro-Uppsalan faction arrived with three lawyers (two Quakers and a Lutheran), along with Naesman, Peter Tranberg, and a Philadelphia merchant named Peter Koch—at the time all leading proponents of Uppsala's cause and mode of piety in the Delaware Valley. After arbitration failed, they went to trial. The constable brought Bryzelius into the crowded courtroom, before Judge Hinckman, the grand jury, five Swedish attestors, and his adversaries, including the thirteen men from the pro-Uppsalan faction in Raccoon who had just been fined for their assault on the pro-Moravians, as well as the pro-Uppsalan preachers and lawyers. Bryzelius told his story, and the charges were dropped, although the judge pronounced that he would not be allowed to preach in the Raccoon church again until the congregation was united. After this, pro-Moravian parishioners from Raccoon immediately announced that Bryzelius could preach in their houses until then. A jury member then shook his hand, and some gentlemen from Philadelphia praised Bryzelius for not allowing himself to be examined by the Uppsalan pastors while in arbitration. This was more than Bryzelius's furious adversaries could take, and one of them—a man who had locked the church door at Raccoon to keep the pro-Moravians out and had just been himself fined by the court—flew into a rage and had to be held down by seven men. This so shocked the other adversaries that they apologized to Bryzelius and offered to make peace with him. According to the Moravian pastor, this included even Naesman, who said that he would no longer preach against Bryzelius. For a time after this the Moravian had no trouble preaching in English and Swedish in New Jersey, including in Raccoon, with more listeners than ever.[28]

The shocking courtroom scene and the verdicts in Woodbury created sympathy for the Moravian cause among the New Jersey Swedes and shifted the tide in the conflict back in favor of the Moravians and against the Uppsalan preachers and their supporters. Bryzelius kept returning to Raccoon and other communities, and Nyberg visited as well, although they were not allowed to preach in the church. Meanwhile his duties in Philadelphia prevented Naesman from preaching more than once per month in Raccoon, and he complained that the pro-Moravian faction still attacked him maliciously, spreading lies to get him removed from the Raccoon pulpit. By early August 1744 a pro-Uppsalan council member collected signatures for a request to Uppsala for a new minister, but he sent the petition through the Swedish Lutheran pastor in Philadelphia, Laurentius Nyberg. Meanwhile the Moravians were popular again and could put enough preachers in the field to keep their supporters satisfied, while the pro-Uppsalan faction waited for a response from Uppsala to their petition, unaware that Nyberg was with the Moravians and never forwarded it to Sweden. Discredited by the events in the Gloucester County courthouse, many enemies of the Moravians either switched sides or kept their distance. Naesmann, now descending into the depths of his misogynist paranoia, blamed all of his troubles on the Moravians, and according to rumor kept three loaded guns hanging in his house, swearing to shoot dead any Moravian he caught at night.[29]

As with the Arch Street community in Philadelphia, the religious violence at Raccoon was not about property or a struggle between the laity and the clergy for control of the church. In this case the pro-Uppsalan faction won the church building by force, but conflict in the community continued and for a time worsened because they were fighting about more than a building. Instead, the pro-Uppsalan faction wanted to remove Moravian influence from all of Raccoon. But their attempt to use the courts against the pro-Moravian faction backfired, and instead of sealing the victory, as it had done in Philadelphia, the shocking court-room debacle insured that the conflict would continue. Moreover, in Raccoon the battle lines were not drawn between those for or against increased lay or clerical power. Instead, ordinary male and female parishioners and church councilmen rallied behind the pastors who promoted the form of religious order that they wanted.

The importance of gender issues to the conflict in Raccoon is best revealed in the showdowns between Naesman and Bryzelius. Until the arrival of Acrelius in 1749 Naesman was the primary proponent of Uppsala's orthodox position in the Delaware Valley. It was Naesman who led the charge against the ecumenical, female-oriented piety represented by Bryzelius and his followers. (His Uppsalan colleague, Peter Tranberg, for the most part refused to get involved outside of his parish in Wilmington, Delaware.) The fact that these two pastors and their supporters clashed in the church and the courthouse represents direct evidence that confessional and gender issues motivated not only the pastors, but also their followers—ordinary Lutheran men and women. Naesman and other pastors sent by Uppsala to the region were familiar with Moravian activities and the beliefs and practices of the count's group. Uppsala informed them of the Moravian threat with letters, polemics, and briefings before they departed for North America. Essentially the Uppsalan pastors brought the critique of Moravian confessional and gender order to the Delaware Valley communities and disseminated the message among church members in Raccoon and elsewhere where violent attacks occurred. The support ordinary men and women gave to Naesman during these encounters suggests that many people in Raccoon heard the message, believed it, and attacked, in the way they often did in this era when they felt their community was threatened. The fact that the man in the courthouse who attempted to attack Bryzelius so shocked the Uppsalan pastors present and caused them to apologize to the Moravian suggests that there may have been some disjunction between the way the clergy and the laity felt about the use of violence. Communal religious violence from the lower orders was often unsanctioned by proper religious authority in this era. But the presence of Bryzelius and Naesman, together with Naesman's misogynist cries when the chips were down, suggest that gender and confessional issues were important in the conflict. Further, the views of the Uppsalan pastors on gender and confessional issues were clear, as it is clear that they hoped to drive the Moravians out of the Swedish Lutheran communities in the Delaware Valley. The fact that this ultimately happened and that it was ordinary people in the communities (not the church or the state) that did it, suggests that the Uppsalans were ultimately successful in dealing with the Moravian threat.

When word finally arrived from Uppsala that these ecumenical Moravians were really deluded liars utterly condemned in Sweden, the tide began to turn in Raccoon, as it did elsewhere in the Swedish communities of the Delaware Valley. Not only had the Moravian pastors been lying, it seemed, but the women preachers they were beginning to use in the Swedish communities were part of a much deeper and dangerous threat to proper gender order in the spiritual realm and the community that was associated with the work of Satan. With this news the pro-Uppsalan faction in Raccoon, still in possession of the church building, went on the offensive again to remove the Moravian threat from the community itself, and ultimately they succeeded in pushing the Moravians out of Raccoon permanently.[30]

Lancaster, Pennsylvania

The fight for German Lancaster turned violent in late 1745 and 1746, when a series of clashes occurred between pro- and anti-Moravian factions in the Lutheran church. Several accounts of the conflict have survived, including one by Laurentius Nyberg, the Swedish Moravian pastor who led one of the German Lutheran factions in Lancaster, as well as an anti-Moravian account from Mühlenberg, who came to the town during the immediate aftermath of the violence and tried unsuccessfully to settle the conflict. These, along with newspaper accounts, portray a new community fighting over control of sacred and secular space in a colony where the two were supposed to be kept separate.[31] The new town of Lancaster was important to all sides because it was a rapidly growing county seat with a number of satellite congregations. Like York, whoever controlled Lancaster had a major advantage in these other congregations as well. Newspaper coverage was extensive, and before the conflict ended the governor and preachers from throughout the province were involved.

As was often the case, the Moravians moved into Lancaster early and quickly established a strong support base because of their willingness to commit a good pastor and provide other assistance for free. They assigned Nyberg to Lancaster in December 1743, who immediately began preaching in German to large crowds. As his success continued, the Lutherans began building a new stone church building, which Nyberg consecrated in November 1744.[32]

By the autumn of 1745 things were going so well for the Moravian mission in Lancaster that Spangenberg asked Nyberg to find a meeting place for their upcoming synod, and this sparked the community violence. Nyberg spoke with the mayor to receive permission to use the courthouse and worked hard on other local arrangements for the conference. He saw to it that the horses were stabled, ordered bread to be baked and an ox killed and roasted for the some two hundred persons who attended, and boarded sixteen of them himself. Nyberg's energetic support of the Moravian conference baffled some of the elders who did not like the group. Many began to speculate that Nyberg might be connected to the Moravians. The elders warned Nyberg of pending trouble at the conference, but he continued the preparations, procuring the key to the courthouse and posting a guard at the entrance to the building and another on the stairwell. The synod then met on the upper floor, and when they refused to admit several "honorable and moderate citizens" the trouble began. According to Nyberg, Justice of the Peace Edward Smout attended the synod and had to quell a riot intended to disrupt it. While this action gained them sympathy with Smout, the uproar continued all night until the Moravian synod participants left town. One account noted that the crowd pelted Spangenberg with mud during the commotion.[33]

The trouble continued four days later on Sunday, 12 December—what Nyberg described in his journal as a "Day of Darkness." After the anti-Moravian riot at the courthouse the Lutheran congregation began dividing over Nyberg. Many believed he was a Moravian, not a true Lutheran, and wanted him removed from their church, while others did not care about this and wanted to keep him. As Nyberg approached the entrance the disaffected people cried out against him as he passed by, "There is the Wounds-preacher, the Blood-Preacher." The next day three men went to Governor George Thomas and lodged a disturbing the peace complaint against Nyberg. On the following Sunday the "whole Town & Country" crowded into the church, laughing, grinning, bawling, quarreling, and some even cursing loudly. One group surrounded the altar, while another guarded the path to the pulpit. All the while someone played the new organ, and everything was in "the most horrible Confusion." Finally the organ player stopped, and Nyberg stood up on a pew to speak. He told the crowd that many thought he was the cause of the disorder, but this simply was not true. No one could prove anything against his doctrine or morals, and he reminded them that Martin Luther once said "Where the Gospel is preach'd, there it causeth Tumult." His preaching and their actions had now made it clear what Luther meant. Nyberg proclaimed that he would not give in and told the crowd that he would preach Christ crucified, which meant blood and wounds and everything else. Those that could not hear this Gospel were excused. Accordingly many went out of the church, and those who remained bonded to become the pro-Moravian faction of the Lutheran church.[34]

Now the issues were out in the open in Lancaster, and battle lines were drawn. This was no showdown between the clergy and the laity over how to share power in their church. It was about whether this Lutheran community wanted Moravians and all that they represented in its midst. They were now aware that the Moravians did not adhere to Lutheran orthodoxy and that they offered a radical alternative to what male and female relations should be. They knew from the polemics, sermons, and rumors circulating in Lancaster and throughout the Delaware Valley that the Moravians maintained strange views about the Trinity, bizarre spiritual relationships with Jesus, and irregular practices regarding the family in their closed communities. The Moravian synod, Nyberg and his assistants, and the polemics and rumors informed them on these issues. Many Lancaster Lutherans *wanted* what the Moravians offered, including their ecumenical, gender alternative. Many others did not, and when they jeered the "blood and wounds" preacher, using that well-known short expression for everything that was wrong with the Moravians during this period, it indicated that they now believed that a dangerous Satanic threat had emerged in their community, as it had elsewhere in the region and apparently throughout British North America and the Protestant Atlantic world, if one believed the polemics.

In January 1745 tensions between the pro- and anti-Moravian factions reached a boiling point, and people began attending church wearing guns and swords. Justice of the Peace Smout begged Nyberg not to preach there until tempers cooled, but Nyberg and his supporters insisted. They approached the church for a service, but found a huge lock on the door. While they worked to break the lock, a disorderly crowd of about eighty people in the anti-Moravian faction gathered to stop them. Mühlenberg called the women in the crowd "brave," but Nyberg wrote that they were outrageous, and some pinched him as he passed through the crowd. The women were less delicate with Christopher Frantz, an innocent bystander whom they attacked and beat severely. Smout proclaimed the King's peace and literally read the riot act, but no one listened to him since he had been so friendly toward the Moravians. Instead of dispersing, some of the crowd declared they were ready to lose their heads for Luther, to which their opponents answered, "But alas! not your fingers for Christ." According to reports Mühlenberg heard a few days later, Nyberg's supporters then ran full force toward the sacristy door. Their opponents tried to block them, and during the melee a deacon grabbed Nyberg by the neck, but the pro-Moravian crowd had them outnumbered and forced their way in. The victors sang "Don't Despair, Thou Little Flock" ("Verzage nicht du

Häuflein klein") and "If God is for me what is it, that Men can do to me?" and then Nyberg preached "with uncommon feeling of our Saviour's Nearness." During the service a "wicked Woman" standing in the church door cried out, "The Devil absolutely helps that Man to preach!" and then ran away. The men and women of the anti-Moravian faction knew that Zinzendorf's blood and wounds style and strange ecumenism were the work of the Devil, and they had to continue the fight to remove this threat from their community.[35]

In the next few days both sides pled their cases to higher secular authorities, but no one was in the mood to compromise or otherwise seek a peaceful solution, and the conflict continued. The governor recommended arbitration by the Lutheran pastors of the colony, but, when Nyberg convinced him that they were all Hallensians and Uppsalan pastors who would never give him a fair hearing, the governor agreed to allow him to preach until a decision came from Uppsala about whether Nyberg was a Lutheran in good standing in Sweden, or a Moravian imposter. But the anti-Nyberg faction knew what they were dealing with now—the Moravian threat had come to Lancaster, and they were not about to allow Satan to take over the Lutheran church while awaiting word from overseas about whether they should. When Nyberg's group approached for their next service, seventy men and women of the anti-Moravian faction defied the governor's order and stood before the door. This time the pro-Moravians could not get in. Both sides exchanged abusive language as the Nyberg group managed to break the lock, but the door was nailed shut, and they could not in. The pro-Moravians then left and pressed charges against nine of the opposing party for hindering their worship in defiance of the governor's order. Meanwhile the anti-Moravian group asked two Hallensians, Mühlenberg and Peter Brunnholtz, as well as another Lutheran pastor named Tobias Wagner, to intervene, and they came on 31 January 1746. Nyberg knew that he could not win against this group and refused to attend the meeting.[36]

The grand jury trial took place in the Lancaster courthouse in early February 1746, where all of the trouble had begun a few weeks earlier, and it became a local sensation that could be followed throughout the region in Christopher Saur's newspaper. It involved two issues, the attack by the anti-Moravian women on Christopher Frantz and the charges against the nine men who defied the governor's order and hindered Nyberg from preaching in the church. In spite of the overwhelming evidence that the pro-Nyberg faction had legally occupied the church building and had been violently attacked by their enemies, the grand jury was packed by the anti-Moravian faction and refused to pursue either case. They thought that Christopher Frantz, who was badly beaten by women in the crowd, was an "Ignoramus" who rarely went to church anyway and thus was unworthy of any sympathy. It was none of his business what happened there, and he should not have been hanging around, getting mixed up with the pro-Nyberg group. On the contrary, the grand jury believed that there was good reason to complain against Nyberg because of his connection to the dangerous Moravians. Their church, their sacred space, had to be protected from this group that was attempting to violate it, and this made the violence against them appear justified.[37]

Defeated in the streets and by a grand jury packed by their enemies, the Moravians in the Lutheran community of Lancaster were reeling and tried to defend themselves in the newspapers, but this only made matters worse for them. Four members of the pro-Moravian faction published an article in Saur's newspaper that explained their position and accused Mühlenberg of manipulation when he tried and failed to intervene and resolve the church dispute.[38] A month later, six anti-Moravian elders and members of the church council retorted angrily in a two-and-one-half page article that represented the views, fears, and motivations of the people who violently attacked the pro-Nyberg faction. They accused the pro-Moravian authors of the previous article of making unfounded assertions and unfairly attacking Mühlenberg. It was Nyberg, a dangerous, arrogant Moravian and not a true Lutheran, who had started the whole problem in Lancaster. They resorted to violence only against Nyberg, not his followers in the church, and it was the Nyberg faction that had gone to court. It was Nyberg who refused arbitration by the judges or with the Lutheran pastors. They had called Mühlenberg to preach, who was good enough to do so in an open field to avoid trouble, instead of in the church. They had made their decision about whether a preacher could be both a Moravian and a Lutheran: it was impossible. Now they were not about to be drawn into the Moravian net and become a part of that group's ecumenical, blood and wounds form of religion and community. This was a Lutheran church, and they were not going to let the Moravians and their supporters tell them what to do in it—as the Moravians were trying to do in Lutheran and Reformed churches all over the province. Nyberg wanted to take their church, their houses, their plantations, and everything they had and bring them under Count Zinzendorf's yoke. They would have none of it. The church was theirs, they had the deed, and the governor agreed.[39]

At this point the Moravians gave up and withdrew from the Lutheran church in Lancaster, although this did not completely end the tensions in town. Nyberg was tired of the "confusions" at the church every Sunday and began preaching in the courthouse. The anti-Moravian faction dug out the cornerstone of the church that Nyberg had laid because they were afraid that the Moravians might return and try to claim the

church. Nyberg recorded in his journal that there was uncommon commotion on these matters throughout the land that summer, with Mühlenberg traveling and stirring up trouble against the Moravians.[40] The
now separated pro-Moravian Lutheran faction remained influential in
Lancaster and built a new church. Although it was no longer Lutheran,
it continued to attract some Lancaster Germans and worried Mühlenberg, who wrote in his journal in May of 1748 that "Lancaster is an
important station in which the Herrnhuters have gained a secure foot-
hold, and we must either drive them out or they us."[41]

But the Lutheran pastors only succeeded in dividing Lancaster, as
they had done in Philadelphia, Raccoon, and many other communities,
and could not win it over. Gabriel Naesman began preaching there occasionally, but he charged the community the extraordinary fee of £5 per
visit, perhaps once again reminding people of one reason why they had
liked the Moravians in the first place: they preached for free and were
good at it. Mühlenberg believed that the Moravians also played a role in
the failure of his colleague, Johann Nicolaus Kurtz, to hold Lancaster.
Kurtz struggled at this time with his preaching and diplomatic skills in
this difficult situation, and he also needed to be paid. By 1747 his congregation no longer wanted him, and Mühlenberg sent Handschuh as a
replacement the following year. Unfortunately for the Hallenisans, Handschuh had to leave in 1751, and they did not send another pastor to Lancaster until 1769. The Hallensian pastors had helped insure a Moravian
defeat there, but they could not win this important community themselves and extend their denominational establishment to Lancaster until
much later.[42]

As in Philadelphia, there is evidence that issues of authority and confessionalism motivated the assaults on the Moravians, while the role of
gender must be inferred. The newspaper articles written by the anti-
Moravian elders stressed not what the Moravians did wrong, but that
Nyberg was a Moravian, not a Lutheran, and thus had no authority to
preach in their church. Perhaps some people did not *want* to publish
unpleasantries regarding gender, marriage, and sex practices in the
local newspaper, although there is a brief reference to Nyberg marrying
a young Moravian woman who was chosen for him by lot. The voice of
ordinary parishioners is once again essentially absent in the records, but
there are two hints that they may have thought something more sinister
was going on than confessional and authority issues. The first lay in the
cries of the crowd toward Nyberg during the "Day of Darkness" that he
was the "Wounds-preacher, the Blood-Preacher." The second occurred
a month later when the anti-Moravian woman interrupted Nyberg's service and charged that the Devil was the Moravian's assistant. Both of
these condemnations refer not to notions of authority, but rather to

actual Moravian beliefs and practices during this period and the printed accusations and rumors by many of their enemies that connected these beliefs and practices to the work of the Devil. Lastly, when their opponents asked the Hallensians to intervene in the conflict, this brought the full weight of the critique of Moravians described earlier down on the small group working in Lancaster, including the extreme language used to condemn their challenge to gender and confessional order.

As the religious alternatives and conflict turned the Delaware Valley into a burnt-over district, these decisions and struggles transformed the religious landscape of the region. The Moravians could and did field enough effective preachers to care for most of the German and Swedish communities, and that was their greatest asset in the struggle, but they were unprepared to handle the resistance they encountered in many of those places. After many early victories, the Moravians began succumbing to the pressure, rumors, conflict, and violence, and many of their preachers could be seen running terror-stricken back to Bethlehem after encounters with their enemies in the embattled communities throughout the region. Sometimes the pro-Moravian factions won violent battles with their enemies, but they were losing the war. As long as enough members supported them, the Moravian preachers kept returning to the embattled Lutheran and Reformed communities, but support for them eventually began to fade away. While Moravian preachers had served in at least 102 German-speaking congregations and at least 38 others from 1740 to 1748, they served in only 48 and 20 respectively during the period 1749 to 1755, and many of these visits were either brief or to small congregations that would ultimately become separate Moravian communities instead of Lutheran, Reformed, or something else.[43]

While the Moravians retreated from the Lutheran and Reformed communities in the late 1740s and early 1750s and began to devote more of their energies to building up their closed communities, to their economic activities (to include trade with other colonists), and to their slave and Indian missions throughout the Americas, the Lutheran and Reformed pastors and their supporters gained influence in the communities the Moravians left behind and began building the patriarchal, denominational establishments that transformed the religious landscape of the Delaware Valley, although they struggled in places like Lancaster. By 1752 eight Hallensian pastors worked in the field and provided the most important leadership in the new Lutheran ministerium, which quickly extended its influence to German Lutheran congregations throughout the mid-Atlantic colonies. The Amsterdamers had eleven pastors working in the field by 1752, who led the new German Reformed coetus in the region. Meanwhile six Uppsalan pastors worked in the Swedish communities from 1749 to 1755 and controlled the ground in the Swedish Lutheran parishes.[44]

On the eve of the French and Indian War the factions supported by the three religious centers in Europe had won the war against the Moravians in the Lutheran and Reformed communities, and clashes between the groups usually only occurred when the Hallensians, Amsterdamers, and Uppsalans ventured into the closed Moravian settlements. In June of 1754 two Uppsalan pastors (Acrelius and Unander), a Halle pastor (Brunnholtz), and a German Lutheran layman visited Bethlehem, hoping to deliver a letter to Spangenberg. Their escort was Paul Daniel Bryzelius, the Moravian preacher who had been involved in the conflict at Raccoon. Bryzelius may have hoped that they would see the Moravians' better side in Bethlehem and that this would improve relations between the groups. They never met Spangenberg in Bethlehem, however, and instead argued tensely with other Moravians for two days. From the beginning Acrelius was suspicious and cynical. Moreover, he found nothing about the now famous Moravian settlement impressive except for their music, and even on this subject he could not resist attacking them: he condemned their hymnal, especially the infamous Twelfth Appendix, which contained the sensual imagery that had so horrified their opponents.[45]

Acrelius and Unander argued constantly and aggressively with various Moravian spokesmen during their visit to Bethlehem. An old Swiss man named Johann Jacob Lescher greeted them with the controversial kiss, apparently on the mouth, which displeased Acrelius, who wrote that the man stank of tobacco. Acrelius questioned Christian Thomas Benzien about how they raised their children to be infected by religious enthusiasm (*Enthusiasteri*). They met another Swede who Acrelius believed was being held against his will there by the crafty Moravians, who "have many arts to retain such simple strangers in their clutches if they see that they are useful to them."[46] Unander questioned the inscription above the entrance to the Single Brothers House, "Father and Mother and Dear Husbands, Honor the Young Man's Plan" (Vater und Mutter und lieber Mann, Habt Ehre vorm Jünglings Plan"), but their host refused to explain its meaning, only referring to it as something mysterious with which he did not agree. (Was this a reference to the Trinity? Was it a reference to all aspects of Christ's function and being?) Acrelius snidely condemned Moravian hospitality, which he had heard was highly regarded, and decided that Bethlehem was in decline because it was a place where people went after they failed elsewhere. As the Lutherans were parting they fired one last shot at the Moravians, expressing general condemnation of their movement and activities. Brunnholtz said that he had been trained in Halle, from where such errors never had emanated. Their Moravian guide responded that if August Hermann Francke (the founder of Halle pietism) were still alive, he would surely side with the Moravians. Temperatures rose to the boiling point again, but the Lutherans decided just to stop and leave. They had already defeated the Moravians in the Lutheran communities, and there was no need to go after Bethlehem itself.[47]

Acrelius's remarks about his visit to Bethlehem in 1754 and other comments in his history written two years later reveal how deep the wounds of the earlier conflicts had been, how well both parties still remembered some of the major events of that conflict, and the continuing mistrust between the groups. Acrelius championed Mühlenberg for having challenged Zinzendorf face-to-face over a decade earlier in Philadelphia, and he praised Naesman for leading the anti-Moravian charge at Raccoon, as well as the faction there that had violently attacked Bryzelius. A year earlier Acrelius had made a similar visit to the cloister at Ephrata, but with a different outcome. Although he argued many points of doctrine and practice with Conrad Beissel and others in the cloister, their debates remained civil and Acrelius departed on good terms. This was not possible with the Moravians, for whom he reserved not the least modicum of respect. When writing his history of New Sweden from 1756 to 1759 after returning to Europe, Acrelius was still concerned about a Moravian conspiracy in the colonies.[48]

The three most important church opponents of the Moravians—the Hallensians, the Amsterdamers, and the Uppsalans—experienced further difficulties and successes after defeating the Moravians as they moved toward building their denominational establishments. The Hallensians for the most part organized and directed the Lutheran governing body in the colonies, but they never received enough support from Halle fully to implement the program they wanted, and internal problems wracked many of their congregations in subsequent years. Yet the Lutheran denomination did slowly emerge from these difficult beginnings. The Amsterdamers had more success earlier, but remained plagued by internal troubles as well. Although schism and realignment lay in their future, the German Reformed denomination did take root and develop in the aftermath of the Moravian conflict. On the other hand, Uppsala's plan for the Delaware Valley, to revive the lost ethnic ideal of a Swedish-language denominational church directed by them, eventually faltered. The Swedes were a dying ethnic group and moved increasingly toward English-language services and the Anglican Church, causing Uppsala to withdraw from the region. There would be no "Swedish Lutheran" denomination in North America until the late nineteenth century, when Swedish immigration increased dramatically. But before its demise in the eighteenth century the Swedish church,

played a critical role in defeating the Moravian threat to denominationalism and gender order in the Delaware Valley.[49]

While it is difficult to find indisputable evidence demonstrating that
gender and confessional issues motivated ordinary Lutheran and
Reformed colonists to attack the Moravians and their supporters in the
Delaware Valley communities, this seems to have been the case. It is
clear that both issues played a critical role in the conflict with the Moravians throughout the Atlantic world, and that the problems in North
America were part of this larger conflict. It is also clear that defending
gender and confessional order were important to the European clergy
who struggled against the Moravians in the very communities where the
religious violence occurred, and in some cases those clergy became
directly involved in the violence. Moreover, even those who did not nevertheless insured that the Delaware Valley communities were informed
of Atlantic events by infusing them with inflammatory anti-Moravian
polemics, sermons, and rumors that stressed how Count Zinzendorf and
his followers violated gender and confessional order in dangerous ways.

Another way to assess whether tensions regarding gender motivated
the religious violence in these communities is to ask whether the Moravians and their supporters would have been physically attacked if they
had *not* violated the prevailing gender order. Probably not. Their enemies used their gender transgressions more than anything else to convince men and women in the communities that the Moravians were not
merely a problem but a serious Satanic threat. If the Moravians had not
violated gender boundaries, then the mission of the itinerant preachers
sent from Bethlehem to the Lutheran and Reformed communities
would not have been so devastated when the people who lived there discovered they were really "Moravians." Indeed, it was difficult enough
for their opponents to remove them from these communities when people *were* aware of the gender transgressions, primarily because the people from Bethlehem otherwise seemed to be so appealing to most
Lutheran and Reformed colonists.

Would the Moravians and their supporters have been physically
attacked had they not violated the confessional order? Probably not.
Other groups on both sides of the Atlantic believed in a female Trinity,
allowed women to preach, and lived in cloistered communities that violated mainstream gender values. Although many religious authorities
disliked these radicals, they were often tolerated because they kept to
themselves and were *not* ecumenical or expansive like the Moravians.
Thus they represented no serious threat to the orthodox churches. This
was especially true in Pennsylvania, where there was no state church, and

in a few territories along the Rhine and elsewhere where rulers granted such radicals safe havens.

But the religious violence did take place. Ordinary men and women chose sides, for and against the Moravians, and fought for control of their communities and the nature of the religious order that would characterize them. There clearly was a "theistic free market of religion and choice" between religious communities in the Middle Colonies, as one historian has noted, but the commitment to proper gender and confessional order within them was strong, and this meant that upstanding community members policed boundaries against intruders and demanded or even coerced compliance within, violently if need be.[50] The radical Moravians were winning in the Delaware Valley communities until they encountered such community members, who in factional conflict reacted violently against them to defend sacred communal space and values, including gender and confessional order. To those who supported patriarchal, confessional communal order, religious violence was a logical and necessary measure to take in the absence of state church authority to stop the Moravians. And they did stop them, thus limiting radical religion in this colonial environment.

How far could radicalism go in North America? It could go as far as ordinary people in communities flooded by information and advocates for and against it wanted it to go. In a colonial environment where the tensions and choices regarding religious freedom and order seemed to be almost a daily, conscious part of life, many men and women in these communities decided that radicalism had gone far enough, and they stopped it.

Conclusion: The Limits of Radical Religion in America

Although the social and political conditions in British North America created a much greater potential for radical religion to flourish there than in Europe in the eighteenth century, there were definite limits to how far religious radicalism could develop in the colonies. When the radical Moravians adopted an ecumenical position and then tried to extend their message to the rapidly growing Lutheran and Reformed communities of the mid-Atlantic colonies, claiming a legitimate right to do so, they eventually provoked a violent response that defeated their movement. In Europe the intrusions on Lutheran and Reformed gender order could not seriously threaten the large state churches and masses of population in the Protestant territories, but the early success in the American setting, the Moravians' particular aggressiveness (Zinzendorf himself arrived to lead the assault), and their new doctrines and practices, combined with the printed alarms raised in Europe to create a major and distinctively colonial crisis. The sheer if at first veiled aggressiveness of the Moravian assault alone does much to explain the violence of colonial Lutheran and Reformed reactions. Time and again the question came down to the parishioners' outrage that an illegitimate claim to their religion and literally to their churches was being forced on them by a group they increasingly perceived as illegitimate within their polity and more aggressive than Christian discourse allowed. Crowds of shouting Moravians, claiming one's home church while posing as the legitimate holders of church order and peaceful Christians, would have made any non-Moravian furious. It became clear to many that Zinzendorf was directing the fulfillment of his real dream to take over an entire European society from within, lock, stock, and barrel. But this alone cannot explain the fury of colonial reactions, for the law usually upheld the claims of the anti-Moravian factions to their churches. The Moravians lost the majority of cases brought by or against them in the courts, yet the violence of their opponents only increased apace, as did their willingness, unusual in the colonial context, to submit to the nearly patriarchal leaders and order of the European churches, as if seeking a refuge from hell. And that is precisely what they were doing, for fragmentary but convincing evidence indicates time and again that the real fears of colonial Lutherans and Calvinists were those first put on paper by European anti-Moravian leaders, and adopted with a special edge of terror by vulnerable American believers. Although in Europe it was hard to believe that transgressions of gender order could provoke a spiritual battle, in colonial Pennsylvania and surrounding areas, where all beliefs and all order were partial and constantly eroded by popular willfulness and competing views, the sudden totality of the Moravian assault and its simultaneously revealed, wildly transgressive views, overwhelmed believers, threatening them with a literal fear of hell and sending them flying into the arms of the very European clergy whose authority they had long resisted. The very disorder, as recent immigrants saw it, inherent in Pennsylvania society, coalesced into the Moravian challenge, and it was this that had sent them fleeing to whatever conventional order offered itself. Zinzendorf had got it all wrong: he had picked the wrong, not the right, context for his experiment at conquest. North America, especially Pennsylvania, was simply *too* unstable for a Moravian victory.

Thus North America offered radicals the most potential in the Protestant Atlantic world, but was also extremely hard on them when they violated gender and confessional order as they developed in the eighteenth century. In some ways it is surprising that the Moravians received as much support as they did, especially after their identity became known. In fact, many Lutheran and Reformed colonists wanted the Moravian preachers and more female ways, and when forced to fight for it they did—and lost. What is important is not that the Moravians were a small group that tried something big and failed—this in and of itself is hardly important in the grand scheme of the colonial history of British North America or the Atlantic world. Instead, what is important is that the Moravian challenge and the response by their enemies illustrate the opportunity and limits to radical religion in America.

The social conditions in British North America led to the greatest potential for success for the Moravians and also led to the most violent response toward them. Inversion and radical religious views had a chance in these colonies because of rapid economic and demographic growth, diversity, and religious tolerance, but these same conditions prevented the realization of any grand schemes for radical religion: British North American colonists would not submit to any larger, external religious authority, even a relatively loose, ecumenical one, nor would their weak or nonexisting apparatus protect those who tried from the violent resistance of other colonists. The radicals who challenged the church establishments, as well as the ministers and most of the supporters who fought against the radicals, were immigrants. In many ways what happened in the North American Lutheran and Reformed communities was an extension of old conflicts in Europe, now fought under new conditions that, at least initially, favored the radicals. It was only through well-organized and financed migrations from Europe to the colonies that the Moravians were able to achieve their early advantage among other immigrants. Much as in Europe, a patriarchal, confessional religious culture predominated in British North America, and although North America became one place, perhaps the best place, in the Atlantic world where all of these attributes could be significantly challenged because these colonies tolerated radical immigrants, North America itself would not become radical: although initially allowed, radicals had to be defeated when they became too strong, and many like the Moravians, Quakers, Baptists, and Methodists eventually abandoned most of their radical beliefs and practices in order to gain acceptance in the new denominational culture developing in the United States. Thus the radicals limited themselves, a process that actually began much earlier, as soon as their women preachers emphasized obedience to the women in their audiences.

This book suggests that gender and confessional issues may have been the central problems in the struggle with radical religion in the German and Swedish communities of British North America. Whether radicals like Moravians or pastors like those from the Halle, Amsterdam, and Uppsala, Europeans coming to America were trying, in their own words, to establish some kind of "order" in the colonies where so many diverse people had settled so quickly. Gender order was critical to their view of order. To those following Protestant orthodoxy this meant a male deity, a male ecclesiastical hierarchy, and male control of religious communities in clearly defined denominational establishments. "Disorder" meant, among other things, female power run amok, which could be seen in the radical gospel of femaleness in the Trinity, women preaching, strange marriage and sex practices that undermined the patriarchal family, and ecumenism, which left families and communities exposed to incursions by improper, disorderly, and ill-intentioned male and female preachers. The threat of disorder was magnified in North America, and one issue or critique of the Moravians that continually emerged was that they threatened immigrant communities with elite ideas from old Europe about what ordinary men and women should do. Many immigrants found at least some of these ideas attractive, but others quickly adjusted to an environment with no nobility in the colonies and resented counts, barons, and even bishops with grand plans who attempted to establish authority over them and give women more power than they should have.

The innovative beliefs and practices by radicals like the Moravians became part of the larger reevaluation of gender order in colonial North America. The Moravian challenge and defeat represents one of many historical cases in which the orthodoxy of a male Trinity and overwhelmingly male control of communities survived a challenge and emerged intact. This is important to the thesis held by many historians that the "feminization" of the Protestant religion in America occurred after 1800, meaning that female participation, influence, and content increased during this era. My findings concerning the radical Moravian challenge in the Atlantic world support the view that these elements were present in the eighteenth century, before a reaction set in that suppressed them. This suggests that if "feminization of religion" occurred, then it was not a linear development from the eighteenth to the nineteenth century, but instead an ambiguous progression, with cyclical challenges and defeats and continuing male power, both symbolic and actual. Furthermore, if this feminization occurred, then it took place without a permanent or lasting transformation in male gendered symbols of power, which may explain why achieving gender equality, spiritually and in religious institutions, was not possible. This demonstrates the limits of what radical religion could accomplish in North America.[1]

Europeans became increasingly interested in these religious developments in eighteenth-century North America, and some tried and failed to control them, as they failed to control so many other aspects of life in colonial North America. This was demonstrated in their attempts to build religious regimes in North America that would impress Protestant pietists in Europe. European religious rivalries and goals made a difference in North America, and what happened there mattered to religious leaders in Europe. But the transatlantic evangelical awakening of the eighteenth century ran a different course in North America and shaped religious culture in the colonies in different ways. A struggle broke out among colonists as to whether more or less European influence and control in their religious affairs should exist, and this was part of a larger struggle over the entire relationship between the colonies and Europe that led to revolution and independence. One result of this struggle and separation was that Protestant religion became increasingly vibrant, active, and influential in American culture, whereas it began a long, slow decline in European culture. Diversity and tolerance in North America led to volunteerism (not coercion) and increasing religiosity to this very day, whereas the lack of these elements in Europe led to anticlericalism and secularization, even as the evangelical Protestant awakening and pietism continued. As for religious radicalism, it remained prolific in America despite the defeats in the eighteenth century. Religious radicals continued to view America as an asylum in the nineteenth century, but they never became powerful enough to take over the mainstream, an aspect of American religious culture that exists to this day.

Appendix 1. Anti-Moravian Polemics Written, Published, or Reprinted in North America, 1741–1763

Polemics Written by Radical Pietists

Eckerlin, Israel. *Ein Kurtzer Bericht von den Ursachen, Warum die Gemeinschaft in Ephrata sich mit dem Grafen Zinzendorf und seinen Leuten Eingelassen . . .* Germantown, Pa.: Christopher Saur, 1743. Eckerlin was a member of the Ephrata cloister in Pennsylvania.

Frey, Andreas. *. . . seine Declaration, oder: Erklärung Auf welcher Weise er unter die sogenannte Herrnhuter Gemeine gekommen . . .* Germantown, Pa.: Christopher Saur, 1748. Frey was a former Moravian.

Gruber, Johann Adam. "Ausführliche Nachricht von Zinzendorfs Unternehmungen in Pennsylvanien, 1742–1743." In "Americanische Nachrichten von Herrnhutischen Sachen," 87–872 in Fresenius, *Bewährte Nachrichten von Herrnhutischen Sachen*, vol. 3, here Part 3, Nr. 1, 97–236. Authorship attributed to Gruber in John Philip Boehm, *Life and Letters of Reverend John Philip Boehm*, ed. William J. Hinke (Philadelphia: Reformed Church of the United States, 1916), 366. Gruber was a member of the groups known as the "Inspired."

———. *Einfältige Warnung- und Wächter-Stimme an die Seelen dieser Zeit* (1741). Printed in Fresenius, *Bewährte Nachrichten von Herrnhuter Sachen*, 4 vols. (Frankfurt am Main: Johann Leonard Buchner and Heinrich Ludwig Broenner, 1746–1751), vol. 3, 297–303.

———. *Eines Geringen Bericht, was zwischen ihm und Herrn Ludwig und andern seiner Zugehörigen, in der Herrnhuter Sache . . .* Germantown, Pa.: Christopher Saur, 1743.

———. *Kurtzer doch nöthiger Bericht wegen der vor sechs Jahren verfassten und nun ohne mein Wissen, Befragen und Willen . . . von andern herausgegebenen Schrift . . .* Germantown, Pa.: Christopher Saur, 1742.

———. *Ein Zeugniß eines Betrübten, der seine Klage ausschüttet über die unzeitige, eingenmächtige übereylte Zusammen-Beruffung und Sammlung verschiedener Partheyen und erweckten Seelen so unter Nahmen Immanuels vorgegeben wird.* Germantown, Pa.: Christopher Saur, 1742?, dated end of December 1741.

Hildebrand, Johannes. *Mistisches und kirchliches Zeuchnüs Der Brüderschaft in Zion . . .* Germantown, Pa.: Christopher Saur, 1743. Hildebrand was a member of the Ephrata cloister.

———. Report on Eschenbach and Zinzendorf in Oley, Pennsylvania (1742). Written in Pennsylvania and published in Fresenius, *Bewährte Nachrichten von Herrnhutischen Sachen*, vol. 3, 504–10.

———. *Schriftmässiges Zeuchnüss Von dem Himmlischen und Jungfräulichen Gebährungs-Werck . . .* Germantown, Pa.: Christopher Saur, 1743.

————. *Wohlgegründetes Bedencken der Christlichen Gemeine in und bey Ephrata . . . Bey veranlassung Eines von der so genannten Herrenhutischen Gemeine erhaltenes Briefs.* Germantown, Pa.: Christopher Saur, 1743.

Reynier, Jean François (Johann Franz). "Das Geheimnis der Zinzendorfischen Secte." Written in Pennsylvania, published in Fresenius, *Bewährte Nachrichten von Herrnhutischen Sachen,* vol. 1, 321–479. Reynier was a former Moravian.

Volck, Alexander. *Das Entdeckte Geheimnis der Bosheit der Herrnhutischen Secte.* Reprint of 1748 edition published in Frankfurt am Main and Leipzig. Philadelphia: Johann Boehm, 1749. Volck was a former Moravian.

Other Authors

Anonymous. *Erweiterte Vorschläge, zu einem dauerhaften Frieden zwischen dem hochgebornen Herrn Nicolaus Ludewig . . . von Zinzendorff . . .* Germantown, Pa.: Christopher Saur, 1749.

Berkenmeyer, Wilhelm Christoph. *Geheime und öffentliche Ansprache, samt einer Schluss-rede, an Herren Johann Christopher Hartwick, mit Etlichen zur Erläuterung, und zur Entdeckung des Cripto-Herrnhuthianismi. . . .* New York: J. Zenger, 1749. Berkenmeyer was a German Lutheran pastor in New York.

Boehm, Johann Philip. *Abermahlige treue Warnung und Vermahnung an meine sehr werthe und theuer geschätzte Reformierte Glaubens-verwandte . . .* Philadelphia: Cornelia Bradford and Isaiah Warner, 1743. Boehm was a German Reformed pastor sponsored by the Classis of Amsterdam.

————. *Getreuer Warnungs Brief an die Hochteutsche Evangelisch Reformierten Gemeinden und alle deren Glieder, in Pennsylvanien, Zur getreuen Warschauung, vor denen Leuthen, welche unter dem nahmen von Herrn-Huther bekandt seyn . . .* Philadelphia: Andrew Bradford, 1742.

Bruin, F. de, Gerhardus Kulenkamp, and A. Buurt. *Nadere Trouhartige Waarschouwinge, Tegen de Verleinduengen der Herrnhutters. . . .* Reprint of 1750 original published in Amsterdam. New York, 1763. The authors were members of the state church council (*kerkenraad*) in the Netherlands.

Crellius, Joseph. *Compendious Extract: Containing the Chiefest Articles of Doctrine and most remarkable Transactions of Count Lewis of Zinzendorf and the Moravians! Together with the most material Objections of some of their Antagonists.* Philadelphia: Andrew Bradford, 1742. Crellius was a Unitarian.

Duyckinck, Gerardus. *A Short Tho True Account of the Establishement and Rise of the Church so Called Moravien Brethren.* New York: Henry de Foreest, 1744. Duyckinck was from an affluent Dutch family in New York.

Finley, Samuel. *Satan strip'd of his angelick Robe . . .* Philadelphia: William Bradford, 1743. Referring to Moravian sermons preached in Pennsylvania, 1742–43. Finley was a New Light Presbyterian minister.

Güldin, Samuel. . . . *Unpartheyisches Zeugnüß ueber die neue Vereinigung aller Religions-Partheyen in Pensylvanien.* Germantown, Pa.: Christopher Saur, 1743. Güldin was an independent German Reformed pastor from Switzerland.

Hancock, John. *The Examiner, OR, Gilbert against Tennent. Containing a Confutation of the Reverend Mr. Gilbert/ Tennent, and his ADHERENTS.* Boston, 1743. Reprinted and sold by Benjamin Franklin in Philadelphia, 1743. Contains anti-Moravian material.

Lischy, Jacob. *Eine Warnende Wächter-Stimm An alle Gott und Jesum liebende Seelen . . .* Germantown, Pa.: Christopher Saur, 1749. Lischy was a former Moravian.

————. . . . *Zweyte Declaration Seines Sinnes an Seine Reformierte Religions-Genossen in Pensilvanien.* Germantown, Pa.: Christopher Saur, 1748.

"A Protestation of the Several Members of the Protestant Lutheran and Reformed Religions in the City of Philadelphia, jointly concerned in the Lease of their Meeting-House in Arch-Street, about the late Commotion which happened on Sunday the 18th of July 1742." Broadside published in 1742, probably in Philadelphia. Case 2, #12–1, Hinke Collection, Archives of the Evangelical and Reformed Historical Society.

Rimius, Henry. *A Candid Narrative of the Rise and Progress of the Herrnhuters . . .*, Reprint of 1753 original published in London. Philadelphia: W. Bradford, 1753. Although Heinrich Rimius was Prussian, he published the original in English. A German translation appeared in Coburg the same year.

Tennent, Gilbert. *The Necessity of holding fast the Truth . . . Relating to Errors, lately vented by some Moravians in those Parts . . .* Boston: S. Kneeland and T. Green, 1743. Tennent was a New Light Presbyterian minister.

Tersteegen, Gerhard. *Warnungs-Schreiben wider die Leichtsinnigkeit, Worin die nothwendige Verbindung der Heiligung mit der Rechtfertigung, Wie auch was Gesetzlich und was Evangelisch ist,* reprint of 1747 original published in Solingen. Germantown, Pa.: Christopher Saur, 1748. Tersteegen was an influential Reformed mystical pietist in the German territories.

Whitefield, George. *An Expostulatory Letter, Adressed to Nicholas Lewis, Count Zinzendorf.* Reprint of 1753 original published in London. Philadelphia: William Bradford, 1753. Whitefield was an extremely popular revival preacher from the Church of England who toured the North American colonies several times.

Note: Fresenius also published numerous other short documents in *Bewährte Nachrichten von Herrnhutischen Sachen* that attacked the Moravians and were written in North America.

Sources: Primarily Dietrich Meyer, ed., *Bibliographisches Handbuch zur Zinzendorf-Forschung* (Düsseldorf: Kornelius Kaspers, 1987), and Karl John Richard Arndt and Reimer C. Eck, eds., and Gerd-J. Bötte, Werner Tannhof, and Annelies Müller, comps., *The First Century of German Language Printing in the United States of America* (Göttingen: Niedersächsisches Staats- und Universitätsbibliothek, 1989).

Appendix 2. Court Cases, Arrests, Imprisonment, and Pursuits of Moravian Preachers in the Mid-Atlantic Colonies of British North America, 1742–1747

1. 1742, New York: Count Zinzendorf and daughter Benigna were fined 6s by a judge for violating the Sabbath. (Authorities found them writing that day, which was not allowed.)

Source: Karl W. Westmeier, "Out of a Distant Past: A Challenge for Modern Missions from a Diary of Colonial New York (Shekomeko, N.Y., 1744)," *Transactions of the Moravian Historical Society* 27 (1992): 67–86.

2. 1742, Philadelphia. Court case resulting from the July 1742 assault on the Moravian preacher Johann Christoph Pyrlaeus in the church on Arch Street. Of the three men accused of rioting and assault, Philip Bunkart was found guilty of assault, but not rioting, and Casper Klinker and Daniel Milner were acquitted.

Source: Court Judgment against the Moravians for the 18. Jul 1742 Tumult in the Church (City of Philadelphia, 21 January 1744), R.14.A.13 49, Unity Archives, Herrnhut.

3. 1743, Philadelphia. Lawsuit involving the July 1742 attack on Pyrlaeus. It was settled in February 1743, and the Moravians lost.

Sources: Muhlenberg, *Journal*, 29, 31 December 1742, 14 February 1743; Mühlenberg to Francke and Ziegenhagen, 17 March 1743.

4. 1742/1743, Philadelphia. Zinzendorf appears to have won a slander case against Jacob Bauerle of Lancaster. Bauerle had circulated a fabricated story claiming that Zinzendorf had threatened to have the men who attacked Pyrlaeus in Philadelphia hanged.

Source: Report of Rev. John Boehm to the Synods, 8 July 1744, translated and reprinted in James I. Good and William J. Hinke, eds., *Minutes and Letters of the Coetus of the German Reformed Congregations* (Philadelphia: Reformed Church of the United States, 1903), 17–31, here 24–25.

5. 1743, Connecticut. Moravian missionaries Joseph Shaw, Johanna Mack, Johann Martin Mack, and Johann Christoph Pyrlaeus were arrested for itineracy, interrogated in a crowded room, and then brought to the governor. Johanna Mack was released on her own recognizance because she was sick. Pyrlaeus was acquitted on a technicality. Johann Martin Mack and Shaw were fined £100 New England currency.

Source: Johann Christoph Pyrlaeus, Pyrlaeussens Diarium wegen seiner und der Brüder Gefangenschaft in Neu England, 18–24 June 1743, R.14.A.36.4, Unity Archives.

6. 1743, Cohansey, N.J. After a tense confrontation between factions in the church, Moravian pastor Leonhard Schnell was arrested by mistake (the warrant listed another Moravian named Paul Daniel Bryzelius), questioned, and released.

Source: Leonhard Schnell's Nachricht von seinen Predigten u. Besuch in Cohansie, in West Jersey, March-April 1743, here entry for April 7, MJMO H592a, Hinke Manuscript Collection, Archives of the Evangelical and Reformed Historical Society, Lancaster.

7. 1744, New York. Moravian pastors Joseph Shaw, Gottlob Büttner, and Joachim Sensemann at the Indian mission in Shekomeko summoned to appear before the governor and his council for violating the new anti-itinerant law against Indian missionaries. They were ordered to cease preaching and to depart the colony.

Source: Governor's Council Minutes, 5, 26 July, 1, 11 August 1744, in E.G. O'Callaghan, ed., *The Documentary History of the State of New York*, vol. 3 (Albany, N.Y.: Weed, Parsons, & Co., 1850), 613–17.

8. 1744, New York. Moravian pastors Gottlob Büttner, Christian Rauch, and Johann Martin Mack were arrested for violating the new anti-itinerant law against Indian missionaries. They appeared before a judge at Poughkeepsie. After Rauch argued with the judge over swearing the oath they were released.

Source: Christian Rauch, Br. Rauch's Relation von dem letzten tryal in Bikipsi. Dec. 1744, ZK #7, Letters and Documents Relating to the Reformed Church of Pennsylvania, 1743–1746, compiled by William J. Hinke, Archives of the Evangelical and Reformed Historical Society.

9. 1744, Gloucester County, N.J. Members of the anti-Moravian faction fined for attacking pro-Moravian members in the church at Raccoon.

Source: Court of General Sessions and County Court of Gloucester convened 27 March 1744 o.s., here the session meeting on the morning of 29 March 1744, Gloucester County, New Jersey Court Minute Books, 1686–1747, Gloucester County Historical Society, Woodbury, N.J.

10. 1744, Gloucester County, N.J. Bryzelius arrested for Raccoon violence and acquitted at tumultuous grand jury hearing.

Sources: Paul Daniel Bryzelius, Br. Bricelii Bericht von seiner Arbeit unter den Schweden eingegeben im Anfang des Jahrs 1745, here 13 March—7 April 1744 n.s., JA I 13, Moravian Archives, Bethlehem, and Court of General Sessions and County Court of Gloucester convened 27 March 1744 o.s., here the session meeting on the afternoon of 29 March 1744, Gloucester County, New Jersey Court Minute Books, 1686–1747, Gloucester County Historical Society.

11. 1745, New York. Moravian missionaries Friedrich Post and David Zeisberger, Jr., were arrested at Canajoharie and brought to New York City in February 1745 for violating the colony's anti-itineracy law. They were questioned before the governor and his council and then jailed for seven weeks because they refused to swear an oath of allegiance. Pennsylvania Governor Thomas intervened and they were released.

Source: Earl P. Olmstead, *David Zeisberger: A Life Among the Indians* (Kent, Ohio: Kent State University Press, 1997), 33–36; J.Taylor Hamilton and Kenneth G. Hamilton, *History of the Moravian Church* (Bethlehem, Pa.: Moravian Church, 1987), 136.

12. 1745, Lancaster, Pa. December 1745 courthouse violence led to a disturbing the peace complaint against pastor Laurentius Nyberg and the Moravians. Nyberg appeared before the governor and was released.

Sources: Laurentius Nyberg, A Short Sketch of the Awakening about Lancaster near Conestoga, Warwick (now Lititz), Quittoppehille (now Hebron near Lebanon), Yorktown on the Cadores, in Pensilvanien, & Monocasy in Maryland, in North America, by Br. Nyberg, from 1743 till 1748 (1749), here 25 December 1745, R.14.A.40.2, Unity Archives; Muhlenberg, *Journal*, February 1746; *Hoch-Deutsche Pennsylvanische Berichte*, 16 March 1746, Nr. 68.

13. 1746, Lancaster, Pa. January 1746 violence in the Lutheran church led to a trial in February. Nine men in the anti-Moravian faction accused of assaulting pro-Moravians and Nyberg were acquitted.

Sources: *Hoch-Deutsche Pennsylvanische Berichte*, 16 March 1746, Nr. 68; Nyberg Diary, 1743–1749, here 16–17 February 1746 n.s.; Muhlenberg, *Journal*, 4–6 February 1746 o.s.

14. 1746, Lancaster, Pa. Moravian Heinrich Antes was summoned from Bethlehem to Lancaster to answer charges to a full courtroom with several justices that the Moravians in Bethlehem were taking in "French Indians" and had 3,000 men armed with muskets and bayonets who were about to attack the Pennsylvania settlers. After Antes's testimony the charges against the Moravians were dropped and the man who made the accusations was fined nine shillings for court costs.

Source: Heinrich Antes, Bericht von seine reise nach Newtown (Lancaster), und was sich dort zugetragen, als er das Justusamt übernommen, R.14.A.36.9, Unity Archives.

15. 1747, Virginia. Moravian itinerant preachers Leonhard Schnell and Vitus Handrup, working in the Shenandoah Valley, were pursued by a justice of the peace from Fredericktown (Winchester) for violating the governor's anti-itineracy edict. Schnell and Handrup avoided capture by escaping across the Potomac River into Maryland.

Source: "Diary of the Journey of Rev. L. Schnell and V. Handrup to Maryland and Virginia, May 29th to August 4, 1747," trans. and ed. William J. Hinke and Charles E. Kemper, *Virginia Magazine of History and Biography* 12, 1 (July 1904): 55–61, esp. entries for 22 and 27 July 1747.

Appendix 3. Pastors and Assistants Sent by the Four Competing European Religious Centers to Work in the Lutheran and German Reformed Communities in the Mid-Atlantic Colonies of British North America, 1726–1754

A. Pastors and Assistants Sent by the Lutheran Pietist Center in Halle

Name	Dates of service	Congregations served to 1754
Heinrich Melchior Mühlenberg	1742–1787	Philadelphia, New Hanover, Providence, Germantown, Trinity (N.Y.)
Johann Nicolaus Kurtz	1745–1789	New Hanover, Tulpehocken, Lancaster, Earl
Peter Brunnholtz	1745–1757	Philadelphia, Germantown
Johann Helfrich Schaum	1745–1778	Philadelphia, Raritan (N.J.), York, Tohickon, Conewago, Pikestown, Frederick, Bermudian
Johann Friedrich Handschuh	1748–1764	Lancaster, Beaver Creek, Earl, Germantown
Johann Albert Weygand	1748–1770	Raritan (N.J.), Pluckemin (N.J.)
Johann Diedrich Matthias Heintzelmann	1751–1756	Philadelphia
Friedrich Schultz	1751–1756	New Hanover, Providence, Indianfield, New Goshenhoppen, Tohickon

Note: Does not include congregations visited. Unless otherwise noted, all congregations were in Pennsylvania.

Source: Charles H. Glatfelter, *Pastors and People: German Lutheran and Reformed Churches in the Pennsylvania Field, 1717–1793*, 2 vols. (Breinigsville, Pa.: Pennsylvania German Society, 1980, 1981), vol. 2, 107–8, 190.

B. Pastors and Assistants Supported or Sent by the Classis of
Amsterdam

Name	Dates of service	Congregations served to 1754
Johann Philip Boehm*	1729–1749	Falkner Swamp, Skippack, Whitemarsh, Philadelphia, Providence, Coventry, Whitpain, Tulpehocken, Oley, Egypt
P. H. Dorius*	1737–1748	New and Old Goshenhoppen, Egypt
C. L. Schnorr*	1744–1748	Lancaster, Tulpehocken, Eastcamp/Germantown (N.Y.)
J. B. Rieger*	1745–1769	Seltenreich, Hill/ Schaeffer's
G. M. Weiss*	1746–1761	Old and New Goshenhoppen, Great Swamp
Michael Schlatter	1746–1790	Philadelphia, Germantown, Whitpain; Amwell, Rockaway, Fox Hill (N.J.)
J. D. C. Bartholomae	1748–1751	Tulpehocken (Host and Trinity)
J. J. Hochreutiner	1748	Lancaster
J. P. Leydich	1748–1784	Falkner Swamp, Providence
J. C. Steiner	1749–1762	Philadelphia, Germantown, Whitpain
T. Frankenfeld	1752–1755	Frederick, Monocacy, Conococheague (Md.), Conewago
H. W. Stoy	1752–1801	Tulpehocken (Host and Trinity)
P. W. Otterbein	1752–1813	Lancaster
J. C. Rubel	1752–1784	Philadelphia (one faction)
J. Waldschmidt	1752–1786	Cocalico, Muddy Creek, Reyer's, Seltenreich, Blaser's
J. J Wissler	1752–1754	Egypt, Jordan, Heidelberg

* Not sent by Amsterdam but sponsored by or connected to the Classis after arriving. Only
dates of service while connected to Amsterdam are included.
Note: This table includes many congregations only visited by the Amsterdam pastors;
however, it does not include the parishes where Schlatter itinerated, from northern
Virginia to New York, early in his service. Unless otherwise noted, all congregations were
in Pennsylvania.
Source: Glatfelter, *Pastors and People*, vol. 2, 38–39, 117, 190.

C. PASTORS SUPPORTED OR SENT BY THE LUTHERAN CONSISTORY IN UPPSALA, SWEDEN

Name	Dates of service	Parishes served
Andrew Windrufv	1726–1728	Penns Neck (N.J.)
Peter Tranberg	1726–1748	Penns Neck/Raccoon (N.J.), Christina (Wilmington, Del)
John Eneberg	1730–1742	Wicaco (Philadelphia), Christina
John Dylander	1737–1741	Wicaco
Olaf Malander	1737–1742	Penns Neck/Raccoon
Gabriel Naesman	1743–1751	Wicaco
Laurentius Nyberg	1744–1746	Wicaco
John Sandin	1748	Penns Neck/Raccoon
Peter Kalm	1748–1751	Penns Neck/Raccoon
Israel Acrelius	1749–1756	Christina
Eric Unander	1749–1762?	Penns Neck/Raccoon, Christina
Olof Parlin	1750–1757	Wicaco
Johann Abraham Lidenius, Jr.	1750–1753ff	Penns Neck/Raccoon, Maurice River (N.J.), Manathanin, Reading, Little Conestoga, Amasland, Marlborough, Marcus Hook, Folk's Manor, Molatton, Christina

Note: Unless otherwise noted, all parishes were in Pennsylvania. Dates of service refer to the period supported by Uppsala only. Malander and Nyberg, for example, joined the Moravians after the dates listed.
Source: Israel Acrelius, *A History of New Sweden*, trans. William R. Reynolds (Philadelphia: Historical Society of Pennsylvania, 1874).

D. PASTORS AND ASSISTANTS EMPLOYED BY THE MORAVIANS

Name	Dates of service	Colony and ethnic or religious group served
Georg Böhmsch	1734–1737	Pa., Schwenkfelders
Christoph Baus	1734–39,1743–46	Pa., English, Germans, Schwenkfelders
August Gottlieb Spangenberg	1736–39, 1744–45, 1748	N.Y., Md., Va., N.J., Swedes, English, Germans
Anna Caritas Nitschmann	1740–1742	Pa., Germans, Quakers
Johanna Sophia Molther	1741–1742	Pa., Germans
Benigna von Zinzendorf	1741–1742	Pa., Germans, English
Nicolaus Ludwig von Zinzendorf	1741–1743	Pa., Germans

Name	Dates of service	Colony and ethnic or religious group served
Heinrch Almers	1742–1744	N.Y.
Rosina Almers	1742	N.Y.
Andreas (slave from St. Thomas)	1742	N.Y., blacks
Heinrich Antes	1742–1746	Pa.
Johannes Bechtel	1742–1745	Pa., Germans, Reformed
Gottlieb Bezold	1742–1743, 1745	Pa.
Johann Brandmüller	1742–1749	Pa., Md., Va., Germans, Reformed
David Bruce	1742–1747	Pa., Irish, English, German Reformed
Paul Daniel Bryzelius	1742–1745	Pa., N.J., Swedes, Germans
Gottlob Büttner	1742–1744	Pa., N.Y.
Andreas Eschenbach	1742–1745	Pa., N.J.
Andreas Frey	1742	Pa.
Georg Harden	1742, 1744	Pa., N.Y.
Johann Christoph Heine	1742	Pa.
Johann Georg Heydecker	1742, 1744	Pa.
Anna Maria Kohn	1742–1744	Pa., Germans
Jacob Kohn	1742–1745	Pa., Germans
Jacob Lischy	1742–1747	Pa., German and Swiss Reformed
Valentin Lohans	1742	N.Y., blacks
Johann Adam Luckenbach	1742, 1745	Pa.
Johann Adolph Mayer	1742	Pa.
Johann Philipp Meurer	1742–1748, 1752–53	Pa., N.J., Germans
Michael Micksch	1742	Pa.
Johann Rosina Micksch	1742	Pa.
Abraham Meinung	1742–1745	Pa.
Judith Meinung	1742–1743	Pa.
Friedrich Martin	1742	Pa.
John Oakley	1742–1745	Del., Pa., N.J., Germans, English
Christian Post	1742, 1745	Pa., N.Y.
Johann Christoph Pyrlaeus	1742–1747	Pa., N.Y., Germans, English
Christian Rauch	1742–1753	N.Y., Pa., blacks, Germans, Reformed
Owen Rice	1742–1745, 1748	Pa., Md., Va., English
Elisabeth Rice	1742–1743	Pa., English
Reinhold Ronner	1742,1745	Pa.
Joseph Shaw	1742–1745	Pa., N.Y.
Georg Schneider	1742–1745	Pa.
Leonhard Schnell	1742–1747, 1749	Pa., N.Y., N.J., VA, Germans
Bernhard Steinbach	1742	Pa.
Frau Baus	1743	Pa., English
Johann David Bischoff	1743	Pa.

Name	Dates of service	Colony and ethnic or religious group served
Peter Böhler	1743–1744	Pa.
Johann Jacob Döhling	1743–1745	Pa.
Hector Gambold	1743–1745	N.Y.
Gottfried Haberecht	1743	N.Y.
Conrad Harding	1743–1744	N.J., Pa.
Robert Hussey	1743–1746	Pa., Germans
Herr Lesley	1743	N.Y.
Abraham Müller	1743–1746	Pa., Dunkers
Laurentius Nyberg	1743–1749	Pa., German Lutherans, Swedes
Jacob Vetter	1743–1747	Pa., N.Y., Germans
Jost Vollert	1743	Pa., German and Swiss Reformed
Georg Wiesner	1743	N.Y.
Andreas Brocksch	1744, 1747	Pa.
Anna Elisabeth Brocksch	1744, 1747	Pa.
Regina Dorothea Bryzelius	1744	N.J., Swedes
Margaretha Büttner	1744	N.Y.
William Edmunds	1744	N.Y.
Johann Georg Hantsch, Jr.	1744–1747	Pa., Germans
Regina Hantsch	1744–1747	Pa., Germans
Frau Heydecker	1744	Pa.
Johann Martin Mack	1744–1745	Pa.
Christina Meurer	1744	Pa.
Johann Wolfgang Michler	1744–1745	Pa.
Rosina Michler	1744–1745	Pa.
Joseph Müller	1744	Pa.
Georg Niecke	1744–1746	Pa., Md.
David Nitschmann	1744	Pa.
Georg Nixdorf	1744–1745, 1753	Pa., Germans
Susanna Nixdorf	1744	Pa.
Joseph Powell	1744–1747	N.Y.
Martha Powell	1744	N.Y.
Anna Elizabeth Rauch	1744, 1747, 1753	N.Y., Pa., Germans
Abraham Reincke	1744–1745, 1753	N.Y., Pa., N.J., Swedes, Germans
Christoph Schütze	1744	Pa.
Joachim Sensemann	1744–1745	N.Y., N.J., Swedes
Maria Spangenberg	1744–1745	N.Y.
David Zeisberger	1744–1745	Pa., N.Y., Germans
Anna Maria Brandmüller	1745	Pa., Germans, Reformed
James Burnside	1745–1746	N.Y., Md.
John Bull	1745	Pa.
Christoph Demuth	1745	Pa.
Edward Evans	1745–1746	Pa., English
Johann Christoph Francke	1745	Pa.
Christina Francke	1745	Pa.

Name	Dates of service	Colony and ethnic or religious group served
Christian Fröhlich	1745,1747, 1752	Pa., Md., Va, blacks
James Greening	1745	Pa.
Elizabeth Greening	1745	Pa., English
Johann Georg Hantsch, Sr.	1745–1748	Pa.
Anna Regina Hantsch	1745	Pa.
Hans Georg Kelchner	1745	Pa.
Mary Lischy	1745	Pa., Germans, Reformed
Johannes Münster	1745	Pa.
Rosina Münster	1745	Pa.
Daniel Neubert	1745–1747, 1753	Pa., Germans
Rosina Neubert	1745–1747	Pa., Germans
Thomas Noble	1745	N.Y.
Jasper Payne	1745,1747	Pa., N.Y., Md., Va, Germans, Dutch, English, blacks
Matthias Reutz	1745, 1748	Pa., Md., Va
Andreas Schober	1745	Pa.
Nathanael Seidel	1745–1749, 1752	N.Y., Pa., Md., Germans
Anton Seiffert	1745	N.Y.
Richard Utley	1745, 1753	Pa., Md., English
Anton Wagner	1745–1746, 1752	Pa., Germans
Thomas Yarrell	1745, 1753–1754	Pa.
Jacob Adolph	1746	Pa., Germans
Heinrich Beck	1746–1747, 1753	Pa., Germans
Johannes Bruckner	1746	Pa., Germans
Wilhelm Frey	1746	Pa., Dunkers
Johann Georg Hantsch Sr. or Jr.?	1746–1748	Pa., N.J., Germans, Swedes
Georg Neisser	1746–1747, 1753	Pa., Germans
Catharina Neisser	1746–1747	Pa., Germans
Christoph Powell	1746	Pa., Germans
Elisabeth Wagner	1746	Pa., Germans
J. Christian Friedrich Cammerhoff	1747	Pa., Germans
Matthias Gottlieb Gottschalk	1747–1748	Pa., N.J., Germans, Swedes
Vitus Handrup	1747	Pa., Germans
Johann Christoph Höpfner	1747, 1752	Pa., Germans
Peter Leonhard	1747–1748	Pa., Germans
John Eric Westmann	1747	Pa., Md., Germans
Herr Hopson	1748	Md., Va
Sven Roseen	1748–1749	Pa., N.J., Md., Germans, English
John Wade	1748	Pa., Del, N.J., Quakers
Anna Margaretha Roseen	1749	Pa., Md.

Name	Dates of service	Colony and ethnic or religious group served
Christian Philip Bader	1752–1753	Pa., Md., Germans
Johann Jost Eigenbrodt	1752	Md.
Matthias Hehl	1752–1757, 1768	Pa., N.J., Germans
Frau Roesler	1752	Pa., Germans
Gottfried Roesler	1752	Pa., N.J.
Catharina Binder	1753	Pa., Md.
Anna Maria Hehl	1753	Pa., Germans
Ludwig Huebner	1753	Pa., Germans
John Leighton	1753–1754	N.Y., New England
Elizabeth Payne	1753	Pa., English
Anna Ramberger	1753–1756	Pa., Md., Germans
Sarah Utley	1753	Md.
Johann Michael Graff	1754	Pa., Germans
Justine Gertraut Graff	1754	Pa., Germans

Notes. In most cases where an ethnic group was not listed it was Germans. The lists include Moravian men and women who have been identified as having preached, taught, or otherwise led significant religious activities while on assignment in non-Moravian communities. It should be taken as a minimum figure. Those who were exclusively school teachers or Indian missionaries are not included, although some of the above Moravians worked with Indians or in schools in addition to their other duties.

Sources: Moravian itinerant (*Landprediger*) diaries, correspondence by and about itinerants, and synods minutes in the Moravian Archives, the Unity Archives, and the Archives of the Evangelical and Reformed Historical Soceity, as well as *The Bethlehem Diary*, vols. 1–2.

Notes

Introduction

1. My definition of radicalism goes beyond that of most historians of German pietism, who have stressed institutional issues, separatism, and mysticism in their definitions of radicalism or "radical pietism." See Hans Schneider, "Der radikale Pietismus im 18. Jahrhundert," in Martin Brecht and Klaus Deppermann, eds., *Geschichte des Pietismus*, vol. 2, *Der Pietismus im achtzehnten Jahrhundert* (Göttingen: Vandenhoeck and Ruprecht, 1995), 107–97; Johannes Wallmann, *Der Pietismus* (Göttingen: Vandenhoeck and Ruprecht, 1990), 80–108; Chauncey David Ensign, "Radical German Pietism c. 1675–c. 1760" (Ph.D. diss., Boston University, 1955), 1.

2. An enormous literature on the Great Awakening exists. For a recent study that includes much of this literature and explains how the movement received its name see Frank Lambert, *Inventing the "Great Awakening"* (Princeton, N.J.: Princeton University Press, 1999).

3. Most historians of German pietism place the Moravians in a distinct branch of the movement, separate from the radical pietists. See Dietrich Meyer, "Zinzendorf und Herrnhut," in Brecht and Deppermann, *Geschichte des Pietismus*, vol. 2, 5–106; Wallmann, *Der Pietismus*, 108–23; F. Ernest Stoeffler, *German Pietism in the Eighteenth Century* (Leiden: Brill, 1973), 131–67; Ensign, "Radical German Pietism," 378–87.

4. For a good overview of the renewed *Unitas Fratrum* see J. Taylor Hamilton and Kenneth G. Hamilton, *History of the Moravian Church: The Renewed Unitas Fratrum, 1722–1957* (Bethlehem, Pa.: Moravian Church, 1967). On the place of the Moravians in the evangelical pietist movement see W. R. Ward, *The Protestant Evangelical Awakening* (Cambridge: Cambridge University Press, 1992), 116–59, and Meyer, "Zinzendorf und Herrnhut," in Brecht and Deppermann, *Geschichte des Pietismus*, vol. 2, 5–106.

5. Arthur J. Freeman, *An Ecumenical Theology of the Heart: The Theology of Count Nicholas Ludwig von Zinzendorf* (Bethlehem, Pa.: Moravian Church, 1998); Craig D. Atwood, *Community of the Cross: Moravian Piety in Colonial Bethlehem* (University Park: Pennsylvania State University Press, 2004); Beverly Prior Smaby, *The Transformation of Moravian Bethlehem: From Communal Mission to Family Economy* (Philadelphia: University of Pennsylvania Press, 1988); Smaby, "Female Piety Among Eighteenth-Century Moravians," *Pennsylvania History* 64 (special supplement) (Summer 1997): 151–67; Hans-Walter Erbe, *Herrnhaag: Eine religiöse Kommunität im 18. Jahrhundert* (Hamburg: Wittig, 1988); Otto Uttendörfer, *Zinzendorf und die Frauen: Kirchliche Frauenrechte vor 200 Jahren* (Herrnhut: Verlag der Missionsbuchhandlung, 1919). Moravian theology and practice varied over place and time. The above brief description refers to both in their closed communities through-

out the Atlantic world in the mid-eighteenth century, approximately until Zinzendorf's death in 1760. There is a large and growing literature on pietism and its goals. See, for example, Wallmann, *Der Pietismus*, or Stoeffler, *German Pietism in the Eighteenth Century.*

6. There is a large and growing body of literature on Halle pietism. For introductions see Wallmann, *Der Pietismus*, 36–79, Stoeffler, *German Pietism in the Eighteenth Century*, 1–87, and Martin Brecht, "Der Hallische Pietismus in der Mitte des 18. Jahrhunderts—seine Ausstrahlung und sein Niedergang," in Brecht and Deppermann, *Geschichte des Pietismus*, vol. 2, 319–57. On women and Halle pietism see Ulrike Witt, *Bekehrung, Bildung und Biographie: Frauen im Umkreis des Halleschen Pietismus* (Tübingen: Max Niemeyer Verlag, 1996).

7. Johannes Van Den Berg, "Die Frömmigkeitsbestrebungen in den Niederlanden," in Brecht and Deppermann, *Geschichte des Pietismus*, vol. 2, 542–87; Gerald F. De Jong, *The Dutch Reformed Church in the American Colonies* (Grand Rapids, Mich.: W.B. Eerdmans, 1978); James Tanis, "Reformed Pietism in Colonial America," in F. Ernest Stoeffler, ed., *Continental Pietism and Early American Christianity* (Grand Rapids, Mich.: W.B. Eerdmans, 1976), 34–73.

8. Ingrun Montgomery, "Der Pietismus in Schweden im 18. Jahrhundert," in Brecht and Deppermann, *Geschichte des Pietismus*, vol. 2, 489–522.

9. "Confessional order" or "confessionalism" refers to a religious style that emphasizes doctrinal purity as defined in written creeds, support of the state established church, clearly distinguishable boundaries between churches, and patriarchal authority within the church. See Chapter 2 for a fuller explanation.

10. Natalie Zemon Davis, *The Return of Martin Guerre* (Cambridge, Mass.: Harvard University Press, 1983), and Davis, "On the Lame," in AHR Forum: *The Return of Martin Guerre, American Historical Review* 93, 3 (June 1988): 572–603.

11. See Patricia U. Bonomi, *Under the Cope of Heaven: Religion, Society, and Politics in Colonial America*, updated ed. (New York: Oxford University Press, 2003), who stresses volunteerism, and Jon Butler, *Awash in a Sea of Faith: Christianizing the American People* (Cambridge, Mass.: Harvard University Press,1990), who stresses coercion.

12. Unless otherwise noted, all translations in this work are my own.

13. Mühlenberg's journal is published in English translation only; however, his correspondence has been published in German. See *The Journals of Henry Melchior Muhlenberg*, ed. and trans. Theodore G. Tappert and John W. Doberstein, 3 vols. (Philadelphia: Muhlenberg Press, 1942–1958), and *Die Korrespondenz Heinrich Melchior Mühlenbergs aus der Anfangszeit des deutschen Luthertums in Nordamerika*, ed. Kurt Aland and Hermann Wellenreuther, 5 vols. (Berlin: de Gruyter, 1986–2002). The first two volumes of an English translation are now complete, and they cover the critical years of this study (1740–1752). See *The Correspondence of Heinrich Melchior Mühlenberg*, ed. and trans. John W. Kleiner and Helmut T. Lehman (Camden, Me: Picton Press, 1993–1997). My references will be to the dates of Mühlenberg's letters, so that readers may look up either version. Direct quotations in the text will be from the English version, with the original German provided in parentheses or in a note.

14. Lambert, *Inventing the "Great Awakening"*; Frank Lambert, *"Pedlar in Divinity": George Whitefield and the Transatlantic Revivals* (Princeton, N.J.: Princeton University Press, 1994); Harry S. Stout, *The Divine Dramatist: George Whitefield and the Rise of Modern Evangelicalism* (Grand Rapids, Mich.: W.B. Eerdmans, 1991); Karl John Richard Arndt, Reimer C. Eck, et al., eds., *The First Century of German Language Printing in the United States of America*, 2 vols. (Göttingen: Niedersäch-

siche Staats- und Universitätsbibliothek Göttingen, 1989); Susan O'Brien, "A Transatlantic Community of Saints: The Great Awakening and the First Evangelical Network, 1735–1755," *American Historical Review* 91, 4 (October 1986): 811–32.

15. The first edition of the most important Moravian hymnal of the period appeared in 1735: *Das Gesang-Buch der Gemeine in Herrn-Huth* (Herrnhut: Waysen-Hause, 1735). From 1737 to 1747 twelve appendices and four "addenda" (*Zugaben*) were published. The entire collection, often called the *Herrnhuter Gesangbuch* (hereafter referred to as the *Moravian Hymnal*) appeared in numerous editions. I am using the third edition (*Christliches Gesang-Buch der Evangelischen Brüder-Gemeinen*, 1741) because it has been reprinted in Erich Beyreuther, Gerhard Meyer, and Gudrun Meyer-Hickel, eds., *Nikolaus Ludwig von Zinzendorf: Materialien und Dokumente*, series 4, vol. 3, parts 1–3 (Hildesheim: Georg Olms Verlag, 1981). These three volumes contain the hymns in the form used by the Moravians during the period of investigation.

Chapter 1

1. Aaron Spencer Fogleman, *Hopeful Journeys: German Immigration, Settlement, and Political Culture in Colonial America, 1717–1775* (Philadelphia: University of Pennsylvania Press, 1996); Patricia U. Bonomi, *Under the Cope of Heaven: Religion, Society, and Politics in Colonial America* (Oxford: Oxford University Press, 2003); Jon Butler, *Becoming America: The Revolution Before 1776* (Cambridge, Mass.: Harvard University Press, 2000), 185–224; Sally Schwartz, *"A Mixed Multitude": The Struggle for Toleration in Colonial Pennsylvania* (New York: New York University Press, 1987); J. William Frost, *A Perfect Freedom: Religious Liberty in Pennsylvania* (Cambridge: Cambridge University Press, 1990); Dietmar Rothermund, *The Layman's Progress: Religious and Political Experience in Colonial Pennsylvania, 1740–1770* (Philadelphia: University of Pennsylvania Press, 1961); Thomas J. Müller, *Kirche zwischen zwei Welten: Die Obrigkeitsproblematik bei Heinrich Melchior Mühlenberg und die Kirchengründung der deutschen Lutheraner in Pennsylvania* (Stuttgart: Franz Steiner Verlag, 1994); A. G. Roeber, *Palatines, Liberty, and Property: German Lutherans in Colonial British America* (Baltimore: Johns Hopkins University Press, 1993); Charles H. Glatfelter, *Pastors and People: German Lutheran and Reformed Churches in the Pennsylvania Field, 1717–1793*, 2 vols. (Breinigsville, Pa.: Pennsylvania German Society, 1980, 1981); Marilyn J. Westerkamp, *Triumph of the Laity: Scots-Irish Piety and the Great Awakening, 1625–1760* (Oxford: Oxford University Press, 1988); Richard W. Pointer, *Protestant Pluralism and the New York Experience: A Study of Eighteenth-Century Religious Diversity* (Bloomington: Indiana University Press, 1988).

2. For literature on radical pietism in addition to Willi Temme, *Krise der Leiblichkeit: Die Sozietät der Mutter Eva (Buttlarsche Rotte) und der radikale Pietismus um 1700* (Göttingen: Vandenhoeck and Ruprecht, 1998), and Barbara Hoffmann, *Radikalpietismus um 1700: Der Streit und das Recht auf eine neue Gesellschaft* (Frankfurt: Campus Verlag, 1996), see Hans Schneider, "Der radikale Pietismus im 18. Jahrhundert," in Martin Brecht and Klaus Deppermann, eds., *Geschichte des Pietismus*, vol. 2, *Der Pietismus im achtzehnten Jahrhundert* (Göttingen: Vandenhoeck and Ruprecht, 1995), 107–97; Chauncey David Ensign, "Radical German Pietism c. 1675–c. 1760" (Ph.D. diss., Boston University, 1955); Johannes Wallmann, *Der Pietismus* (Göttingen: Vandenhoeck and Ruprecht, 1990); F. Ernest

Stoeffler, *German Pietism in the Eighteenth Century* (Leiden: Brill, 1973), 168–216; E. G. Alderfer, *The Ephrata Commune: An Early American Counterculture* (Pittsburgh: University of Pittsburgh Press, 1985); Donald F. Durnbaugh, *Fruit of the Vine: A History of the Brethren, 1708–1995* (Elgin, Ill.: Brethren Press, 1997); Jeff Bach, *Voices of the Turtledoves: The Sacred World of Ephrata* (University Park: Pennsylvania State University Press, 2003); Wolfgang Breul-Kunkel and Lothar Vogel, eds., *Rezeption und Reform: Festschrift für Hans Schneider zu seinem 60. Geburtstag* (Darmstadt: Verlag der Hessischen Kirchengeschichtlichen Vereinigung, 2001); Jutta Taege-Bizer, "Katharina Elisabeth Schütz (1652–1721)—eine pietistische Bürgerin mit Eigensinn," in Gisela Engel, Ursula Kern, and Heide Wunder, eds., *Frauen in der Stadt: Frankfurt im 18. Jahrhundert* (Königsstein: Ulrike Helmer Verlag, 2002), 177–92.

3. M. A. Gruber, ed., "The Newborn," *The Penn Germania: A Popular Journal of German History and Ideas in the United States* 13 (1912): 336–64; John Joseph Stoudt, "Matthias Baumann, The New Born," *Historical Review of Berks County* (Fall 1978): 136–47.

4. See Stephan Goldschmidt, *Johann Konrad Dippel (1673–1734): seine radikalpietistische Theologie und ihre Entstehung* (Göttingen: Vandenhoeck and Ruprecht, 2001). On Johann Konrad Dippel as the possible inspiration for Mary Shelley's *Frankenstein*, see Radu Florescu, *In Search of Frankenstein* (New York: Warner Books, 1976). On German radical pietism as a movement, to include its transatlantic connections, see Schneider, "Der radikale Pietismus im 18. Jahrhundert."

5. Klaus Deppermann, "Pennsylvanien als Asyl des frühen deutschen Pietismus," *Pietismus und Neuzeit* 10 (1982): 190–212; Elisabeth W. Fisher, "'Prophesies and Revelations': German Cabbalists in Early Pennsylvania," *Pennsylvania Magazine of History and Biography* 109 (1985): 299–333; Friedrich de Boor, "Anna Maria Schuchart als Endzeit-Prophetin in Erfurt, 1691/92," *Pietismus und Neuzeit* 21 (1995): 148–83; Julius F. Sachse, *The German Pietists of Provincial Pennsylvania* (Philadelphia: Julius F. Sachse, 1895); Julius F. Sachse, ed., "The Diarium of Magister Johannes Kelpius," part 27 of *Pennsylvania: The German Influence in its Settlement and Development: A Narrative and Critical History*, in *The Pennsylvania German Society, Proceedings and Addresses*, vol. 25 (Lancaster, Pa., 1917), pp. 2–100; Oswald Seidensticker, "The Hermits of the Wisahickon," *Pennsylvania Magazine of History and Biography* 11 (1887): 427–41; Bach, *Voices of the Turtledoves*, 8–24.

6. Fogleman, *Hopeful Journeys*, 100–126; Schneider, "Der radikale Pietismus im 18. Jahrhundert."

7. The *Haarlemse Courant* article was reprinted in the *Büdingischen Sammlung Einiger in die Kirchen-Historie Einschlagender Sonderlich neuerer Schrifften*, 3 vols. (Büdingen: Johann Christoph Stöhr, 1740–1745), here vol. 2, part 12 (1743), Nr. 10, 849–51. This work, hereafter referred to as the *Büdingische Sammlung*, was reprinted in *Nikolaus Ludwig von Zinzendorf: Ergänzungsbände zu den Hauptschriften*, ed. Erich Beyreuther and Gerhard Meyer (Hildesheim: Georg Olms Verlag, 1965–1971), vols. 7–10. See also the 1 March 1743 article by Johann Jacob Müller in the *Amsterdammer Courant*, in which he belittles Zinzendorf's activities and complaints in Pennsylvania, reprinted in *Büdingischen Sammlung*, vol. 3, part 15, Nr. 19, 336–37.

8. The best comprehensive study that investigates the North American Great Awakening as part of the transatlantic evangelical revival and demonstrates the international aspects of this event, including the importance of the German pietist components is W. R. Ward's, *The Protestant Evangelical Awakening* (Cam-

bridge: Cambridge University Press, 1992); see especially 241–95 for developments in North America. See also older works by F. Ernest Stoeffler, *The Rise of Evangelical Pietism* (Leiden: Brill, 1965) and Stoeffler, *Continental Pietism and Early American Christianity* (Grand Rapids, Mich.: William B. Eerdmans, 1976.) Other studies with a significant transatlantic component that focus on individuals or single religious groups include Frank Lambert, *Pedlar in Divinity: George Whitefield and the Transatlantic Revivals, 1737–1770* (Princeton, N.J.: Princeton University Press, 1994); Harry S. Stout, *The Divine Dramatist: George Whitefield and the Rise of Modern Evangelicalism* (Grand Rapids, Mich.: W.B. Eerdmans, 1991); Sung-Duk Lee, *Der deutsche Pietismus und John Wesley* (Giessen: Brunnen Verlag, 2003); Bernard Semmel, *The Methodist Revolution* (New York: Basic Books, 1973); Leigh E. Schmidt, *Holy Fairs: Scottish Communions and American Revivals in the Early Modern Period* (Princeton, N.J.: Princeton University Press, 1989); Westerkamp, *Triumph of the Laity* on the Scots-Irish Presbyterians; Roeber, *Palatines, Liberty, and Property*; and Müller, *Kirche zwischen zwei Welten* on German Lutherans; Rebecca Larson, *Daughters of Light: Quaker Women Preaching and Prophesying in the Colonies and Abroad, 1700–1775* (New York: Knopf, 1999) on the Quakers; Elisabeth W. Sommer, *Serving Two Masters: Moravian Brethren in Germany and North Carolina, 1727–1801* (Lexington: University Press of Kentucky, 2000) on Moravians in Germany and North Carolina. Susan O'Brien, "A Transatlantic Community of Saints," *American Historical Review* 91, 4 (October 1986): 811–32; Lambert, *Inventing the "Great Awakening"*, has one chapter on the transatlantic aspects of the movement, including discussion and a list of the "revival magazines" (see 151–79); Robert E. Cazden, *A Social History of the German Book Trade in America to the Civil War* (Columbia, S.C.: Camden House, 1984), 3–31. On newspaper coverage of Whitefield and Zinzendorf's meeting see Saur's *Der Hoch-Deutsch Pennsylvanische Geschicht-Schreiber* 36 (Germantown), 16 July 1743. See also Saur's coverage of European state presure on the Moravians and their pending migrations to America in *Pennsylvanische Berichte* (Germantown), 16 December 1750.

9. Johann Philip Fresenius, ed., "Americanische Nachrichten von Herrnhutischen Sachen," in Fresenius, ed., *Bewährte Nachrichten von Herrnhutischen Sachen*, 4 vols. (Frankfurt: Johann Leonard Buchner and Heinrich Ludwig Broenner, 1746–51), here vol. 3 (1748), 87–872.

10. See Marianne S. Wokeck, *Trade in Strangers: The Beginnings of Mass Migration to North America* (University Park: Pennsylvania State University Press, 1999), 45–46, who has recently revised upward estimates of total German-speaking immigration during this period. For the number who were not Lutheran and Reformed, see Fogleman, *Hopeful Journeys*, 101–7.

11. Mack Walker, *The Salzburg Transaction: Expulsion and Redemption in Eighteenth-Century Germany* (Ithaca, N.Y.: Cornell University Press, 1992) and George Fenwick Jones, *The Salzburger Saga: Religious Exiles and Other Germans Along the Savannah* (Athens: University of Georgia Press, 1984). "Greater Pennsylvania" refers to Pennsylvania and the areas in surrounding colonies settled largely by people from Pennsylvania and maintaining economic ties to the colony. Greater Pennsylvania extended from parts of New Jersey to the southern backcountry, as far south as North Carolina. See Carl Bridenbaugh, *Myths and Realities: Societies of the Colonial South* (Baton Rouge: Louisiana State University Press, 1952; reprint New York: Atheneum, 1963), 119–26, esp. 127. See also Parke Rouse, *The Great Wagon Road from Philadelphia to the South* (New York: McGraw-Hill, 1973), and Bernard Bailyn, with the assistance of Barbara DeWolfe, *Voyagers to the West: A Passage in the Peopling of America on the Eve of the Revolution* (New York: Knopf, 1986), 14–17.

Some historians extend the boundaries of Greater Pennsylvania as far south as the South Carolina or even Georgia backcountry. However, in my study of German immigration into the colonies I found few settlers from the north venturing past North Carolina, while the vast majority of immigrants in the South Carolina and Georgia backcountry came through the port cities in those colonies. See Fogleman, *Hopeful Journeys*, 8–11.

12. For historians taking a negative view of religious developments in Pennsylvania in this era, stressing confusion, indifference, and hostility, see Charles H. Maxson, *The Great Awakening in the Middle Colonies* (Chicago: University of Chicago Press, 1920); Martin E. Lodge, "The Crisis of the Churches in the Middle Colonies, 1720–1750," *Pennsylvania Magazine of History and Biography* 95 (1971): 195–220; John B. Frantz, "The Awakening of Religion Among the German Settlers in the Middle Colonies," *William and Mary Quarterly* 33 (1976): 266–88. Jon Butler argues that renewal and development in religious culture took place from 1680 to 1760 without a "Great Awakening," but that coercion, not freedom or volunteerism, was the dynamic that led to this. See Butler, *Awash in a Sea of Faith: Christianizing the American People* (Cambridge, Mass.: Harvard University Press, 1990), 98–163 and "Enthusiasm Described and Decried: The Great Awakening as Interpretive Fiction," *Journal of American History* 69 (1982): 305–25.

For historians viewing Pennsylvania religious culture in a much more positive way, stressing growth, volunteerism, and stability even among the larger church groups, see Patricia U. Bonomi, "'Watchful Against the Sects': Religious Renewal in Pennsylvania's German Congregations, 1720–1750," *Pennsylvania History* 50, 4 (1983): 273–83, and Bonomi, *Under the Cope of Heaven*, as well as Schwartz, *A Mixed Multitude*, 1–15, 81–119. Rothermund, *The Layman's Progress*, 1–15, and J. William Frost, *A Perfect Freedom: Religious Liberty in Pennsylvania* (Cambridge: Cambridge University Press, 1990), stress tension between religious groups, but to them the problems were between church groups and the smaller separatists that pushed the limits of religious freedom in the colony. Their overall assessments of religious culture in Pennsylvania before the Great Awakening are essentially positive.

13. For Saur's attacks on Penn family see Fogleman, *Hopeful Journeys*, 138–42. See also the letter Saur cosigned in 1738 that condemns conditions for immigrants, reprinted in Donald F. Durnbaugh, ed., *The Brethren of Colonial America: A Source Book on the Transplantation and Development of the Church of the Brethren in the Eighteenth Century* (Elgin, Ill.: Brethren Press, 1967), 42–53.

14. Saur, *Hoch-Deutsch Pennsylvanische Geschichts-Schreiber* 45, 16 April 1744.

15. See the *Einwohner-Neukommer* dialogues in the almanacs for the years 1751–1753 in *Der Hoch-Deutsch Americanische Calender* (Germantown, Pa.: Christopher Saur, 1750–1752).

16. For the Mittelberger quotes see Gottlieb Mittelberger, *Journey to Pennsylvania*, ed. and trans. Oscar Handlin and John Clive (Cambridge, Mass.: Belknap Press of Harvard University Press, 1960), 48. The original quotes are "von der vielen Sekten blindem Eifer" and "Pennsylvania ist der Bauern ihr Himmel, der Handwerksleute ihr Paradies, der Beamten und Prediger ihre Hölle." Gottlieb Mittelberger, *Reise nach Pennsylvanien im Jahr 1750 und Rückreise nach Deutschland im Jahr 1754* (Stuttgart: Gottlieb Friderich Jenisch, 1756), here the reprint edited by Jürgen Charnitzky (Sigmaringen: Jan Thorbecke Verlag, 1997), 124.

17. "Hier ist keine Obrigkeit, die Ältesten und Vorsteher gelten nicht. Die Leute folgen ihnen nicht sondern ein jeder ist frey und thut was er beliebt." Mühlenberg to Gotthilf August Francke and Friedrich Michael Ziegenhagen, 3 December 1742.

18. Mühlenberg to Francke and Ziegenhagen, 1 July 1743; Mühlenberg, *Journal*, April, May 1747. The quotation is from Muhlenberg's *Journal*, late November 1750.

19. Mühlenberg to Ziegenhagen, Francke, Johann August Majer, 20 December 1749.

20. Mühlenberg to Gabler, 22 December 1749; Mühlenberg, *Journal*, February 1751; Mühlenberg to Francke and Ziegenhagen, 22 September 1743. The first quotation comes from Muhlenberg, *Journal*, Introduction, 1751, and the second from the *Journal*, 12 December 1745.

21. Muhlenberg, *Journal*, January 1747, esp. 138.

22. The original of the quotation is "Summa, es ist wol keine Secte in der Welt die hier nicht geheget und gepfleget wird. Es giebt hier Leute fast von allen Nationen in der Welt. Was man in Europa nicht dultet, das findet hier Platz." Mühlenberg to Prof. Dr. Joachim Oporin, 12 August 1743.

23. Muhlenberg, *Journal*, 23 June 1747, January 1754.

24. Muhlenberg, *Journal*, 20 June 1747.

25. Mühlenberg to Francke and Ziegenhagen, 24 May 1747; Muhlenberg, *Journal*, 20, 22, 23, 26 June 1747, 23 August 1750; Johann Friedrich Vigera to Johann Martin Boltzius, 24 August 1750, in Eva Pulgram, Magdalena Hoffman-Loerzer, and George Fenwick Jones, trans. and eds., *Detailed Reports on the Salzburger Emigrants Who Settled in America*, vol. 14 (Athens: University of Georgia Press, 1989), 122, 231n17. For a brief biography of Carl Rudolph see Glatfelter, *Pastors and People*, vol. 1, 113.

26. Saur, *Pennsylvanische Berichte*, 16 August 1753.

27. "und haben ihm sein hoch-ehrwürdiges Priester-Fell recht schaffen abgetroschen, daß dem Herrn Seel-Sorger sein Kitzel vergangen: Ein mehreres davon ist daselbst zu hören." Saur, *Pennsylvanische Berichte*, 16 August 1753.

28. Saur, *Pennsylvanische Berichte*, 1 August 1754.

29. Mühlenberg to Francke, Ziegenhagen, and Majer, 30 October 1746; Mühlenberg to Francke and Ziegenhagen, 15 June 1751; Mühlenberg, *Journal*, 6 March 1745, 12 December 1745, March/April, 1 May 1750, February, 7 April, 11 August 1751, March, 2 June 1752. For a critical view of Mühlenberg and his attitudes toward women and wives see Barbara Cunningham, "An Eighteenth-Century View of Femininity as Seen through the Journals of Henry Melchior Muhlenberg," *Pennsylvania History* 43, 3 (July 1976): 197–212. For another, less critical view on Mühlenberg and his wife and family, see Paul A. W. Wallace, *The Muhlenbergs of Pennsylvania* (Philadelphia: University of Pennsylvania Press, 1950).

Chapter 2

Epigraph: "Ich will auch in solchen gefährlichen Ehelichen Gemeinschafts-Sachen den Leser nicht lang unter die alten Ketzer-Register weisen; dann in unsern neuen Zeiten, Gott seys geklagt! das betrübte Exempel von der Mutter Eva und ihren Cammeraden allzubekant ist." Georg Jacob Sutor, "Licht und Warheit, bestehend in einer Untersuchung der Secten-Thorheit, besonders der gantz neuen, unter dem Namen Herrnhuter bekannten . . . ," in Fresenius, *Bewährte Nachrichten von Herrnhutischen Sachen*, vol. 1 (1746), 623–910, here 783.

1. The most important recent work on the Mother Eva Society is by Barbara Hoffmann, *Radikalpietismus um 1700: Der Streit um das Recht auf eine neue Gesell-*

schaft (Frankfurt: Campus Verlag, 1996), esp. 112–15 on female circumcision, and Willi Temme, *Krise der Leiblichkeit: Die Sozietät der Mutter Eva (Buttlarsche Rotte) und der radikale Pietismus um 1700* (Göttingen: Vandenhoeck and Ruprecht, 1998), esp. 353–54 on circumcision. For a brief overview see Martin H. Jung, *Frauen des Pietismus: Zehn Porträts von Johanna Regina Bengel bis Erdmuthe Dorothea von Zinzendorf* (Gütersloh: Gütersloher Verlagshaus, 1998), 141–53.

2. Temme and Hoffmann disagree on some of these points. Hoffmann, for example, questions whether the ritual for men with Eva was repeated, and she is not even sure that it involved sex (115–20). Temme is sure (358–61).

3. My views on these issues have been largely shaped by the following literature: Joan Wallach Scott, *Gender and the Politics of History* (New York: Columbia University Press, 1988), especially 1–50; Lynn Hunt, ed., *The New Cultural History* (Berkeley.: University of California Press, 1989); Rebekka Habermas, "Geschlechtergeschichte und 'anthropology of gender': Geschichte einer Begegnung," *Historische Anthropologie* 1 (1993): 485–509; Victoria E. Bonnell and Lynn Hunt, eds., *Beyond the Cultural Turn: New Directions in the Study of Society and Culture* (Berkeley: University of California Press, 1999); Lynn Abrams and Elizabeth Harvey, eds., *Gender Relations in German History: Power, Agency, and Experience from the Sixteenth to the Twentieth Century* (Durham, N.C.: Duke University Press, 1997), especially therein Heide Wunder, "Gender Norms and Their Enforcement in Early Modern Germany," 39–56. On the concept of *Handlungsräume* see Heide Wunder, *Er ist die Sonn', sie ist der Mond: Frauen in der Frühen Neuzeit* (Munich: C.H. Beck, 1992), 205–41; Lyndal Roper, *The Holy Household: Women and Morals in Reformation Augsburg* (Oxford: Clarendon Press, 1989); Lyndal Roper, *Oedipus and the Devil: Witchcraft, Sexuality and Religion in Early Modern Europe* (London: Routledge, 1994), esp. 37–52; Natalie Zemon Davis, "City Women and Religious Change," 65–95, and "Women on Top," 124–51, in Davis, *Society and Culture in Early Modern France* (Stanford, Calif.: Stanford University Press, 1975); Mary Beth Norton, *Founding Mothers and Fathers: Gendered Power and the Forming of American Society* (New York: Knopf, 1996), 203–39 on communities, 240–77 on gossip, 359–99; and Merry E. Wiesner, *Women and Gender in Early Modern Europe*, 2nd ed. (Cambridge: Cambridge University Press, 2000).

4. Abrams and Harvey, *Gender Relations in German History*, esp. 3–9; Clifford Geertz, *The Interpretation of Cultures: Selected Essays* (New York: Basic Books, 1973), 87–125, here esp. 90; Victor Turner, *The Ritual Process: Structure and Anti-Structure* (Chicago: Aldine, 1969), 1–93; Nigel Barley, *Symbolic Structures: An Exploration of the Culture of the Dowayos* (Cambridge: Cambridge University Press, 1983), 11–49; Scott, *Gender and the Politics of History*, especially 28–50; Caroline Walker Bynum, *Jesus as Mother: Studies in the Spirituality of the High Middle Ages* (Berkeley: University of California Press, 1982); Roper, *Oedipus and the Devil*; Wiesner, *Women and Gender in Early Modern Europe*; Wunder, "Gender Norms and Their Enforcement"; Caroline Walker Bynum, Steven Harrell, and Paula Richman, eds., *Gender and Religion: On the Complexity of Symbols* (Boston: Beacon Press, 1986).

5. See, for example, Rosemary Radford Ruether, *Womanguides: Readings Toward a Feminist Theology* (Boston: Beacon Press, 1985); Mary Daly, "The Qualitative Leap Beyond Patriarchal Religion," *Quest* 1 (1974); Gail Ramshaw Schmidt, "Lutheran Liturgical Prayer and God as Mother," *Worship* 52 (November 1978); Rosemary Radford Ruether, *Sexism and God-Talk: Toward a Feminist Theology* (Boston: Beacon Press, 1983); Elisabeth Schüssler Fiorenza, *In Memory of Her: A Feminist Theological Reconstruction of Christian Origins* (New York: Crossroad, 1983); G. R. Schmidt, "De Divinis Nominibus: The Gender of God," *Worship* 56

(1982); Carol Christ, "Symbols of Goddess and God in Feminist Theology," in *The Book of the Goddess Past and Present: An Introduction to Her Religion*, ed. Carl Olson (New York: Crossroad, 1983); Elaine Pagels, "What Became of God the Mother? Conflicting Images of God in Early Christianity," *Signs: Journal of Women in Culture and Society* 2 (Winter, 1976); Mary Daly, *Beyond God the Father: Toward a Philosophy of Women's Liberation* (Boston: Beacon Press, 1973); Patricia Wilson-Kastner, *Faith, Feminism, and the Christ* (Philadelphia: Fortress Press, 1983); Elizabeth A. Johnson, *She Who Is: The Mystery of God in Feminist Theological Discourse* (New York: Crossroad, 1992); Ruth C. Duck, *Gender and the Name of God: The Trinitarian Baptismal Formula* (New York: Pilgrim Press, 1991); Elizabeth Rankin Geitz, *Gender and the Nicene Creed* (Harrisburg, Pa.: Morehouse, 1995).

For a critique of the feminist theologians, see Alvin F. Kimel and Catherine Mowry LaCugna, eds., *Speaking of the Christian God: The Holy Trinity and the Challenge of Feminism* (Leominster: Gracewing; Grand Rapids, Mich.: W.B. Eerdmans, 1992), and LaCugna, *God for Us: The Trinity and Christian Life* (New York: HarperSan Francisco, 1991). For a response to this view see David S. Cunningham, *These Three Are One: The Practice of Trinitarian Theology* (Malden, Mass.: Blackwell, 1998).

6. Philip Walker Butin, *Revelation, Redemption, and Response: Calvin's Trinitarian Understanding of the Divine-Human Relationship* (New York: Oxford University Press, 1995); Samuel M. Powell, *The Trinity in German Thought* (Cambridge: Cambridge University Press, 2001).

7. Socinians believed that Christ was a man, though one whom God created as perfect and with special authority and a revelation of his will. Arians recognized that Christ was more than a mere human, yet inferior to God. See Conrad Wright, *The Beginnings of Unitarianism in America* (Boston: Star King Press of Beacon Press, 1955), 4, 201–2. See also Earl Morse Wilbur, *A History of Unitarianism: Socinianism and Its Antecedents* (Cambridge, Mass.: Harvard University Press, 1945).

8. Martin Luther, "Eine kurze Form der Zehn Gebote, eine kurze Form des Glaubens, eine kurze Form des Vaterunsers (1520)," in *Martin Luther: Die reformatorischen Grundschriften*, ed. Horst Beintker, 4 vols., here vol. 4, *Die Freiheit eines Christen* (Munich: Deutscher Taschenbuch Verlag, 1983), 49–79. Cunningham, for example, addresses the early modern understanding of the passive female role in conception (see *These Three Are One*, 55–88). Mary E. Fissell, *Vernacular Bodies: The Politics of Reproduction in Early Modern England* (Oxford: Oxford University Press, 2004), esp. 32–35, 197–203, found that a popular medical text in sixteenth-century England altered a German text that had stressed passivity among women during conception and replaced it with a view that elevated the role of women during the process. Furthermore, popular Restoration texts provided varying views, but favored the notion of a more active role for women.

9. Butin, *Revelation, Redemption, and Response*.

10. John Calvin, *Institutes of the Christian Religion*, ed. John T. McNeill, trans. Ford Lewis Battles (Philadelphia: Westminster Press, 1960), here vol. 1, Book I, Chapter 13, 120–59.

11. Huldrych Zwingli, "Schriftpredigt (1522)," in *Zwingli Hauptschriften*, ed. Fritz Blanke, Oskar Farner, and Rudolf Pfister (Zurich: Zwingli-Verlag, 1940), vol. 1, 59–119, esp. 64–78. See also Zwingli, "Marienpredigt (1522)," *Hauptschriften*, vol. 1, 121–64; "Credo-Predigt (1528)," *Hauptschriften*, vol. 2 (1941), Part II, 15–65.

12. Menno Simon, "A Confession of the Triune, Eternal, and True God, Father, Son, and Holy Ghost," in *The Complete Works of Menno Simon* (Elkhart, Ind.: John F. Funk and Brother, 1871, rep. Aylmer, Ont.: Pathway Publishers, 1983), Part II, 183–88.

13. Powell, *The Trinity in German Thought*, 31–59; Gerhard Wehr, *Jakob Böhme* (Reinbek: Rowohlt Taschenbuch Verlag, 1971), 76–68; *Confessie ende Vredehandelinge, Geschiet tot Dordrecht, A° 1632* (Harlem, 1633), 15, 22, 29; William S. Babcock, "A Changing of the Christian God: The Doctrine of the Trinity in the Seventeenth Century," *Interpretation* 45, 2 (April 1991): 133–46.

14. Powell, *The Trinity in German Thought*, 60–103, Amy Plantinga Pauw, *"The Supreme Harmony of All": The Trinitarian Theology of Jonathan Edwards* (Grand Rapids, Mich.: W.B. Eerdmans, 2002).

15. Powell, *The Trinity in German Thought*, 60–103.

16. Wiesner, *Women and Gender in Early Modern Europe*, 222–25, and Wunder, *Er ist die Sonn', sie ist der Mond*, 217–41. On restrictions against Calvinist women preaching, see Davis, "City Women and Religious Change." On women playing significant roles (including preaching) in Lollard communities in England until the early sixteenth century, see Shannon McSheffrey, *Gender and Heresay: Women and Men in Lollard Communities, 1420–1530* (Philadelphia: University of Pennsylvania Pess, 1995).

17. Wiesner, *Women and Gender in Early Modern Europe*, 242–45; Jeremy Gregory, "Gender and the Clerical Profession in England, 1650–1850," in R. N. Swanson, ed., *Gender and Christian Religion* (Woodbridge: Boydell, 1998), 235–71; and Phyllis Mack, *Visionary Women: Ecstatic Prophesy in Seventeenth-Century England* (Berkeley: University of California Press, 1992). Mack's work focuses on Quakers; however, she does have a lot of important information on other radical groups in which women had a high profile, including prophesying and preaching.

18. Mack, *Visionary Women*, and Mack, "Gender and Spirituality in Early English Quakerism, 1650–1665," in Elisabeth Potts Brown and Susan Mosher Stuard, eds. *Witnesses for Change: Quaker Women over Three Centuries* (New Brunswick, N.J.: Rutgers University Press, 1989), 31–63; Jean R. Soderlund, "Women's Authority in Pennsylvania and New Jersey Quaker Meetings, 1680–1760," *William and Mary Quarterly* 44 (1987): 722–49; Kate Peters, "Women and Discipline in the Early Quaker Movement," in Swanson, *Gender and Christian Religion*, 205–34.

19. Laurel Ulrich Thatcher, *Good Wives: Image and Reality in the Lives of Women in Northern New England, 1650–1750* (New York: Knopf, 1980), 215–26; Catherine A. Brekus, *Strangers and Pilgrims: Female Preaching in America, 1740–1845* (Chapel Hill: University of North Carolina Press, 1998), 27–33, and Marilyn J. Westerkamp, *Women and Religion in Early America, 1600–1850: The Puritan and Evangelical Traditions* (London: Routledge, 1999), 19–24, 39–45.

20. On the early pietist movement and the origins of "radical pietism" see Schneider, "Der radikale Pietismus im 18. Jahrhundert"; Johannes Wallmann, *Der Pietismus* (Göttingen: Vandenhoeck and Ruprecht, 1990), 80–108; F. Ernest Stoeffler, *German Pietism in the Eighteenth Century* (London: E.J. Brill, 1973), 168–216; Chauncey David Ensign, "Radical German Pietism" (Ph.D. diss., Boston University, 1955); numerous essays in Martin Brecht et al., eds., *Geschichte des Pietismus*, vol. 1, *Der Pietismus vom siebzehnten bis zum frühen achtzehnten Jahrhundert* (Göttingen: Vandenhoeck and Ruprecht, 1993). On the Gnostic elements of this movement that emphasize female qualities of God see, e.g., Verena Wodtke,

ed., *Auf den Spuren der Weisheit: Sophia-Wegweiserin für ein neues Gottesbild* (Freiburg im Breisgau: Herder, 1991), esp. Ruth Albrecht, "'Der einzige Weg zur Erkenntnis Gottes'—Die Sophia-Theologie Gottfried Arnolds und Jakob Böhmes," 102–17; Thomas Schipflinger, *Sophia-Maria: A Holistic Vision of Creation*, trans. James Morgante (York Beach, Me.: Samuel Weiser, 1998). See also Gottfried Beyreuther, "Sexualtheorien im Pietismus" (Ph.D. diss., Munich, 1963), 15–29.

21. The best overview of the early development of Halle, the role of women, and relations with the radicals is UlrikeWitt, *Bekehrung, Bildung, und Biographie: Frauen im Umkreis des Halleschen Pietismus* (Halle: Franckesche Stiftungen, 1996), 21–86. On Schuchart see Friedrich de Boor, "Anna Maria Schuchart als Endzeit Prophetin in Erfurt, 1691/62," *Pietismus und Neuzeit* 21 (1995): 148–831. For other women playing important leadership roles in the pietist movement see Jutta Taege-Bizer, "Katharina Elisabeth Schütz (1652–1721)—eine pietistische Bürgerin mit Eigensinn," in Gisela Engel, Ursula Kern, and Heide Wunder, eds., *Frauen in der Stadt: Frankfurt im 18. Jahrhundert* (Königsstein: Ulrike Helmer Verlag, 2002), 177–92; and Martin H. Jung, *Frauen des Pietismus* (Gütersloh: Gutersloher Verlagshaus, 1998).

22. Taege-Bizer, "Katharina Elisabeth Schütz"; Witt, *Frauen im Umkreis des Halleschen Pietismus,* and Martin Brecht, "Der Hallische Pietismus in der Mitte des 18. Jahrhunderts," in *Geschichte des Pietsimus,* Brecht and Klaus Deppermann, eds., vol. 2, *Der Pietismus im achtzehnten Jahrhunderton* (Göttingen : Vandenhoeck and Ruprecht, 1995), 319–57, on Halle's new trends.

23. Gregory, "Gender and the Clerical Profession in England."

24. W. R. Ward, *Protestant Evangelical Awakening* (Cambridge: Cambridge University Press, 1992); Richard P. Heitzenrater, *Wesley and the People Called Methodists* (Nashville, Tenn.: Abingdon Press, 1995), 193, 234–37, 247–48, 276, 298, 312–13; Margaret P. Jones, "From 'The State of My Soul' to 'Exalted Piety': Women's Voices in the *Arminian/Methodist Magazine, 1778–1821*," 273–86, in Swanson, *Gender and Christian Religion.*

25. Brekus, *Strangers and Pilgrims,* 23–67; Westerkamp, *Women and Religion in Early America,* 84–103; Rhys Isaac, *The Transformation of Virginia, 1740–1790* (Chapel Hill: University of North Carolina Press, 1982); Cynthia Lynn Lyerly, *Methodism and the Southern Mind, 1770–1810* (New York: Oxford University Press, 1998); Susan Juster, *Disorderly Women: Sexual Politics and Evangelicalism in Revolutionary New England* (Ithaca, N.Y.: Cornell University Press, 1994), 1–107; Dee E. Andrews, *The Methodists and Revolutionary America, 1760–1800: The Shaping of an Evangelical Culture* (Princeton, N.J.: Princeton University Press, 2000), 100.

26. Brekus, *Strangers and Pilgrims,* 23–67, and Juster, *Disorderly Women,* 1–107.

27. Mary Maples Dunn, "Latest Light on Women of Light," in Brown and Stuard, eds., *Witnesses for Change,* 71–85; Jack D. Marietta, *The Reformation of American Quakerism, 1748–1783* (Philadelphia: University of Pennsylvania Press, 1984); Soderlund, "Women's Authority in Pennsylvania and New Jersey Quaker Meetings."

28. Larson, *Daughters of Light.*

29. Westerkamp, *Women and Religion in Early America,* 84–103; Juster, *Disorderly Women,* 108–44, Brekus, *Strangers and Pilgrims,* 23–67; Andrews, *The Methodists and Revolutionary America,* 99–122; Larson, *Daughters of Light.*

30. A. G. Roeber, *Palatines, Liberty, and Property* (Baltimore: Johns Hopkins University Press, 1993)

31. Wunder, "Gender Norms and Their Enforcement," and Davis, "City Women and Religious Change" and "Women on Top."

32. Westerkamp, *Women and Religion in Early America*, 84–103; Brekus, *Strangers and Pilgrims*, 23–113; Juster, *Disorderly Women*; Dunn, "Latest Light on Women of Light"; Larson, *Daughters of Light*; Soderlund, "Women's Authority in Pennsylvania and New Jersey Quaker Meetings."

33. This discussion does not address the "Shorter thesis," which argues that a lower-class sexual revolution took place in the late eighteenth and nineteenth centuries, since it has been heavily criticized. See Edward Shorter, "Illegitimacy, Sexual Revolution, and Social Change in Modern Europe," *Journal of Interdisciplinary History* 2 (1971): 237–72, and opposing views in Robert I. Rotberg and Theodore K. Rabb, eds., *Marriage and Fertility: Studies in Interdisciplinary History* (Princeton, N.J.: Princeton University Press, 1980). The phenomenon he addresses clearly began in the aftermath of the Reformation, not in the late eighteenth century. Also excluded is Foucault, who has also come under fire, yet remains important. His transition and its causes are more associated with transitions from the late eighteenth to the nineteenth centuries, after the period of study here. See Michel Foucault, *History of Sexuality*, vol. 1, trans. Robert Hurley (New York: Pantheon, 1978).

34. See Richard van Dülmen, *Kultur und Alltag in der Frühen Neuzeit*, vol. 2, *Dorf und Stadt 16.—18. Jahrhundert* (Munich: C.H. Beck, 1992), 232–35; Wunder, *Er ist die Sonn', sie ist der Mond*, 57–88; Roper, *Oedipus and the Devil*, 37–52; Roper, *The Holy Household*, 1–5; Joel F. Harrington, *Reordering Marriage and Society in Reformation Germany* (Cambridge: Cambridge University Press, 1995); Thomas Max Safley, *Let No Man Put Asunder: The Control of Marriage in the German Southwest: A Comparative Study, 1550–1600* (Kirksville, Mo.: Sixteenth Century Journal Publishers, 1984).

35. I am using the definition of sex employed by Richard Godbeer, that is, "erotically charged interactions tending toward though not necessarily including genital orgasm." See *Sexual Revolution in Early America* (Baltimore: Johns Hopkins University Press, 2002), 11.

36. Godbeer, *Sexual Revolution in Early America*, 11–12.

37. Merry E. Wiesner-Hanks, *Christianity and Sexuality in the Early Modern World: Regulating Desire, Reforming Practice* (London: Routledge, 2000), 2–19, 59–100, 253–67.

38. For good overviews of the issues among the reformers and debates among scholars about the reformers' views on marriage and sex see Wiesner-Hanks, *Christianity and Sexuality in the Early Modern World*, 63–67; Harrington, 48–100; Isabel V. Hull, *Sexuality, State, and Civil Society in Germany, 1700–1815* (Ithaca, N.Y.: Cornell University Press, 1996), 17–22; Calvin, *Institutes of the Christian Religion*, vol. 1, Book 2, Chapter 8, 405–8.

39. For Luther's views see the following in *D. Martin Luthers Werke, Kritische Gesamtausgabe*: "Ein Sermon von dem Ehlichen Stand" (1519), vol. 2 (Weimar: H. Böhlaus, 1884), 162–71; "Vom ehelichen Leben" (1522), vol. 10, pt. 2 (1907), 267–304; "Von Ehesachen" (1530), vol. 30, pt. 3 (1910), 198–248; Luther's letter to three nuns, 6 August 1524, Correspondence series, vol. 3 (1933), 326–28; as well as and "The Babylonian Captivity of the Church" (1520), in *Martin Luther: Three Treatises from the American Edition of Luther's Works*, ed. and trans. A. T. W. Steinhäuser, Frederick C. Ahrens, and Abdel Ross Wentz, 2nd rev. ed. (Philadelphia: Fortress Press, 1970), 113–260, and "Die dankbare Schätzung des Ehestandes (1531)," in *Predigten über den Weg der Kirche*, ed. Erich Widmann (Güthersloh: Gütersloher Verlagshaus, 1977), 177–83.

40. My interpretation stressing ambiguity in Luther's view on marital sex dif-

fers significantly from that of others who emphasize that he viewed sex within marriage as a positive good in an unqualified way. See Hull, *Sexuality, State, and Civil Society in Germany*, 17–22; Safley, *Let No Man Put Asunder*, 11–40; Lyndal Roper, "Luther: Sex, Marriage and Motherhood," *History Today* 33 (December 1983): 33–38; Olavi Lähteenmaki, *Sexus und Ehe bei Luther* (Turku, 1955); G. Beyreuther, *Sexualtheorien im Pietismus*, 9–15. Weisner Hanks, *Christianity and Sexuality in the Early Modern World*, 63–64, expresses some reservations, but essentially supports this view. For views stressing ambiguity, see Reinhold Seeberg, "Luthers Anschauung von dem Geschlechtsleben und der Ehe und ihre geschichtliche Stellung," *Luther-Jahrbuch: Jahrbuch der Luther-Gesellschaft* 7 (1925): 77–122, here 113–15, on the specific point of Luther and marital sex, and Roper, *Oedipus and the Devil*, 94–97, on the general instability of the reformers' marriage doctrine. See also Rüdiger Schnell, *Sexualität und Emotionalität in der vormodernen Ehe* (Cologne: Böhlau Verlag, 2002).

41. Simon Schama, *The Embarrassment of Riches: An Interpretation of Dutch Culture in the Golden Age* (New York: Knopf, 1987), 423–24. The quote is from Johan de Brune, *Emblemata of Sinnewerk* (Amsterdam, 1624), 9, as cited by Schama.

42. Fritz Tanner, *Die Ehe im Pietismus* (Zurich: Zwingli-Verlag, 1952), 180–209; Beyreuther, *Sexualtheorien im Pietismus*, 66–69; Siegmund Jacob Baumgarten, *Theologisches Bedencken*, 7 vols. (Halle: Johann Andreas Baur, 1742–1750), here vol. 2, 85–104, vol. 3, 261–64, vol. 4, 1–64, vol. 5, 273–83, vol. 6, 165–270, vol. 7, 38–48, 71–94; Muhlenberg, *Journal*, January 1747 and 22 May 1752 (p. 326n). For Mühlenberg's misogyny see Barbara Cunningham, "An Eighteenth-Century View of Femininity," *Pennsylvania History* 43 (1976): 197–212.

43. Edmund S. Morgan, "The Puritans and Sex," *New England Quarterly* 15 (1942): 591–607; Edmund S. Morgan, *The Puritan Family: Religion and Domestic Relations in Seventeenth-Century New England*, enlarged ed. (New York: Harper and Row, 1966), 29–64; Ulrich, *Good Wives*, 106–125; Roger Thompson, *Sex in Middlesex: Popular Mores in a Massachusetts County, 1649–1699* (Amherst: University of Massachusetts Press, 1986), 190–200; Edmund Leites, *The Puritan Conscience and Modern Sexuality* (New Haven, Conn.: Yale University Press, 1986), 1–21, 75–104; Godbeer, *Sexual Revolution in Early America*, 52–83; Amanda Porterfield, *Female Piety in Puritan New England: The Emergence of Religious Humanism* (New York: Oxford University Press, 1992), 14–39.

44. Ulinka Rublack, *Magd, Metz' oder Mörderin: Frauen vor frühneuzeitlichen Gerichten* (Frankfurt am Main: Fischer Taschenbuch Verlag, 1998), 199–235; Wunder, *Er ist die Sonn', sie ist der Mond*, 155–172.

45. Stefan Breit, *"Leichtfertigkeit" und ländliche Gesellschaft: Voreheliche Sexualität in der frühen Neuzeit* (Munich: R. Oldenbourg, 1991), and Rainer Beck, "Illegitimität und voreheliche Sexualität auf dem Land, Unterfinning, 1671–1770" in Richard van Dülmen, ed., *Kultur der einfachen Leute: Bayrisches Volksleben vom 16. bis zum 19. Jahrhundert* (Munich: C.H. Beck, 1983), 112–50.

46. John E. Knodel, *Demographic Behavior in the Past: A Study of Fourteen German Village Populations in the Eighteenth and Nineteenth Centuries* (Cambridge: Cambridge University Press, 1988), 209–349, esp. 214. See also Beck, "Illegitimität und voreheliche Sexualität," who found decreasing but still relatively high premarital conception rates in one community in Bavaria.

47. Rodger C. Henderson, *Community Development and the Revolutionary Transition in Eighteenth-Century Lancaster County, Pennsylvania* (New York: Garland, 1989), 83, 153–56, 219–20, 244–45. Although a large majority of the population Henderson analyzed were ethnically German, unfortunately he did not distin-

guish between ethnic and religious groups in his analysis, so it cannot be stated for certain that these rates apply to "Germans." For premarital conception rates in New England, England, Virginia, New Jersey, and France see Daniel Scott Smith and Michael S. Hindus, "Premarital Pregnancy in America, 1640–1971: An Overview and Interpretation," *Journal of Interdisciplinary History* 5, 4 (Spring 1975): 537–70, here 561–64. Although there are clearly limits to what demographic analysis can tell us about sexual behavior, premarital conception rates are a robust measure of this one aspect of that behavior at the community level.

48. Schama, *The Embarrassment of Riches*, 438–40.

49. For a collection of essays that summarizes much of the work by historical demographers in the 1970s on this subject see Peter Laslett, Karla Oosterveen, and Richard M. Smith, eds., *Bastardy and Its Comparative History: Studies in the History of Illegitimacy and Marital Nonconformism in Britain, France, Germany, Sweden, North America, Jamaica and Japan* (Cambridge, Mass.: Harvard University Press, 1980). See Laslett, "Introduction," 23, for the figures on England.

50. Rita Bake and Birgit Kiupel, *Unordentliche Begierden: Liebe, Sexualität und Ehe im 18. Jahrhundert* (Hamburg: Ernst Kabel Verlag, 1996), 73–155.

51. Steven Ozment, *Flesh and Spirit: Private Life in Early Modern Germany* (New York: Viking, 1999), 3–52, 260–68.

52. Godbeer, *Sexual Revolution in Early America*; Mary Beth Norton, "Gender, Crime, and Community in Seventeenth-Century Maryland," in James A. Henretta, Michael Kammen, and Stanley N. Katz, eds., *The Transformation of Early American History: Society, Authority, and Ideology* (New York: Knopf, 1991), 123–50; Cornelia Huges Dayton, *Women Before the Bar: Gender, Law, and Society in Connecticut, 1639–1789* (Chapel Hill: University of North Carolina Press, 1995), 157–230.

53. Robert Dimit, "European Emotion Before the Invention of Emotions: The Passion of the Mind," Steven C. Bullock, "The Rages of Governor Francis Nicholson: Anger, Politeness, and Politics in Provincial America," and Elena Carrera, "The Role of Emotions in Seventeenth-Century Spirituality: Affective Hermeneutics," all in Vera Lind and Otto Ulbricht, eds., "Emotions in Early Modern Europe and Early America," in preparation.

54. Richard Godbeer, "Love Raptures: Marital, Romantic, and Erotic Images of Jesus Christ in Puritan New England, 1670–1730," *New England Quarterly* 68 (1995): 355–84; Marilyn J. Westerkamp, "Engendering Puritan Religious Culture in Old and New England," *Pennsylvania History* 64 (1997): 105–22, who points out that Puritan *men* were being spiritually ravished by Christ.

55. Ruth H. Bloch, "Changing Conceptions of Sexuality and Romance in Eighteenth-Century America," *William and Mary Quarterly* 60, 1 (January 2003): 13–42.

56. Wunder, *Er ist die Sonn', sie ist der Mond*, 80–88; Stephan Buchholz, *Recht, Religion und Ehe: Orientierungswandel und gelehrte Kontroversen im Übergang vom 17. zum 18. Jahrhundert* (Frankfurt am Main: Vittorio Klostermann, 1988), 117–24; Anne-Charlott Trepp, *Sanfte Männlichkeit und selbständige Weiblichkeit: Frauen und Männer im Hamburger Bürgertum zwischen 1770 und 1840* (Göttingen: Vandenhoeck and Ruprecht, 1996), 39–171; Bake and Kiupel, *Unordentliche Begierden*; Vera Lind, "Das Scheitern eines neuen Lebensentwurf und einer neuen Konzeption der Liebe (1775): Der Historienmaler Philip Peter Pfeifer: Ein Leben in Bildern," in Martin Rheinheimer, ed., *Subjektive Welten: Wahrnehmung und Identität in der Neuzeit* (Neumünster: Wachholtz Verlag, 1998), 137–54.

57. Bloch, "Changing Conceptions of Sexuality and Romance in Eighteenth-Century America." Bloch also introduces the notion of commerce into these

changes, as well as evangelical religion, discussed above. She sees this an important part of what would become the nineteenth-century cult of domesticity.

58. On Wesley, see Bufford W. Coe, *John Wesley and Marriage* (Bethlehem, Pa.: Lehigh University Press and Associated University Presses, 1996), 52–79, 126–30. For Mühlenberg's views on marriage see Cunningham, "An Eighteenth-Century View of Femininity."

59. For overviews of these developments see Wiesner-Hanks, *Christianity and Sexuality in the Early Modern World*, 147–78, 216–52, and Godbeer, *Sexual Revolution in Early America*, 1–11, 117–224, 335–39. For specific studies on regions of British North America see Kathleen M. Brown, *Good Wives, Nasty Wenches, and Anxious Patriarchs: Gender, Race, and Power in Colonial Virginia* (Chapel Hill: University of North Carolina Press, 1996); Peter H. Wood, *Black Majority: Negroes in Colonial South Carolina from 1670 Through the Stono Rebellion* (New York: Knopf, 1974), 97–103, 233–38; Kirsten Fischer, *Suspect Relations: Sex, Race, and Resistance in Colonial North Carolina* (Ithaca, N.Y.: Cornell University Press, 2002); Jennifer M. Spear, "Colonial Intimacies: Legislating Sex in French Louisiana," *William and Mary Quarterly* 60, 1 (January 2003): 75–98; Daniel H. Usner, Jr., *Indians, Settlers, and Slaves in a Frontier Exchange Economy: The Lower Mississippi Valley Before 1783* (Chapel Hill: University of North Carolina Press, 1992). On Woodmason see Charles Woodmason, *The Carolina Backcountry on the Eve of the Revolution: The Journal and Other Writings of Charles Woodmason, Anglican Itinerant*, ed. Richard J. Hooker (Chapel Hill: University of North Carolina Press, 1953). On Wesley see Aaron S. Fogleman, "Shadow Boxing in Georgia: The Beginnings of the Moravian-Lutheran Conflict in British North America," *Georgia Historical Quarterly* 83, 4 (Winter 1999): 629–59, here 649–53.

60. On the changing nature of same-sex relations in the colonies during the eighteenth century see Clare A. Lyons, "Mapping an Atlantic Sexual Culture: Homoeroticism in Eighteenth-Century Philadelphia," *William and Mary Quarterly* 60, 1 (January 2003): 119–54. On masturbation see Brian D. Carroll, " 'I Indulged my Desire too Freely': Sexuality, Spirituality, and the Sin of Self-Pollution in the Diary of Joseph Moody, 1720–1724," *William and Mary Quarterly* 60, 1 (January 2003): 155–70, and Thomas W. Laqueur, *Solitary Sex: A Cultural History of Masturbation* (New York: Zone Books, 2003).

61. Wunder, "Gender Norms and Their Enforcement," and Godbeer, *Sexual Revolution in Early America*, 227–339.

62. Bach, *Voices of the Turtledoves*; E. G. Alderfer, *The Ephrata Commune* (Pittsburgh: University of Pittsburgh Press, 1985); Donald F. Durnbaugh, *Fruit of the Vine* (Elgin, Ill.: Brethren Press, 1997), 87–102; James E. Ernst, *Ephrata: A History* (Allentown, Pa.: Pennsylvania German Folklore Society, 1963); Walther C. Klein, *Johann Conrad Beissel: Mystic and Martinet, 1690–1768* (Philadelphia: University of Pennsylvania Press, 1942); Julius Friedrich Sachse, *The German Sectarians of Pennsylvania, 1708–1742, A Critical and Legendary History of the Ephrata Cloister and the Dunkers*, vol. 1 (Philadelphia: J.F. Sachse, 1899), reprint (New York: AMS Press, 1971).

63. I would like to thank Jonathan Yonan for his helpful comments on confessionalism that greatly assisted me in the development of my views on the subject.

64. Gerhard Johannes Raisig, *Theologie und Frömmigkeit bei Johann Philipp Fresenius: Eine Studie zur Theorie und Lebenspraxis im Pietismus der frühen Aufklärung* (Frankfurt am Main: Peter Lang, 1975). Numerous essays in Engel, Kern, and Wunder, *Frauen in der Stadt*, addresses the radical religious culture developing in Frankfurt, focusing on women (see especially Pia Schmid, "Brüderische

Schwestern—Frankfurter Herrnhuterinnen des 18. Jahrhunderts in ihren Lebensläufen," 161–75, and Taege-Bizer, "Katharina Elisabeth Schütz."

65. Martin Greschat, ed., *Orthodoxie und Pietismus* (Stuttgart: W. Kohlhammer Verlag, 1982); Wallmann, 36–79 and 123–43; Stoeffler, *German Pietism in the Eighteenth Century*, 1–130; Brecht, "Der Württembergische Pietismus," in Brecht and Deppermann, *Geschichte des Pietismus*, vol. 2, 225–95; Hartmut Lehmann, *Pietismus und weltliche Ordnung in Württemberg vom 17. bis zum 20. Jahrhundert* (Stuttgart: W. Kohlhammer Verlag, 1969), 22–134.

66. On Halle's increasing conservatism and changing attitudes toward women see Brecht, "Der Hallische Pietismus in der Mitte des 18. Jahrhundert," and Paul Knothe, "Siegmund Jakob Baumgarten und seine Stellung in der Aufklärungstheologie," *Zeitschrift für Kirchengeschichte* n.s. 46, 9 (1928): 491–536; Martin Schloemann, *Siegmund Jacob Baumgarten: System und Geschichte in der Theologie des Überganges zum Neuprotestantismus* (Göttingen: Vandenhoeck and Ruprecht, 1974); Ward, *The Protestant Evangelical Awakening*, 54–92; and Witt, *Frauen im Umkreis des Halleschen Pietismus*. In this respect the Hallensians differed significantly from the Lutheran pietists in Württemberg, who continued to promote a high profile role for women throughout the eighteenth century. See also Ulrike Gleixner, *Pietismus und Bürgertum: Eine historische Anthropologie der Frömmigkeit: Württemberg, 17.—19. Jahrhundert* (Göttingen: Vandenhoeck and Ruprecht, 2005).

67. Patricia U. Bonomi, *Under the Cope of Heaven: Religion, Society, and Politics in Colonial America* (Oxford: Oxford University Press, 2003); Jon Butler, *Awash in a Sea of Faith* (Cambridge, Mass.: Harvard University Press, 1990), 37–193; Joyce D. Goodfriend, *Before the Melting Pot: Society and Culture in Colonial New York City, 1664–1730* (Princeton, N.J.: Princeton University Press, 1992); Westerkamp, *Women and Religion in Early America*, 75–103; Brekus, *Strangers and Pilgrims*, 23–113.

68. As quoted in Hoffmann, *Radikalpietismus um 1700*, 116.

69. Hoffmann, 136–62. On the importance and use of polemical literature in general during this era see Martin Gierl, *Pietismus und Aufklärung: Theologische Polemik und die Kommunikationsreform der Wissenschaft am Ende des 17. Jahrhunderts* (Göttingen: Vandenhoeck and Ruprecht, 1997).

70. Hoffmann, *Radikalpietismus um 1700*, 136–62; Temme, *Krise der Leiblichkeit*; Schneider, "Der radikale Pietismus im 18. Jahrhundert," 133–35; Sutor, "Licht und Warheit," in Fresenius, *Bewährte Nachrichten*, vol. 1, 783. Fresenius also compared Moravian beliefs and practices regarding female power to the Mother Eva Society in his commentary on Pastor Johann Christoph Schinmeyer's correspondence, in Fresenius, *Bewährte Nachrichten*, vol. 3, 41–52. On Baumgarten see *Theologische Bedencken*, vol. 5, 451–52, and vol. 6, 833, 848–50. Alexander Volck also compared the Moravians to the Mother Eva Society in *Das Entdeckte Geheimnis der Bosheit der Herrnhutischen Secte* (Frankfurt: Heinrich Ludwig Brönner, 1748, here reprint of Philadelphia edition: Johann Boehm, 1749), 50–54.

Chapter 3

Epigraph: Mühlenberg to Israel Acrelius, 22 June 1750.

1. Most Moravian historians have downplayed or ignored the issues of their so-called "Sifting Period" (*Sichtungszeit*). Many documents from this era were destroyed by archivists in the late eighteenth and early nineteenth centuries, in

part because Moravian leadership was embarrassed by their contents and hoped to promote a better image of the church by writing new histories of the movement without such documents. See Paul M. Peucker, "'In Staub und Asche': Bewertung und Kassation im Unitätsarchiv, 1760–1810," in Rudolf Mohr, ed., *"Alles ist euer, ihr aber seit Christi": Festschrift für Dietrich Meyer* (Cologne: Rheinland-Verlag, 2000), 127–58. Recently some Moravian historians have begun reinterpreting this era of their history. See Craig D. Atwood, *Community of the Cross: Maravian Piety of Colonial Bethlehem* (University Park: Pennsylvania State University Press, 2004), 11–19; Paul Martin Peucker, "'Inspired by the Flames of Love': Homosexuality and Moravian Brothers Around 1750," *Journal of the History of Sexuality*, forthcoming; Peucker, "'Blut auf unsre grünen Bändchen': Die Sichtungszeit in der Herrnhuter Brüdergemeine," *Unitas Fratrum* 49/50 (2002): 41–94; Hans-Walther Erbe, *Die Herrnhaag-Kantate von 1739: Ihre Geschichte und ihr Komponist, Philipp Heinrich Molther* (Hamburg: Friedrich Wittig Verlag, 1982); Hans-Walther Erbe, "Herrnhaag—Tiefpunkt oder Höhepunkt der Brüdergeschichte?" *Unitas Fratrum* 26 (1989): 37–51.

2. My emphasis here on gender is only part of the complex Moravian views on the Trinity in this era. There is a large and growing literature on the subject by Moravian historians, and most emphasize, as I do, that the Trinity was an extremely important concept to the Moravians at this time. I am stressing the gender of the Trinity and its importance because this was the aspect of Moravian views that their enemies condemned most harshly. That is, it was Moravian views of a female Trinity that became the most important part of the conflict. For Moravian views of the Trinity generally, see Peter Zimmerling, *Gott in Gemeinschaft: Zinzendorfs Trinitätslehre* (Gießen-Basel: Brunnen, 1991); Gary Steven Kinkel, *Our Dear Mother the Spirit: An Investigation of Count Zinzendorf's Theology and Praxis* (Lanham, Md.: University Press of America, 1990); Arthur J. Freeman, *An Ecumenical Theology of the Heart* (Bethlehem, Pa.: Moravian Church of America, 1998), 70–123.

3. Nicolaus Ludwig von Zinzendorf, *Sieben Letzte Reden, So Er in der Gemeine, Vor seiner am 7. Aug. erfolgen abermahligen Abreise nach Amerika, gehalten* (Büdingen: Johann Christoph Stöhr, 1743), reprinted in *Nikolaus Ludwig von Zinzendorf: Ergänzungsbände zu den Hauptschriften*, ed. Erich Beyreuther and Gerhard Meyer (Hildesheim: Georg Olms Verlag, 1965–1971), vol. 2, 1–78, here 8–9, and August Gottlieb Spangenberg, *Darlegung richtiger Antworten auf mehr als dreyhundert Beschuldigungen gegen den Ordinarium Fratrum* (Leipzig: Marchesche Buchhandlung, 1751), 232–33, reprinted in *Ergänzungsbände zu den Hauptschriften*, vol. 5. For the newspaper article referring to Christ as the Creator see Thurnstein (Zinzendorf), open letter printed in the *Pennsylvania Gazette*, 7 April 1742, 3. Zinzendorf refers to Christ as the Creator in a sermon preached in Philadelphia in 1742 as well. See Zinzendorf, "Sermon Held in the Brethren's Church in Philadelphia on the Second Sunday in Advent, 1742," 119–31, here 122–23, in *A Collection of Sermons from Zinzendorf's Pennsylvania Journey, 1741–1742*, ed. Craig D. Atwood, trans. July Tomberlin Weber (Bethlehem, Pa.: Moravian Church of America, 2001). See also Freeman's analysis of this concept in *An Ecumenical Theology of the Heart*, 83–84, 168–69, and Otto Uttendörfer, *Zinzendorf und die Mystik* (Berlin: Christlicher Zeitschriften-Verlag, 1952), 338–44. For a more thorough analysis of the Christ as Creator concept among the Moravians, see Atwood, *Community of the Cross*, 77–83, 144–48, 152–54.

For the polemics attacking the Moravian view of Christ as the Creator see Fresenius, *Bewährte Nachrichten von Herrnhutischen Sachen*, here vol. 1, 158–59, 166, and vol. 3, 950–56. Johann Philip Boehm, *Getreue Warnungs-Brief an die Hochteutsche Evangelisch Reformierten Gemeinden und alle deren Glieder, in Pensylvanien* (Philadelphia: Andrew Bradford, 1742); Gerardus Kulenkamp et al., *Nadare Trouhartige Waarschouwinge, Tegen de Verleidingen der Herrnhuters* (Amsterdam: Loveringh and Borstius, 1750), 16–30. See also Johann Georg Walch, *Theologisches Bedencken von der beschaffenheit der Herrnhutischen secte und wie sich ein landes-herr in ansehung zu verhalten habe* (Frankfurt am Main: Johann Leonhard Buchner, 1747), 55–56.

4. See Nicolaus Ludwig von Zinzendorf, *Pennsylvanische Nachrichten vom dem Reiche Christi* (1742), reprinted in *Hauptschriften*, vol. 2, "Der öffentlichen Gemeinreden im Jahr 1747, erster Theil, Anhang" (1748), reprinted in *Hauptschriften*, vol. 4, 1–14, 368–73. For a translation of Zinzendorf's Germantown sermon, see "The First Sermon in Pennsylvania held in Germantown in the Reformed Church on December 20/31, 1741," in *A Collection of Sermons from Zinzendorf's Pennsylvania Journey*, 19–29, especially 21–22, 24, 26. A number of historians have analyzed the eighteenth-century Moravian view of the Holy Spirit as mother, the most important of whom are Craig Atwood, "The Mother of God's People: The Adoration of the Holy Spirit in the Eighteenth-Century Brüdergemeine," *Church History* 68, 4 (December 1999): 886–909, esp. 892–95; Atwood, *Community of the Cross*, 64–70, 154–56; Zimmerling, *Gott in Gemeinschaft*; Kinkel, *Our Dear Mother the Spirit*. See also Freeman, *An Ecumenical Theology of the Heart*, 88–90, 105–23; Jörn Reichel, *Dichtungstheorie und Sprache bei Zinzendorf: 12. Anhang zum Herrnhuter Gesangbuch* (Bad Homburg: Gehlen, 1969), 29–64, esp. 61–63; F. Ernest Stoeffler, *Mysticism in the German Devotional Literature of Colonial Pennsylvania* (Allentown, Pa.: Pennsylvania German Folklore Society, 1950), 67–90.

5. See entries for 5 December 1744, 1 January, 15 April 1745 in Vernon H. Nelson et al., eds., and Kenneth G. Hamilton and Lothar Madeheim, trans., *The Bethlehem Diary*, vol. 2 (Bethlehem, Pa.: Moravian Archives, 2001), 162, 193, 274, and Gemein-Diarium 1747, Beilage 79, reprinted in Hans-Christoph Hahn and Hellmut Reichel, *Zinzendorf und die Herrnhuter Brüder: Quellen zur Geschichte der Brüder-Unität von 1722 bis 1760* (Hamburg: Friedrich Wittig Verlag, 1977), 299–301. For criticism of the Moravian view of the Holy Spirit as mother, see Johann Georg Walch, *Theologisches Bedencken*, 7 vols. (Halle: Johann Andreas Baur, 1742–1750), 44–60, and Jacob Siegmund Baumgarten, *Theologisches Bedencken* (Frankfurt am Main: Johann Leonhard Buehrer, 1747), vol. 5, 438, vol. 6, 771–72. For the booklet of daily readings, see *Ein Büchlein von Gott dem Heiligen Geiste des selbständigen Weisheit und Unser aller Mutter* (Barby, 1756).

6. Other examples can be found in hymns 1872, introduction and verses 1–5; 1887, verses 6–7; 1896 (The "Te Matrem"), introduction and verse 5, and 2188, verse 14, *Moravian Hymnal*.

7. "Amen, Amen, und doch ists auch vom heilgen Geiste wahr." See August Gottlieb Spangenberg, *Apologetische Schluß-Schrifft: Worinn über tausend Beschuldigungen gegen die Brüder-Gemeinen und Ihren zeitherigen Ordinarium nach der Wahrheit beantwortet werden*, 2 vols. (Leipzig: Marchesche Buchhandlung, 1752), reprinted in *Hauptschriften*, 124–25, 185–89.

8. Zinzendorf, "Naturelle Reflexiones über allerhand Materien, nach der Art, wie er bei sich selbst zu denken gewohnt ist" (1747), in *Ergänzungsbände zu den Hauptschriften*, vol. 5, 62; Spangenberg, *Apologetische Schluß-Schrifft*, 187–89. Among those who attacked the Moravian belief in the Holy Spirit as mother were Fresenius, who called this "a great mystery of evil" ("ein groses Geheimnis der Bosheit," see *Bewährte Nachrichten*, vol. 1, 166); Baumgarten, who saw their belief in the Holy Ghost as mother not as an allegory, but rather as a view of its essen-

tial nature as the mother of believers (*Theologisches Bedencken*, vol. 6, 811); anon., *Erweiterte Vorschläge zu einem dauerhalten Frieden zw. Sr. Excellenz dem Herrn Grafen Nicolaus Ludewig von Zinzendorff und der Creutz-Luft-Holtz-Wurm-Gemeine an Einem, Und deren Feinden am andern Theile . . .*" (Germantown, Pa.: Christopher Saur, 1749), 45.

9. Although Moravian historians have studied various controversial aspects of the group's views on gender, sexuality, the Holy Spirit as mother, bridal mysticism, and unusual views of Christ's side wound that the group held during this period, the interpretation of Jesus as female or androgynous is new and so will be explained at length here. I introduced this concept in Fogleman, " 'Jesus ist weiblich': Die herrnhutische Herausforderung in den deutschen Gemeinden Nordamerikas im 18. Jahrhundert," *Historische Anthropologie* 9, 2 (2001): 167–94, and Fogleman, "Jesus Is Female: The Moravian Challenge in the German Communities of British North America," *William and Mary Quarterly* 60, 2 (April 2003): 295–332. (I would like to thank the *William and Mary Quarterly* for granting permission to use some of this material in this book.) Since then some Moravian historians have briefly addressed this concept as well, but they either deemphasize its importance or do not connect it to the larger, controversial challenge by Moravians to gender order and hence part of the transatlantic conflict between the Moravians and their numerous enemies. See Peucker in " 'Blut' auf unsre grünen Bändchen," and again in "Inspired by Flames of Love"; Atwood, *Community of the Cross*, 110–11; and Peter Vogt, " 'Ehreligion': The Moravian Theory and Practice of Marriage as a Point of Contention in the Conflict Between Ephrata and Bethlehem," *Communal Societies: Journal of the Communal Studies Association* 21 (2001): 37–48, here 42.

10. "seine *Pleura* ist die *Matrix*, in der mein Geist gezeuget und getragen worden ist," Nicolaus Ludwig von Zinzendorf, "Ein und zwanzig Discurse über die Augsburgische Confession, gehalten vom 15. Dec. 1747. bis zum 3. Mart. 1748" (1748), reprinted in *Hauptschriften*, vol. 6, 91–106, esp. 101–5.

11. Spangenberg, *Apologetische Schluß-Schrifft*, 124–25, 187–88.

12. *Das Marschesche Gesangbuch* (Herrnhut: M. Christian Gottfried Marchen, 1731), number 1041; *Das Gesang-Buch der Gemeine in Herrn-Huth* (Herrnhut: Waysen-Hause, 1735), number 820; *Das Gesang-Buch der Gemeine in Herrn-Huth* (Herrnhut: Waisen-Hause, 1737), number 820; *Alt- und neuer Brüder-Gesang* (London: Haberkorn- and Gussischen Schriften, 1753), number 1507. The 1778 hymnal uses a different text, as do subsequent hymnals (see, e.g., *Gesangbuch zum Gebrauch der evangelischen Brüdergemeinen* (Barby: Friedrich Spellenberg, 1778), number 508.

13. Ruth H. Bloch, "Changing Conceptions of Sexuality and Romance in Eighteenth-Century America," *William and Mary Quarterly* 60, 1 (January 2003): 18–21, 30–34; Cynthia Lynn Lyerly, *Methodism and the Southern Mind* (New York: Oxford University Press, 1998), 146–75; Susan Juster, *Disorderly Women: Sexual Politics and Evangelicalism in Revolutionary New England* (Ithaca, N.Y.: Cornell University Press, 1994), 37, 62–68.

14. Nicolaus Ludwig von Zinzendorf, *Nine Public Lectures on Important Subjects in Religion Preached in Fetter Lane Chapel in London in the Year 1746*, trans. and ed. George W. Forell (Iowa City: University of Iowa Press, 1973), as cited in Freeman, *An Ecumenical Theology of the Heart*, 193; Freeman, 192–205; Hans-Christoph Hahn and Helmut Reichel, eds., *Zinzendorf und die Herrnhuter Brüder* (Hamburg: Friedrich Witter Verlag, 1977), 296–303; Otto Uttendörfer, *Zinzendorf und die Mystik* (Berlin: Christian Zeitschriften-Verlag, 1952), 344–50; Erbe, Herrnhaag,

95–104; Craig D. Atwood, "Sleeping in the Arms of Christ: Sanctifying Sexuality in the Eighteenth-Century Moravian Church," *Journal of the History of Sexuality* 8, 1 (July 1997): 25–51, here 33–39; Atwood, *Community of the Cross*, 190–94; Peucker, "Inspired by Flames of Love"; Peucker, "Blut' auf unsre grünen Bändchen," 63–65.

15. Christian Renatus Zinzendorf, the son of the count and countess, wrote a poem to his parents and Anna Nitschmann, in which he praised how they were all made into little sisterly souls by the side wound of Christ. See Lieder an und von Christian Renatus von Zinzendorf aus der Sichtungszeit, number 7 (verse 6), R.20.E.36, Unity Archives, Herrnhut. See also Gemein-Diarium 1747, in Hahn and Reichel, *Zinzendorf und die Herrnhuter Brüder*, 302, Atwood, "Sleeping in the Arms of Christ," 36–37, and Peucker, "Inspired by Flames of Love." The idea of a female soul inflamed the wildest imagination of opponents like the Heinrich Rimius, who concluded that to the Moravians male body parts must be detached at burial—see Henry Rimius, *A Candid Narrative of the Rise and Progress of the Herrnhuters* (London: A. Linde, 1753, reprinted Philadelphia: W. Bradford, 1753), 59–60. Kulenkamp and other Reformed theologians in Amsterdam attacked the Moravians on this as well, and Baumgarten condemned their beliefs that all souls are female and that after death men become women. See Kulenkamp et al., *Nadare Trouhartige Waarschouwinge*, 33–35, and Baumgarten, *Theologisches Bedencken*, vol. 6, 763–64, 795. On this belief among mystics see Wiesner-Hanks, *Christianity and Sexuality in the Early Modern World*, 44. On the Puritans see Susan Hardman Moore, "Sexing the Soul: Gender and the Rhetoric of Puritan Piety," in R. N. Swanson, ed., *Gender and Christian Religion* (Woodbridge: Boydell Press, 1998), 175–86.

16. "Nimm Ihn ins Cabinet, Wo man so zwischen Zweÿ, n redt, Wo man eins caressiert, Vor Liebs-Feur inspirirt, Einander schätzelt und küßt, Mit Haut und Haaren auffrißt." See Lieder an und von Christian Renatus von Zinzendorf, number 2, verses 4–5 and number 7, verse 12. On Zinzendorf's reprimand to the Herrnhaag community see points 19 and 20 in Craig D. Atwood, "Zinzendorf's 1749 Reprimand to the *Brüdergemeine*," *Transactions of the Moravian Historical Society* 29 (1996): 59–84.

17. Peucker, "Inspired by Flames of Love." For Bothe's polemic, which Peucker addresses, see Heinrich Joachim Bothe, *Zuverläßige Beschreibung des nunmehro ganz entdeckten Herrnhutischen Ehe-Geheimnisses*, 2 vols. (Berlin: self published, 1751–1752), esp. vol. 1, 41, 112.

18. In 1752 the single brothers in London questioned Christian Renatus Zinzendorf's view of the gender of Jesus. This occurred when Moravians were beginning to renounce many of these beliefs and practices. They resented his confusion over whether the Savior was a "man or woman person" ("Manns- oder Weibsperson") and linked this to the earlier teachings of the celibate radical pietist Johann Georg Gichtel and his followers. See Minutes of the Single Brothers Synod, London, Session II, 19 December 1752, R.2.A.32b, p. 80, Unity Archives, Herrnhut.

Of the above solutions, both Atwood and Peucker stress the androgynous view of human males (not Christ) and in Peucker's case the homoerotic solution (see Atwood, *Community of the Cross*, 91–95, and Peucker, "Inspired by Flames of Love"). When these authors do mention female characteristics assigned to Christ it is only the motherly qualities, and not the erotic qualities. This omission may be a problem, since they both stress erotic spiritual relations between believers and Christ in general and that the side hole or wound was central to the sensual feelings involved. Also, while Peucker has found credible evidence of homoerotic practices among Moravians and that some single brothers held these views toward Christ, I wonder if he does not overemphasize the importance of the side wound as anus interpretation since Christ already had one (making such new imagery redundant). Furthermore, my emphasis on the side wound as vagina instead of anus seems more in line with numerous historical examples and later interpretations, as will be shown. It is my view that the Moravians worked with *all* these solutions during this period of spiritual innovation and experimentation, more or less along the lines described by Atwood, Peucker, and myself. However, the assignment of female characteristics to the Trinity fitted into the larger pattern of challenges to traditional gender order by the Moravians and was the most inflammatory to their enemies. Hence this contributed the most to the religious conflict that is the subject of this book.

19. Religious art and images were an important part of Moravian devotion and worship in the mid-eighteenth century. Sacred paintings were often the center pieces in their places of worship, and their most prolific painter of the era, Valentin Haidt, produced dozens of portraits of Moravian men and women, as well as religious scenes and images. See Vernon H. Nelson, "John Valentine Haidt's Theory of Painting," *Transactions of the Moravian Historical Society* 23, 3–4 (1977–1984): 70–77.

20. Many of the cards are located in M135 and M136, Unity Archives, Herrnhut. On paintings in worship places see the prints in anon., *Kurze, zuverläßige Nachricht Von der, unter dem Namen der Böhmisch-Mährischen Brüder bekanten, Kirche UNITAS FRATRUM Herkommen, Lehr-Begrif* (1757). For Mariane von Watteville's work see M163, Unity Archives. The original of the expression is "O, ich erfreu, ich erfreu mich sehr, das ich gefunden das Wunden Meer, da bin ich ein seeliges Sündelein. Ich habe alles."

21. For the use of the little cards in the instructions to married couples on how to have sex see Item 12, Einige Punckte zur Einleitung in die Ehe (n.d.), in 4. Die einzelnen Departements und Geschaeftszweige der Unitäts-Ältesten Conferenz C. Chorsachen. II. Ehechor 8. (hereafter referred to as "Married Choir Materials"), R.4.C.II.8; Unity Archives, Herrnhut. There are references to Moravians using little cards with side wound verses in card games in their Wetteravian settlements and as tree decorations in the Single Brothers' House of Bethlehem. While it is likely that these were similar to those I examined in the Unity Archives in Herrnhut, it is still not certain. On the card games see A.P. Hecker, *Gespräch eines evangelisch-lutherischen Predigers mit einem, der über 6 Jahr sich zu der Gemeine der sogenannten Mährischen Brüder gehalten* (Berlin: Buchhandlung der Real-Schule, 1751), 19. On the tree and room decorations see Oct. 15, 1748, Relation von dem vom 12/23–16/27 Oct. Synod, Moravian Archives, Bethlehem and Atwood, *Community of the Cross*, 162.

22. David Morgan, *Visual Piety: A History and Theory of Popular Religious Images* (Berkeley: University of California Press, 1998), 97–123; David Freedberg, *The Power of Images: Studies in the History and Theory of Response* (Chicago: University of Chicago Press, 1989); Jeffrey F. Hamburger, *Nuns as Artists: The Visual Culture of a Medieval Convent* (Berkeley: University of California Press, 1997); Martin Scharfe, *Evangelische Andachtsbilder: Studien zu Intention und Funktion des Bildes in der Frömmigkeitsgeschichte vornehmlich des schwäbischen Raumes* (Stuttgart: Verlag Müller & Griff, 1968), 1–37, 78–139.

23. There is a significant literature on the Gnostic and Sophia traditions since early Christianity. For an overview see Thomas Schipflinger, *Sophia-Maria: A*

Holistic Vision of Creation (York Beach, Me.: S. Wieser, 1998) and Roelof van den Broek and Wouter J. Hanegraaff, *Gnosis and Hermeticism from Antiquity to Modern Times* (Albany: State University of New York Press, 1998). Also, there are several good studies of early modern mystics that present useful overviews of the older traditions and how they influenced seventeenth- and eighteenth-century mystics. See, for example, Wodtke, *Auf den Spuren der Weisheit*, especially Albrecht, "Der einzige Weg zur Erkenntnis Gottes," and E. G. Alderfer, *The Ephrata Commune* (Pittsburgh: University of Pittsburgh Press, 1985), 5–6, 14–26, 108, 112.

24. Caroline Walker Bynum, *Jesus as Mother: Studies in the Spirituality of the High Middle Ages* (Berkeley: University of California Press, 1992), 110–69, esp. 161–62. Wiesner-Hanks's work supports Bynum's on this point (see *Christianity and Sexuality in the Early Modern World*, 44). And see Barbara Newman, *From Virile Woman to WomanChrist: Studies in Medieval Religion and Literature* (Philadelphia: University of Pennsylvania Press, 1995).

25. Phyllis Mack, *Visionary Women* (Berkeley: University of California Press, 1992), 114–15; Albrecht, "Der einzige Weg zur Erkenntnis Gottes"; Schipflinger, *Sophia-Maria*; Beyreuther, *Sexualtheorien im Pietismus*, 15–29; Amanda Porterfield, *Female Piety in Puritan New England* (New York: Oxford University Press, 1992), 61–62, 80–81, 94–95.

26. See Jeff Bach, *Voices of the Turtledoves: The Sacred World of Ephrata* (University Park: Pennsylvania State University Press, 2003), 25–67, 97–114; Alderfer, *The Ephrata Commune*, 108–12; Donald F. Durnbaugh, "Ephrata: An Overview," in Wolfgang Breul-Kunkel and Lothar Vogel, eds., *Rezeption und Reform: Festschrift für Hans Schneider zu seinem 60. Geburtstag* (Darmstadt: Verlag der Hessischen Kirchengeschichtlichen Vereinigung, 2001), 251–65, esp. 255; F. Ernst Stoeffler, *Mysticism in the German Devotional Literature of Colonial Pennsylvania* (Allentown: Pennsylvania German Folklore Society, 1950), 43–65.

27. Bloch, "Changing Conceptions of Sexuality and Romance," 32–34; Rachel Wheeler, "Women and Christian Practice in a Mahican Village," *Religion and American Culture: A Journal of Interpretation* 13, 1 (2003): 27–67, esp. 45–56; Nardi Reeder Campion, *Ann the Word: The Life of Mother Ann Lee, the Founder of the Shakers* (Boston: Little and Brown, 1976), 39–49; Catherine A. Brekus, *Strangers and Pilgrims: Female Preaching in America, 1740–1845* (Chapel Hill: University of North Carolina Press, 1998), 27–33, 211–12; John K. Thornton, "'I Am the Subject of the King of Congo': African Political Ideology and the Haitian Revolution," *Journal of World History* 4, 3 (1993): 181–214, here 194.

28. Henry Rimius, *Candid Narrative* (London: A. Linde, 1753), 43–45.

29. Alexander Volck, *Das Entdeckte Geheimnis der Bosheit der Herrnhutischen Secte* (Frankfurt: Heinrich Ludwig Broenner, 1748, reprint Philadelphia, 1749), 30–35. Volck finds this evidence in, e.g., Hymn 1944, verse 4 and Hymn 2104, verse 4, *Moravian Hymnal*.

30. Gerardus Kulenkamp, *De naakt ontdekte enthusiastery, geest-dryvery, en bedorvene mystikery der zo genaamde Herrnhuthers*, 2 vols. (Amsterdam: Adriaan Wor and Erve G. Onder de Linden, 1739–1740), vol. 2, 426–52, esp. 435–43.

31. See Muhlenberg, *Journal*, 26 June 1747, and Mühlenberg to Israel Acrelius, 22 June 1750.

32. There is a large and growing literature on Moravian communities in the eighteenth century. See, for example, Atwood, *Community of the Cross*; Beverly Prior Smaby, *Transformation of Moravian Bethlehem: From Communal Mission to Family Economy* (Philadelphia: University of Pennsylvania Press, 1988); Gillian Lindt Gollin, *Moravians in Two Worlds: A Study of Changing Communities* (New York:

Columbia University Press, 1967); Joseph Mortimer Levering, *A History of Bethlehem, Pennsylvania, 1741–1892, with Some Account of its Founders and their Early Activity in America* (Bethlehem, Pa.: Times Publishing Co., 1903); Daniel B. Thorp, *The Moravian Community in Colonial North Carolina: Pluralism on the Southern Frontier* (Knoxville: University of Tennessee Press, 1989); Elisabeth W. Sommer, *Serving Two Masters: Moravian Brethren in Germany and North America, 1727–1801* (Lexington: University Press of Kentucky, 2000); Paul M. Peucker, *s'Heerendijk: Herrnhutters in IJsselstein, 1736–1770* (Zutphen: Walburg Pers, 1991); Aaron Spencer Fogleman, "The Decline and Fall of the Moravian Community in Colonial Georgia: Revising the Traditional View," *Unitas Fratrum* 48 (2001): 1–22; Erbe, *Herrnhaag*; Hahn and Reichel, *Zinzendorf und die Herrnhuter Brüder*, 178–349.

33. See, for example, Katherine Carté Engel, "The Stranger's Store: Moral Capitalism in Moravian Bethlehem, 1753–1775," *Early American Studies* 1, 1 (Spring 2003): 90–126, and Thorp, *Moravian Community in Colonial North Carolina*, 107–47, on Wachovia. On discipline see Sommer, *Serving Two Masters*, 53–54 and esp. 184n60.

34. Fogleman, *Hopeful Journeys*, 107–25, and Aaron S. Fogleman, "Moravian Immigration and Settlement in British North America, 1734–1775," *Transactions of the Moravian Historical Society* 29 (1996), 23–58.

35. See especially Atwood, *Community of the Cross*, 173–78. For more on the Moravian choir system on both sides of the Atlantic see Gollin, *Moravians in Two Worlds*, 67–109; Thorp, *The Moravian Community in Colonial North Carolina*, 58–80; Sommer, *Serving Two Masters*, 29–31; Peucker, *s'Heerendijk*, 101–22, esp. 115–18.

36. The most thorough study of Herrnhaag that does not shy away from addressing the controversies there is Erbe, *Herrnhaag*. Recently Peucker ("Blut' auf unsre grünen Bändchen" and "Inspired by the Flames of Love") has directly dealt with historically controversial issues that took place in Herrnhaag as well.

37. Erbe, *Herrnhaag*, 13–35. See translations of some of this imagery in Atwood, *Community of the Cross*, App. 3.

38. Erbe, *Herrnhaag*, 36–123.

39. "Nachdem Tags vorher die Brr. in Hhaag mit einem erstaunl. Gefühl, *alle* zu led. Schw. angenommen u. declariert worden, so haben wir diesen Abend diese erstaunl. Sache auch erfahren u. sind von dem th. (theuren) Hertzel Ren. Rubusch u. Caillet dazu singen segnet worden mit Hand-Auflegung, es war Abd. Mhl. u. Fusswaschen; ich gieng mitten aus dem Fieber heraus u. nach Bethlehem." Diarium oder Journal gehalten von Johann Christoph Becker und angefangenen A.C. 1732 in Ravensburg. See entry for 7 December 1748. R.21.A.196, Unity Archives. See Peucker, "Inspired by the Flames of Love" and "Blut' auf unsre grünen Bändchen" for more on the details and context of Moravians' views on gender developed at Herrnhaag.

40. Erbe, *Herrnhaag*, 124–54.

41. At least 103 Moravian immigrants in the North American colonies came directly from Herrnhaag and at least 23 others from elsewhere in Wetteravia. Of these, 62 went immediately to Bethlehem and 20 others to nearby Nazareth upon arrival in North America. Most of the remainder settled elsewhere in Pennsylvania. At some point virtually all of the immigrants from Wetteravia probably lived in or at least visited Bethlehem. This information was compiled from a database of Moravian immigrants in colonial North America (see Fogleman, "Moravian Imigration and Settlement in British North America," esp. 50n1, which explains the sources used in compiling the database).

Atwood, *Community of the Cross*, and Smaby, "Female Piety Among Eighteenth-Century Moravians," provide by far the most extensive work on the liturgical aspects of life in Bethlehem that treats many of the controversial issues involving women and gender addressed in my work. Other studies of Bethlehem that treat important aspects of communal life there include Smaby, *Transformation of Moravian Bethlehem*; Gollin, *Moravians in Two Worlds*; Hellmuth Erbe, *Bethlehem, Pa: Eine kommunistische Herrnhuter Kolonie des 18. Jahrhunderts* (Herrnhut, Pa.: G. Winter, 1929; Levering, *A History of Bethlehem, Pennsylvania*.

42. Atwood, *Community of the Cross*, 115–70.

43. Atwood, *Community of the Cross*, 141–70.

44. Atwood, *Community of the Cross*, 173–221, and Smaby, "Female Piety among Eighteenth-Century Moravians."

45. For a brief summary of Zinzendorf's views on marriage and the liturgical and spiritual meaning of sex between husband and wife see Hahn and Reichel, *Zinzendorf und die Herrnhuter Brüder*, 296–303; Vogt, "Ehereligion"; Atwood, *Community of the Cross*, 91–95, 152–54, 190–94.

46. Hahn and Reichel, *Zinzendorf und die Herrnhuter Brüder*, 246–49; A number of historians have briefly treated use of the lot by the Moravians. See, for example, Peucker, '*s-Heerendijk*, 118–20; Sommer, *Serving Two Masters*, 86–109; Gollin, *Moravians in Two Worlds*, 50–63. Anti-Moravian polemicists referred to this practice as well. See Volck, *Das Entdeckte Geheimnis der Bosheit der Herrnhutischen Secte*, 14–16, who refers to fourteen couples married in one ceremony in Herrnhaag, and Sutor, "Licht und Wahrheit," 690–91.

47. Foreword, addenda to the Twelfth Appendix, *Moravian Hymnal*, n.p.

48. Atwood, *Community of the Cross*, 185–94; Atwood, "Sleeping in the Arms"; Smaby, *The Transformation of Moravian Bethlehem*, 100–105; Sommer, *Serving Two Masters*, 44–45, 69–78; Vogt, "*Ehereligion*," 42–43. On Zinzendorf's affair with Nitschmann see Volck, 66–70, and Muhlenberg, *Journal*, 5 July 1747. John R. Weinlick maintains, however, that Zinzendorf was not unfaithful to his first wife. See *Count Zinzendorf: The Story of His Life and Leadership in the Renewed Moravian Church* (Bethlehem, Pa.: Moravian Church, 1984), 225–27.

49. Item 3, Married Choir Materials, R.4.C.II.8, Unity Archives.

50. Item 12, Married Choir Materials, R.4.C.II.8, Unity Archives; *Bethlehem Diary*, vol. 2, 18 February 1745, 223.

51. Hahn and Reichel, *Zinzendorf und die Herrnhuter Brüder*, 296–303, esp. the excerpt from the *Jüngerhaus-Diarium*, Supplement 76 (1750) referring to couples having sex in the presence of others. On the Mahican woman see Rahel to Maria Spangenberg, August 1745, Box 319, Folder 1, Item 10, Moravian Archives, Bethlehem. For more on the Cabinet, or little cabinet (*Cabinetgen*), see Lieder an und von Christian Renatus von Zinzendorf, number 2 (verse 5) and number 7 (verse 12), R.20.E.36, Unity Archives. For historians' treatments of these issues see Erbe, "Herrnhaag—Tiefpunkt oder Höhepunkt?" 42–43; Smaby, *The Transformation of Moravian Bethlehem*, 103; Erbe, *Bethlehem, Pa.*, 38–39; Atwood, "Sleeping in the Arms," 39–44, and *Community of the Cross*, 185–88.

52. Defining what is meant by women "preaching" in the eighteenth century is not an easy task. The terms "prophesying" or "exhorting" were often used to describe the work of unordained women in the early modern period who had no permanent posts as heads of congregations, yet spoke to groups about faith, the power of God, Jesus, and the like, sometimes in an ecstatic manner warning of the approaching apocalypse. I am using the term "preaching" to refer to Moravian women (some of whom were ordained) who traveled with their hus-

bands to Lutheran, Reformed, and other communities and met with groups of women outside church services, and also to women like Anna Nitschmann, who spoke before groups of non-Moravian men and women, sometimes in meeting houses. Nitschmann preached in a confident style without notes, conscious that she was a model to women in her audiences. See Lucinda Martin, "Möglichkeiten und Grenzen geistlicher Rede von Frauen in Halle und Herrnhut," *Pietismus und Neuzeit* 29 (2003): 80–100. In North America, informal lay "preaching" by men was common and carried with it significant authority in the German communities, where there were few properly ordained European pastors. Thus Moravian men and women performing similar roles represented a significant threat to many, and the anti-Moravian polemics severely condemned the group for allowing women (as well as untrained men) to carry out such "preaching" in these communities.

53. ". . . ein Schwesterherz ist ein treues Herz," as quoted in Uttendörfer, *Zinzendorf und die Frauen,* 13.

54. Nicolaus Ludwig von Zinzendorf, "Reden vor Frauen-Personen gehalten in Philadelphia alle ab," R.14.A.38.1a.3, Unity Archives, and Uttendörfer, *Zinzendorf und die Frauen,* 5–19. For recent literature on Moravian women, see Beverly Prior Smaby, "Forming the Single Sisters' Choir in Bethlehem," *Transactions of the Moravian Historical Society* 28 (1994): 1–14; Smaby, "Female Piety Among Eighteenth Century Moravians"; Katherine M. Faull, ed. and trans., *Moravian Women's Memoirs: Their Related Lives, 1750–1820* (Syracuse, N.Y.: Syracuse University Press, 1997); Peter Vogt, "A Voice for Themselves: Women as Participants in Congregational Discourse in the Eighteenth-Century Moravian Movement," in Beverly Mayne Kienzle and Pamela J. Walker, eds., *Women Preachers and Prophets Through Two Millennia of Christianity* (Berkeley: University of California Press, 1998), 227–47.

55. Hahn and Reichel, *Zinzendorf und die Herrnhuter Brüder,* 292–95; Uttendörfer, *Zinzendorf und die Frauen,* 36–66. In her study of the single sisters choir in Bethlehem, Smaby also concludes that Zinzendorf's attempt to empower women was limited (see "Female Piety Among Eighteenth Century Moravians"). See also Lucinda Martin, "Möglichkeiten und Grenzen geistlicher Rede von Frauen in Halle und Herrnhut," *Pietismus und Neuzeil* 29 (2003): 80–100.

56. Nitschmann and Zinzendorf's activities are documented in the sources listed below. Molther is connected to Nitschmann and Zinzendorf's preaching tour in an anonymous article printed in Fresenius, "Americanische Nachrichten von Herrnhutischen Sachen," 140.

57. J. Taylor Hamilton and Kenneth Hamilton, *History of the Moravian Church* (Bethlehem, Pa.: Moravian Church, 1967), 86.

58. Nitschmann's views are in a series of 21 letters she wrote from 1740 to 1742. See R.20.B. 20a and R.14.A.26.66–82, Unity Archives. For her diary see Diarium der Schwester Anna Nitschmannin Von Ihre Reysse nacher Pennsylvanien (hereafter Nitschmann Travel Diary,1740), R.14.A.26.65.

59. As quoted in Uttendörfer, *Zinzendorf und die Frauen,* 27.

60. Nitschmann Travel Diary, 1740; Anna Nitschmann to the Moravians in Holland, Wetteravia, Herrnhut, April 1741, R.14.A.26, Nr. 68; Nitschmann to Benigna Zinzendorf, April 1741, Nr. 71; Nitschmann to Sister Augustina, April 1741, Nr. 72; Nitschmann to Anna Pisch, April 1741, Nr. 73; Nitschmann to Isaac LeLong, May 1741, Nr. 74; Nitschmann to Count Zinzendorf, 3 May 1741?, Nr. 75; Nitschmann to Sister Hutton et al., 12 June 1741, Nr. 77; Nitschmann to LeLong, 18 March 1742, Nr. 80.

61. Benigna von Zinzendorf to the Moravians in Europe, 30 May 1742, R.14.A.26, Nr. 84; Benigna Zinzendorf to the Single Sisters and Older Girls Choir in Herrnhaag, 16 June 1742, Nr. 85; Benigna Zinzendorf to her mother, 30 July 1742, Nr. 86; Benigna Zinzendorf to the Elders' Choir, 31 July 1742, Nr. 87. Some of these events are briefly summarized in A. Katherine Miller, trans., "Benigna's First Visit to North America," *Transactions of the Moravian Historical Society* 27 (1992): 62–66, a translation of a contemporary biography.

62. Reiße Diarium der 2 Ledigen Schwestern Anna Ramsbergerin und Maria Catharina Binderin von ihrem Besuch der Ledigen Weibs-Leute im Lande (hereafter Ramsberger and Binder Diary, 4 March to 24 April 1753), R.14.Aa.19, Unity Archives.

63. *Ein ABC Buch bey allen Religionen ohne billigen Anstoß zu gebrauchen* (Germantown, Pa.: Christopher Saur, 1738).

64. Brandmüller's Diarum vom 1sten biß 24ten Sept. 1745 St.V. (hereafter Brandmüller Diary, 1–24 September 1745) and Continuation Brandmüller's Diarii (hereafter Brandmüller Diary, 26 October 1745 to 11 January 1746), MJMO H592A, and David Bruce Diary, 19 June to 7 August 1745, MK G326, all in the Hinke Manuscript Collection, Archives of the Evangelical and Reformed Historical Society, Lancaster.

65. Anonymous, Diaria von Besuchsreisen verschiedenen Brüder in Pensylvanien, Virginien, Neu England, Maryland, N. York, July–September 1742, R.14.A.36.1; Andreas Eschenbach, Diarium von Brud. Eschenbachs aus Neu-Hanover in Pensylvanien d.d. 22 May/3 Jun 1743 (hereafter Eschenbach Diary, 22 May to 3 June 1743), which was attached to the Bethlehem community diary, R.14.Aa.10–11; Matthias Hehl, Kurze Beschreibung meiner Reise mit meiner Frau zur visitation in denen Landgemeinen Warwick, Lancaster . . . vom 6ten Nov. 1755 bis 5. Mart 1756 (hereafter Hehl Diary, 6 November 1755 to 5 March 1756), R.14.A.36.21, which notes that Anna Ramsberger met with twelve single women in Heidelberg in 1755; Frau Gottfried Roesler, Diarium eines Land Besuchs derer led. Manns Personen u. grossen Knaben in Pensilvanien (hereafter Frau Roesler Diary, 20 June to 12 August 1752), R.14.A.36.11, all in the Unity Archives. Jacob Lischy and Christian Rauch, Visitations-Reise und Predigten in den Reformierten Gemeinde Pennsylvaniae (here after Lischy and Rauch Diary, February 1745), Jacob Lischy, Relation von meiner Reise seitdem Br. Rauch von mir ist (hereafter Lischy Diary, 23 February to 28 May 1745), and Jacob Lischy, Diarium von Monath August St.V. 1745 (hereafter Lischy Diary, 14 August to 9 September 1745), all in the Hinke Manuscript Collection, MJMO H592a, Archives of the Evangelical and Reformed Historical Society. Travel Diary of Jasper Payne, 1753, translated and printed in William N. Schwarze and Ralf Ridgway Hillmann, ed. and trans., *The Dansbury Diaries: Moravian Travel Diaries, 1748–1755, of the Reverend Sven Roseen and Others in the Area of Dansbury, now Stroudsburg, Pa.* (Camden, Me.: Picton Press, 1994), 108–14.

66. Joachim Lange, *Lebenslauf, Zur Erweckung seiner in der Evangelischen Kirche Stehenden . . . Nebst einem Anhange Väterliche Warnung . . . vor dem Herrenhutischen Kirchenwesen und Missionswercke* (Halle: Christian Peter Francken, 1744), 346–58; Walch, *Theologisches Bedencken,* 107–10 and 187–98; Fresenius' own commentary in *Bewährte Nachrichten,* vol. 1, 890; anon., "Ausführliche Nachricht von Zinzendorfs Unternehmungen in Pennsylvanien, 1742–1743," in Fresenius, "Americanische Nachrichten von Herrnhutischen Sachen," 97–236, esp. 130, 140, 146 (William J. Hinke, *Life and Letters of the Reverend John Philip Boehm: Founder of the Reformed Church in Pennsylvania, 1683–1749* (Philadelphia: Reformed Church of

the United States, 1916), 366, attributes authorship to Johann Adam Gruber); Ernst Salomon Cyprian, "Letztes Votum, die herrnhutische Secte betreffend," in Fresenius, vol. 3, 1–24, here 11–12; Sutor, "Licht und Wahrheit," 680–82, 713–38. Mühlenberg to Francke, Ziegenhagen, and Johann August Majer, 30 October 1746. For Naesman's comments on the Moravians see Gabriel Naesman to Bishop Beronius, 14 November 1745, Amandus Johnson Papers, MSS 41, Box 59, Folder 3, Archivum Americanum, vol. 1, 1724–1780, pp. 108–127, here 122. Balch Institute for Ethnic Studies, now a part of the Historical Society of Pennsylvania, Philadelphia. The letter by Naesman to Beronius in Uppsala is an English translation by Amandus Johnson of the original Swedish (see ibid., Box 65, Folder 11, Photostats). I would like to thank John Fea for pointing out the existence, location, and importance of the Naesman letter.

67. For Heidelberg see, e.g., Eschenbach Diary, 22 May to 3 June 1743; *Bethlehem Diary*, vol. 2, e.g., 18 April 1745; Leonhard Schnell, Diarium seiner Landreise (hereafter Schnell Diary, 21 October to 1 November 1745) and Christian Rauch, Diarium (hereafter Rauch Diary, 6 February to 14 November 1746), MJMO H592a, and Schnell, Auszüge aus Leonhardt Schnell's Diarium (hereafter Schnell Diary, 10 January to 17 November 1746), MJMO H592 vol. 1, Hinke Manuscript Collection, Archives of the Evangelical and Reformed Historical Society. On women in the Great Awakening see Juster, *Disorderly Women*, 14–107; Brekus, *Strangers and Pilgrims*, 23–67; Westerkamp, *Women and Religion in Early America*, 73–130.

68. For Moravian women working as Indian missionaries see Carola Wessel, *Delaware-Indianer und Herrnhuter Missionare im Upper Ohio Valley, 1772–1781* (Tübingen: Max Niemeyer Verlag, 1999), e.g., 118–20; Jane T. Merritt, *At the Crossroads: Indians and Empires on a Mid-Atlantic Frontier, 1700–1763* (Chapel Hill: University of North Carolina Press, 2003), esp. 3 and 143–47; Amy C. Schutt, "Female Relationships and Intercultural Bonds in Moravian Indian Missions," in William A. Pencak and Daniel K. Richter, eds., *Friends and Enemies in Penn's Woods: Indians, Colonists, and the Racial Construction of Pennsylvania* (University Park: Pennsylvania State University Press, 2004). On the total number of female Moravian immigrants in the colony and the number of men and women involved in preaching or mission work, see Fogleman, "Moravian Immigration and Settlement in British North America," 23, and Fogleman, *Hopeful Journeys*, 111.

69. By 1760 at least 420 female acolytes, 199 deaconesses, and fourteen presbyters worked in the Moravian church (see Martin, "Möglichkeiten und Grenzen geistlicher Rede von Frauen," 86). Many of these worked in North America. The Bethlehem church book lists 127 men who were ordained as episcopus (bishop), ordinarius (high-ranking pastor), or deaconus (low-ranking pastor) and 60 women (all deaconesse) who were working in the northern provinces of North America before 1790. Of these, 60 men and 14 women were working before 1750. Additionally some men and women were acolytes and teachers. See Bethlehemisches Kirchen-Buch (Bethlehem church book), vol. 2, Moravian Archives, Bethlehem. For explanations of the various offices see Vernon H. Nelson, "Ordination in the Moravian Church in America, 1736–1790," (unpublished typescript, Moravian Archives, Bethlehem, 1996) and Smaby, "Female Piety Among Eighteenth-Century Moravians." On leadership opportunities for women see also Uttendörfer, *Zinzendorf und die Frauen*, 20–35; Hahn and Reichel, *Zinzendorf und die Herrnhuter Brüder*, 292–95, 454–61; Vogt, "A Voice for Themselves."

70. *Pennsylvania Gazette*, Nr. 741, 24 February 1743.
71. Atwood, *Community of the Cross.*

Chapter 4

Epigraph: *Büdingische Sammlung*, vol. 3, part 14 (1744), Nr. 11, 188–252. The first quote is on p. 200 and the verse on p. 204. Zinzendorf's last speech before returning to Europe, given to the Brethren gathered at Stephan Benezet's house in Philadelphia, 29 December 1742/9 January 1743, printed in *Büdingische Sammlung*, vol. 3, Part 14, 188–252, here 200, 204.
    1. Arthur J. Freeman, *An Ecumenical Theology of the Heart* (Bethlehem, Pa.: Moravian Church of America, 1998). For more on Zinzendorf's ecumenism see also A. J. Lewis, *Zinzendorf: The Ecumenical Pioneer: A Study in the Moravian Contribution to Christian Mission and Unity* (Philadelphia: Westminster Press, 1962).
    2. Erich Beyreuther, *Der Junge Zinzendorf* (Marburg an der Lahn: Verlag der Francke-Buchhandlung, 1957), 83–120.
    3. Zinzendorf's ecumenical views are explained with numerous full text documents showing in their origins in Hans-Christoph Hahn and Hellmut Reichel, *Zinzendorf und die Herrnhuter Brüder: Quellen zur Geschichte der Brüder-Unität von 1722 bis 1760* (Hamburg: Friedrich Wittig Verlag, 1977), 373–78. For literature see Liev Aalen, "Die Theologie des Grafen von Zinzendorf: Ein Beitrag zur 'Dogmengeschichte des Protestantismus'," in Martin Greschat, ed., *Zur Neueren Pietismusforschung* (Darmstadt: Wissenschaftliche Buchgesellschaft, 1977), 319–53, here 328–31; John J. Stoudt, "Pennsylvania and the Oecumenical Ideal," *Bulletin of the Theological Seminary of the Reformed Church in the United States* 12, 4 (October 1941): 171–97; Stoudt, "Count Zinzendorf and the Pennsylvania Congregation of God in the Spirit: The First American Oecumenical Movement," *Church History* 9 (1940): 366–80. On Philip Jacob Spener see his *Pia Desideria* (Frankfurt am Main: Johann Diederich Fritgen, 1675); Johannes Wallmann, "Philip Jakob Spener," in Martin Greschat, ed., *Orthodoxie und Pietismus* (Stuttgart: W. Kohlhammer, 1982), 205–23. On the Puritans see Edmund S. Morgan, *Visible Saints: The History of a Puritan Idea* (New York: New York University Press, 1963).
    4. On Zinzendorf's early ecumenical plans and relations with other groups, see Hahn and Reichel, *Zinzendorf und die Herrnhuter Brüder*, 390–96, 408–11; Dietrich Meyer, "Nikolaus Ludwig Graf von Zinzendorf (1700–1760)," in Heinrich Fries and Georg Gretschmar, eds., *Klassiker der Theologie*, 2 vols. (Munich: C.H. Beck, 1981, 1983), vol. 2, 22–38, esp. 26–29. On Moravian work in the Netherlands see Wilhelm Lütjeharms, *Het Philadelphisch-Oecumenisch Streven der Herrnhutters in de Nederlanden in de Achttiende Eeuw* (Zeist: Zendingsgenootschap der Evang. Broedergemeente, 1935), 1–70, 125–78, and Paul M. Peucker, *s'Heerendijk: Herrnhutters in IJsselstein, 1736–1770* (Zutphen: Walburg Pers, 1991). On Dippel see Stephan Goldschmidt, *Johann Konrad Dippel (1673–1734): Seine radikalpietistische Theologie und ihre Entstehung* (Göttingen: Vandenhoeck and Ruprecht, 2001).
    5. Aaron S. Fogleman, "Shadow Boxing in Georgia: The Beginnings of the Moravian-Lutheran Conflict in British North America," *Georgia Historical Quarterly* 83, 4 (Winter 1999): 629–59. Most literature emphasizes that the Moravians left Georgia because of the pressure to bear arms in the war against the Spanish, but there is ample evidence left by the Moravians themselves indicating that internal dissension was the most important cause. See Aaron Spencer Fogleman,

"The Decline and Fall of the Moravian Community in Colonial Georgia: Revising the Traditional View," *Unitas Fratrum* 48 (2001): 1–22.

6. Johann Adam Gruber's union call, "Gründliche An- und aufforderung an die Ehmahlig erweckte hier und dar zerstreuete Seelen dieses Landes, In oder ausser Partheyen, zur Neuen Umfassung, Gliedlicher Vereinigung, und Gebets-Gemeinschaft" (1736), was published in Philadelphia in what Fresenius called a heavily edited version in the ecumenical synod minutes of 1742 by Benjamin Franklin (see next note). Fresenius claimed to have published an unedited version in *Bewährte Nachrichten von Herrnutischen Sachen*, vol. 3, 351–80. The Moravians also printed it in the *Büdingische Sammlung*, vol. 3, 13–39. Heinrich Antes's "Circular Letter" ("Circular-Schreiben") was published by Franklin in the 1742 synod minutes as well. On Anna Nitschmann's residence at the Wiegner house, where the Skippack Brethren met, see Anna Nitschmann to the Communities in Holland, Wetteravia, and Herrnhut, April 1741, R.14.A.26, Nr. 68, Unity Archives. On the failure of the Moravian Schwenkfelder mission see Horst Weigelt, "The Emigration of the Schwenkfelders from Silesia to America," 2–15, and John B. Frantz, "Schwenkfelders and Moravians in America," 101–11, in Peter C. Erb, ed., *Schwenkfelders in America* (Pennsburg, Pa.: Schwenkfelder Library, 1987); August Gottlieb Spangenberg, *Leben des Herrn Nicolaus Ludwig Grafen und Herrn von Zinzendorf und Pottendorf*, 8 vols. (Barby, 1773–1775), vol. 4, 803–4, reprinted in Beyreuther et al., *Materialien und Dokumente*, vol. 2, parts 1–8; Spangenberg's letters dated 16 June and 11 July 1735 in George Fenwick Jones and Paul M. Peucker, trans. and ed., "'We Have Come to Georgia with Pure Intentions': Moravian Bishop August Gottlieb Spangenberg's Letters from Savannah, 1735," *Georgia Historical Quarterly* 82, 1 (Spring 1998): 84–120. *George Whitefield's Journals*, 27 November 1739, 24, 25 April 1740 (Edinburgh: Banner of Truth Trust reprint, 1960), 357–58, 412–13. Stoudt places Whitefield's sermon at Christoph Wiegner's house (see "Count Zinzendorf and the Pennsylvania Congregation of God in the Spirit," 370). Christopher Saur published German translations of Whitefield's sermons and a letter the next year. See *Von Georg Weitfields Predigten, Der Erste Theil, Nebst einer Einleitung und Copia eines Briefs von Neu-Yorck: Aus dem Englischen ins Hoch Deutsche übersetzt* (Germantown, Pa.: Christopher Saur, 1740).

7. Stoudt, "Pennsylvania and the Oecumenical Ideal" and Stoudt, "Count Zinzendorf and the Pennsylvania Congregation of God in the Spirit." For the ecumenical synod conference minutes. *Authentische Relation Von dem Anlass, Fortgang und Schlusse Der am 1sten und 2ten Januarii Anno 1741/2 In Germantown gehaltenen Versammlung Einiger Arbeiter Derer meisten Christlichen Religionen Und Vieler vor sich selbst Gott-dienenden Christen-Menschen in Pennsylvania . . .* (Philadelphia: Benjamin Franklin, 1742). The minutes have been reprinted three times, first in Zinzendorf's *Pennsylvanische Nachrichten von dem Reiche Christi* (1742), 47–66, which was itself reprinted in Zinzendorf, *Hauptschriften*, vol. 2, part B, 1–238. The most comprehensive and best edited version is by Peter Vogt, who recently completed a bilingual edition with minutes from all seven of the ecumenical conferences that includes a useful introduction. See Peter Vogt, *Authentische Relation . . .* , vol. 30 in Beyreuther et al., *Materialien und Dokumente* (Hildesheim: Georg Olms Verlag, 1998). On the Council of Basel see Remigius Bäumer, ed., *Die Entwicklung des Konziliarismus: Werden und Nachwirkung der konziliaren Idee* (Darmstadt: Wissenschaftliche Buchgesellschaft, 1976). For newspaper coverage of the synods, including announcements of the meetings, advertisements for sale of the minutes, and published letters about the debates and issues that arose dur-

ing the meetings see Franklin's *Pennsylvania Gazette*, Nr. 691–696 (10 March to 15 April 1742), as well as Christopher Saur's *Hoch-Deutsch Pensylvanische Geschichts-Schreiber*, Nr. 19 (16 February 1742).

8. Vogt, *Authentische Relation*, 1–37. The original of the last quote (p. 8) is "Die Gemeine Gottes im Geist, durch die gantze Welt, welche da ist Sein Leib, nehmlich die Fülle Deß der alles in allen erfüllet, die ist unzählbar, und ihre Glieder sind an Orten zu finden, wo man sie nimmermehr suchen solte." Vogt's volume provides a contemporary unpublished English translation, but there are problems with this version. Therefore, the English translations presented here are my own. See Vogt, editor's introduction, xxvi–xxx.

9. Vogt, *Authentische Relation*, 8–9, 119–20.

10. On the eve of the ecumenical conferences the Inspired member of the Skippack Brethren, Johann Adam Gruber, attacked Zinzendorf and the Moravians in a polemic entitled *Ein Zeugniß eines Betrübten, der seine Klage ausschüttet über die unzeitige, eingenmächtige übereylte Zusammen-Beruffung und Sammlung verschiedener Partheyen und erweckten Seelen so unter Nahmen Immanuels vorgegeben wird* (Germantown, Pa.: Christopher Saur, December 1741).

11. Stoudt attributed the failure of the ecumenical conferences to incompatible views of the church, Gruber's resistance, Zinzendorf's personality, and timing (i.e., Zinzendorf was dealing with first generation immigrants who had recently been persecuted in Europe and were unwilling to give up any of their religious freedom up to serve his purposes). See Stoudt, "Count Zinzendorf and the Pennsylvania Congregation of God in the Spirit," 378–80.

12. Hahn and Reichel, *Zinzendorf und die Herrnhuter Brüder*, 412–17; Irina Modrow, *Dienstgemeine des Herrn: Nikolaus Ludwig von Zinzendorf und die Brüdergemeine seiner Zeit* (Hildesheim: Georg Olms Verlag, 1994), 118–43; Lütjeharms, *Het Philadelphisch-Oecumenisch Streven der Herrnhutters in de Nederlanden*, 149–78; Freeman, *An Ecumenical Theology of the Heart*, 3–4, 95, 248–49, 270; J. Taylor Hamilton and Kenneth Hamilton, *History of the Moravian Church* (Bethlehem, Pa.: Moravian Church, 1967), 101–2, 157–58, 163.

13. *Bethlehem Diary*, vol. 2, 22 May 1745.

14. For the number and percentage of Moravian pastors among all those working in the Pennsylvania field see Aaron S. Fogleman, "Religious Conflict and Violence in German Communities During the Great Awakening," Tables 1 and 2, in Jean R. Soderlund and Catherine S. Parzynski, eds., *Backcountry Crucibles: The Lehigh Valley from Settlement to Steel* (Bethlehem, Pa: Lehigh University Press, forthcoming). See also Tables 2 and 3 of this volume. The number of schools, which is impressionistic and probably only a portion of the total, is based on Moravian itinerant diaries (e.g., Brandmüller, 1745–46, Archives of the Evangelical and Reformed Historical Society), correspondence by and about itinerants, and synod minutes in Bethlehem, Lancaster, and Herrnhut, as well as *The Bethlehem Diary*, vols. 1–2, and Pyrlaeus Notebook, R.27.375, Unity Archives.

15. *Bethlehem Diary*, 14 June 1742 o.s., vol. 1, 17–20; Beverly Prior Smaby, *The Transformation of Moravian Bethlehem: From Communal Mission to Family Economy* (Philadelphia: University of Pennsylvania Press, 1988); Craig D. Atwood, *Community of the Cross: Moravian Piety in Colonial Bethlehem* (University Park: Pennsylvania State University Press, 2004); Joseph M. Levering, *A History of Bethlehem, Pennsylvania* (Bethlehem: Times Publishing Co., 1903); Gillian Lindt Gollin, *Moravians in Two Worlds: A Study of Changing Communities* (New York: Columbia University Press, 1967).

16. See, for example, Jacob Lischy, Relation von meiner Reise seitdem Br. Rauch von mir ist (hereafter Lischy Diary, 23 February to 28 May 1745), MJMO H592a, William J. Hinke Manuscript Collection, Archives of the Evangelical and Reformed Historical Society.

17. Schnell Diary, 10 January to 17 November 1746.

18. Lischy, for example, accomplished this in Bern and in Tulpehocken (see Lischy Diarium, hereafter Lischy Diary, 5–19 April 1743, R.14.A.36. 2–3, 5, Unity Archives). For Spangenberg see Br. Josephs Land-Besuch, JE III 3e, Moravian Archives (hereafter Spangenberg Report, 8 February to 4 March 1748).

19. Zinzendorf's last speech before returning to Europe, 29 December 1742/9 January 1743, in *Büdingische Sammlung*, vol. 3, part 14, Nr. 8, 215–16, 247–52. A 49-point plan for work in America is outlined in Kurtze Relation von dem General Synod gehalten in Friedrichstown (Frederick, Pennsylvania), March 1745, sixth session minutes, in Auszüge aus den Verhandlungen der Pennsylvanischen Synoden, 1745–1748, MKX G326, Archives of the Evangelical and Reformed Historical Society. See also *Bethlehem Diary*, vol. 1, 1742–1744, ed. and trans. Kenneth G. Hamilton (Bethlehem, Pa.: Moravian Archives, 1971), 4, 17 November 1742, 112–13, 118, the entry for 16 December 1742 (129–30) on the follow-up conference, and *Bethlehem Diary*, vol. 2, 23 January 1744 (25), 26 April 1744 (129–30). On the success of Moravian overseas migrations see Aaron S. Fogleman, *Hopeful Journeys: German Immigration, Settlement, and Political Culture in Colonial America, 1717–1765* (Philadelphia: University of Pennsylvania Press, 1996), 113–26, and Fogleman, "Moravian Immigration and Settlement in British North America, 1734–1775," *Transactions of the Moravian Historical Society* 29 (1996): 23–58.

20. Fogleman, *Hopeful Journeys*, 104–5.

21. See *Bethlehem Diary*, vol. 2, 30 November 1744 (160) and subsequent entries on Spangenberg's return. For his activities and impact during field tours in Pennsylvania, Maryland, and Virginia see Spangenberg Report, 8 February to 4 March 1748, and Kurze Nachricht von Br. Joseph's und Matth. Reuzen's Besuch und Land-Prediger-Reise durch Maryland und Virginien . . . (hereafter Spangenberg and Reutz Report, 30 June to 18 August 1748), JE III 3f, Moravian Archives; Anonymous Diary, 2–7 November 1746, and Lischy Diary, 23 February to 28 May 1745.

22. Zinzendorf, *A Collection of Sermons from Zinzendorf's Pennsylvania Journey*, ed. Craig D. Atwood, trans. Julie Tomerlin Weber (Bethlehem, Pa.: Moravian Church of America, 2001), esp. editor's introduction, xvi–xviii.

23. About 60 percent of the white colonists attended church regularly during this period. See Patricia U. Bonomi and Peter R. Eisenstadt, "Church Adherence in the Eighteenth-Century British American Colonies," *William and Mary Quarterly* 39 (April 1982), 245–86.

24. Br. John Oakley's Journal of his Visit in West Jersey In the Year 1743 (hereafter Oakley Journal, 23 May to 4 June 1743), JD II 1b, Moravian Archives.

25. Rauch Diary, 6 February to 14 November 1746, and Br. Leonhard Schnells Reise-Diarium von Seinem und Br. Joh. Brandmüllers Land-Besuch in die oberen Theile von Virginien (hereafter Schnell and Brandmüller Diary, October–December 1749), R.14.A.36.10, Unity Archives.

26. Br. Abr. Reincke's Relation von seiner Reisse und Aufenthalt in Oblong, Dutchess County, New York Gouvernement (hereafter Reincke Diary, July–September 1753), R.14.A.36, Unity Archives.

27. Roseen Diaries for 17 September to 21 October 1748, 22 November 1748

to 3 January 1749, 7 to 28 February and 6 to 25 March 1749, et al., *Dansbury Diaries*. Ultimately Roseen did not want to continue working in the area, hoping to work instead as a full-fledged Indian missionary. Bethlehem reassigned him to Maryland in the autumn of 1749, and he died in 1750. Five years later when war came the Delawares wiped out the Dansbury mission. For a similar interpretation of shared space in the area slightly to the west of where Roseen worked see Jane T. Merritt, *At the Crossroads: Indians and Empires on a Mid-Atlantic Frontier, 1700–1763* (Chapel Hill: University of North Carolina Press, 2003).

28. Eschenbach Diary, 22 May to 3 June 1743; Diarium der 2 Br. Joh Hantsch und Jacob Adolph von ihrer Besuch in Pinsilvanien den ledigen leuthe (hereafter Hantsch and Adolph Diary, 6 February to 23 March 1746), JB II 2f, Moravian Archives; Schnell Diary, 10 January to 17 November 1746. Nyberg, Rice, Reutz, and Reincke consecrated the new Swedish church at Morris River on 18 December 1746. Laurentius Nyberg, A Short Sketch of the Awakening about Lancaster near Conestoga, Warwick, Quittoppehille, Yorktown on the Cadores, in Pensilvanien, & Monocasy in Maryland, in North America (hereafter Nyberg Diary, 12 December 1743 to 20 November 1749), R.14.A.40.2, Unity Archives. Schnell, Brandmüller, Rauch, Cammerhoff, and the Roseens worked together in and around York and then as far south as Monocacy in the autumn of 1749, before Schnell and Brandmüller toured the Shenandoah Valley. Schell and Brandmüller Diary, October–December 1749.

29. Heinrich Antes, "Circular-Schreiben" (December 1741).

30. Lischy Diary, 5–19 April 1743.

31. Jerome H. Wood, Jr., *Conestoga Crossroads, Lancaster, Pennsylvania, 1730–1790* (Harrisburg: Pennsylvania Historical and Museum Commission, 1979), 47.

32. Nyberg Diary, 1743–1749. Nyberg's attempt to work for both Bethlehem and Uppsala would eventually cause problems in Lancaster (see Chapter 7).

33. Schnell Diary, 10 January to 17 November 1746.

34. Johann Jacob Döhling, Christian Rauch, Joseph Müller, Johann Philipp and Christina Meurer, Leonhard Schnell, Johann Georg and Anna Regina Hantsch, and others preached regularly in Macungie in 1744, see *Bethlehem Diary*, vol. 2, e.g., 19, 26 January, 9 February 1744 (22–23, 26, 33).

35. Bruce Diary, 19 June to 7 August 1745; Br. Jn Oakley's Journal of his Journey from Pensilvania to Lewis Town (hereafter John Oakley Journal, 1–17 August 1742), JD II 1; John Wade's Journal of his Itinerant Preaching, 8 February to 1 April 1748(?), JF IV 1; Abraham Müller: Journal of his Visits among the Baptists, 8 to 28 March 1745 o.s., JC III 4, and Abraham Müller and Wilhelm Frey: Journal of his Visits among the Baptists, 9 October to 6 November 1746, JC III 4a; all in the Moravian Archives.

36. Charles H. Glatfelter, *Pastors and People: German Lutheran and Reformed Churches in the Pennsylvania Field, 1717–1793*, 2 vols. (Breinigsville, Pa.: Pennsylvania German Society, 1980, 1981), vol. 2, *The History*, 84–87, provides a good overview of Lischy and his work.

37. See Lischy Diary, 5–19 April 1743; Lischy and Rauch Diary, February 1745, and Lischy Diaries for the following dates: 29 April to 5 May 1743, 23 February to 28 May and 14 August to 9 September 1745, and a Lischy diary/letter from mid-1744, all in the Archives of the Evangelical and Reformed Historical Society. See also *Bethlehem Diary*, vol. 2, e.g., 9, 16, 17, 19, and 20 March 1745 (241, 245–49). Eventually Lischy left the Moravians after becoming involved in a notorious scandal.

38. Rauch Diary, 6 February to 14 November 1746 and Auszüge aus Rauchs

Diarium (hereafter Rauch Diary, 23 January to 30 June 1747), MJMO H592–592a, William J. Hinke Manuscript Collection.

39. Mühlenberg addressed the doctor shortage in a letter to Ziegenhagen, 22 September 1743. Later he and other Hallensian pastors were bleeding patients. For examples of Moravian itinerants bleeding patients in their communities, see Rauch Diary 6 February to 14 November 1746, e.g., 10 July 1746; Rauch Diary, 23 January to 30 June 1747, e.g. 18 April 1747; Schnell Diary, 10 January to 17 November 1746, e.g., 15 October and 5 November 1746. On the Jesuits see James Axtell, *The Invasion Within: The Contest of Cultures in Colonial North America* (New York and Oxford: Oxford University Press, 1985). For Zinzendorf's warning against competing with Hallensians see his last speech before returning to Europe, 29 December 1742/9 January 1743, 240–43. See Renate Wilson, *Pious Traders in Medicine: A German Pharmaceutical Network in Eighteenth-Century North America* (University Park: Pennsylvania State University Press, 2000), on the Halle medical establishment in North America.

40. Farley Grubb, "Colonial Immigrant Literacy: An Economic Analysis of Pennsylvania-German Evidence," *Explorations in Economic History* 24 (January 1987): 63–76.

41. Zinzendorf's last speech before returning to Europe, 240–43.

42. Muhlenberg, *Journal*, 12 December 1745.

43. Mühlenberg to Ziegenhagen, 24 May 1747.

44. Muhlenberg, *Journal*, December 1746. In November 1746 someone visited York, Lancaster, and Muddy Creek, where they discussed building a school in each place. Anon. Diary, 2–7 November 1746.

45. See William J. Hinke, ed. and trans., "Diary of the Rev. Michael Schlatter: June 1–December 15, 1746," *Journal of the Presbyterian Historical Society* 3, 3 (September 1905): 105–21; 4, 13 (January 1906); 158–76 (hereafter Schlatter Diary, 1746), here entry for 23 October 1746.

46. Mühlenberg to Francke, Ziegenhagen, and Majer, 30 October 1746, and Schlatter Diary, 23 October 1746. A. G. Roeber has thoroughly analyzed how concerns over property rights shaped internal politics and policy in German Lutheran churches during this era. See *Palatines, Liberty, and Property: German Lutherans in Colonial British America* (Baltimore: Johns Hopkins University Press, 1993), 243–82. See also Jon Butler, *Awash in a Sea of Faith: Christianizing the American People* (Cambridge, Mass.: Harvard University Press, 1990), 98–128, who describes the wave of church building that took place throughout the colonies during the mid-eighteenth century.

47. Zinzendorf instructed all of the brethren and sisters in Pennsylvania not to accept payment for preaching. If they did, they were on the direct path toward becoming spiritual slaves. However, they may accept needed goods (like a preaching gown) to carry out their tasks. See Zinzendorf's last speech before returning to Europe, 230–35.

48. Lischy's Diary, 29 April to 5 May 1743.

49. Nyberg Diary, 1743–49.

50. When Mühlenberg helped the Lutherans in Tulpehocken write a call for a pastor he included in the document that the pastor would receive 5s for funerals and 6s for marriages. He also noted that one of his Hallensian colleagues, Johann Nicolaus Kurtz, charged 1s for a baptism and 5–8s for a funeral and seemed to be making a lot of money from it. Furthermore, Mühlenberg heard that Gabriel Naesman, the Uppsalan pastor, was charging Lancaster £5 for each visit, but that they could not afford it, and so Naesman resigned after four visits—something the Moravians could and did exploit. See Muhlenberg, *Journal*,

12 December 1745 and 6–7 July 1747. For other examples of Mühlenberg referring to the problem of Moravian competition by preaching for free see Muhlenberg, *Journal*, December 1746 and May 1748; Mühlenberg to Francke, 17
March 1743, for the period 14–18 February 1743; Mühlenberg to Francke and
Ziegenhagen, 6 June 1743; Mühlenberg to Boltzius, 15 March 1744; Mühlenberg to Ziegenhagen, 6 March 1745; Mühlenberg to Francke and Ziegenhagen,
24 May 1747.

51. Johann Philip Boehm had no respect for the Moravian practice. To him
the Moravian preachers were enthusiasts and fanatics, like the "strolling Jews"
who went about adjuring evil spirits—the Apostle Paul had warned against them.
Boehm railed against the blood and wounds message of the Moravian itinerants
and wrote that since they preached for free it was a sign that they were false
prophets, using this as a trick to get people's possessions. See Boehm's polemic,
*Abermahlige treue Warnung und Vermahnung an meine sehr werthe und theurer geschät-
zte Reformirte Glaubens-verwandte* . . . (Philadelphia: Cornelia Bradford and Isaiah
Warner, 1743), reprinted in English in Boehm, *Life and Letters of Reverend John
Philip Boehm: Founder of the Reformed Church in Pennsylvania, 1683–1749*, ed. William J. Hinke (Philadelphia: Reformed Church of the United States, 1916), 373–
84. Michael Schlatter was obsessed with pastor salaries as well. After preaching
his first sermon in Pennsylvania on 18 September 1746 his first order of business
with his new congregation in Philadelphia was to secure his salary, which he set
at £30 Pennsylvania currency per annum. In Germantown that afternoon he
received an additional commitment of £25 per annum. Schlatter Diary, 18 September 1746.

52. Katherine Carté Engel, "The Stranger's Store: Moral Capitalism in Mora-
vian Bethlehem, 1753–1775," *Early American Studies* 1, 1 (Spring 2003): 90–126;
Hahn and Reichel, *Zinzendorf und die Herrnhuter Brüder* 320–31; Hamilton and
Hamilton, *History of the Moravian Church*, 107–13; Edmund de Schweinitz, *The
Financial History of the Province and Its Sustentation Fund* (Bethlehem: Moravian
Church, 1877), 3–29.

53. Nyberg Diary, 1743–1749.

54. Schnell and Brandmüller Diary, October–December 1749; Br. Nathanaels
u. Westm. Bericht von ihrer Reise durchs Land (hereafter Seidel and Westman
Diary, 17 November to 5 December 1747), JE II 4c, Moravian Archives; Lischy
Diary, 23 February to 28 May 1745; Hantsch and Adolph Diary, 6 February to 23
March 1746; Nathanael Seidels Diarium von seinem Land Visitation von Bethlehem bis über die Susquehanna (hereafter Seidel Diary, 25 July to 15 August
1747), JE II 4a, Moravian Archives; Sven Roseen Diary, 11–30 July 1748.

55. For Heidelberg see, e.g., Eschenbach Diary, 22 May to 3 June 1743; *Bethlehem Diary*, vol. 2, e.g., 18 April 1745; Schnell Diary, 21 October to 1 November
1745; Schnell Diary, 10 January to 17 November 1746; Rauch Diary, 6 February
to 14 November 1746. On women in the Great Awakening see Juster, 14–107,
Brekus, 23–67, Westerkamp, *Women and Religion in Early America*, 73–130.

56. Fogleman, *Hopeful Journeys*, 60–65.

Chapter 5

1. See Jean François Reynier (Johann Franz Regnier), "Das Geheimnis der
Zinzendorfischen Secte," in Johan Philip Fresenius, ed., *Bewährte Nachrichten von
Herrnhutischen Sachen*, 4 vols. (Frankfurt and Leipzig: Johann Leonard Buchner
and Heinrich Ludwig Broenner, 1746–51), vol. 1, 321–479. For the sections Fresenius refused to print, see Alexander Volck, *Das Entdeckte Geheimnis der Bosheit*

der Herrnhutischen Secte (Frankfurt: Heinrich Ludwig Broenner, 1748, reprint Philadelphia, 1749), 28–56, 65–66. These Moravian practices are also discussed and attacked in the anonymous parody, *Erweiterte Vorschläge, zu einem dauerhaften Frieden zwischen Sr. Excellenz dem Herrn Nicolaus Ludewig von Zinzendorff* (Germantown, Pa.: Christopher Saur, 1749).

2. Christopher Saur to ? , 16 November 1747, Johann Adam Gruber to Andreas Gross, 29 November 1747, Johann Christian Sieberberg to Andreas Gross, 30 November 1747, all in Fresenius, *Bewährte Nachrichten*, vol. 3, 837–43.

3. Henry Rimius, *A Candid Narrative of the Rise and Progress of the Herrnhutters* (London: A. Linde, 1753), 61–65.

4. Jacob Siegmund Baumgarten, *Theologische Bedencken* (Halle: Johann Andreas Baur, 1742–1750), vol. 6, 762–70.

5. George Jacob Sutor, "Licht und Wahrheit," in Fresenius, *Bewährte Nachrichten*, vol. 1, 690–91. Sutor also accused Moravians of brutally beating their children, and he condemned their hierarchical, autocratic socioeconomic organization, 692–97.

6. Volck, Foreword, and Reynier, "Das Geheimnis der Zinzendorfischen Secte," 477–78.

7. On German-language books in this era see Karl John Richard Arndt et al., eds., *The First Century of German Language Printing* (Göttingen: Niedersächsische Staats- und Universitätsbibliothek, 1959), vol. 1; Robert E. Cazden, "The Provisioning of German Books in America During the Eighteenth Century," *Libri 23* (1973): 81–108; Cazden, *A Social History of the German Book Trade in America* (Columbia, S.C.: Camden House, 1984); James N. Green, "The Book Trade in the Middle Colonies, 1680–1720," 199–223, and A. Gregg Roeber, "German and Dutch Books and Printing," 298–313, in Hugh Amory and David D. Hall, eds., *A History of the Book in America*, vol. 1, *The Colonial Book in the Atlantic World* (Cambridge: Cambridge University Press, 2000); John Warwick Montgomery, "The Colonial Parish Library of Wilhelm Christoph Berkenmeyer," *Papers of the Bibliographical Society of America* 53, 2 (1959): 114–49; Klaus G. Wust, "German Books and German Printers in Va.," *Rockingham Recorder 2*, 2 (May 1958): 24–29. On German immigrant literacy see Farley Grubb, "Colonial Immigrant Literacy: An Economic Analysis of Pennsylvania-German Evidence," *Explorations in Economic History* 24 (January 1987): 63–76, who presents evidence that German immigrant illiteracy during his period was only 29%—at least comparable to and probably significantly lower than in the European populations from which the immigrants came or the rest of colonial population in America (see 64–67). See Martin Gierl, *Pietismus und Aufklärung: Theologische Polemik und die Kommunikationsreform der Wissenschaft am Ende des 17. Jahrhunderts* (Göttingen: Vandenhoeck and Ruprecht, 1997).

8. Dietrich Meyer, ed., *Bibliographisches Handbuch zur Zinzendorf-Forschung* (Düsseldorf: Kornelius Kaspers, 1987), has catalogued 385 anti-Moravian polemics published from 1727 to 1764, and this does not include translations, reprints, and subsequent editions, of which there were many. Of these polemics 339 (88 percent) were published from 1738 to 1755, the era in which the Moravian threat in the Atlantic world peaked and then declined. A few of these polemics have been collected and reprinted in Erich Beyreuther and Gerhard Meyer, eds., *Antizinzendorfia aus der Anfangszeit 1729–1735*, vol. 14, and *Antizinzendorfiana II*, vol. 15, in Beyreuther, Meyer, and Molnár, *Materialien und Dokumente*, 2nd series, but the most inflammatory works by Fresenius, Volck, Reynier, and others are not included in this collection. For this reason Meyer's work should be used as the basis for studying eighteenth-century anti-Moravian polemics.

9. Joachim Lange, *Lebenslauf* (Halle: Christ. Peter Francke, 1744). The writings of Lange and other Halle theologians like Bogatzky and Baumgarten make it clear that their most important criticism of the Moravians was not their lack of emphasis on a difficult, emotional conversion experience, or *Bußkampf*, as is often emphasized in the literature on Lutheran pietism, but rather a range of issues that can be summed up as a clash over beliefs and practices concerning gender, proper doctrine, and respect for the boundaries of the Lutheran church.

10. Carl Heinrich von Bogatzky, *Güldnes Schatz-Kästleins der Kinder Gottes* (Breslau, 1718). It is a prayer book with adages from and about the Bible. An edition was published in Philadelphia in 1811. The last (67th) edition was published by Halle: Buchhandlung des Waisenhauses, 1924.

11. Carl Heinrich von Bogatzky, *Nöthige Warnung und Verwahrung vor dem Rückfall, Nebst einem zwiefachen Anhange und einem erbaulichen Briefe, worrinen die Herrnhuter nach Wahrheit und Liebe beurtheilet werden* (Halle: Waisenhaus, 1750), 108–14, 321–36; Bogatzky, *Aufrichtige und an alle Kinder Gottes gerichtete Declaration über Eine gegen Ihn herausgekommene Herrnhutische Schrift . . .* (Halle: Waisenhaus, 1751), Introduction, 15–20, 39–47, 59–70, 75–93, 124–28. See also John Kelly, *The Life and Work of Charles Henry von Bogatzky, Author of "The Golden Treasury": A Chapter from the Religious Life of the Eighteenth Century* (London: Religious Tract Society, 1889), esp. 51, 64–133.

12. Martin Brecht, "Der Hallische Pietismus in der Mitte des 18. Jahrhunderts," in Brecht and Depperman, eds., *Geschichte des Pietismus* (Göttingen: Vandenhoeck and Ruprecht, 1995), vol. 1, 319–57; Paul Knothe, "Siegmund Jakob Baumgarten und seine Stellung in der Aufklärungstheologie," *Zeitschrift für Kirchengeschichte* 49 n.s. 9 (1928): 491–536; Martin Schloemann, *Siegmund Jacob Baumgarten* (Göttingen: Vandenhoeck and Ruprecht, 1974); Baumgarten, *Theologische Bedencken.*

13. Baumgarten, *Theologische Bedencken,* vol. 1, 123–74.

14. Baumgarten, *Theologische Bedencken,* vol. 3, Introduction.

15. Baumgarten, *Theologische Bedencken,* vol. 4, 128–86, 314–690.

16. Baumgarten, *Theologische Bedencken,* vol. 5, 211–52, 361–464, 451–52, 833, 848–50.

17. ". . . das durch und durch höchst ärgerliche Weiber-Lied." See Baumgarten, *Theologische Bedencken,* vol. 5, 444. Other hymns in the Twelfth Appendix and addenda of the *Moravian Hymnal* that Baumgarten condemned in this context because of their extremely sensual or sexual nature include numbers 1945 (verses 1–2), 2096 (verses 2 and 5), 2156 (verse 8), 2281, and 2289 (verse 12). See Baumgarten, vol. 5, 444–46, 764, and vol. 6, 762–70, 785.

18. Baumgarten, *Theologische Bedencken,* vol. 6, 669–898.

19. *Väterlicher Hirten-Brieff an die blühenden Reformierte Gemeine in Amsterdam* (Amsterdam: Kirchenrat, 1738), here a reprint in German translation in *Büdingische Sammlung,* vol. 2, part 9, 289–339 (Leipzig: D. Korte, 1742), available in a modern reprint in Beyreuther and Meyer, *Ergänzungsbände zu den Hauptschriften,* vol. 8, and Kulenkamp, *De naakt ontdekte enthusiastery,* vol. 1, 52–200, vol. 2, 203–68. For a brief biography of Kulenkamp see Paul M. Peucker, "Kulenkamp, Gerardus," in *Biografisch Lexicon voor de Geschiedenis van het Nederlands Protestantisme,* vol. 4 (Kampen, 1998), 275–76.

20. Kulenkamp, *De naakt ontdekte enthusiastery,* vol. 2, 268–375.

21. Kulenkamp, *De naakt ontdekte enthusiastery,* vol. 2, 376–425.

22. Kulenkamp, *De naakt ontdekte enthusiastery,* vol. 2, 426–52.

23. Kulenkamp et al., *Nadere Trouwhartige Waarschouwinge*, 6–15.

24. Kulenkamp et al., *Nadere Trouwhartige Waarschouwinge*, 16–30.

25. *Nadere Trouwhartige Waarschouwinge*, 30–33.

26. *Nadere Trouwhartige Waarschouwinge*, 33–35.

27. "Dit is nu een uitgemaakte zaak, dat in die Gemeente eene Antichrist-liche heerschappy van menschen plaats heeft, en dat den Graf eene meer dan Pausselyke macht is opgedragen." *Nadere Trouwhartige Waarschouwinge*, 48. Kulenkamp's discussion of the above Moravian beliefs was based on his reading of the following numbered hymns in the *Moravian Hymnal*: 6, 12, 18, 20, 25, 42, 70, 71, 102, 111, 122, 176, 216/verse 1, 221/verse 7, 222, 268/verse 3, 365, 386, 412/verse 3, 433, 503, 520, 544/ verse 7, 690, 714, 726, 732, 738, 741, 804, 807, 878, and 909.

28. Uppsala Consistory to Peter Koch, 4 September 1745, *Records of the Swedish Lutheran Churches at Raccoon and Penn's Neck, 1713–1786*, trans. and comp. Federal Writer's Project of the Works Progress Administration, State of New Jersey, 1938, 46–52, and Naesman to Beronius, 14 November 1745.

29. Uppsala Consistory to Peter Koch, 4 September 1745.

30. Gabriel Naesman to Beronius, 14 November 1745.

31. Baumgarten, *Theologisches Bedencken*. For another critique viewing Moravian destruction of the proper nuclear family as a threat to the state see Stollberg, in Fresenius, *Bewährte Nachrichten*, vol. 2, 1–164, here 157–64. For another attack on the Moravians that linked their transgressions regarding gender, marriage, and sex to a political threat to the state see Rimius, *A Candid Narrative*.

32. Gerhard Johannes Raisig, *Theologie und Frömmigkeit bei Johann Philipp Fresenius: Eine Studie zur Theorie und Lebenspraxis im Pietismus der frühen Aufklärung* (Frankfurt am Main: Peter Lang, 1975).

33. The full title is *Johann Philip Fresenius, /Evangelischen Predigers und Pastoris an der Sanct Peters- /Kirche zu Franckfurt am Mayn, / Bewährte Nachrichten/ von/ Herrnhutischen/ Sachen*, 4 vols. (Frankfurt am Main: Johann Leonard Buchner, 1746–1751).

34. Fresenius, *Bewährte Nachrichten*, vol. 1, 477–78, 766–85; vol. 2, 153–57, 259–64; vol. 3, 115–99, 303–94, 410–520, 601–3, 627–33, 765–73, 785–90, 798–99, 809–18, 822–30, 877–976.

35. Fresenius, vol. 1, 608–14, 678–82; vol. 2, 3–18; vol. 3, 212–15, 231, 747–62.

36. Fresenius, vol. 1, 357–64, 493–502, 678–79, 686–87, 695–97, 726–27, 785–90, 813–27; vol. 2, 3–18, 259–64; vol. 3, 160–68, 269–92, 585–88, 597, 747–62.

37. Fresenius, vol. 1, 133–44,166–67, 602–3; vol. 3, 638–39, 950–56.

38. Fresenius, vol. 1, 168, 604–8, 690–91, 698–702, 783–85, 872–73; vol. 2, 3–18, 536; vol. 3, 76, 722–28, 830–37.

39. Fresenius, vol. 1, 680–82, 713–38, 783, 806–13, 890; vol. 3, 11–12, 41n, 45–52, 61–63, 140–46, 830–37.

40. Fresenius, vol. 1, 369–70, 692–93, 698–702, 829–34; vol. 2, 157–64, 604–9; vol. 3, 201–4, 722–28, 740–42; vol. 4, 60–69.

41. "Diese überheilige Gemeine siehet einer zusamen geschworen Rotte von Räubern und öffentlichen Land-Betrüger ähnlicher, als einem heiligen Volck, wenn man sie recht ansiehet." Fresenius, vol. 1, 898.

42. Fresenius, vol. 1, 168.

43. Fresenius, vol. 1, 98–99, 158–59, 167–68, 477–78; vol. 2, 271; vol. 3, 61, 601–3, 616, 619, 644–45.

44. Alexander Volck's *Das Entdeckte Geheimnis der Bosheit der Herrnhutischen Secte* initially appeared in Frankfurt and Leipzig (Heinrich Ludwig Brönner, 1748) and was reprinted in Philadelphia (Johann Boehm, 1749). Fresenius printed Reynier's "Das Geheimnis der Zinzendorfischen Secte" and Sutor's "Licht und Wahrheit," in *Bewährte Nachrichten von Herrnhutischen Sachen,* vol. 1, 321–479, 640–842. Christopher Saur published Andreas Frey's *Declaration, Oder: Erklärung, Auf welche Weise, und wie er unter die sogenannte Herrnhuter Gemeine gekommen . . .* (Germantown, Pa.: Christopher Saur, 1748), which was reprinted the following year in Frankfurt and Leipzig. Saur also printed and sold Johannes Hildebrand's *Wohlbegründetes Bedencken der Christlichen Gemeine in und bey Ephrata. . . .* (Germantown, Pa.: Christopher Saur, 1743) for 6p. See the ad in his newspaper, the *Hoch-Deutsch Pennsylvanische Geschichts-Schreiber,* Nr. 38, 16 September 1743. Other important polemics written by radicals in Pennsylvania who were not ex-Moravians include those by Johann Adam Gruber (of the Inspired radical pietist group) and Israel Eckerlin and Johannes Hildebrand of the Ephrata cloister (see Appendix 1).

45. Volck, *Das Entdeckte Geheimnis der Bosheit,* 14–16, 21–28, 50–54, 59–62, 65–70, 73–74. See Saur's ad for Volck's book in *Pennsylvanische Berichte,* Nr. 114, 1 December 1749.

46. Frey, *Declaration, Oder,* 33–38, 62, 74–75.

47. Volck, Introduction, 2, 7–11, 14–16, 28–43, 45–47, 50–54, 94–95.

48. Hartmut Lehmann, *Pietismus und weltliche Ordnung in Württemberg* (Stuttgart: W. Kohlhammer Verlag, 1969), 62–134, and the following essays in Brecht and Deppermann, *Geschichte des Pietismus,* vol. 2: Martin Brecht, "Der Württembergische Pietismus," 225–95; Manfred Jakubowski-Tiessen, "Der Pietismus in Niedersachsen," 428–45; Ingun Montgomery, "Der Pietismus in Norwegen im 18. Jahrhundert," 472–88; Pentti Laasonen, "Der Pietismus in Finnland im 17. und 18. Jahrhundert," 523–41.

49. On Halle's increasing conservatism and changing attitudes toward women see Brecht, "Der Hallische Pietismus in der Mitte des 18. Jahrhundert," and Knothe, "Siegmund Jakob Baumgarten und seine Stellung in der Aufklärungstheologie"; Schloemann, *Siegmund Jacob Baumgarten*; W. R. Ward, *The Protestant Evangelical Awakening* (Cambridge: Cambridge University Press, 1992), 54–92; and Ulrike Witt, *Bekehrung, Bildung und Biographie* (Halle: Franckesche Stiftungen, 1996).

For an overview of the Halle-Herrnhut rivalry in many of the territories where it took place see Dietrich Meyer, "Zinzendorf und Herrnhut," in Brecht and Deppermann, *Geschichte des Pietismus,* and Ward, *The Protestant Evangelical Awakening,* 116–59. For its origins in Zinzendorf's youth see Erich Beyreuther, *Der Junge Zinzendorf* (Marburg: Verlag der Francke-Buchhandlung, 1957), 83–120. For a detailed analysis on developments between Zinzendorf and Halle up to and after the beginning of the Moravian mission to Georgia in 1735 see Fogleman, "Shadow Boxing in Georgia." On the rivalry in North America see Walther H. Wagner, *The Zinzendorf-Muhlenberg Encounter: A Controversy in Search of Understanding* (Bethlehem, Pa.: Moravian Historical Society, 2002), and Aaron Fogleman, "Hallesche Pietisten und Herrnhuter in Nordamerika," *Pietismus und Neuzeit* 29 (2003): 148–78. There are several other relevant articles in this issue of *Pietismus und Neuzeit,* which is dedicated to relations between Halle and Herrnhut in this era.

50. Jakubowski-Tiessen, "Der Pietismus in Dänemark und Schleswig-Holstein," and Jakubowski-Tiessen, "Hallischer Pietismus und Herrnhutertum in Dänemark," *Pietismus und Neuzeit* 29 (2003): 134–47.

51. Fogleman, "Shadow Boxing in Georgia."

52. H. Römer, *Geschichte der Brüdermission auf den Nikobaren und des "Brüdergartens" bei Trankebar* (Herrnhut: Missionsbuchhandlung, 1921), 14–27, and J. Taylor Hamilton and Kenneth G. Hamilton, *History of the Moravian Church: The Renewed Unitas Fratrum, 1722–1957* (Bethlehem, Pa.: Moravian Church, 1967), 305–6.

53. The pastoral letter was translated into German and published. See *Väterlicher Hirten-Brieff an die bluehenden Reformierte Gemeine in Amsterdam* (Amsterdam: Kirchenrath, 1738); Paul M. Peucker, "Der Amsterdamer Hirtenbrief vom 1738" (unpublished manuscript); Peucker, " 'Godts Wonderen met zyne Kerke': Isaäc LeLong (1683–1762) en de Herrnhutters," *De Achttiende Eeuw* 25, 2 (1993): 151–85; Wilhelm Lütjeharms, *Het Philadelphisch-oecumenisch Streven der Herrnhutters in de Nederlanden in de achttiende eeuw* ; Van Den Berg, "Die Frömmigkeitsbestrebungen in den Niederlanden"; John Exalto and Jan-Kees Karels, *Waakzame wachters en kleine vossen: Gereformeerden en herrnhutters in de Nederlanden, 1734–1754* (Heerenveen: Uitgeverij Groen, 2001).

54. Hamilton and Hamilton, *History of the Moravian Church*, 56–57.

55. Römer, *Geschichte der Brüdermission auf den Nikobaren und des "Brüdergartens" bei Trankebar*, 24–25, and Hamilton and Hamilton, 58–59.

56. See numerous letters from Reynier and other Moravian missionaries in Suriname reprinted in Fritz Staehelin, ed., *Die Mission der Brüdergemeine in Suriname und Berbice in achtzehnten Jahrhundert: Eine Missionsgeschichte hauptsächlich in Briefen und Originalberichten*, 3 vols. (Herrnhut: Verein für Brüdergeschichte, 1913–1920), here reprint Beyreuther, Meyer, and Molnár, *Materialien und Dokumente*, vol. 28, parts I, II.1, and II.2 (Hildesheim: Georg Olms Verlag, 1997), 41–79.

57. Montgomery, "Der Pietismus in Schweden im 18. Jahrhundert."

Chapter 6

1. "Etliche Pläne von Gemeinen in Pensylvanien," in *Büdingische Sammlung*, vol. 3, 71–76, and *Bethlehem Diary*, vol. 1, entry for 17 July 1743, p. 157. The original of the quote is: "einige bekamen ein Zittern in allen Gliedern, einige fangen jämmerlich im Schlaf an zu schreyen, und so sie erweckt werden, sagen sie, der Graf Zinzendorf sey da und greife mit ausgestreckten Armen nach ihnen. Andern kommen gantze Truppen und Menge Herrnhuter vor, und ängsten sie." Anonymous, "Ausführliche Nachricht," 234–35.

2. Naesman to Beronius, 14 November 1745.

3. Mühlenberg to Johann Philip Fresenius, 15 November 1751.

4. For Moravian problems with Lutherans and colonial authorities in Virginia during the 1740s see the following translations of Moravian itinerant diaries by William J. Hinke and Charles E. Kemper in *Virginia Magazine of History and Biography*: "Extracts from the Diary of Leonhard Schnell and Robert Hussey, of Their Journey to Georgia, November 6, 1743–April 10, 1744," 11, 3 (January 1904): 370–93; "Diary of the Journey of Rev. L. Schnell and V. Handrup to Maryland and Virginia, May 29 to August 4, 1747," 12, 1 (July 1904): 55–61; "Extracts from the Diary of Bro. Gottschalk's Journey Through Maryland and Virginia, March 5–April 20, 1748," 12, 1 (July 1904): 62–76; "Extracts from the Diary of John Brandmüller of Their Journey to Virginia, October 12–December 12, 1749" (hereafter Schnell and Brandmüller Diary, October–December 1749), 11, 2 (October 1903): 113–31. For the Moravian tours among the Dunkers see

Müller Diary, 8–29 March 1745 and Müller and Frey Diary, 9 October–6 November 1746. For the Dunker response see Dunker leaders in Pennsylvania to Joseph Müller, 12 February 1750, reprinted in English translation in Donald F. Durnbaugh, *The Brethren in Colonial America* (Elgin, Ill.: Brethren Press, 1967), 312–50. For Bradford's anti-Moravian articles see *American Weekly Mercury*, 7–14 April 1743, Nr. 1214.

5. The conflict with the Moravians during the Great Awakening fits a pattern outlined by J. M. Bumsted and John E. Van de Wetering, *What Must I Do to Be Saved? The Great Awakening in Colonial America* (Hinsdale, Ill.: Dryden Press, 1976), esp. 96–126, of three factions, which they label the Opposition (Old Lights and Old Sides), Moderates (who accept revival innovations to preserve existing social and religious order), and Radicals (who promote a fundamental reordering of tradition). Their work is largely a New England, Calvinist-centered study that does not address gender issues, but the principle of three factions and radicalism is valid for the Moravian and other conflicts that they do not address.

6. Milton J. Coalter, Jr., *Gilbert Tennent, Son of Thunder: A Case Study of Continental Pietism's Impact on the Great Awakening in the Middle Colonies* (New York: Greenwood Press, 1986), 91–112; Coalter, "The Radical Pietism of Count Nicholas Zinzendorf as a Conservative Influence on the Awakener Gilbert Tennent," *Church History* 49 (1980): 35–46, and Marilyn J. Westerkamp, *Triumph of the Laity* (New York: Oxford University Press, 1988), 207–8, 213. Finley and Tennent published several anti-Moravian polemics in 1743; see Dietrich Meyer, ed., *Bibliographisches Handbuch zur Zinzendorf-Forschung* (Düsseldorf: Kornelius Kaspers, 1987). Also, Tennent wrote a harsh letter to Whitefield dated 5 June 1742 in which he criticized him for favoring the Moravians, reprinted in Dietmar Rothermund, *The Layman's Progress: Religious and Political Experience in Colonial Pennsylvania, 1740–1770* (Philadelphia: University of Pennsylvania Press, 1961), 148. And he responded to Zinzendorf's questions and answers in Franklin's *Pennsylvania Gazette*, 19 May, 30 June, 7 July 1743, Nr. 753, 759, 760. See also the full-page article in the *American Weekly Mercury* with excerpts from Tennent's polemic *The Necessity of Holding Fast the Truth*, warning against false teachers, schisms, confusions, and seducers (16–24 March 1743, Nr. 1211). For Blair's exchange with the Moravians see Blair to Peter Böhler, 14 March 1743, Böhler to Blair, 18 March 1743, and Blair to Böhler, 25 March 1743 in Peter Böhler Box, 256G, Controversies and Religious Questions Folder, Nr. 3 i–iii, Moravian Archives. In March 1744 Boehm informed Holland that they were not interested in a union with the Presbyterians. See Boehm et al. to Synods of Holland, 18 March 1744, in Boehm, *Life and Letters*, 386–405, here 391–92. For more precise documentation of the failed Presbyterian-Reformed union talks see James I. Good, "Early Attempted Union of Presbyterians with Dutch and German Reformed," *Journal of the Presbyterian Historical Society* 3 (1905–1906): 122–37.

7. J. Taylor Hamilton and Kenneth G. Hamilton, *History of the Moravian Church* (Bethlehem, Pa.: Moravian Church, 1967), 76–81; Richard P. Heitzenrater, *Wesley and the People Called Methodists* (Nashville, Tenn.: Abingdon Press, 1995), 58–73, 106–24, 141–46; for excerpts from Wesley's journal that outline his changing relationship with the Moravians see Albert C. Outler, ed., *John Wesley* (New York: Oxford University Press, 1964), "The Rift with the Moravians," 353–76, here 367–76; James Nelson, "John Wesley and the Georgia Moravians," *Transactions of the Moravian Historical Society* 23, 3–4 (1977–1984): 17–46; Sung-Duk Lee, *Der deutsche Pietismus und Wesley* (Giessen: Brunner Verlag, 2003).

8. There are a number of letters that outline the above relationships. Some

of these that highlight the turning points are Whitefield to the Fetter Lane Society, 12 June 1739; Whitefield to James Hutton, 7 June 1740; Whitefield to J. B. in London, 2 July 1740; Whitefield to Howel Harris, 24 September 1740; Whitefield to James Hutton, 24 November 1740; Whitefield to James Habersham, 25 March 1741; Whitefield to Peter Böhler, 10 October 1741; Whitefield to Mr. F. in Pennsylvania, 22 September 1742; all in *The Letters of George Whitefield, for the Period 1734–1742*, ed. S. M. Houghton (Edinburgh: Banner of Truth Trust, 1976); George Whitefield, "An Expostulary Letter, Adressed to Nicholas Lewis, Count Zinzendorff, and Lord Advocate of the Unitas Fratrum" (London: G. Keith, 1753, 3rd ed. reprinted in Philadelphia by William Bradford, 1753). On the importance of Hutton and his loss to Whitefield's publishing see Frank Lambert, *Pedlar in Divinity: George Whitefield and the Transatlantic Revivals, 1737–1770* (Princeton, N.J.: Princeton University Press, 1994), 88–89.

9. Pyrlaeussens Diarium wegen seiner und der Brüder Gefangenschaft in Neu England (hereafter Pyrlaeus Diary, 17–24 June 1743), R.14.A.36.4, Unity Archives.

10. Governor's Council Minutes for 5 and 26 July and 1 and 11 August 1744, E. B. O'Callaghan, ed., *Documentary History of the State of New York*, vol. 3 (Albany: Weed, Parsons, and Co., 1850), 613–17; "Rauch's Relation von dem letzten tryal in Bikipsi (Poughkeepsie). Dec. 1744," in Letters and Documents Relating to the Reformed Church of Pennsylvania, 1743–1746, ZK #7, Archives of the Evangelical and Reformed Historical Society.

11. Earl P. Olmstead, *David Zeisberger: A Life Among the Indians* (Kent, Ohio: Kent State University Press, 1997), 32–41.

12. 18 July 1744, *Bethlehem Diary*, vol. 1, p. 201.

13. Heinrich Antes Bericht von seine reise nach Newtown, und was sich dort zugetragen, als er Justusamt übernommen (hereafter Antes Report, 17 June 1746), R.14.A.36.9, Unity Archives.

14. Stefan Hertrampf, *"Unsere Indianer-Geschwister waren lichte und vergnügt": Die Herrnhuter als Missionare bei den Indianern Pennsylvanias 1745–1765* (Frankfurt am Main: Peter Lang, 1997), 308–28.

15. For Horsmanden's report and the correspondence regarding it see New York Council Chamber Meeting, 27 November 1744, pp. 2861–62; Zinzendorf to the Board of Trade, 31 December 1744, p. 2865; Board of Trade to Governor Clinton, 28 June 1745, p. 2874; Daniel Horsmanden's Response to Inquiry by the Board of Trade, May 1746, pp. 2906–8; Gov. Clinton to Board of Trade, 21 June 1746, p. 2917. All the above are from Hugh Hastings, ed., *Ecclesiastical Records of the State of New York*, 5 vols. (Albany: J.B. Lyon Company, State Printers, 1901–1905), here vol. 4 (1902), for the years 1725–1750.

16. Horsmanden, New York Council Report, 27 November 1744. In 1741 Horsmanden presided over the controversial investigation and proceedings of the conspirators in the "Negro plot," and he published the minutes in 1744.

17. Mühlenberg to Ziegenhagen, 3 December 1742, Mühlenberg to Francke and Ziegenhagen, 12 and 17 March 1743, and editor's note in Heinrich Melchior Mühlenberg, *Die Korrespondenz Heinrich Melchior Mühlenbergs*, ed. Kurt Aland (Berlin: de Gruyter, 1986–), xviii–xix; Heinrich Melchior Mühlenberg, *Selbstbiographie, 1711–1743*, ed. W. Germann (Allentown, Pa.: Brobst, Diehl and Co., 1881), e.g., 122–29, 212, 216. See also the following documents reprinted in *Nachrichten von den vereinigten Deutschen Evangelisch-Lutherischen Gemeinen in Nord-America, absonderlich in Pensylvanien*, ed. D. Johann Ludewig Schulze, here expanded edition by W. J. Mann, B. M. Schmucker, and W. Germann, vol. 1

(Allentown, Pa.: Brobst, Diehl & Co., 1886), hereafter cited as *Hallesche Nachrichten*: "Kurtze Nachricht von einigen Evangelischen Gemeinen in America, absonderlich in Pensylvanien," 1744 (pp. 9–22); Daniel Weisiger to Francke, 23 September 1734 (p. 56); Francke to Ziegenhagen, 14 March 1736 (pp. 60–61); Lutherans in Philadelphia, Providence, and New Hanover to Francke, 6 December 1736 (pp. 62–63); Lutherans in Philadelphia to Ziegenhagen, 6 December 1736 (pp. 63–64); and Lutherans in Philadelphia, Providence, and New Hanover to Ziegenhagen, 15 October 1739 (pp. 67–70). For a brief treatment of these developments by recent historians see Charles H. Glatfelter, *Pastors and People: German Lutheran and Reformed Churches in the Pennsylvania Field, 1717–1793* (Breinigsville, Pa.: Pennsylvania German Society, 1980–1981), vol. 2, 31–35, and Thomas Müller, *Kirche zwischen zwei Welten* (Stuttgart: Franz Steiner Verlag, 1994), 179–83.

18. For good overviews of Halle Pietism during this period that include the overseas mission see Martin Brecht, "Der Hallische Pietismus in der Mitte des 18. Jahrhunderts," in *Geschichte des Pietismus*, vol. 2, *Der Pietismus im achtzehnten Jahrhunderton*, ed. Martin Brecht and Klaus Deppermann (Göttingen : Vandenhoeck and Ruprecht, 1995) and W. Reginald Ward, *The Protestant Evangelical Awakening* (Cambridge: Cambridge University Press, 1992). On the work of the Halle pietists in the colonies see Müller, *Kirche zwischen zwei Welten*; A. G. Roeber; *Palatines, Liberty, and Property: German Lutherans in Colonial British America* (Baltimore: Johns Hopkins University Press, 1993); Renate Wilson, *Pious Traders in Medicine: A German Pharmaceutical Network in Eighteenth-Century North America* (University Park: Pennsylvania State University Press, 2000); Leonard R. Riforgiato, *Missionary of Moderation: Henry Melchior Muhlenberg and the Lutheran Church in English America* (Lewisburg, Pa.: Bucknell University Press, 1980); Theodore C. Tappert, "The Influence of Pietism in Colonial American Lutheranism," in F. Ernest Stoeffler, *Continental Pietism and Early American Christianity* (Grand Rapids, Mich.: W.B. Eerdmans, 1976), 13–33; Wolfgang Splitter, *Pastors, People, Politics: German Lutherans in Pennsylvania, 1740–1790* (Trier: Wissenschaftlicher Verlag, 1998); Stephen L. Longenecker, *Piety and Tolerance: Pennsylvania German Religion, 1700–1850* (Metuchen, N.J.: Scarecrow Press, 1994).

In addition to Mühlenberg's correspondence and journal, see his official reports to Halle and other documents from the Lutheran pastors in North America. They were published serially by Halle and then collectively in D. Johann Ludewig Schulze, *Nachrichten von den vereinigten Deutschen Evangelisch-Lutherischen Gemeinen in Nord-America, absonderlich in Pensylvanien* (Halle: Waisenhaus, 1787). In the next century an expanded edition of these *Hallesche Nachrichten* (Halle Reports) with the same title appeared, edited by W. J. Mann, B. M. Schmucker, and W. Germann, 2 vols. (Allentown, Pa.: Brobst, Diehl and Co., 1866, 1895). While the *Hallesche Nachrichten* are a useful source, they were heavily censored by the authorities in Halle, who omitted or altered many important passages on the conflict with the Moravians. This is not only true of the eighteenth-century published editions, but even for the nineteenth-century edition, which is also incomplete. For these reasons I have consulted the complete manuscript diaries in the Lutheran Archives Center in Philadelphia and the Archives of the Francke Foundations in Halle, Germany and have avoided the *Hallesche Nachrichten* for the most part.

19. See Wilson, *Pious Traders in Medicine*, 129–47, for the mechanics of the trade in the colonial era. Thomas Müller discovered that Francke began sending printed materials to Pennsylvania so he could control the theological content

of what Lutherans received in the colony. Both Francke and Friedrich Michael Ziegenhagen in London doubted Mühlenberg's abilities as a theologian and for this reason did not honor his request for a printing press, which he might misuse in destructive theological debates. See Müller, *Kirche zwischen zwei Welten*, 188–89.

20. Mühlenberg to Francke, 7 May 1742; Mühlenberg to Francke and Ziegenhagen, 17 March 1743; Francke to Mühlenberg, 17 September 1747; Mühlenberg to Francke and Ziegenhagen, 15 June 1751; Mühlenberg to Francke, 22 February 1752; Francke to Pennsylvania pastors, 31 July 1752; Muhlenberg, *Journal*, 24 October 1742 and 14 February 1743; Francke to Brunnholtz, 3 August 1749 (which contains the above quotation), in Halle Documents, ed. William Julius Mann and W. Germann, vol. 2, 943–48, here 945, PM 28 TH 18, Lutheran Archives Center, Philadelphia. From 1744 to 1756 Halle sent its Delaware Valley pastors polemics written by their own theologians, namely Lange (*Lebenslauf*), Baumgarten (*Theologische Bedencken*, vols. 2–8, as they appeared), and Bogatzky (*Nöthige Warnung*, nine copies, *Aufrichtige . . . Declaration*, eleven copies, and *Evangelische Uebung das wahren Christenthums . . .* (Halle: Waisenhaus, 1750), three copies). They also sent their pastors the *Acta Historias Ecclesiastica* (a periodical that contained excerpts and summaries of anti-Moravian writings), volumes of Fresenius's *Bewährte Nachrichten von Herrnhutischen Sachen* as they appeared, Volck's *Entdeckte Geheimnis der Bosheit* (two copies), and Becherer's *Nöthige Prüfung*. See Lieferungen nach Pennsylvanien, 1740–1768, pp. 11–17, 29–30, 39–41, 47–50, 61–69, 99, 111–19, AFSt/M 4 G 6–11, and Hn Pastor Handschuchs Diaria (hereafter Handschuh Diary, 13 January 1748 to 2 March 1753), here 4 October 1751, AFSt/M 4 H 10, Archives of the Francke Foundations, Halle.

21. Becherer's work was published in Frankfurt am Main by Johann Benjamin Andrea in 1748, and contained a forward written by Fresenius.

22. Mühlenberg to Conrad Weiser, 27 December 1750; Handschuh Diary, 1748–1753, here 28 November 1749 and 4 October 1751, and Diarium von Johann Albert Weygand (hereafter Weygand Diary, 1748–1752, here 13 January 1752, AFSt/M 4 H 6–8, Archives of the Francke Foundations. See Weiser's report on Zinzendorf in Weiser to Brunnholtz, 17 February 1747, Conrad Weiser Correspondence, PW42 D2, Lutheran Archives Center, and see Francke's comment on the report in Francke to Brunnholtz and Mühlenberg, 23 July 1748.

23. In 1749 Johann Martin Boltzius received a large shipment of books from Halle, including Fresenius's *Bewährte Nachrichten*, and planned to read excerpts before the assembly in order to demonstrate yet again the dangers of the Herrnhuters. As late as 1752 he received Johann Georg Walch's *Einleitung in die Religionsstreitigkeiten in und außer der lutherischen Kirche*, which he intended to use along with hymnals and Bibles to fend off the sects, and in 1753 he received Bogatzky's *Nöthige Warnung*. See Boltzius, 19 July 1749, vol. 13, and 2 November 1753, vol. 16, in George Fenwick Jones et al., *Detailed Reports of the Salzburger Emigrants Who Settled in America* (Camden, Me.: Picton Press, 1988).

24. Glatfelter found thirty Lutheran congregations in 1742, the year Mühlenberg began the Hallensian work in the Pennsylvania field, and fifty-three in 1748 (see *Pastors and People*, vol. 2, 52–53, 139). On the Halle pastors' intervention in Lutheran church community disputes see Müller, *Kirche zwischen zwei Welten*, 104–56 and Paul A. W. Wallace, *The Muhlenbergs of Pennsylvania* (Philadelphia: University of Pennsylvania Press, 1950), 48–55. On pastor assignments in 1748 see Muhlenberg, *Journal*, May 1748. For Mühlenberg's attitude toward other Lutheran ministers during this period see his numerous letters to Gotthilf August Francke in Halle and Ziegenhagen in London, e.g., those dated 3

December 1742, 22 September, 25 November 1743, 6 March 1745, as well as his letter to Caspar Stoever, 20 January 1747.

25. On Zinzendorf and Mühlenberg see Walter H. Wagner, *The Zinzendorf-Muhlenberg Encounter* (Bethlehem, Pa.: Moravian Historical Society, 2002); Wolfgang Splitter, *Pastors, People, Politics* (Trier: Wissenschaftlicher Verlag, 1998), 25–27; Wallace, *The Muhlenbergs of Pennsylvania*, 31–33; Muhlenberg, *Journal*, 30 December 1742; Mühlenberg to Providence and New Hanover congregations, 30(?) January 1743; Mühlenberg, *Selbstbiographie*, 141–50.

Three documents that contain Zinzendorf's position on his encounter with Mühlenberg in December of 1742 are Plan einer Unterredung mit Past. Mühlenberg vor Br. Böhler, 1742, Folder IX: Varia June–Dec. 1742, Nr. 7; Zinzendorf to Peter Tranberg, 31 December 1742, Folder IV: Zinzendorf's Letters, 1741–1742, Nr. 8; Zinzendorf to Pennsylvania Lutherans, 13 September 1746, Folder V: Zinzendorf's Letters, 1743–1746, all in Zinzendorf: Box A. Letters, etc.: Till 1749, Moravian Archives, Bethlehem.

Both Hallensian and Moravian documents support the view of Thomas Müller and others that Zinzendorf's journey to Pennsylvania in 1741 accelerated Halle's decision to send a pastor there. See Müller, *Kirche zwischen zwei Welten* 180–81.

26. In Georgia, for example, a tense meeting took place between the Hallensian Johann Martin Boltzius and Spangenberg, with John Wesley as mediator. See Aaron S. Fogleman, "Shadow Boxing in Georgia: The Beginnings of the Moravian-Lutheran Conflict in British North America," *Georgia Historical Quarterly* 83, 4 (Winter 1999): 629–59, here 649–53.

27. 12 February 1746, Nyberg Diary, and 2 May 1748, Handschuh Diary.

28. Israel Acrelius, *Beskrifning om de swenska forsamlingars forna och narwarande tilstand* (Stockholm: Harberg and Hasselberg, 1759). I have used the English translation by William M. Reynolds, *A History of New Sweden; or, The Settlements on the River Delaware* (Philadelphia: Historical Society of Pennsylvania, 1874), here 402–34, and Muhlenberg, *Journal*, March 1756.

29. The Hallensians successfully employed these tactics in Lancaster and Tulpehocken, for example. See Muhlenberg, *Journal*, 13–26 April 1748; Diarium, H. Past. Kurtzens zu Tulpehokin in Pensylvanien (hereafter Kurtz Diary, 1746–1750), 7–27 April 1748, PK 98 A, Lutheran Archives Center; Handschuh Diary, 1748–1753, 14–26 April, 12–19 May 1748.

30. Roeber, *Palatines, Liberty, and Property*, and Müller, *Kirche zwischen zwei Welten*; Kurt Aland, "*Ecclesia Plantanda*: Die ersten brieflichen Dokumente zur Wirksamkeit H. M. Mühlenbergs in den Vereinigten Staaten," in Heinrich Bornkamm, Friedrich Heyer, and Alfred Schindler, eds., *Der Pietismus in Gestalten und Wirkungen* (Bielefeld: Luther-Verlag, 1975), 9–49; Splitter, *Pastors, People, Politics*; Glatfelter, *Pastors and People*, vol. 2, 137–290.

31. Boehm's Reports, *Life and Letters*.

32. Among the more notable defections were a pastor named Peter Müller, who joined the Ephrata cloister, Conrad Weiser, who also joined Ephrata, and Heinrich Antes and Johann Bechtel, who both joined the Moravians. P. H. Dorius to Synodical Deputies, 1 March 1738 (Acts of the Synodical Deputies, vol. 8, p. 610), and Georg Michael Weiss to Classis of Amsterdam, 29 April 1738 (N.B. 473), John Plantinus/C. Van de Bogaarde (Classis of Amsterdam) to Weiss, 13 January 1739 (N.B. 491), ZK#6, Letters and Documents Relating to the Reformed Church, William J. Hinke, comp., Archives of the Evangelical and Reformed Historical Society; Glatfelter, *Pastors and People*, vol. 2, 35–51.

33. Tulpgehocken lay leaders wrote consistories in Zweibrücken, Switzerland, Heidelberg, and Hessen as well, but never received a pastor until Amsterdam finally sent one in 1748. Tulpehocken elders to Boehm, March 1744, reprinted in Boehm, *Life and Letters*, 385–86

34. Johann Philip Boehm, *Getreue Warnungs-Brief an die Hochteutsche Evangelisch Reformierten Gemeinden und alle deren Glieder, in Pensylvanien* (Philadelphia: Andrew Bradford, 1742) and *Abermahlige treue Warnung und Vermahnung an meine sehr werthe und theurer geschätzte Reformirte Glaubens-verwandte . . .* (Philadelphia: Cornelia Bradford and Isaiah Warner, 1743).

35. Glatfelter, *Pastors and People*, vol. 2, 35–134; Report of John Ph. Boehm to the Synods, 8 July 1744, pp. 17–31 in James I. Good and William J. Hinke, trans. and eds., *Minutes and Letters of the Coetus of the German Reformed Congregations in Pennsylvania, 1747–1792, Together with Three Preliminary Reports of Rev. John Philip Boehm, 1734–1744* (Philadelphia: Reformed Church, 1903); Boehm, *Life and Letters*.

36. Schlatter Diary, 1746.

37. Schlatter Diary, October 15–December 15, 1746.

38. Good and Hinke, *Minutes and Letters of the Coetus*; Glatfelter, *Pastors and People*, vol. 2, 112–24, 205–8, 217–21. See also "The Journal of Rev. Michael Schlatter," a heavily edited, incomplete version of the original for the years 1746–1751, in Henry Harbaugh, ed. and trans., *Life of Rev. Michael Schlatter* (Philadelphia: Lindsay and Blakiston, 1857), 87–234 (hereafter Schlatter Journal), 15 October–15 December 1746.

39. See Meyer, *Bibliographisches Handbuch*.

40. Boehm, *Life and Letters*, Good and Hinke, *Minutes and Letters of the Coetus*, Schlatter Diary, 1746.

41. Johann Friedrich Christian Cammerhof to Zinzendorf, 2 July 1748, Epistola XIV, Moravian Archives, also in Cammerhoff-Zinzendorf Correspondence, 1747–1748, Letters and Documents Relating to the Reformed Church of Pennsylvania, ZK #8, Archives of the Evangelical and Reformed Historical Society; Schlatter Diary, 20 November 1747; Glatfelter, *Pastors and People*, vol. 2, 206–37.

42. On Swedish settlements and ethnicity in the eighteenth century see John Fea, "Ethnicity and Congregational Life in the Eighteenth-Century Delaware Valley," *Explorations in Early American Culture* 5 (2001): 45–78; Carol Hoffecker et al., eds., *New Sweden in America* (Newark: University of Delaware Press and Associated University Presses, 1995); Craig Koedel, *God's Vine in This Wilderness: Religion in South Jersey to 1800* (Woodbury, N.J.: Gloucester County Historical Society, 1980); Daniel Lindmark, "Diaspora, Integration, and Cantonization: Swedish Colonial Education from a Theoretical, Comparative, and Concluding Perspective," 15–40, and Lindmark, "Swedish Schooling in Colonial America: From Swedish-Lutheran Education to American Utilitarian Curriculum," 41–86, in Lindmark, ed., *Education and Colonialism: Swedish Schooling Projects in Colonial Areas, 1638–1878* (Ulmeå: Grafikerna Livréna i Kungälv, 2000).

43. Acrelius, *History of New Sweden*, 203–41, 263–94, 314–27. On education see Lindmark, "Swedish Colonial Education from a Theoretical, Comparative, and Concluding Perspective," 15–40, and Lindmark, "Swedish Schooling in Colonial America," 41–86. On the contrast between the social-religious landscapes of Sweden and the Delaware Valley in the mid-eighteenth century see Kenneth A. Lockridge, "Overcoming Nausea: The Brothers Hesselius and the American Mystery," *Common-Place* 4, 2 (January 2004).

44. The older literature on the Moravian-Swedish Lutheran conflict in the Delaware Valley generally favors one side or the other in its narrative and use of

sources. See, for example, Acrelius, *History of New Sweden*, for the Swedish Lutheran point of view, and J. Taylor Hamilton, "A Sketch of Moravian Activity in New Sweden and Its Vicinity," *Transactions of the Moravian Historical Society* 4 (1895): 163–86, for the Moravian point of view. John Fea's account, "Ethnicity and Congregational Life in the Eighteenth-Century Delaware Valley," *Explorations in Early American Culture* 5 (2001): 45–78, represents a critical, evenhanded analysis, but without the use of Moravian sources.

45. The ten communities were Wicaco (Philadelphia), Christina, Kingsessing, Upper Merion, Manatawny in Pennsylvania; Raccoon, Penns Neck, Maurice River, Oldman's Creek (Pile's Grove) in New Jersey, and an area near the Potomac, probably around Hagerstown in Maryland.

46. Mühlenberg to Ziegenhagen, 6 June 1743, and Acrelius, *History of New Sweden*, 241–46. Additionally, Nyberg sometimes left his post among the German Lutherans at Lancaster to visit the Swedes at Manatawny, where he preached in three languages (Swedish, English, and German) on the same day. See, e.g., his entry for October 1745, Nyberg Diary, 1743–1749.

47. Acrelius, Nyberg, and Mühlenberg provide three different, yet corroborating views of this meeting. See Acrelius, *History of New Sweden*, 245–49; Nyberg to Paul Daniel Bryzelius, spring 1745, translated and printed in Rothermund, *The Layman's Progress*, 154–58; Nyberg Diary, 1743–1749, here 14 April 1744; Mühlenberg to Ziegenhagen and Francke, 24 May 1744.

48. Cammerhof to Zinzendorf, Anna Nitschmann, and Johannes von Watteville, 10 February 1748 n.s., R.14.A.28.5, Unity Archives; Nyberg Diary, 1743–1749; Schnell and Brandmüller Diary, October–December 1749; Reise Diarium der 2 Brüder Johannes and Matehs Gottlieb Gottschalk (hereafter Hantsch and Gottschalk Diary, 23 March to 20 April 1747), JB II 2c; Mein 4tes Landbesuch in den Jerseys (hereafter Gottschalk Diary, 29 June to 9 July 1747), JB I 5; Nyberg to Bethlehem Congregation, 8 March 1748, JD I 4, Moravian Archives; Naesman to Beronius, 14 November 1745; Acrelius, *History of New Sweden*, 252–53, 294–313; Lockridge, "Overcoming Nausea."

49. For a Moravian account of the tour of Abraham and Sara Reincke see Diarium von ihrer Besuchs-Reiße unter die Schweden in Racoon, Pens Neck u. Morris River (hereafter Reincke and Sensemann Diary, 26 March to 10 April 1745), R.14.A.36.7, Unity Archives; *Bethlehem Diary*, vol. 2, entries for 9, 11, 13, 14, 18, 20, 24, April and 7, 9, 19, 23, 30 May 1745 n.s., 268–73 and 281, 297, 299, 305, 309, 314. For Naesman's response see Naesman to Beronius, 14 November 1745.

50. Nyberg Diary, 1743–1749, and the following documents reprinted in *Records of the Swedish Lutheran Churches at Raccoon and Penn's Neck, 1713–1786*, trans. and comp. Federal Writer's Project of the Works Progress Administration, State of New Jersey, 1938. Minutes of Racoon church council meeting, 1745? (42); Ecclesiastical Consistory of Uppsala to Peter Koch, 4 September 1745 (46–52); Uppsala Consistory to Swedish Lutheran Congregations in America, 12 August 1747 (53–57); Uppsala Consistory to Israel Acrelius, 28 February 1750 (69–70). See also Acrelius, *History of New Sweden*, 335.

51. *Vernünftige Warnung vor Irrthume von Gleichgültigkeit der Gottesdienste* (Gotha: Johann Andreas Reyher, 1744). Eric Beckman's Swedish translation, *Fœrnuftig Warning/Fœr/ Then Wifarlsen,/Som woro alla sætt, at tjena GUD . . .*, was published in Stockholm in 1748 by Lars Salvii. For the transport to the Delaware Valley see Acrelius, *History of New Sweden*, 368.

52. The translation of Johann Georg Walch's work, *Theolgiska Betænkande Om*

Then Herrnhutiska Sectens Beskaffenhet, was published in Stockholm in 1748 by Lars Salvii.

53. Acrelius, 253–55, 336–39, 366–68. An older Swedish work by Otto Norberg addresses Acrelius' pastor's attempt to repair the damage to the Swedish Lutheran Church caused by the battle with the Moravians in *Svenska krkans mission vid Delaware* (Stockholm: A.V. Carlson, 1893). I would like to thank Kenneth Lockridge for pointing out the importance of Norberg's work on these developments.

54. Acrelius, *History of New Sweden,* 244, 336.

Chapter 7

1. Charles H. Glatfelter, *Pastors and People: German Lutheran and Reformed Churches in the Pennsylvania Field, 1717–1793* (Breinigsville, Pa.: Pennsylvania German Society, 1980–1981), vol. 2, 81–96.

2. For a brief background of the Swedish community at Manatawny and the Molatton church see Glatfelter, *Pastors and People,* vol. 1, 248.

3. For Bryzelius's account see Br. Bricelii Bericht von seiner Arbeit unter den Schweden eingegeben im Anfang des Jahrs 1745, which covers the period 13 January 1743 to 12 January 1745 (hereafter Bryzelius Report, 1743–1745), especially the entry for 20 January 1743, JA I 13, Moravian Archives. Bryzelius's own account of the assault by Falk is corroborated by Muhlenberg, *Journal,* March 1748.

4. For published documents on these developments in Coventry see "Vocation by Coventry Township to Jacob Lischy, 10 April 1743, in *Büdingische Sammlung,* vol. 3 (1744), Nr. 34, 109–10; Boehm, *Abermahlige treue Warnung und Vermahnung an meine sehr werthe und theurer geschätzte Reformirte Glaubens-verwandte* . . . (Philadelphia: Cornelia Bradford and Isaiah Warner, 1743); Jacob Lischy, *Jacob Lischys Reformierten Predigers Declaration seines Sinnes. An seine Reformierte Religions-Genossen In Pennsylvanien* (Germantown, Pa.: Christopher Saur, 1743). For manuscripts see Jacob Lischy to Brother Andreas, 1743, R.14.A.36.6, Unity Archives; Lischy Diaries, 5–19 April 1743 and 29 April to May 12, 1743 and 23 February to 28 May and 14 August to 9 September 1745; Jacob Lischy's Aufrichtige Relation vom Anfang und Fortgang der Reformierten Sache in Pennsylvanien (hereafter Lischy Report, 8 December 1744) and Lischy and Rauch Diary, February 1745; Johann Brandmüller, Diarium, (hereafter Brandmüller Diary, 8 April to 6 May 1745) and Auszug aus Leonhardt Schnell's Gemeine-Bericht (hereafter Schnell Report, 1745), both in the William J. Hinke Manuscript Collection, MJMO H592–592a; Schnell Diary, 10 January to 17 November 1746; Rauch Diaries, 6 February to 14 November 1746 and 23 January to 30 June 1747. For background literature, see Glatfelter, *Pastors and People,* vol. 1, 277–79, vol. 2, 85–87, and Boehm, *Life and Letters,* 79–81.

5. Lischy Report, 8 December 1744; Lischy and Rauch Diary, February 1745 (here February 17–18); Lischy Diaries, 23 February to 28 May 1745 (here March 30, April 2, 15, 22, 24, May 6, 14) and 14 August to 9 September 1745 (here August 15, 28, September 2); Brandmüller Diary, 1–24 September 1745 (here September 13, 19).

6. VII. Relation und Verlaß des Bruder Synodi gehalten zu Creutz-Creek an der Susquehanna, Oct. 30 segn. 1746 (hereafter Moravian Synod Minutes, 30 October 1746), MKX G326, Auszüge aus den Verhandlungen der Pennsylvanischen Synoden, 1745–1748, compiled by William J. Hinke, Archives of the Evan-

gelical and Reformed Historical Society; Rauch Diaries, 6 February to 14 November 1746 (here 23 October to 2 November 1746) and 23 January to 30 June 1747 (here 5–7, 10, 11 February, 7–14 April, May, June 1747); Diarium deß Bruder Heinrich Becks u. Jacob Adolph (hereafter Beck and Adolph Diary, 8–29 October 1746), here October 25–26, JA I 3, Moravian Archives; Seidel and Westman Diary, November to December 1747 (here December 17).

7. For literature on the long history of factional conflict at Tulpehocken see Glatfelter, *Pastors and People*, vol. 1, 258–64; Francis Jennings, "Incident at Tulpehocken," *Pennsylvania History* 35 (1968): 335–55; Theodore Emanuel Schmauk, *A History of the Lutheran Church in Pennsylvania (1638–1820) from the Original Sources* (Philadelphia: General Council Publication House, 1903), vol. 1, 493–501ff; J. Taylor Hamilton, "The Confusion at Tulpehocken," *Transaction of the Moravian Historical Society* 4 (1895): 237–73, which also contains some documents; and Christopher Saur's newspaper, *Pennsylvanische Berichte*, 16 October 1747, Nr. 87.

For Moravian sources on their work and conflict in Tulpehocken, see Johann Philip Meurer's Bericht ans Consistorium in Philadelphia (5 November 1742 o.s.), *Büdingische Sammlung*, vol. 2 (1743), Part 12, Nr. 5, 832–45, and vol. 3 (1744), Part 13, Nr. 22, 78–79; *Die Confusion von Tulpehocken* (Philadelphia: Benjamin Franklin, 1742); vi. Verlass der Pensylvanischen Religions Conferenz, gehalten zu Philadelphia, den 31ten Julii, sequentibus Anno Christi vati 1746 (hereafter Synod Minutes, 31 July 1746), MKX G326, Archives of the Evangelical and Reformed Historical Society; *Bethlehem Diary*, vol. 1, 4 October 1743 and 26 May 1744; Büttner to ? , 17 April 1742, and Meurer to ? , 5/16 November 1742, in Fresenius, vol. 3, "Americanische Nachrichten von Herrnhutischen Sachen," part 3, Nr. 31, 541–61.

For Hallensian sources on the Moravian conflict in Tulpehocken see Weiser to Spangenberg, 13 February 1748 (1747?) and Weiser to Brunnholtz, 16 February 1747, Conrad Weiser Correspondence, PW42 D1, Lutheran Archives Center; Weiser to ? , September 1747, in Fresenius, vol. 3, part 3, Nr. 63, 822–30. (The first Weiser letter describing the tense visit by two Moravians to his house may be misdated as 1748. Weiser refers elsewhere to such a visit in February 1747.) Kurtz Diary, 2–4 February, 22 April, 24 August, 25, 27 September 1747, 17–18 April, 5 September 1748, 13 May and 30 September 1749, 7, 16, 30 May 1750; Handschuh Diary, 17, 22 April 1748; Mühlenberg to Francke and Ziegenhagen, 25 November 1743 and 12 December 1745; Muhlenberg, *Journal*, 12 December 1745, 6–7 July 1747, 17–18 April 1748.

8. Historians of the Middle Colonies have been especially important in promoting this thesis. See Dietmar Rothermund, *The Layman's Progress: Religious and Political Experience in Colonial Pennsylvania, 1740–1770* (Philadelphia: University of Pennsylvania Press, 1961); Marilyn J. Westerkamp, *Triumph of the Laity: Scots-Irish Piety and the Great Awakening, 1625–1760* (New York: Oxford University Press, 1988); Wolfgang Splitter, *Pastors, People, Politics: German Lutherans in Pennsylvania, 1740–1790* (Trier: Wissenschaftlicher Verlag, 1998). Roeber's work stressing the importance of property issues in support of the "layman's progress" thesis can be found in A. G. Roeber, *Palatines, Liberty, and Property: German Lutherans in Colonial British America* (Baltimore: Johns Hopkins University Press, 1993) and "Germans, Property, and the First Great Awakening: Rehearsal for a Revolution?" in *The Transit of Civilization from Europe to America: Essays in Honor of Hans Galinsky*, ed. Winfried Herget and Karl Ortseifen (Tübingen: Gunter Narr Verlag, 1986), 165–84. For examples of general studies of the Great Awakening

that include at least parts of this interpretation see Alan E. Heimert, *Religion and the American Mind: From the Great Awakening to the Revolution* (Cambridge, Mass.: Harvard University Press, 1966), Richard Hofstadter, *America at 1750: A Social Portrait* (New York: Knopf, 1971), 269–93. Patricia U. Bonomi, *Under the Cope of Heaven: Religion, Society, and Politics in Colonial America* (New York: Oxford University Press, 1986) supports the thesis generally, but notes that latitudinarianism actually declined during the Great Awakening and clerical authority increased (39–85, esp. 73–74). Rhys Isaac, *The Transformation of Virginia* (Chapel Hill: University of North Carolina Press, 1982) also supports the thesis generally, but stresses that there was a triangular struggle in the Virginia Anglican communities among the gentry, the vestry, and ordinary people. Jon Butler, "Enthusiasm Described and Decried," *Journal of American History* 69 (1982): 302–5, on the other hand, rejects the notion that the religious renewal movements of the mid-eighteenth century were related to the democratic struggles at the local level during the Revolution.

9. See, for example, Natalie Zemon Davis, "The Rites of Violence," in Davis, *Society and Culture in Early Modern France* (Stanford, Calif.: Stanford University Press, 1975), 152–87, esp. 153. To Davis, this kind of behavior was more normal than pathological in the early modern era.

10. Henry S. Dotterer, *Rev. John Philip Bœhm* (Philadelphia, 1890), 8–15; Boehm, *Getreuer Warnungs Brief*; "Acten-mässiger Bericht von wieder Aufrichtung der verfallenen Lutherischen Kirche-Sachen in Pensylvanien im Jahr 1742"; a pro-Moravian account in *Büdingische Sammlung*, vol. 3, part 16, Nr. 51, 579–86.

11. Pro-Moravian accounts: "Extract from Species Facti on the Philadelphia Tumult (Philadelphia, 5 August 1742)," in *Büdingische Sammlung*, vol. 3, part 13 (1744), Nr. 24, 80–86; Relation von dem Tumult in der Kirche zu Philadelphia, 26 July 1742, R.14.A.13.25, Unity Archives. Anti-Moravian accounts: Muhlenberg, *Journal*, 29 December 1742, including the quote in English; Heinrich Melchior Mühlenberg, *Selbstbiographie, 1711–1743*, ed. W. Germann (Allentown, Pa.: Brobst, Diehl and Co., 1881), 139–41, including the quotation in German; anonymous broadside, "A Protestation of the Several Members of the Protestant *Lutheran* and *Reformed* Religions in the City of *Philadelphia*" (1742), Case 2, #12–1, Hinke Manuscript Collection, Archives of the Evangelical and Reformed Historical Society; Boehm, *Getreuer Warnungs Brief*; anonymous (probably Gruber), "Ausführliche Nachricht," 205–7. Newspaper accounts included views from both sides.

In the above broadside ("A Protestation . . .") some of the people involved in the attack on Pyrlaeus claimed that a heated argument broke out, they led Pyrlaeus by the arms out into the street, during which time pushing, elbowing, and scolding took place on both sides, but that no blows were struck. Instead the anti-Moravian leaders urged their followers to take the matter up with the magistrates. Given what was at stake and the confusion, arguing, and tension present, not to mention the violence described by their opponents and the violence the anti-Moravian faction did admit to, it is difficult to image that the group that attacked Pyrlaeus exercised this much restraint.

12. Thurnstein (Zinzendorf), *Pennsylvania Gazette*, 26 August 1742, Nr. 715, p. 3.

13. "Remarks on Count Zinzendorff's Memorandum," *American Weekly Mercury*, 26 August–2 September 1742, p. 4.

14. Anti-Moravian accounts: Boehm, 23 August 1742, *Life and Letters*, 366–70;

Mühlenberg, *Selbstbiographie*, 139–41; "Ausführliche Nachricht," 205–7. Pro-Moravian accounts: "Acten-mässiger Bericht"; Extract from Species Facti on the Philadelphia Tumult"; Relation von dem Tumult in der Kirche zu Philadelphia, 26 July 1742.

15. Relation von dem Tumult in der Kirche zu Philadelphia, 26 July 1742, R.14.A.13.25.

16. "Ausführliche Nachricht," 205–8.

17. Mühlenberg, *Selbstbiographie*, 139–41; Muhlenberg, *Journal*, 29 December 1742 (pp. 75–76).

18. Declaration to the Court by Zinzendorf concerning the Pyrlaeus tumult, R 14.A.13.26, Unity Archives, and Court Judgment against the Moravians for the 18. Jul 1742 Tumult in the Church (City of Philadelphia, 21 January 1744 o.s.), R.14.A.13.49; Boehm Report to the Synods, 8 July 1744, 24–25; Mühlenberg to Ziegenhagen and Francke, 17 March 1743; Muhlenberg, *Journal*, 14 February 1743.

19. "Ausführliche Nachricht," 214. According to the same anti-Moravian account, one of the pro-Moravians who broke open the church door for Pyrlaeus was supposed to have gone to jail but was released (208).

20. *Aufrichtige Nachricht ans Publicum, Über eine Von dem Holländischen Pfarrer Joh. Phil. Böhmen bei Mr. Andr. Bradford edirte Lästerschrift Gegen Die so gennanten Herrnhuter* . . . (Philadelphia: Benjamin Franklin, 1742), extract reprinted in *Büdingischen Sammlung*, vol. 2, Part 12 (1743), pp. 888–906, here 903. Arndt, Eck, et al., *First Century of German Printing*, attribute authorship to Zinzendorf, but the text suggests the author was Georg Neisser. See also Peter Böhler, Phila., mense Dec 1742, Die Abolitions-Schrifft wegen des Mr. Boehms, *Büdingische Samm-lungen*, vol. 3, Part 13, Nr. 38, 91–95, and Richard Peters to Thomas Penn, 15 January 1743, Letter Books, Richard Peters, 1737–1750, Historical Society of Pennsylvania, Philadelphia.

21. This happened during the violence at Coventry as well, during the faceoff in the church between the Moravian pastor Jacob Lischy and his supporters and the Amsterdamer Johann Philip Boehm (see earlier discussion in this chapter).

22. John Fea briefly addresses the violence at Raccoon using primarily pro-Uppsalan sources, and places it in the larger context of the decline of Swedish ethnic congregational life in the region during the mid-eighteenth century. See Fea, "Ethnicity and Congregational Life in the Eighteenth-Century Delaware Valley," *Explorations in Early American Culture* 5 (2001): 45–75, here 53–56.

23. The Moravian account of these events is in Bryzelius Report, 1743–1745, especially 23 December 1743. The Uppsalan version is in Naesman to Beronius, 14 November 1745. Also, Acrelius left a brief account of the violence, based on what his colleague (Naesman) had told him Israel Acrelius, trans. William M. Reynolds, *A History of New Sweden; or, The Settlements on the River Delaware* (Philadelphia: Historical Society of Pennsylvania, 1874), 333–34.

24. Naesman to Beronius, 14 November 1745; Bryzelius Report, 1743–1745, here 23 December 1743.

25. See Westerkamp, *Triumph of the Laity*; Rothermund, *Layman's Progress*; Roeber, *Palatines, Liberty, and Property*; Isaac, *The Transformation of Virginia*.

26. Bryzelius Report, 1743–1745, accounts from March 1744; Naesman to Beronius, 14 November 1745; *Records of the Swedish Lutheran Churches at Raccoon and Penn's Neck, 1713–1786*, trans. and comp. Federal Writer's Project of the Works Progress Administration, State of New Jersey, 1938, 40–41.

27. Bryzelius Report, 1743–1745. Bethlehem followed these developments

closely, and worried. See *Bethlehem Diary*, vol. 2, entries for 22 January 1744 n.s. (p. 24); February 29 (40), which notes that Bryzelius returned from Raccoon "because his life is not safe there, his enemies rage so"; March 9 (46); April 2 (53), which notes that Böhler told a group of "pilgrims" that Bryzelius had been arrested while traveling to Raccoon and the constable was trembling, unable to sleep that night; April 10 (56); October 3 (141); December 22 (169). For Acrelius's remarks see Acrelius, *History of New Sweden*, 333–34.

28. The primary documentation of the trial and courtroom scene is in Bryzelius Report, 1743–1745, accounts from April 1744. The court records for this case, while brief, corroborate Bryzelius's view. See Court of General Sessions and County Court of Gloucester convened 27 March 1744 o.s., Gloucester County, New Jersey Court Minute Books, 1686–1747 (Gloucester County Historical Society). Some details concerning the case are also in Naesman to Beronius, 14 November 1745, Acrelius, *History of New Sweden*, 333–34, and Reincke and Sensemann Diary, 26 March to 10 April 1745.

29. Nyberg Diary, entry for 8 November 1744; Naesman to Beronius, 14 November 1745; Acrelius, *History of New Sweden*, 334–35; Reincke and Sensemann Diary, 26 March to 10 April 1745.

30. Uppsala Consistory to Peter Koch (Philadelphia), 4 September 1745.

31. Thomas J. Müller provides a good overview of the basic problems between the pro-and anti-Moravian factions in *Kirche zwischen zwei Welten* (Stuttgart: Franz Steiner Verlag, 1994),118–29, although his analysis is based primarily on evidence from Halle-Lutheran sources. See also Jerome H. Wood, *Conestoga Crossroads, Lancaster, Pennsylvania, 1730–1790* (Harrisburg: Pennsylvania Historical and Museum Commission, 1979), 184–86, who also relies primarily on Hallensian sources.

32. Nyberg Diary, 1743–1749. See Nyberg's discussion of the circumstances of his call to Lancaster, the trip from Sweden, joining the Moravians, etc., which is at the beginning of the diary.

33. Nyberg Diary, entry for 8 December 1745; anonymous, *Hoch-Deutsche Pennsylvanische Berichte*, 16 March 1746, Nr. 68; Wood, *Conestoga Crossroads*, 184–85.

34. Nyberg Diary, 12, 19 December 1745.

35. Nyberg Diary, 22 January 1746; Muhlenberg, *Journal*, February 1746; Mühlenberg to Francke and Ziegenhagen, 12 December 1745; *Hoch-Deutsche Pennsylvanische Berichte*, 16 March 1746, Nr. 68.

36. Muhlenberg, *Journal*, February 1746; anonymous, *Hoch-Deutsche Pennsylvanische Berichte*, 16 March 1746, Nr. 68; Nyberg Diary, 25 December 1745, 12 February 1746. There is a lot about the Lancaster dispute in Mühlenberg's correspondence for early 1746. See his synopsis in a letter of 15 November 1751 to Fresenius, in which he looks back on those events. Conrad Weiser proposed a peace plan allowing both sides to use the church, but they could not agree on the details and took their case to the governor (see Muhlenberg, *Journal*, 7 February 1746). See also Müller, *Kirche zwischen zwei Welten*, 124–29.

37. Nyberg Diary, 17 February 1746; Muhlenberg, *Journal*, 6 February 1746; *Hoch-Deutsche Pennsylvanische Berichte*, 16 March 1746, Nr. 68. Some details are also in the issue of 16 June 1746.

38. Sebastian Graff, Johan Michael Immel, Jacob Schlauch, and Matheus Jung's open letter to Saur, printed in *Hoch-Deutsche Pennsylvanische Berichte*, 16 May 1746, Nr. 70.

39. Philip Schauffelberger, Ludwig Stein, Adam Simon Kuhn, Jacob Jayser,

Michael Groß, and Bernhart Hubele to Saur, printed in *Hoch-Deutsche Pennsylvanische Berichte*, 16 June 1746, Nr. 71.

40. Nyberg Diary, 17 February, 31 May, 9 June 1746.

41. Nyberg Diary, 22 September, 11 December 1746, and Muhlenberg, *Journal*, 5 May 1748.

42. Muhlenberg, *Journal*, 28–30 June, 6–7 July 1747, and Glatfelter, *Pastors and People*, vol. 1, 316–18.

43. See Moravian synod minutes, itinerant (*Landprediger*) diaries, and correspondence by and about itinerants in the Moravian Archives, the Unity Archives, the *Bethlehem Diary*, vols. 1–2, and the Archives of the Evangelical and Reformed Historical Society.

44. Compiled from information in the numerous diaries and correspondence of the Halle and Amsterdam pastors and Glatfelter, *Pastors and People*, vol. 1 and the tables in vol. 2, 52–53, 139, and from Acrelius, *History of New Sweden*.

45. Acrelius, *History of New Sweden*, 402–26.

46. Acrelius, *History of New Sweden*, 430.

47. Acrelius, *History of New Sweden*, 418–34.

48. Acrelius, *History of New Sweden*, 248–49 and 373–401.

49. See Fea, "Ethnicity and Congregational Life," on the decline of the Swedish language and religious-ethnic identity in the second half of the eighteenth century. Fea argues that parishioners sacrificed their ethnic identity and joined the Anglicans for the stability that church offered.

50. The quotation is from Bonomi, *Under the Cope of Heaven*, who stresses volunteerism in American religious communities and culture. On the other hand Jon Butler, *Awash in a Sea of Faith: Christianizing the American People* (Cambridge, Mass.: Harvard University Press, 1990), stresses coercion.

Conclusion

1. For a good explanation of the feminization thesis see Ann Douglas, *The Feminization of American Culture* (New York: Knopf, 1977), and Barbara Welter, "The Feminization of American Religion, 1800–1860," in Welter, ed., *Dimity Convictions: The American Woman in the Nineteenth Century* (Athens: Ohio University Press, 1976), 83–102. More recently Susan Juster, *Disorderly Women: Sexual Politics and Evangelicalism in Revolutionary New England* (Ithaca, N.Y.: Cornell University Press, 1994) has examined this idea in a more complex way and found that feminization early in the radical history of Baptists in Connecticut gave way to mainstream views. The difference between the Connecticut Baptists and the Lutheran and Reformed communities is that both the impulse toward feminization and the reaction to it began during the Great Awakening in the latter communities, where as the reaction among the Baptists did not occur until the Revolutionary era. See also Amanda Porterfield, *Female Piety in Puritan New England* (New York: Oxford University Press, 1992), who found that women dominated church membership throughout New England by the 1680s and that female imagery and piety was important from the beginning of Puritan settlement in North America (esp. 116–53).

Bibliography of Primary Sources

Archival

UNITY ARCHIVES, HERRNHUT (GERMANY)

Correspondence, Reports, Diaries, and Synod Minutes

Johann Christian Friedrich Cammerhof correspondence, 1748, R.A.28.5
Jacob Lischy to Brother Andreas, 1743, R.14.A.36.6, Nr. 6
Anna Nitschmann correspondence from Pennsylvania, 1740–1742, R.A.26.66–82
August Gottlieb Spangenberg, Letters from America, 1736–1739, R.14.A.18.1
Benigna Zinzendorf correspondence from Pennsylvania, 1742, R.14.A.26
Zinzendorf correspondence with Pennsylvania, 1734–1740, R.14.1.21
Heinrich Antes Bericht von seine reise nach Newtown, 17 June 1746, R.14.A.36.9
Johann Christoph Pyrlaeus Notebook, R.27.375
Zinzendorf, Kurtze Relation von Pensylvanien, 1742, R.14.A.15.1a
Johann Christoph Becker, Diarium oder Journal angefangen A.C. 1732, R.21.A.196
Bethlehem Diary, 1746, R.14.Aa. Nr. 13
Zinzendorf, Diarium an die Gemeinen, 1742, R.14.A.13.37
Minutes of the Single Brothers Synod, London, 1752, R.2.A.32b

Itinerant Preacher (Landprediger) Diaries

Anonymous, July–September 1742, R.14.A.36.1
Andreas Eschenbach, Diarium . . . aus Neu-Hanover, 22 May–3 June 1743, R.14.Aa. Nr.10.11
Matthias Hehl, Kurze Beschreibung meiner Reise, 6 November 1755–5 March 1756, R.14.A.36.21
Matthias and Anna Maria Hehl, Relation von . . . Reise ins Land, 6 September–3 October 1753, R.14.A.36.17
Johann Christoph Höpfner, Diario von Swatara, 12 January–14 March 1752, R.14.Aa.18
John Leighton, Journal thro' New England, 29 November 1753–March 1754, R.A.36.18
Jacob Lischy Diarum, 5–19 April 1743, R.14.A.36.2
Jacob Lischy Diarum, 29 April–12 May 1743, R.14.A.36.3
Johann Philipp Meurer, Diario von York an der Catores (extract), 4 January–26 February 1752, R.14.Aa.18
Anna Nitschmann, Diarium . . . Von Ihre Reyße nacher Pensylvanien, 1740, R.14.A.26.65
Laurentius Nyberg, A Short Sketch of the Awakening, 12 December 1743–20 November 1749, R.14.A.40.2

Johann Christoph Pyrlaeus, Diarium wegen seiner . . . Gefangenschaft, 17–24 June 1743, R.14.36.4

Anna Ramsberg and Maria Catharina Binder, Reiße Diarium, 4 March–24 April 1753, R.14.Aa.19

Abraham Reincke, Relation von seiner Reiße, July–September 1753, R.14.A.36.7

Abraham Reincke and Joachim Sensemann, Diarium, 26 March–10 April 1745, R.14.A.36.7

Frau Gottfried Roesler, Diarium eines Land Besuchs, 20 June to 12 August 1752, R.14.A.36.11

Leonhard Schnell and Johann Brandmüller, Reiße-Diarium, October–December 1749, R.14.A.36.10

Nathanael Seidel and Christian Philip Bader, Reise-Diarum, 31 January–23 March 1752, R.14.Aa.18

Anton Wagner, Diario von Quittopehille, 19 January–6 March 1752, R.14.Aa.18

Other

Court Judgment Against the Moravians, Philadelphia, 21 January 1744, R.14.A.13.49

Declaration of the Court by Zinzendorf concerning the Pyrlaeus tumult, 1742, R.14.A.13.26

Relation von dem Tumult in der Kirche zu Philadelphia, 26 July 1742, R.14.A.13.25

Ehechor, Chorsachen (Married Choir Materials), R.4.C.II.8.3

Lieder an und von Christian Renatus von Zinzendorf aus der Sichtungszeit, R.20.E.36

Mariane von Watteville, Lebenslauf (Memoir), R.22. Nr. 80

Zinzendorf, Reden vor Frauens-Personen, Philadelphia, R.14.A.38.1a.3

MORAVIAN ARCHIVES, BETHLEHEM (PENNSYLVANIA)

Itinerant Preacher (Landprediger) Diaries and Reports

Christoph Baus and Johann Georg Hantsch, Journal . . . in the country, 5–18 March 1745, JA I 1

Heinrich Beck and Jacob Adolph, Diarium, 8–29 October, 1746, JA I 3

Paul Daniel Bryzelius, Bericht von seiner Arbeit, 13 January 1743–12 January 1745, JA I 13

Abraham Bünniger, Diaria, 30 Dec 1746–31 Jan 1747 and 15 April–14 May 1747, JA I 14

Matthias Gottlieb Gottschalk, Mein 4tes Landbesuch in den Jerseys, 29 June–9 July 1747, JB 1 5

Johann Georg Hantsch Diarium, 12 March–26 April 1747, JB II 1

Johann Georg Hantsch, Diarium, 28 July–30 August 1747, JB II 1c

Johann Georg Hantsch and Jacob Adolph, Diarium, 6 February–23 March 1746, JB II 2f

Johannes Hantsch and Matthias Gottlieb Gottschalk, Reise Diarium, 23 March–20 April 1747, JB II c

Abraham Müller, Journal of his Visits among the Baptists, 8–28 March 1745, JC III 4

Abraham Müller and Wilhelm Frey, Journal of his Visits, 9 October–6 November 1746, JC III 4a

John Oakley, Journal of his Journey from Pensilvania to Lewis Town, 1–17 August 1742, JD II 1

John Oakley, Journal of his Visit in West Jersey, 23 May to 4 June 1743, JD II 1b
Nathanael Seidel, Diarium von seinem Land Visitation, 25 July–15 August 1747, JE II 4a
Nathanael Seidel and Eric Westman, Bericht von ihrer Reise, 17 Nov–5 Dec 1747, JE 4c
August Gottlieb Spangenberg, Br. Josephs Land-Besuch, 8 February–4 March 1748, JE III 3e
August G. Spangenberg and Matthaeus Reutz, Kurtze Nachricht, 30 June–18 August 1748, JE III 3f
John Wade, Journal of his Itinerant Preaching, 8 February–1 April 1748(?), JF IV 1

Other

Bethlehemisches Kirchen-Buch (Bethlehem church book), vol. 2
Peter Böhler Box, Controversies and Religious Questions Folder, Nr. 3 i–iii, 256G
Laurentius Nyberg to Bethlehem Congregation, 8 March 1748, JD I 4
Rahel to Maria Spangenberg, August 1745, Box 319, Folder 1, Item 10
Brandmüller-Zinzendorf correspondence, 1748, JA I 7c
Zinzendorf correspondence, 1743–1746, Zinzendorf: Box A. Letters, etc.: Till 1749
Reports from Pennsylvania Synods, 1747–1748

ARCHIVES OF THE EVANGELICAL AND REFORMED HISTORICAL SOCIETY OF THE UNITED CHURCH OF CHRIST, LANCASTER, PENNSYLVANIA

William J. Hinke Manuscript Collection, MJMO H592–592a (primarily *Landprediger* diaries)

Anonymous Diary, 2–7 November 1746
Johann Brandmüller, Diaria, 8 April–6 May 1745, 1–24 September 1745, 26 October 1745–11 Jan 1746
David Bruce, Extract from his Plan among the English, 1746
Jacob Lischy, Aufrichtige Relation vom Anfang . . . der Reformierten Sache, 8 December 1744
Jacob Lischy, Relation von meiner Reise, 23 February–28 May 1745
Jacob Lischy, Diarium, 14 August–9 September 1745
Jacob Lischy and Christian Rauch, Visitations-Reise und Predigten, February 1745
Christian Rauch, Diarium, 6 February–14 November 1746
Christian Rauch, Auszüge aus seinem Diarium, 23 January–30 June 1747
Leonhard Schnell, Nachricht von seinen Predigten u. Besuch, March–April 1743
Leonhard Schnell, Auszug aus seinem Gemeine-Bericht, 1745
Leonhard Schnell, Diarum seiner Landreise, 21 October–1 November 1745
Leonhard Schnell, Auszüge aus seinem Diarium, 10 January–17 November 1746

Letters and Documents Relating to the Reformed Church, 1743–1746, compiled by William J. Hinke, ZK #6–8 (primarily minutes, reports, correspondence, and other documents)

Johann Bechtel—Zinzendorf correspondence, 1745
Cammerhoff—Zinzendorf correspondence, 1747–1748

Classis of Amsterdam, correspondence with Pennsylvania Pastors, 1739
Peter Heinrich Dorius Report, 1 March 1738
Jacob Lischy, Specification seiner Gemeinden, wie sie stehen und versorgt werden können, 1744
Christian Rauch, Relation von dem letzten Tryal in Bikipsi (Poughkeepsie, N.Y.), December 1744
Tulpehocken elders to Johann Philip Boehm, 1744
Georg Michael Weiss Report, 29 April 1738

Auszüge aus den Verhandlungen der Pensylvanischen Synoden, 1745–1748, compiled by William J. Hinke, MKX G326

David Bruce, Diary 19 June to 7 August 1745
Synod Minutes, 1745–1748

Archives of the Francke Foundations, Halle

Peter Brunnholtz, Diarum, 1744–1745, AFSt/M 4 A 2
Johann Friedrich Handschuh, Diaria, 1748–1753, AFSt/M 4 H 10
Lieferungen nach Pennsylvanien, 1740–1768, AFSt/M 4 G 6–11
Johann Albert Weygand, Diarum, 1748–1752, AFSt/M 4 H 6–8

Lutheran Archives Center, Philadelphia

Halle Documents, edited by William Julius Mann and W. Germann, vol. 2, PM 28 TH 18
Johann Nicolaus Kurtz, Diarium, 1746–1750, PK 98 A
Johann Helfrich Schaum, Diarium, 1748, PS 313 A
Johann Helfrich Schaum correspondence, 1743–1753, PS 313 E 1–2 and PS 313 C
Conrad Weiser correspondence, 1747, PW42 D1–2

Historical Society of Pennsylvania, Philadelphia

Richard Peters to Thomas Penn, 15 January 1743, Richard Peters Letter Books, 1737–1750
Gabriel Naesman to Bishop Mag. Beronius, 14 November 1745, Amandus Johnson Papers, Archivum Americanum, vol. 1, Box 59, Folder 3, MSS 41 and Box 65, Folder M, Photostats, in the collections of the Balch Institute for Ethnic Studies

Gloucester County Historical Society, Woodbury, New Jersey

Court of General Sessions and Country County Court of Gloucester, New Jersey Court Minute Books, 1686–1747, here 1744

Printed Primary Sources

Newspapers and Almanacs

Pennsylvania Gazette. Philadelphia: Benjamin Franklin, 1742–1747
American Weekly Mercury. Philadelphia: Andrew Bradford, 1742–43

Hoch-Deutsch Pensylvanische Geschichts-Schreiber. Germantown: Christopher, 1742–1744

Hoch-Deutsche Pennsylvanische Berichte. Germantown: Christopher Saur, 1745–1746

Pennsylvanische Berichte. Germantown: Christopher Saur, 1746–1754

Der Hoch-Deutsch Americanische Calender. Germantown: Christopher Saur, 1750–1752

BOOKS, PAMPHLETS, AND BROADSIDES

Ein ABC Buch bey allen Religionen ohne billigen Anstoß zu gebrauchen. Germantown, Pa.: Christopher Saur, 1738.

Acrelius, Israel. *A History of New Sweden; or, The Settlements on the River Delaware.* Trans. William R. Reynolds. Philadelphia: Historical Society of Pennsylvania, 1874.

Aland, Kurt, ed. *Die Korrespondenz Heinrich Melchior Mühlenbergs aus der Anfangszeit des deutschen Luthertums in Nordamerika,* vol. 1. Berlin: de Gruyter, 1986.

Alt- und neuer Brüder-Gesang . . . London: Haberkorn and Gussichen Schriften, 1753.

Anonymous (perhaps Johann Adam Gruber). "Ausführliche Nachricht von Zinzendorfs Unternehmungen in Pennsylvania, 1742–43." In "Americanische Nachrichten von Herrnhutischen Sachen," in *Bewährte Nachrichten von Herrnhutischen Sachen,* ed. Johann Philip Fresenius. Frankfurt am Main: Heinrich Ludwig Broenner, 1748, vol. 3, 97–236.

Aufrichtige Nachricht Ans Publicum, Über eine Von dem Holländischen Pfarrer Joh. Phil. Böhmen bei Mr. Andr. Bradford edirte Lästerschrift Gegen Die so gennanten Herrnhuter . . . Philadelphia: Benjamin Franklin, 1742.

Authentische Relation Von dem Anlass, Fortgang und Schlusse Der . . . Versammlung Einiger Arbeiter Derer meisten Christlichen Religionen Und Vieler vor sich selbst Gottdienenden Christen-Menschen in PENNSYLVANIA. Philadelphia: Benjamin Franklin, 1742. Reprint, edited by Peter Vogt, in Erich Beyreuther, Matthias Meyer und Amedeo Molnár, eds., *Nikolaus Ludwig von Zinzendorf, Materialien und Dokumente,* vol. 30. Hildesheim: Georg Olms Verlag, 1998.

Baumgarten, Jacob Siegmund. *Theologische Bedencken.* 7 vols. Halle: Johann Andreas Baur, 1742–1750.

The Bethlehem Diary, vol. 1, 1742–1744. Ed. and trans. Kenneth G. Hamilton. Bethlehem: Moravian Archives, 1971.

The Bethlehem Diary, vol. 2, 1744–1745. Ed. Vernon H. Nelson et al, trans. Kenneth G. Hamilton and Lothar Madeheim. Bethlehem, Pa.: Moravian Archives, 2001.

Beyreuther, Erich and Gerhard Meyer, eds. *Antizinzendorfia.* In Erich Beyreuther, ed., *Nikolaus Ludwig von Zinzendorf, Materialien und Dokumente,* vols. 14–16. Hildesheim: Georg Olms Verlag, 1976 and 1982.

Boehm, Johann Philip. *Abermahlige treue Warnung und Vermahnung an meine sehr werthe und theurer geschätzte Reformirte Glaubens-verwandte . . .* Philadelphia: Cornelia Bradford and Isaiah Warner, 1743.

———. *Getreuer Warnungs Brief an die Hochteutsche Evangelisch Reformirten Gemeinden und alle deren Glieder, in Pensylvanien, Zur getreuen Warschauung, vor denen Leuthen, welche unter dem nahmen von Herrn-Huther bekandt seyn . . .* Philadelphia: Andrew Bradford, 1742.

———. *Life and Letters of Reverend John Philip Boehm: Founder of the Reformed Church in Pennsylvania, 1683–1749.* Ed. William J. Hinke. Philadelphia: Reformed Church of the United States, 1916.

Bogatzky, Carl Heinrich von. *Aufrichtige und an alle Kinder Gottes gerichtete Declaration über Eine gegen Ihn herausgekommene Herrnhutische Schrift . . .* Halle: Waisenhaus, 1751.

———. *Güldnes Schatz-Kästleins der Kinder Gottes.* Breslau, 1718.

———. *Nöthige Warnung und Verwahrung vor dem Rückfall, Nebst einem zwiefachen Anhange und einem erbaulichen Briefe, worrinen die Herrnhuter nach Wahrheit und Liebe beurtheilet werden.* Halle: Waisenhaus, 1750.

Bothe, Heinrich Joachim. *Zuverläßige Beschreibung des nunmehro ganz entdeckten Herrnhutischen Ehe-Geheimnisses . . . ,* 2 vols. Berlin: self published, 1751–1752.

Bruin, F. de, Gerardus Kulenkamp, and A. Buurt. *Nadare Trouhartige Waarschouwinge, Tegen de Verleidingen Der Herrnhuters.* Amsterdam: Loveringh and Borstius, 1750.

Ein Büchlein van Gott dem Heiligen Geiste der selbständigen Weisheit und Unser aller Mutter. Barby, 1756.

Büdingische Sammlung Einiger in die Kirchen-Historie Einschlagender Sonderlich neuerer Schrifften, 3 vols. Büdingen: Johann Christoph Stöhr; Leipzig: D. Korte, 1740–1745. Reprinted in Erich Beyreuther and Gerhard Meyer, eds., *Nikolaus Ludwig von Zinzendorf, Ergänzungsbände zu den Hauptschriften,* vols. 7–10. Hildesheim: Georg Olms Verlag, 1965–1971.

Calvin, John. *Institutes of the Christian Religion.* 2 vols. Ed. John T. McNeill, trans. Ford Lewis Battles. Philadelphia: Westminster Press, 1960.

Christliches Gesang-Buch, der Evangelischen Brüder Gemeinen vom 1735. Third ed., with twelve appendices and supplements. Ebersdorf, 1741–1748. Reprinted in Erich Beyreuther, Gerhard Meyer, and Gudrun Meyer-Hickel, eds., *Nikolaus Ludwig von Zinzendorf, Materialien und Dokumente,* vol. 3, parts 1–3. Hildesheim: Georg Olms Verlag, 1981.

Confessie ende Vredehandelinge, Geschiet tot Dordrecht, Aᵒ 1632. Harlem, 1633.

Cyprian, Ernst Salomon. "Letztes Votum, die herrnhutische Secte betreffend (1745)." In Johann Philipp Fresenius, ed., *Bewährte Nachrichten von Herrnhutischen Sachen,* vol. 3, 1–24. Frankfurt am Main and Leipzig: Heinrich Ludwig Broenner, 1748.

———. *Vernünftige Warnung vor Irrthume von Gleichgültigkeit der Gottesdienste.* Gotha: Johann Andreas Reyher, 1744.

The Dansbury Diaries: Moravian Travel Diaries, 1748 and 1755, of the Reverend Sven Roseen and Others in the Area of Dansbury, now Stroudsburg, Pa. Ed. and trans. William N. Schwarze and Ralf Ridgeway Hillmann. Camden, Me.: Picton Press, 1994.

Detailed Reports on the Salzburger Emigrants Who Settled in America, vols. 14 and 16. Ed. and trans. Eva Pulgram, Magdalena Hoffman-Loerzer, Georg Fenwick Jones, and Renate Wilson. Athens: University of Georgia Press, 1989, 1991.

Documentary History of the Evangelical Lutheran Ministerium of Pennsylvania and Adjacent States. Proceedings of the Annual Conventions from 1748 to 1821. Philadelphia: Lutheran Church, 1898.

Durnbaugh, Donald F., ed. *The Brethren in Colonial America: A Source Book on the Transplantation and Development of the Church of the Brethren in the Eighteenth Century.* Elgin, Ill.: Brethren Press, 1967.

Ecclesiastical Records of the State of New York, vol. 4. Ed. Hugh Hastings. Albany: J.B. Lyon Company, State Printers, 1902.

Erweiterte Vorschläge, zu einem dauerhalten Frieden zw. Sr. Excellenz dem Herrn Grafen

Nicolaus Ludewig von Zinzendorff und der Creutz-Luft-Holtz-Wurm-Gemeine an Einem, Und deren Feinden am anderen Theile. Germantown, Pa.: Christopher Saur, 1749.

Faull, Katherine M., ed. and trans. *Moravian Women's Memoirs: Their Related Lives, 1750–1820.* Syracuse, N.Y.: Syracuse University Press, 1997.

Fresenius, Johann Philip, ed. *Bewährte Nachrichten von Herrnhutischen Sachen.* 4 vols. Frankfurt am Main: Johann Leonard Buchner and Heinrich Ludwig Broenner, 1746–1751.

Frey, Andreas, *Declaration, Oder: Erklärung, Auf welche Weise, und wie er unter die sogenannte Herrnhuter Gemeine gekommen . . .* Germantown, Pa.: Christopher Saur, 1748.

Das Gesang-Buch der Gemeine in Herrn-Huth. Herrnhut: Waysen-Hause, 1735.

Das Gesang-Buch der Gemeine in Herrn-Huth. Herrnhut: Waysen-Hause, 1737.

Gesangbuch zum Gebrauch der evangelischen Brüdergemeinen. Barby: Friedrich Spellenberg, 1778.

Good, James I. and William J. Hinke, trans. and eds. *Minutes and Letters of the Coetus of the German Reformed Congregations in Pennsylvania, 1747–1792, Together with Three Preliminary Reports of Rev. John Philip Boehm, 1734–1744.* Philadelphia: Reformed Church, 1903.

Gruber, Johann Adam. *Ein Zeugniß eines Betrübten, der seine Klage ausschüttet über die unzeitige, eingenmächtige übereylte Zusammen-Beruffung und Sammlung verschiedener Partheyen und erweckten Seelen so unter Nahmen Immanuels vorgegeben wird.* Germantown, Pa.: Christopher Saur, December 1741.

Güldin, Samuel, . . . *Unpartheyisches Zeugnüß Ueber Die Neue Vereinigung Aller Religions-Partheyen In Pensylvanien.* Germantown: Christopher Saur, 1743.

Hahn, Hans-Christoph and Hellmut Reichel, eds. *Zinzendorf und die Herrnhuter Brüder: Quellen zur Geschichte der Brüder-Unität von 1722 bis 1760.* Hamburg: Friedrich Wittig Verlag, 1977.

Hecker, A. P. *Gespräch eines evangelisch-lutherischen Predigers mit einem, der über 6 Jahr sich zu der Gemeine der sogenannten Mährischen Brüder gehalten.* Berlin: Buchhandlung der Realschule, 1751.

Hildebrand, Johannes. *Wohlbegründetes Bedencken der Christlichen Gemeine in und bey Ephrata . . .* Germantown, Pa.: Christopher Saur, 1743.

Hinke, William J. and Charles E. Kemper, eds. and trans. "Moravian Diaries of Travels Through Virginia." *Virginia Magazine of History and Biography* 11, 3 (January 1904): 370–93; 12, 1 (July 1904): 55–61, 62–76; 11, 2 (October 1903): 113–31.

Jones, George Fenwick and Paul Martin Peucker, trans. and ed. "'We Have Come to Georgia with Pure Intentions': Moravian Bishop August Gottlieb Spangenberg's Letters from Savannah, 1735." *Georgia Historical Quarterly* 82, 1 (Spring 1998): 84–120.

Kelpius, Johannes. "The Diarium of Magister Johannes Kelpius." Ed. and trans. Julius Friedrich Sachse. Part 27 of *Pennsylvania: The German Influence in Its Settlement and Development: A Narrative and Critical History.* In *The Pennsylvania German Society, Proceedings and Addresses,* vol. 25, 2–100. Lancaster, Pa.: Pennsylvania German Society, 1917.

Kulenkamp, Gerardus. *De naakt ontdekte enthusiastery, geest-dryvery, en bedorvene mystikery der zo genaamde Herrnhuthers . . .* 2 vols. Amsterdam: Adriaan Wor and Erve G. Onder de Linden, 1739–1740.

Kurze zuverläßige Nachricht Von der, unter dem Namen der Böhmisch-Mährischen bekanten, Kirche UNITAS FRATRUM Herkommen, Lehr-Begrif . . . 1757.

Lange, Joachim. *Lebenslauf, Zur Erweckung seiner in der Evangelischen Kirche Stehen-den . . . Nebst einem Anhange Väterliche Warnung . . . vor dem Herrenhutischen Kir-chenwesen und Missionswercke.* Halle: Christ. Peter Francken, 1744.

Lischy, Jacob. *Jacob Lischys Reformierten Predigers Declaration seines Sinnes. An seine Reformierte Religions-Genossen In Pennsylvanien.* Germantown, Pa.: Christopher Saur, 1743.

Luther, Martin. "The Babylonian Captivity of the Church (1520)." In *Martin Luther: Three Treatises from the American Edition of Luther's Works.* 2nd rev. ed. ed. and trans. A. T. W. Steinhäuser et al., 113–260. Philadelphia: Fortress Press, 1970.

———. "Die dankbare Schätzung des Ehestandes (1531)." In *Predigten über den Weg der Kirche.* Trans. Erich Widmann, 177–83. Gütersloh: Gütersloher Verlagshaus Mohn, 1977.

———. "Eine kurze Form der Zehn Gebote, eine kurze Form des Glaubens, eine kurze Form des Vaterunsers . . . (1520)." In *Martin Luther: Die reformatori-schen Grundschriften,* vol. 4, *Die Freiheit eines Christen.* Ed. Horst Beintker. Munich: Deutscher Taschenbuch Verlag, 1983.

———. *Martin Luthers Werke, Kritische Gesamtausgabe.* "Ein Sermon von dem Ehlichen Standt (1519)," vol. 2, 162–171; "Vom ehelichen Leben (1522)," vol. 10, pt. 2, 267–304; "Von Ehesachen (1530)," vol. 30, pt. 3, 198–248. Let-ter to three nuns, 6 August 1524, Correspondence Series, vol. 3, 326–28. Wei-mar: Böhlaus, 1884–1933.

Das Marschesche Gesangbuch. Herrnhut: M. Christian Gottfried Marchen, 1731.

Mittelberger, Gottlieb. *Journey to Pennsylvania.* Ed. and trans. Oscar Handlin and John Clive. Cambridge, Mass.: Belknap Press of Harvard University Press, 1960.

———. *Reise nach Pennsylvanien im Jahr 1750 und Rückreise nach Deutschland im Jahr 1754.* Stuttgart: Gottlieb Friderich Jenisch, 1756. Reprint ed. Jürgen Charnitzky. Sigmaringen: Thorbecke, 1997.

Mühlenberg, Heinrich Melchior. *The Correspondence of Heinrich Melchior Mühlen-berg,* vols. 1 and 2. Ed. and trans. John W. Kleiner and Helmut T. Lehmann. Camden, Me.: Picton Press, 1993, 1997.

———. *The Journals of Henry Melchior Muhlenberg,* vol. 1. Edited and translated by Theodore G. Tappert and John W. Doberstein. Philadelphia: Muhlenberg Press, 1942.

———. *Die Korrespondenz Heinrich Melchior Mühlenberg aus der Anfangszeit des deut-schen Luthertums in Nordamerika,* vol. 1. Ed. by Kurt Aland. Berlin and New York: Walter de Gruyter, 1986.

——— *Selbstbiographie, 1711–1743.* Ed. W. Germann. Allentown, Pa.: Brobst, Diehl, and Co., 1881.

Nachrichten von den vereinigten Deutschen Evangelisch- Lutherischen Gemeinen in Nord-America, absonderlich in Pensylvanien. Ed. D. Johann Ludewig Schulze. Here the expanded edition by W. J. Mann, B. M. Schmucker, and W. Germann. 2 vols. Allentown, Pa.: Brobst, Diehl, and Co., 1886, 1895.

O'Callaghan, E. B., ed. *The Documentary History of the State of New York,* vol. 3 Albany: Weed, Parsons and Co., 1850.

"A Protestation of the Several Members of the Protestant *Lutheran* and *Reformed* Religions in the City of Philadelphia." 1742.

Records of the Swedish Lutheran Churches at Raccoon and Penn's Neck, 1713–1786. Trans. and comp. Federal Writer's Project of the Works Progress Administra-tion, State of New Jersey, 1938.

Reynier, Jean François (or Johann Franz Regnier). "Das Geheimnis der Zinzendorfischen Sect." In Johann Philip Fresenius, ed., *Bewährte Nachrichten von Herrnhutischen Sachen*, vol. 1, 321–479. Frankfurt am Main: Johann Leonhard Buchner, 1746.

Rimius, Henry. *A Candid Narrative of the Rise and Progress of the Herrnhuters, Commonly Call'd Moravians or Unitas Fratrum*. London: A. Linde, 1753, and Philadelphia: W. Bradford, 1753.

Schlatter, Michael. "Diary of Rev. Michael Schlatter: June 1–December 15, 1746." Edited and translated by William J. Hinke. *Journal of the Presbyterian Historical Society* 3, 3 (September 1905): 105–21; 4, 1 (January 1906): 158–76.

———. "The Journal of Rev. Michael Schlatter." Ed. and trans. Henry Harbaugh, 87–234. *Life of Rev. Michael Schlatter*. Philadelphia: Lindsay and Blakiston, 1857.

Simon, Menno. "A Confession of the Triune, Eternal, and True God, Father, Son, and Holy Ghost." In *The Complete Works of Menno Simon*, Part II, 183–88. Elkhart, Ind.: John F. Funk and Brother, 1871. Reprint Aylmer, Ont.: Pathway Publishers, 1983.

Spangenberg, August Gottlieb. *Apologetische Schluß-Schrifft, Worinn über tausend Beschuldigungen gegen die Brüder-Gemeinen und Ihren zeitherigen Ordinarium nach der Wahrheit beantwortet werden*, 2 vols. Leipzig: Marchesche Buchhandlung, 1752. Reprinted in Erich Beyreuther and Gerhard Meyer, eds. *Nicolaus Ludwig von Zinzendorf, Ergänzungsbände zu den Hauptschriften*, vol. 3. Hildesheim: Georg Olms Verlag, 1964.

———. *Darlegung richtiger Antworten auf mehr als dreyhundert Beschuldigungen gegen den Ordinarium Fratrum*. Leipzig and Görlitz: Marchesche Buchhandlung, 1751. Reprinted in Erich Beyreuther and Gerhard Meyer, eds., *Nikolaus Ludwig von Zinzendorf, Ergänzungsbände zu den Hauptschriften*, vol. 5. Hildesheim: Georg Olms Verlag, 1964.

———. *Leben des Herrn Nicolaus Ludwig Grafen und Herrn von Zinzendorf und Pottendorf*, 8 vols. Barby, 1773–1775. Reprinted in Erich Beyreuther and Gerhard Meyer, eds. *Nikolaus Ludwig von Zinzendorf, Materialien und Dokumente*, vol. 2, parts 1–8. Hildesheim: Georg Olms Verlag, 1971.

Spener, Philip Jacob. *Pia Desideria*. Frankfurt am Main: Johann Diederich Fritgen, 1675.

Staehlin, Fritz, ed. *Die Mission der Brüdergemeine in Suriname and Berbice im achtzehnten Jahrhundert: Eine Missiongeschichte hauptsächlich in Briefen und Originalberichten*, vol. 1. Herrnhut: Verein für Brüdergeschichte, 1913. Reprinted in Erich Beyreuther, Gerhard Meyer, and Amadeo Molnár, eds., *Nikolaus Ludwig von Zinzendorf, Materialien und Dokumente*, vol. 28, part 1. Hildesheim: Georg Olms Verlag, 1997.

Sutor, Georg Jacob, "Licht und Warheit bestehend in einer Untersuchung der Secten-Thorheit, besonders der gantz neuen, unter dem Namen Herrnhuter bekannten." In Johann Philip Fresenius, ed., *Bewährte Nachrichten von Herrnhutischen Sachen*, vol. 1, 627–842. Frankfurt am Main: Johann Leonhard Bruchner, 1746.

Tennent, Gilbert, *Some Account of the Principles of the Moravians . . .* London: S. Mason, 1743.

Väterlicher Hirten-Brieff an die bluehenden Reformierte Gemeine in Amsterdam. Amsterdam: Kirchenrath, 1738.

Volck, Alexander, *Das Entdeckte Geheimnis der Bosheit der Herrnhutischen Secte*. Frankfurt: Heinrich Ludwig Broenner, 1748. Here reprint of Philadelphia edition, 1749.

Walch, Johann Georg. *Theologisches Bedencken von der Beschaffenheit der Herrnhutischen secte.* Frankfurt am Main: Johann Leonhard Buchner, 1747.

Whitefield, George. *An Expostulary Letter, Adressed to Nicholas Lewis, Count Zinzendorff, and Lord Advocate of the Unitas Fratrum.* London: G. Keith, 1753, 3rd ed. reprinted Philadelphia: William Bradford, 1753.

——. *Von Georg Weitfields Predigten, Der Erste Theil, Nebst einer Einleitung und Copia eines Briefs von Neu-Yorck. Aus dem Englischen ins Hoch Deutsche übersetzt.* Germantown: Christopher Saur, 1740.

——. *George Whitefield's Journals.* Edinburgh: Banner of Truth Trust reprint, 1960.

——. *The Letters of George Whitefield, for the Period 1734–1742.* Ed. S. M. Houghton. Edinburgh: Banner of Truth Trust, 1976.

Woodmason, Charles. *The Carolina Backcountry on the Eve of the Revolution: The Journal and Other Writings of Charles Woodmason, Anglican Itinerant.* Ed. Richard J. Hooker. Chapel Hill: University of North Carolina Press, 1953.

Zinzendorf, Nicolaus Ludwig von. *A Collection of Sermons from Zinzendorf's Pennsylvania Journey, 1741–1742.* Ed. Craig D. Atwood, trans. Julie Tomerlin Weber. Bethlehem, Pa.: Moravian Church of America, 2001.

——. "Ein und zwanzig Discurse über die Augsburgische Confession, gehalten vom 15. Dec. 1747. bis zum 3. Mart. 1748." Reprinted in Erich Beyreuther and Gerhard Meyer, eds. *Nikolaus Ludwig von Zinzendorf, Hauptschriften,* vol. 6, 91–106. Hildesheim: Georg Olms Verlag, 1963.

——. "Naturelle Reflexiones über allerhand Materien, nach der Art, wie er bei sich selbst zu denken gewohnt ist (1747)." *Nikolaus Ludwig von Zinzendorf, Ergänzungsbände zu den Hauptschriften,* ed. Erich Beyreuther and Gehard Meyer, vol. 5. Hildesheim: Georg Olms Verlag, 1965.

——. *Nikolaus Ludwig von Zinzendorf: Texte zur Mission.* Ed. Helmut Binte. Hamburg: Friedrich Wittig Verlag, 1979.

——. "Der öffentlichen Gemeinreden im Jahr 1747, erster Theil, Anhang (1748)." Reprinted in *Nikolaus Ludwig von Zinzendorf, Hauptschriften,* ed. Erich Beyreuther and Gerhard Meyer, vol. 4. Hildesheim: Georg Olms Verlag, 1963.

——. *Pennsylvanische Nachrichten vom dem Reiche Christi* (1742). Reprinted in *Nikolaus Ludwig von Zinzendorf, Hauptschriften,* ed. Erich Beyreuther and Gerhard Meyer, vol. 2. Hildesheim: Georg Olms Verlag, 1963.

——. *Sieben Letzten Reden, So Er In der Gemeine, Vor seiner am 7. Aug. erfolgen abermahligen Abreise nach Amerika, gehalten,* 8–9 (11 June 1741). Büdingen: Johann Christoph Stöhr, 1742. *Nikolaus Ludwig von Zinzendorf, Hauptschriften,* vol. 2, ed. Erich Beyreuther and Gerhard Meyer, Hildesheim: Georg Olms Verlag, 1963.

Zwingli, Huldrych. *Hauptschriften.* Ed. Fritz Blanke, Oskar Farner, and Rudolf Pfister, vols. 1–2, *Zwingli, der Prediger.* Zurich: Zwingli-Verlag, 1940–1941.

Index

Acknowledgments

In the eleven years since this project began I have experienced many things and met many wonderful people on both sides of the Atlantic who helped me. While researching in Germany in 1995, 1996–1997, and 1999 I lived in Göttingen and made numerous extended trips to Halle and Herrnhut to work in the archives. Halle proved to be a fascinating place, undergoing a dramatic transformation in the 1990s. There Eva-Maria Hohlwein, who has since passed away, took me in and told me extraordinary, historic tales of life in the city from her own experiences through four political regimes in the twentieth century. Numerous people associated with the Moravian Church helped me when I stayed in Herrnhut, a fascinating place, as were nearby Zittau, Bautzen, and Görlitz, as they too experienced dramatic change in the 1990s. In Göttingen, Hartmut and Silke Lehmann sometimes astounded me with their generosity and kindness, as they helped make living there extremely pleasant. Göttingen was a place for music and love. When not reading rare books in the old library, looking out the window at a plaque marking where Benjamin Franklin once lived, I played in the MUSA chamber orchestra directed by Rolf Bartels, tangoed in the same place, and met Vera, whom I later married in a wonderful folk wedding fest on a mountain in nearby Dransfeld. On this side of the Atlantic, many people in Philadelphia and Lancaster supported my stay as well, but in Bethlehem and Nazareth people were exceptionally welcoming, as they always have been, especially Otto and Sue Dreydoppel. Here I explored many historic sites and married Vera again in one of them—the Whitefield House in Nazareth—a week after Dransfeld, and this time officially.

While I was traveling to these places, many archivists and librarians assisted me greatly. Thomas Müller guided me through the manuscripts and rare books of the Francke Foundations in Halle. In Herrnhut, Esther von Ungern-Sternberg and especially Paul Peucker helped me in the (Moravian) Unity Archives. Vernon Nelson provided critical assistance in the Moravian Archives in Bethlehem, as he did with my first book. Both he and Paul Peucker continue to provide me with valuable insight into the world of eighteenth-century Moravians. Their interest in my work, together with their knowledge of the sources on both sides of the Atlantic, have played an important role in improving the quality of this book, as they have with many other historians working outside the Moravian tradition. John Peterson of the Lutheran Archives Center in Philadelphia, Kay Schellhase of the Archives of the Evangelical and Reformed Historical Society of the United Church of Christ in Lancaster, and Jim Green of the Library Company of Philadelphia were also very helpful not only in guiding me to needed manuscripts and printed documents, but also in sharing their expertise on them and the period with me.

A number of institutions on both sides of the Atlantic directly funded or otherwise supported this project. Research in Germany was supported by the Alexander von Humboldt Foundation, the Fulbright Program, the Marx Planck Institute for History in Göttingen, and the Interdisciplinary Center for the Study of Pietism in Halle. Support in the United States came from the American Philosophical Society, the McNeil Center for Early American Studies, the International Seminar on the History of the Atlantic World at Harvard University, the University of South Alabama Research Council, and the Northern Illinois University College of Liberal Arts and Sciences and History Department. Also, *The William and Mary Quarterly* allowed me to use the title and material from my article published with them.

I would also like to thank a number of other individuals who helped me in various ways. Vera Lind, Susan Branson, and Kenneth Lockridge read and commented extensively on the entire manuscript, in some cases on more than one version. Kathleen Brown and Daniel Richter not only commented on the entire manuscript, but have also gone to great lengths beyond this to continue to support the project at the McNeil Center in Philadelphia. Richard Dunn, Hans Medick, and Heide Wunder provided encouragement and spent a great deal of time with me and my work as this project developed. Paul Peucker (now at the Moravian Archives in Bethlehem) helped with final preparations, as did Keith Lowman of Northern Illinois University Media Services and Lenny Walther (who prepared the final maps). John Shy and George Jewsbury remain interested and supportive after many years, as did H. James Henderson until his recent death. My former colleagues at the University of South Alabama were helpful in the early phases of this project, especially Michael Monheit, and my new colleagues at Northern Illinois University have supported me in very important ways in recent years, especially Harvey Smith, Heide Fehrenbach, David Kyvig, and Christine Worobec.

Last, I would like to thank my family. This includes my family in North Carolina, in Houston, and in other places to which they have scattered. Above all I am thankful for Salome, who came along late in this project and continues to make life very interesting and enjoyable, and for Vera, to whom this book is dedicated.